Developing Countries and the WTO:
A Pro–active Agenda

Developing Countries and the WTO: A Pro–active Agenda

Edited by

BERNARD HOEKMAN

and

WILL MARTIN

British Library Cataloguing in Publication Data has been applied for

Library of Congree Cataloging in Publication Data has been applied for

Typeset by MHL Typesetting, Coventry

Contents

Foreword   vii

Author Affiliations   ix

Introduction   xi

1   Developing Countries and the Next Round of WTO Negotiations
Rajesh Chadha, Bernard Hoekman, Will Martin, Ademola Oyejide, Mari
Pangestu, Diana Tussie and Jamel Zarrouk   1

2   Two Principles for the Next Round or, How to Bring Developing
Countries in from the Cold
Joseph E. Stiglitz   7

3   Bringing Discipline to Agricultural Policy via the WTO
Kym Anderson   25

4   Liberalising Agriculture and Manufactures in a Millennium Round:
Implications for Developing Countries
Thomas W. Hertel and Will Martin   59

5   Developing Countries in the New Round of GATS Negotiations:
Towards a Pro-Active Role
Aaditya Mattoo   75

6   Options for Improving Africa's Participation in the WTO
Richard Blackhurst, Bill Lyakurwa and Ademola Oyejide   95

7   Implementation of Uruguay Round Commitments: The Development
Challenge
J. Michael Finger and Philip Schuler   115

8   WTO Dispute Settlement, Transparency and Surveillance
Bernard M. Hoekman and Petros C. Mavroidis   131

9   Maximising the Benefits of the Trade Policy Review Mechanism for
Developing Countries
Joseph F. Francois   147

10   Industrial Policy, and the WTO
Bijit Bora, Peter J. Lloyd and Mari Pangestu   167

11 Subsidiarity and Governance Challenges for the WTO: Environmental and Labour Standards
Jim Rollo and L. Alan Winters   185

12 From TRIMs to a WTO Agreement on Investment?
Bernard Hoekman and Kamal Saggi   201

13 Trade Facilitation: Technical Regulations and Customs Procedures
Patrick A. Messerlin and Jamel Zarrouk   215

14 Competition Policy and Intellectual Property Rights in Developing Countries
Keith E. Maskus and Mohamed Lahouel   233

15 Market Access Advances and Retreats: The Uruguay Round and Beyond
J. Michael Finger and Ludger Schuknecht   251

Index   309

Foreword

Perspectives on the role of the trade in development have changed dramatically in recent decades. The earlier enthusiasm for policies of import substitution behind formidable tariff and nontariff barriers has been replaced by a widely-shared agreement that a relatively open trade regime is an important component of a broad-based strategy for development and poverty alleviation.

Developing country policy makers have shown themselves willing to make the difficult political decisions needed to reduce protection and integrate their economies into the world economy. In the Uruguay Round, World Bank research revealed that developing countries were willing to make bigger cuts in their import costs than industrial countries. And these reductions were only part of a broader wave of trade policy reform that swept developing countries during the 1980s and 1990s.

Another manifestation of developing country commitment to relatively open economies has been the increasing numbers of developing countries seeking to join the World Trade Organization (WTO). Since the beginning of the Uruguay Round, 36 countries have joined the WTO. Over two-thirds of the 139 members of the WTO are now developing countries, as are all of the roughly thirty countries currently in the accession process. Further, many developing country members of the WTO are extremely active participants in its activities. In the lead-up to the most recent WTO Ministerial, over half the proposals were submitted by developing countries.

With the broadening of the trading agenda in recent years, the business of the WTO has become extremely complex. Even for the industrial countries, it has become difficult to accurately identify interests and concerns. For developing countries, with widely differing trade interests and levels of administrative capacity, the problem has become even greater. In this situation, there is a great need for objective research to identify trade-related reforms that can help countries achieve their development goals. The set of papers included in this volume makes an important contribution to this objective.

This volume contains papers on the key issues confronting developing countries in the WTO – trade reform, implementation and governance issues and the ever-expanding agenda of 'second-generation' issues. A number of the papers were widely distributed prior to the WTO Ministerial in Seattle, and had a significant impact on the debate. I believe that this collected set of papers will be of great value to analysts and policy makers for many years.

Nicholas Stern
Senior Vice President and Chief Economist
The World Bank

Authors' Affiliations

Kym Anderson	University of Adelaide (Australia) & CEPR
Richard Blackhurst	Graduate Institute for International Studies, Geneva
Bijit Bora	UNCTAD (Geneva) & Flinders University, Australia
Rajesh Chadha	Hindu College, University of Delhi & National Council for Applied Economic Research (New Delhi)
J. Michael Finger	World Bank
Joseph Francois	Erasmus University Rotterdam & CEPR
Thomas W. Hertel	Purdue University
Bernard Hoekman	World Bank & CEPR
Mohamed Lahouel	University of Tunis III & Economic Research Forum for the Arab Countries, Iran and Turkey
Peter J. Lloyd	University of Melbourne
Bill Lyakurwa	African Economic Research Consortium, Nairobi
Will Martin	World Bank
Keith Maskus	University of Colorado in Boulder
Aaditya Mattoo	World Bank
Petros Mavroidis	University of Neuchâtel & CEPR
Patrick A. Messerlin	Institut d'Etudes Politiques de Paris
Ademola Oyejide	University of Ibadan & African Economic Research Consortium (Nairobi)
Mari Pangetsu	Centre for Strategic & International Studies (Jakarta)
Jim Rollo	University of Sussex (Brighton)
Kamal Saggi	Southern Methodist University
Ludger Schuknecht	European Central Bank
Philip Schuler	University of Maryland
Joseph Stiglitz	Brookings Institution
Diana Tussie	Latin American Trade Network and FLACSO (Buenos Aires)
L. Alan Winters	School of Social Sciences, University of Sussex & CEPR
Jamel Zarrouk	Arab Monetary Fund & Economic Research Forum for the Arab Countries, Iran and Turkey

Introduction

This volume collects a number of studies that analyze the multilateral trade negotiating agenda confronting developing countries. The papers were prepared as part of a World Bank research and capacity-building project that seeks to provide practical assistance to developing country policy makers through an integrated program of research, dissemination of knowledge, and policy advice. The 'WTO 2000' project is a collaborative one, involving many analysts associated with research institutes and networks in developing countries, including the Latin American Trade Network (LATN); the Economic Research Forum for the Arab Countries, Iran and Turkey (ERF); the African Economic Research Consortium (AERC); the Coordinated African Program of Assistance on Services (CAPAS); and the Trade Policy Forum of the Pacific Economic Cooperation Council (PECC). The project has benefited from the opportunity to incorporate perspectives from researchers and policy makers in both developed and developing countries. This has helped to generate both innovative ideas and analysis, and to subject these to feedback from practitioners.

Work at the World Bank continues under this project, as well as a closely related project on agricultural trade policy options, and specific research programs on trade in services and the impact of product standards on international trade. All these projects aim to provide information and tools needed by decision makers, analysts and trade negotiators. Outputs include handbooks, seminars and training designed to build capacity in developing countries.

The first chapter of this book provides an overview of the issues and the main messages that emerge from the collaborative research effort, greatly facilitating the task of drafting an Introduction. More details on the project, participating research networks, and additional results and papers on the issues can be obtained from the project's website, www.worldbank.org/trade, which also provides links to partner institution home pages. The authors of the contributions to this volume benefitted from numerous suggestions received from anonymous reviewers, discussants and conference participants. Special thanks go to Rajesh Chadha, Richard Elgin, J. Michael Finger, Carsten Fink, Peter Holmes, Robert Hudec, Friedrich von Kirchbach, Philip Levy, Vivien Liu, Miguel Rodriguez-Mendoza, Marcelo Olarreaga, Claudia Orozco, David Palmeter, Arvind Panagariya,

Randeep Rathindran, Arvind Subramanian, Susan Teltscher, Diana Tussie, Helen Wallace, Joerg Weber, and Alasdair Young for commenting on individual papers. Aime Murigande provided excellent research assistance for the paper by Blackhurst, Lyakurwa and Oyejide.

This project could not have happened without a great deal of support and assistance from our colleagues and friends in partner institutions, other organizations, and the World Bank. We are grateful to the World Bank Institute; the World Bank Research Support Budget (RPO 683-54); the governments of Italy and the Netherlands; and Société Générale de Surveillance (SGS) for financial assistance. We are particularly indebted to the Department for International Development (DFID), United Kingdom, for its generous financial support. We would also like to thank Philip English, of the World Bank Institute, for his superb contribution to the implementation of the project, Ishac Diwan for supporting research capacity-building by the World Bank Institute, and Ana Rivas, Maria Kasilag, Rebecca Martin and Lili Tabada for outstanding administrative assistance. All of our colleagues in the Trade Team of the Development Research Group have also been unstinting in their support, as has been the Group's Director, Paul Collier. Outside the Bank, we have benefited greatly from cooperation with UNCTAD and the World Trade Organization – which kindly hosted the conference at which a number of the papers in this volume were presented. Finally, we extend our thanks to the National Council for Applied Economic Research, New Delhi, the Ministry of Trade of Cote d'Ivoire, the Southern African Development Community secretariat, ERF, LATN, CAPAS, the Trade Policy Forum of PECC, and the Center for Economic Policy Research (CEPR), all of which hosted and helped organize regional meetings and workshops under the auspices of the project.

BH
WM

1

Developing Countries and the Next Round of WTO Negotiations

Rajesh Chadha, Bernard Hoekman, Will Martin, Ademola Oyejide,
Mari Pangestu, Diana Tussie and Jamel Zarrouk

T HE Uruguay Round of multilateral trade talks, concluded in 1994 after eight years of often conflictual negotiations, was a landmark in the history of the trading system. Agriculture and textiles and clothing, two sectors that for all intents and purposes had been removed from the ambit of the GATT, were brought back into the fold. The system of multilateral rules was extended to include intellectual property rights and services, and, because of the Single Undertaking rule, all countries desiring to become members of the new World Trade Organisation (WTO) accepted a variety of disciplines in areas ranging from customs valuation to subsidies. Simulation models suggested that the Round would result in significant welfare gains, especially for those countries that had made the most market-opening commitments (see Martin and Winters, 1996).

Although it was recognised that certain agreements – most notably that related to TRIPs – were not necessarily in the interest of low-income countries and would certainly give rise to short-run costs, many argued that this was more than compensated by the inclusion of agriculture, the commitment to phase out the Multifibre Arrangement (MFA), and the creation of the WTO – which embodied a much stronger enforcement/dispute settlement mechanism than what had prevailed under GATT. More critical observers noted that to a large extent the deal that was struck in the Uruguay Round entailed industrialised country commitments to abolish practices that violated the letter or spirit of the GATT – agricultural intervention, the network of quotas under the MFA, voluntary export restraint agreements – in return for a substantial expansion of the coverage and reach of multilateral disciplines, including new rules on intellectual property and services. As such, it could be argued to be a rather unbalanced outcome.

The Round did little to liberalise trade in agriculture and services. Reflecting this, the Agreement on Agriculture and the GATS included provisions calling for new efforts to reduce trade barriers within five years of the entry into force of the WTO. Other agreements contained review provisions. In order to increase the scope for beneficial trade-offs across issues, a number of governments (led by the EU) argued that rather than pursue only the 'built-in' agenda, it was preferable to launch a full-fledged round of negotiations. The Ministerial meeting that was to launch a new round took place in Seattle at the end of November 1999. It turned out to be a fiasco.

There were a number of reasons for the failure of the Seattle Ministerial to launch a new round. Domestic US politics played a key role. Strong differences on the scope of agricultural liberalisation between the EU on the one hand and the US and other agricultural exporters on the other were also important.[1] But a major factor as well was the unwillingness of many developing countries to consider accepting the agenda that was being pushed by a number of high-income countries in some areas – e.g., inclusion of labour standards – and general dissatisfaction regarding the process through which a negotiating agenda was being crafted. Small countries in particular perceived themselves to be left completely in the cold, not having access to the negotiating fora where potential agenda-setting compromises were being crafted.

The importance accorded to the agenda-setting process by developing countries, and their active participation in the 'pre-negotiation' phase – almost half of all submissions made by WTO members regarding the issues that should be included in the draft Ministerial declaration came from developing countries – reflected widespread perceptions that a *necessary* condition for a balanced negotiating outcome is an agenda that reflects their interests. Of course, this is not a *sufficient* condition. A balanced outcome also requires effective participation in market access bargaining and rule making. Negotiators must come to the table appropriately armed with negotiating briefs that reflect the outcome of analyses and assessments undertaken in capitals. These in turn should be based on consultations and interactions with the private sector, NGOs and the local research communities. Without a local capacity to analyse issues, and mechanisms to feed this analysis into a process of decision-making that in turn is fed to negotiators, developing country governments will find it difficult to defend their interests and to pursue anything but a 'stone-walling' or 'delay' strategy (e.g., seek transition periods). In the Uruguay Round, a pro-active, constructive approach was frequently out of reach for many countries because of resource and research capacity constraints (see Blackhurst, Lyakurwa and Oyejide, this issue).

Efforts have been made by many developing countries to gear up for the next

---

[1] For a concise report see the 11 December, 1999, issue of *The Economist*.

round of negotiations – whenever these may be launched. But, negotiating capacity, however important, is just one element determining final outcomes. Experience suggests that even if notional symmetry prevails in terms of defining the agenda, outcomes are likely to be asymmetric. Under GATT this was exemplified by the gradual *de facto* exclusion of agriculture and textiles and clothing, and the expanding use of various instruments of contingent protection. To some extent these outcomes resulted from developing country negotiating strategies – an insistence on special and differential treatment, and a refusal to engage in reciprocal exchange of liberalisation commitments. Although attitudes towards participation have changed to a very significant extent, asymmetries in negotiating power and capacity remain a fundamental characteristic of the system. In the Uruguay Round this was illustrated, *inter alia*, by the fact that very little, if anything, was done to enhance developing country service export opportunities (e.g., through the movement of natural persons). Moreover, as noted by Finger and Schuler in this issue, the costs of implementing WTO agreements can easily exceed the entire development budget of a least developed country, while not imposing any costs on high-income countries – as disciplines reflect the prevailing status quo in these nations. It is not at all clear from a development perspective that the resources required for implementation of some WTO agreements, whatever the amount might be, would not be better used to build schools or improve infrastructure.

The Uruguay Round illustrated that 'one size fits all' is not a good rule of thumb when it comes to negotiations on the substance of national regulatory regimes. More generally, it revealed that greater participation by developing countries – although a necessary condition for achieving a balanced outcome – will not necessarily have this result. The challenge extends therefore beyond building capacity to define national interests and mobilising domestic resources to participate in negotiations. What is also required are efforts to overcome power asymmetries and create effective incentives for the major traders to grant market access and rule-making concessions that are of interest to developing countries. This can be pursued by seeking to create mechanisms and 'rules of the game' that increase the likelihood of balanced outcomes.

Examples are 'formulae' that allow meaningful linkages to be made across issues and negotiating modalities that aim at achieving greater balance. For example, a country's market access commitments in services on 'mode 4' (movement of persons) might be linked to the volume of that country's exports (see Mattoo, this issue). Another example would be a 'no exceptions' rule aimed at preventing large players from removing certain sectors or modes of supply from the table. In general, the payoffs from effective coalition formation can be significant. This was illustrated in the Uruguay Round, where the successful conclusion of an agreement on agriculture was in no small part due to the formation of the Cairns Group. Clearly such coalitions should be subject-specific, with membership differing across issues. Finally, it is vital that the implications of proposed agreements for developing countries are assessed carefully. In many instances what is required is a project evaluation approach that clearly identifies the costs and benefits of alternative rules (agreements) and generates information on the resource implications associated with adopting a particular set of disciplines.

The chapters included in this volume suggest that participation constraints bias both the process and outcome of negotiations, and that this is especially a problem for least developed countries; that lack of information and limited experience greatly constrains the ability of countries to exploit the 'wiggle room' that is embodied in many WTO agreements; that fulfilment of offers of financial and technical assistance by high-income countries have proven to be disappoint-ing; and that provisions requiring such countries to take into account the interests of developing countries have proven to be meaningless.

The end result has been an absence of 'ownership' of many agreements, and a general suspicion of the WTO. This can only be remedied if the next round results in a more balanced outcome, one that addresses the selective liberalisation and rule-making that has been a characteristic of the system to date. The preconditions for achieving greater balance appear to be there – developing countries have demonstrated a willingness to participate actively and construc-tively in the WTO. This was reflected in the run-up to Seattle and the role played in the process of defining a negotiating agenda. The inability (unwillingness) of the major traders to accept the necessary compromises helped scuttle the talks, but arguably this has helped set the stage for a more balanced agenda to be crafted in the future.

Many of the substantive results of the project are summarised and cited in the chapters included in this book. Among the major conclusions to emerge:

- The potential gains from pursuing a traditional market access agenda (liberalisation of trade in agriculture, manufactures and services) are still huge. Priority should be given to this area, which implies that the agenda should include industrial tariffs. In agriculture substantial reductions in import barriers are required to even begin to approach parity with the treatment of manufactures trade.
- A more balanced outcome requires that OECD countries significantly increase market access for goods and services of export interest to developing countries, especially for services requiring the temporary entry of service providers (movement of natural persons) and labour-intensive manufactures such as clothing. This must also include a willingness to reduce the treat of contingent protection – especially anti-dumping.
- Efforts to introduce labour standards into the WTO and more generally apply national norms extraterritorially should be resisted. Both labour and environ-mental standards should be determined on a national basis or follow norms

agreed under auspices of the relevant specialised multilateral bodies and agreements.

- The increasingly prevalent controversies regarding the effects of national regulatory differences suggest there may be value in creating mechanisms outside the WTO and open to participation by NGOs to discuss the scientific basis of applied or proposed regulatory policies (regarding standards, bio-tech, genetically modified organisms, etc.).

- The transparency of WTO operations should be enhanced, including information collected on policies maintained by members, improved access to WTO databases, the process of negotiation, and dispute settlement. Consideration should also be given to improving the governance structure of the WTO.

- The incentives for developing countries to use dispute settlement provisions to enforce market access rights should be bolstered by creating mechanisms to collect relevant information (better surveillance) and allowing an 'ombudsman' or 'special prosecutor' to bring forward cases on behalf of developing countries. A 'public defender' body may also be beneficial.

- Many least developed countries confront resource constraints that prohibit active participation in WTO processes. Mechanisms to facilitate cooperation and joint action need to be developed.

- Finally, and very importantly, in many areas that have been proposed for the WTO agenda, there is no need to wait for multilateral initiatives. Much of what is required must be pursued at the national level, and includes complementary policies aimed at improving the ability of citizens to exploit trade and investment opportunities consistent with the goal of sustainable development – education, infrastructure, competition and environmental policies, etc.

REFERENCE

Martin, W. and L.A. Winters (eds.) (1996), *The Uruguay Round and the Developing Countries* (Cambridge: Cambridge University Press).

2

Two Principles for the Next Round or, How to Bring Developing Countries in from the Cold

Joseph E. Stiglitz

1. INTRODUCTION

𝕿HE November 1999 WTO Ministerial meeting in Seattle was expected to usher in a new Round of negotiations, the ninth in a series that began in Geneva in 1947. Although WTO members proved unable to launch a Round, efforts will continue in 2000 to develop a negotiating agenda. In this chapter I want to reinforce the call of the WTO's Director-General, Mr. Moore, for the next set of negotiations to be a 'development round.' Basic notions of equity and a sense of fair play require that the next Round reflect developing country interests and concerns more than was the case in earlier Rounds. Seattle demonstrated that without greater balance the success of future negotiations will be imperiled. Dissatisfaction by developing countries regarding the extent to which their interests were reflected was a factor leading to the failure of the Ministerial meeting.

The stakes are high. There is a growing gap between the developed and the less developed countries, highlighted in this year's World Development Report (World Bank, 1999). The international community is doing too little to narrow this gap: aid per capita to the developing world has fallen by nearly a third in the 1990s.[1] Too often, cuts in aid budgets are accompanied by the slogan 'trade, not aid,' exhortations for the developing world to participate fully in the global marketplace, and lectures about how government subsidies and protectionism distort prices and impede growth. All too often there is a hollow ring to these exhortations. As developing countries take steps to open their economies and

---

[1] The figure was US$32.27 in aid per developing-country resident in 1990, but only US$22.41 in 1997 (World Bank Statistical Information and Management Analysis database).

7

expand their exports, in too many sectors they find themselves confronting significant trade barriers (anti-dumping, high tariffs in sectors of natural comparative advantage, like agriculture or clothing) – leaving them, in effect, with neither aid nor trade. In these circumstances, it is not surprising that critics of liberalisation within the developing world quickly raise cries of hypocrisy.

Trade liberalisation will undoubtedly be of benefit to developing countries and the world more generally. But trade liberalisation must be balanced in agenda, process, and outcomes, including not only sectors in which developed countries have a comparative advantage, like financial services, but also those in which developing countries have a special interest, like agriculture and construction services. Account must be taken of the marked disadvantage that developing countries have in participating meaningfully in negotiations. Fifteen Sub-Saharan African WTO members have no trade representative at WTO headquarters in Geneva, as opposed to the WTO average of five staff per mission (Blackhurst, Lyakurwa and Oyejide, 1999). Developing countries face greater volatility, and opening to trade contributes to that volatility; they have weak or non-existent safety nets; and often confront persistent problems of high unemployment. The playing field is not level. Thus, provisions that look fair on the surface may have very different and unequal consequences for developed and less developed countries. The power imbalances at the bargaining table are exacerbated by the imbalance of consequences.

2. TRADE LIBERALISATION: A DEVELOPING COUNTRY PERSPECTIVE

I have argued elsewhere that true development entails a transformation of society (Stiglitz, 1998). For poorer countries especially, excessive protection shields local residents from a key transformation mechanism. Poor countries simply cannot afford the costs of inefficient resource allocation and the reduction of outside flows of investment and ideas resulting from protection. Yet it is also true that in democratic developing countries, governments have to persuade their citizens of the virtues of liberalisation, and there are always demagogues ready to exploit worries about liberalisation – just as there are in more advanced countries. And more developed countries – through both their rhetoric and their actions – have too often failed to be helpful to those genuinely committed to the cause of liberalisation in developing countries. Although they preach the virtues of openness, strong protectionist measures are frequently imposed. What are developing countries to make of the rhetoric in favour of rapid liberalisation, when rich countries with full employment and strong safety nets argue that they need to impose protective measures to help those adversely affected by trade? Or when rich countries play down the political pressures within developing countries – insisting that their polities 'face up to the hard choices' – while excusing their own trade barriers and agricultural subsidies by citing 'political pressures'?

Nowhere is this hypocrisy greater than in the invocation of anti-dumping and countervailing duties. I remember clearly the conversations I had in 1993 with the first deputy prime minister of Russia, as the United States was threatening to invoke dumping duties on Russia's exports of aluminium. He knew, and I knew, and he *knew* that I knew that Russia was not dumping – at least in the sense that any economist would use that term. We both knew that the dumping laws are not based on principles of fair competition; if that was their intention, there would be no problem with harmonising those laws with competition laws. The alleged objective of dumping laws is to prevent predatory pricing, which is already an offence under competition laws. But the criteria for predation under competition laws, which are based on sound economic principles, are far more stringent than those specified under anti-dumping laws. Indeed, according to one calculation made a few years ago, if the standards used under the dumping laws were applied domestically, 18 of the 20 top Fortune 500 firms in the United States could be accused of dumping (Thurow, 1985)! And the resolution of the 'problem' – what amounted to the establishment of an international aluminium cartel *under the auspices of the governments of the advanced market economies* – did little to convince sceptics of the market that anyone truly believed in the competitive marketplace.

To many in the developing world, trade policy in the more advanced countries seems to be more a matter of self-interest than of general principle. When good economic analysis works in favour of self-interest, it is invoked; but when it does not, so much the worse for economic principles. Several recent events have reinforced this impression. Consider the crisis in East Asia. The conditions imposed through the rescue packages included trade liberalisation measures that were unrelated to the crisis (Feldstein, 1998). To many, it seemed simply that those who wanted to force market-opening measures had seized on an opportune time to make use of their temporary power. Subsequent events strengthened the view that market-opening measures were not always advocated with the crisis countries' best interests at heart. As the crisis economies weakened further and excess capacity proliferated, natural market adjustments led to a decline in the prices of a number of commodities, including oil and steel. In capital-intensive industries where short-run marginal costs lie far below long-run marginal costs, this drop in prices can be quite large. This is part of the market-equilibrating forces; it is not dumping, and should not be interpreted as such. Yet, the dumping laws have been invoked in the case of steel.

Sometimes, as I look back at the years I spent at the White House, I think of how much time was spent managing trade issues – from Chinese honey, to Mexican tomatoes and avocados, to agricultural export subsidies provided under the 'Export Enhancement Programme'. Although these cases occupied much of our time and represented the most egregious cases of special-interest politics, they also represented but a small fraction of GDP. That we were able to turn back some protectionist appeals, that we discouraged others from even attempting to get special favours, that apart from aluminium, there was no major expansion of protectionism in a span of four years, gave me some comfort. Yet, I also knew that I should not take too much comfort from this: after all, throughout this period, the United States was enjoying a major economic expansion and unemployment was declining steadily. I worried that protectionist sentiment would soar, and the effectiveness of protectionist measures like anti-dumping appeals would increase, during the next recession – just as it had during the last major recession in the early 1980s. At that time, by one account, non-tariff measures covered two-fifths of all US imports (Nogués, Olechowski and Winters, 1986).

Standard economic analysis argues that trade liberalisation – even unilateral opening of markets – benefits a country: job loss in one sector will be offset by job creation in another, and the new jobs will be higher-productivity than the old. This economic logic requires markets to be working well, however, and in many countries, underdevelopment is an inherent reflection of poorly functioning markets. Thus new jobs are not created, or not created automatically. Moving workers from a low-productivity sector to unemployment does not – let me repeat, does not – increase output. A variety of factors contribute to the failure of jobs to be created, from government regulations, to rigidities in labour markets, to lack of access to capital. But whatever the causes, they have to be addressed simultaneously if we are to make a convincing case for trade liberalisation.

There are some sectors of the economy where the standard competitive paradigm does not work well even in developed countries, let alone developing countries. A stark lesson of the recent East Asia crisis is that weak financial institutions can wreak havoc on an economy, and that strong financial institutions require strong government regulation. But the increased frequency and depth of financial crises in recent years – with close to a hundred countries suffering through such crises over the past quarter-century[2] – shows how hard it is to establish strong financial institutions, even in developed countries. It also demonstrates that liberalisation – including financial sector liberalisation – without the requisite accompanying improvements in regulation and supervision can contribute to financial-sector instability. Such instability has exacted great costs in terms of growth, deepening poverty in the crisis countries.

---

[2] Sixty-nine countries faced severe banking crises between 1977 and 1995. See also World Bank (1999).

3. THE TWO BASIC PRINCIPLES

There are two basic principles that should govern the next set of trade negotiations: *fairness*, and especially fairness to the developing countries, and *comprehensiveness* (the need to include issues that are important to developing countries). Adherence to these principles could hold open the promise of a more liberal, and more equitable trading regime. While participants in previous Rounds have often paid lip service to these principles, they have been honoured mostly in the breach. Future adherence to these principles is, in my mind, absolutely essential for the success of the next Round, and in particular if the developing countries are to become full partners in the process of trade liberalisation.

At first blush, one might ask, how can one object to either principle? Yet closer examination raises doubts about the extent to which previous Rounds have embodied these principles. The Uruguay and previous Rounds focused heavily on liberalising tariffs on manufacturing. They did little to reduce protection in agriculture, a sector in which many developing countries have a comparative advantage.[3] The agricultural liberalisation that occurred was driven largely by the interests of developed exporters such as the United States and Australia, and developing country exporters in the Cairns group. Exporters of tropical products did not play an active role in the design of the agricultural liberalisation agenda. Tariffication of agricultural quotas during the Uruguay Round has left tariffs very high. In advanced industrial economies, the production-weighted average nominal rate of trade assistance to agriculture is 33 per cent – compared with a mere two per cent for other primary and manufacturing industries (Anderson, Hoekman and Strutt, 1999)! Protection to OECD agriculture actually rose, from 32 per cent in 1997 to 37 per cent in 1998 (OECD, 1999). It is understandable if agricultural exporters wonder whether previous Rounds had their best interests at heart.

Moving ahead on agriculture in the next Round would have big payoffs. Abolition of agricultural export subsidies and achievement of sharp cuts in import tariffs would benefit most developing countries. A 40 per cent reduction in agricultural support policies globally would contribute almost exactly the same amount to global welfare as a 40 per cent cut in manufacturing tariffs (Hertel and Martin, 1999). This reflects the huge size of distortions in agriculture relative to manufacturing, despite the fact that manufacturing value added is two-and-a-half times that of agriculture globally.

---

[3] While agricultural liberalisation was undermined by 'dirty tariffication', there was progress in some important cases, such as the reduction in protection in the Japanese markets for wheat, coarse grains and sugar. See Ingco (1996, pp. 444–45).

a. Comprehensiveness, Fairness and Political Success

If trade liberalisation is to survive the political process, it must have clear advocates – those who see themselves as gaining from the multilateral Rounds. Only if there are significant gainers will liberalisation initiatives muster sufficient support. One can see this dynamic play out even in countries seemingly committed to market processes, like the United States. In the intense political battle to get NAFTA and the Uruguay Round ratified, the export industries that benefited from increased market access played a pivotal role. If, by contrast, the trade negotiations are viewed as unfair, then it is not just populist demagogues who will seize upon this unfairness as an excuse for resisting liberalisation, possibly setting back attempts to implement broader-based market reforms as well. The concepts of comprehensiveness and fairness are closely related. Only if the negotiations are sufficiently comprehensive to include the interests of developing countries, and their exporters, is there likely to be success. There are several important dimensions of comprehensiveness.

(i) Sectoral comprehensiveness

Comprehensive negotiations, as opposed to negotiations focusing on a limited number of sectors, provide much more scope for designing policies that will compensate at least countries, and potentially even groups within countries, by including additional items that provide compensation to those who would otherwise lose. Consider France in the Uruguay Round. While many French policy makers thought of themselves as losing from the restraints on farm subsidies included in the Round, they recognised the potential gains to their exporters of services from liberalising trade in services. For the new negotiations to be a success from a developing country perspective it is vital that developing countries be able to identify their objectives in areas such as services, and to pursue them actively.

Recent World Bank research highlights a surprising advantage of a comprehensive approach to future negotiations. Since the built-in agenda for the negotiations includes agriculture and services, one of the primary questions will be whether to include industrial products – an issue that would typically be assumed to be of primary interest to developed countries. However, this should no longer be the case. Manufactures exports now make up over 70 per cent of the exports of developing countries, and seem poised to rise close to 80 per cent by 2005 (Hertel and Martin, 1999). This raises the clear possibility that the developing countries will actually be the predominant beneficiaries of the inclusion of manufacturing in the negotiations – though of course, whether they are depends on the particular manufactured commodities that are included.

Many observers view with great concern the alternative to a new Round of trade negotiations – the sector-by-sector approach. It is not only that progress is likely to be slower under this approach, but also that any successful sectoral liberalisation may actually impede further success in the next multilateral Round. Those who succeed in getting the trade liberalisation measures that they need (like information technology) cease being as potent a force for trade liberalisation as they might otherwise be. With less 'money' on the table for potential exporters, making a deal in other sectors becomes all the more difficult. After they have already cherry-picked their favoured sectors, what can the United States or European governments hope to gain in compensation for the political costs of liberalising the agricultural sector?

(ii) Special interests
There is a certain irony in the way that trade negotiations have typically proceeded. One might have thought that each country would promote liberalisation in those sectors where it had the most to gain from a societal perspective; and similarly, that it would be most willing to give up protectionism in those sectors where protection was costing the most. But political logic prevails over economic logic: after all, if economic logic dominated, countries would engage in trade liberalisation on their own. High levels of protection in a sector are usually indicative of strong political forces, and so these higher barriers may be the last to give way. By the same token, market access initiatives are not determined primarily by considerations of the national interest, but by special interests. When I was at the Council of Economic Advisers, there was an attempt to do it the right way, to ask questions like 'What trade-opening measures would have the largest effect on US income, and which should be given the highest priority, taking also into account our concern with distribution?' But such a strategy based on economic logic would have pushed off the trade agenda many items that were of great interest to special-interest groups, but of little value (and, in some cases, from a broader perspective, arguably of negative value) to the country as a whole. In this context, it should not come as a surprise that this attempt to have economic logic drive the trade agenda was quickly suppressed.

This observation has an important implication. To the extent that major industrial countries have shaped multilateral trade negotiations in the past, then the agenda has presumably reflected not so much their *national* interests, but the interests of certain domestic political forces. Comprehensive multilateral negotiations offer a possibility of taming those forces: the multiplicity of gains across sectors increases the number of potential winners, so that the process can yield an outcome that is closer to a Pareto improvement – economists' jargon for a situation where everyone is better off after the negotiations.

(iii) Liberalisation of services
Services represent an increasing share of GDP in virtually all economies. In the United States, for instance, the share of manufacturing has declined from 28

per cent in 1960 to 18 per cent today; in the UK, from 36 per cent to 21 per cent. In both countries, the share of services has risen by an even greater amount. Even developing countries also have an increasing interest in including services, as their economies shift into those sectors (Mattoo, 1999). But services are different from manufactured goods in several salient ways – ways that make achieving fairness, especially fairness in outcome, far more difficult, and far more difficult than is generally realised. Two examples, liberalisation of financial services, and liberalisation of construction services, illustrate the challenges.

Modern financial markets are clearly important for economic efficiency, and global financial institutions play an important role in promoting global economic integration, including trade expansion. But financial markets are different from ordinary markets, where our standard theorems about the gains from trade liberalisation in the presence of competitive markets apply. The central functions of financial markets are related to the provision of information, and markets for information function differently from markets for ordinary goods and services. This fundamental difference explains why all countries accept a need for financial regulation that all agree would be totally inappropriate for the typical manufacturing sector. Indeed, the global financial crisis of the last eighteen months should have sensitised us to the downside risks of rapid liberalisation of financial markets in countries that lack the appropriate regulatory structure. If domestic banks in the liberalising country are weak, then providing an easy avenue for depositors to switch funds to a safer foreign-owned bank could spark a run on the domestic banking system. Even short of that, the additional competition may erode the franchise value of the bank, and that itself may lead to more risk-taking, or more broadly less prudential behaviour, on the part of domestic banks. Thus, even countries with reasonably good systems of bank regulation will need to tighten up and improve their financial sector regulations even as they liberalise the market more broadly.

In actuality, countries liberalising their financial systems have failed to take these precautions. Typically, these countries have not only have failed to recognise the need to do so, but instead have moved in the opposite direction, loosening their regulatory frameworks in the euphoria of liberalisation. In retrospect, it should be clear to all that in many countries the objective should not have been deregulation, but the establishment of an appropriate regulatory framework. But even with the appropriate objectives, policy makers and regulators would have found the going tough. In country after country, the new foreign entrants into the financial system have recruited away the best and most talented individuals from the government regulating agencies. Unable to compete on salaries, regulatory agencies have found themselves much weaker just at the time that they need to be strengthened. Nor should we ignore the longer-run development problems that can arise when foreign banks displace domestic banks: these foreign banks may focus their lending efforts on providing finance to multinationals or large national firms, but may show little interest in small and medium enterprises, which are often the engines of growth. These fears seem to have been realised in practice.

To be sure, if countries manage to strengthen their financial sector regulation as they liberalise, and if they manage to ensure that funds reach small and medium-sized enterprises and other under-served groups,[4] then financial sector liberalisation has the potential for improving the performance of this vital sector of the economy. The induced competition can be an important spur to efficiency of the sector. But there are clearly examples (Kenya, for example) where foreign entry, even in the presence of financial-sector liberalisation, has failed not only in that objective, but also in the broader objective of reducing interest-rate spreads and bringing down the rates at which funds are available to borrowers. Thus, the liberalisation of financial services in developing countries should be approached with some caution.[5]

(iv) Trade in factors of production

Another type of comprehensiveness that is important to developing countries concerns factors of production. Many developing countries today are raising a key question, perhaps somewhat rhetorically, about the scope of liberalisation: Why is it that there has been so much interest in liberalising movements in goods and in capital – issues of concern to industrial countries – but so little interest in liberalising movements of people, especially unskilled labour, the factor that is of particular interest to developing countries? The issue becomes of central importance once one starts to focus on services. If industrial-country companies are to deliver effectively services like insurance, they must be allowed to have at least some of their key personnel working in the country. Allowing some individuals to enter is thus a corollary to liberalisation of services. But developing countries have an interest in industries like construction; success in these areas may require larger numbers of somewhat less skilled workers. In both cases, the discussion is about temporary work permits, not long-term migration. What is at stake is partly a matter of equity, but there are also issues of efficiency: services and goods, flows of investment and people, are all inter-linked. Barriers in one area limit possibilities in others. That is why it would be desirable to make progress towards an investment agreement – though the agreement needs to be attentive to the concerns of the developing countries as well as the developed.

---

[4] Perhaps by following and broadening the US example of lending obligations to such groups, as under the Community Reinvestment Act.
[5] The same is true in the case of liberalisation of capital flows. I would hate to see openness equated with full liberalisation of capital flows, given that premature liberalisation can have severely anti-developmental effects.

(v) Beyond tariffs

There are many forms of non-tariff barriers to trade (NTBs), and these have multiplied in recent decades as tariff barriers have come down. This is not surprising; after all, the political forces that give rise to high tariffs do not disappear once tariffs are brought down. Rather, they must seek protection through other channels.[6] Unfortunately, these NTBs are far more pernicious than tariffs, precisely because they are so much harder to assess and quantify, and they can exact even higher costs in efficiency terms. And while previous Rounds have addressed some of these issues – through tariffication of agricultural trade barriers, for example – the problem has not gone away.

One notorious form of GATT/WTO-legal NTBs is anti-dumping (AD) duties and countervailing duties. The provisions of dumping laws do not conform to economic principles concerning fair trade, yet developing countries have learned from their more developed trading partners how to use dumping laws to protect themselves. Even as the number of anti-dumping actions initiated in developed economies fell sharply after 1993, the number of actions in developing countries tripled. Even worse, developing countries have trained the weapon of AD against each other: in 1996–97, for example, Argentina, Brazil, India, Indonesia, Korea and Peru all initiated anti-dumping actions against China (Finger, 1998). Although the US has led the way in this form of protection – so that even in 1996–97, it initiated twice as many AD cases as any other jurisdiction – in the long run, competitive and innovative countries like the United States have the most to lose from anti-dumping. Their low profit margins make them particularly vulnerable to charges of selling below 'reasonable costs,' which are assumed to include an arbitrary and sometimes very large profit margin;[7] and falling prices from innovation make it more plausible that charges of injury will be sustained.

The use of countervailing duties has raised similar concerns about non-tariff protectionism. Most economists would agree that if privatisation is carried out via a competitive auction of assets, then the purchaser has not been subsidised. That is, he has paid full market price for the assets that he has purchased, even if the seller, the government, has lost money in the deal. Imagine that one claimed, conversely, that there was a subsidy involved simply because the government had made a mistake in the past and was now being forced to sell the asset below cost. To be consistent, one would have to hold also that a company that purchased assets from a bankrupt firm was being subsidised by the bankrupt firm, if the price it paid for assets was less than the price originally paid by the bankrupt firm. This logic, untenable though it may be,

---

[6] Finger (1998) refers to this phenomenon as the 'fungibility' of protection across different trade-policy instruments.
[7] Some recent cases have assumed a profit margin as high as 30 per cent.

has been used to justify countervailing duties imposed against exports from the transition economies.[8]

But problems arise not only in the anti-dumping and countervailing duty laws, but also in their implementation process, which puts developing countries at a disadvantage. The information requirements imposed on firms charged with dumping are particularly onerous for developing countries, and the default, the reliance on 'best information available' – typically meaning the information supplied by the party alleging dumping – puts developing countries at a further disadvantage. A comprehensive trade negotiation thus must deal not only with the principles underlying the laws, but also with details of their implementation.

There is a simple principle that should underlie our thinking in this area. 'Fair trade' – or as economists put it, fair competition – is important, but the principles that should guide us in assessing whether a firm is engaged in an unfair practice should be the same whether the practice occurs within a country or across borders. Recent cases have made it abundantly clear that price-fixing can occur, for instance, at the international level, just as it can occur within the borders of a country. Anti-dumping is, or should be, concerned with predatory pricing, which is a practice that can undermine the effectiveness of competition. Anti-trust laws have developed relatively clear and implementable standards for whether a given pricing structure is predatory. These are the standards that should be used for transactions that move across borders – that is, for trade. What would happen if these standards were applied? According to one recent analysis of US anti-dumping cases, in more than 90 per cent no intervention was needed to prevent predation, or to protect competition at all (Willig, 1998).

(vi) Promoting competition

Ironically, while 'fair trade' laws have encouraged protectionism under the guise of protecting competition, there has been insufficient progress in attacking competition barriers in areas where they really are important. For instance, some countries have monopoly importers. Reducing tariffs simply gives those importers scope for increasing their profits, rather than facilitating trade; so it should be clear that competition is necessary to realise the full gains from trade. Effective competition policy may also improve the workings of political processes. When competition is muffled, firms and government officials will tend to divide up economic rents – that is, the monopoly profits – in secret. But with vibrant competition, companies have an incentive to make sure rules are clearly defined and that their rivals get no unfair advantages. Competition allows the emergence of multiple important actors, promoting pluralism and ultimately also efficiency. In the international arena, lack of competition may be an important barrier to trade. It may be especially important to new entrants – and many economies in transition

---

[8] And developed economies as well: a case in point was British Steel post-privatisation.

and developing countries are new entrants into a market. Thus, they have a strong interest in seeing these barriers broken down. Earlier, I referred to how the existing aluminium producers in the West worked together, under the umbrella of the anti-dumping duty, to limit Russia's entry into this market.

These considerations suggest that countries should consider initiating multi-lateral negotiations on competition policy. I know that developing countries are far from unanimous on support of such a competition accord. This ambivalence is perfectly consistent with my earlier discussion about the political economy of trade liberalisation. Competition policy has few supporters within any country, other than economists who realise the central role it plays in making markets work perfectly. (Businesses typically believe in the virtues of competition in *other* sectors, arguing that in their own sectors, competition tends to be disruptive.) Given the lack of interest on the part of the vested interests, I am not sanguine about whether there will be any progress in this direction. Yet those of us who believe that trade liberalisation can be an effective tool for development and welfare improvement – but especially if, and in some cases only if, it is accompanied by competition – cannot let this item slip off the agenda without raising our voices.

Some observers have also raised concerns that if competition policy is treated through the WTO, it will be the market-access concerns of developed-country exporters and not those of developing-country consumers that drive competition policy in developing countries (Hoekman and Holmes, 1999). In this view, developing countries would be better off improving their competition policy frameworks unilaterally. Although these are important concerns, promotion of competition policy brings such important benefits that I believe it warrants serious consideration as part of the next Round. A further advantage, of course, is that a competition accord could reduce tolerance for the use of anti-dumping actions as a remedy for alleged predation.

(vii) New trade barriers

Developed countries have shown enormous creativity in *creating* barriers to trade – well beyond the anti-dumping laws and the ways that they are implemented. The most difficult to deal with are those that align protectionist interests with the interests of other pressure groups. Agricultural interests, for example, foment *Jurassic Park* worries about genetic engineering to keep out genetically engineered plants and animals. Of course, where agricultural subsidies are sufficiently high, any technological advance is, perversely, of doubtful value because it increases the demand for agricultural subsidies. Little wonder that opposition to genetic engineering is stronger in those countries with high agricultural protection than in agricultural exporters. The current broad-based opposition to genetically engineered products may provide another means for developed countries to restrict access for unsubsidised exports from developing countries. This is an issue, of course, that currently may be of second-order interest to developing countries. Their immediate concern is simply to gain access to markets and to level the playing field by getting the advanced industrial countries to stop subsidising agriculture. But in the longer run, this issue cannot be ignored. For increases in productivity in the developing countries will depend in part on the improvement in their seeds, and genetic engineering holds open the promise of the most rapid improvement in that productivity. (Interestingly, the charges of anti-competitive practices recently brought against the industry underline the key role of competition policy, if the benefits of these advances are to be shared meaningfully with those in the developing world.)

Other protectionists try to enlist environmental and labour groups for other types of protection. While it is imperative that the international community continue to pursue good environmental policies and core labour standards, it should resist this unholy alliance of interests. Take the example of the environment. Once international agreements are concluded on global environmental issues, like HFCs and greenhouse gases, and if it becomes clear that other enforcement measures have failed, then it may become appropriate to ask whether trade sanctions should be used. But interestingly, there have not been major enforcement problems with the one major international agreement that included binding commitments, the Montreal Convention. If there is a decision eventually to proceed with the use of trade sanctions, it is important that the imposition of the sanctions be delegated to an international body. It should not be left up to individual countries to decide for themselves whether they like or do not like the environmental policy of a trading partner. That would simply be an invitation to new forms of protectionism.

(viii) Trade facilitation

My hope is that the trade negotiations will go beyond stripping down government-created barriers to trade and will work more actively to facilitate trade. We should ask what the barriers to trade are, and how they can be removed. I have already provided one illustration of such barriers: anti-competitive practices. Promoting competition is one area for facilitating trade, if we interpret that concept broadly. But there are also important steps to take in the area of trade facilitation more narrowly. In many developing countries, corruption by customs officials acts as another important barrier to trade. Considerable thought should go into the question of how the international regime can help address this problem – from pre-clearing, to technical assistance, to simplification of classification schemes that leaves less discretion to customs officials.

(ix) Other dimensions of fairness

I have focused so far mainly on the issue of comprehensiveness, arguing that comprehensiveness is in fact necessary for an equitable agreement. But there are other elements of perceived fairness. Over the years, many developing countries have unilaterally (though often under strong pressure) engaged in a wide variety of trade liberalisation measures. As we approach the new Round, those countries need to be given credit for their concessions, in return for making them binding.

Another aspect of fairness entails *sensitivity* to the special needs of developing countries. There are at least three dimensions to this sensitivity. First, developed countries should recognise the higher costs of liberalisation in developing countries, which I discussed earlier. Allowing longer transition times for liberalisation measures, as was done during the Uruguay Round, lowers the cost of adjustment; but in addition to this concession, the more developed countries should consider establishing a formal programme of trade adjustment assistance. And the costs of implementation can be very high. Finger and Schuler, in their paper presented in this volume, argue that implementation of just a few of the Uruguay Round agreements can swallow up a year's worth of development assistance for a country.[9] The World Bank has played an important role in the provision of such support for implementation, and will continue to do so in the future. Nevertheless, more assistance is clearly needed.

The second point has to do with the special problems posed by human needs, like health. It has been alleged that some developed-country drug companies, for instance, sell their drugs to developing countries at prices that exceed their prices in developed-country markets. That they might be able to do so is not surprising: intellectual property rights give drug firms scope for price discrimination; in particular, the larger developed countries with national health systems can win more favourable pricing from pharmaceutical firms.[10] Yet as reasonable and rational as price discrimination might seem for profit-maximising enterprises, to those in less developed countries it appears exploitative. Within the United States and other countries, such exercises of monopoly power – that is, price discrimination not justified by differences in costs of serving different customers – is illegal. It might be appropriate to consider a similar provision in the next round of trade negotiations.[11] We need to explore various ways to achieve the goal of ensuring that developing countries achieve 'most favoured pricing' status.

Third, the negotiations need to pay special attention to the long-term growth aspirations of the less developed countries. This has several dimensions. I have

---

[9] Finger and Schuler (1999). These estimates cover only the budgetary outlays required of the government – for example, for new computer systems and training of personnel – and thus do not encompass any adjustment costs to private-sector firms or workers.

[10] The issue is a complicated once, since standard models of the discriminating monopolist do not adequately describe those markets in which there is a single buyer of prescription drugs (the national health service), for then the appropriate model is that of bilateral monopoly.

[11] In fact, there have been moves by drug manufacturers to try to write restrictions on parallel imports into the WTO, *increasing* the scope for price discrimination. In my view, this would be a risky move in the absence of good recent evidence that shows that price discrimination benefits, rather than harms, developing country consumers.

already referred to one – how poorly designed financial services liberalisation can lead to greater instability and perhaps even starve small and medium enterprises of needed capital. Similarly, definitions of intellectual property rights need to take into account the interests of users of knowledge as well as producers of knowledge. If they do not, then enforcement of those rights may constrain development. (Interestingly, some members of the academic community, which is both a producer and user of knowledge, share the developing-country concern that the international community has yet to strike the right balance between users and producers.)

More problematic in this vein are issues related to *promotion of infant industries*, which has justified so much protectionism in the past. Certain types of technology subsidies were given the 'green light' under the Uruguay Round, but it is clear that developed countries make use of a whole variety of other, hidden subsidies under the rubric of 'defence'. This point was illustrated by the recent debates about dual-use technologies and subsidies to aircraft manufacturers. The technology issues facing developing countries are different, but no less important. These countries must absorb new technologies; and to do so, they must have the space to engage in a process of learning-by-doing, during which costs fall. With imperfect capital markets, firms cannot simply borrow against future profits, and governments may need to step in. We must find some way of accommodating these very real concerns of developing countries.[12]

(x) Trade and the development agenda

Trade liberalisation is necessary but not sufficient for developing countries to reap the full benefits from integration with the world economy. Much of the trade agenda now goes beyond the border into areas of domestic regulation. The ability of a country, and particularly of the more isolated communities within a country, to participate in trade depends importantly upon the quality of the transport and communications infrastructure that allows them to access the world trading system. The new, broader trade agenda involves many issues that are much more difficult to implement than trade liberalisation, which can be implemented at the stroke of a pen. Efficient infrastructure requires years of investment both in the regulatory framework under which it is supplied, and in the infrastructure itself.

---

[12] Article XVIII, Section A, of the GATT does provide an explicit mechanism for infant industry protection, but that provision has been little used, presumably because of the requirement for compensation of trading partners, as well as the backlash in recent years against abuse of infant-industry arguments. But going forward, it will be important to ensure that the legitimate development concerns of poorer countries are reflected in the international trade rules – even while guarding against the development-impeding types of protectionism that have so often been justified using infant-industry arguments. Part of the task will be to preserve and raise awareness of provisions *already* available within the trade rules that may serve some development needs. One example is the Article XIX safeguard provisions, which permit transparent protection of limited duration without requiring compensation.

Improving the efficiency of customs requires strengthening of the Customs Administration in many countries. Establishing a strong financial regulatory structure – so that opening up markets for financial services strengthens economic performance rather than contributing to economic instability – is no easy task, even for more advanced countries.

The broader agenda opens up the prospect that trade liberalisation may yield even more benefits than it has in the past. But from the perspective of the developing country, what is crucial for growth is access to markets abroad, especially in the developed countries. The East Asia miracle was based on export-oriented policies that took advantage of increasing access. Such policies play a critical role in raising quality within the developing countries, in promoting the transfer of technology, and in enforcing the discipline of competition. The development process entails a transformation of society, and openness to the outside in general, and trade in particular, can play a central role in that transformation (Stiglitz, 1998). Retreat from openness would unacceptably delay the development transformation that developing countries sorely need. More is at stake than simply the exploitation of the gains from comparative advantages. Trade is vital to the dynamics of successful development.

The convergence of the trade and development agendas requires greater cooperation between the agencies involved in development policy, and those focused on trade. Such cooperation is one of the key features of the Integrated Framework for Trade-Related Technical Assistance to Least Developed Countries. Clearly, however, the same needs exist in a much broader group of developing countries, and we and our WTO colleagues will need to work closely if we are to achieve our shared objectives in this new era.

4. CONCLUDING REMARKS

The principles of fairness and comprehensiveness are strongly linked. A comprehensive approach to trade will not only be more effective in attaining the objectives of trade liberalisation, but it will also be perceived as fairer. This perception will not only enhance the chances of trade liberalisation within developing countries, but also increase their enthusiasm for a broader range of market reforms. A comprehensive Round that adequately represents the interests of developing countries will deflate the sentiment that market economics is a theory invoked only in the pursuit of developed-country interests, and it will increase awareness that vigorous market competition brings benefits to any economy.

Both the political and economic stakes are high. If we fail – if the developed countries allow their special interests to prevail over their national interests, both in terms of their offers of market access and their demands on the developing world for market access – this will undermine confidence in democratic processes everywhere. Clearly, the developed countries have much to gain from a more integrated global economy, and they have much to gain from reducing their distortionary policies. But they can afford the luxury of the inefficiencies of the existing distortions, and they have demonstrated an impressive capacity to dismiss or overlook the intellectual inconsistencies – to use a mild term – in some of their positions. The developing countries cannot afford such economic distortions; the evidence of the last three decades strongly supports the conclusion that market-oriented policies, including outward-oriented policies, provide their best hope for sustained growth. Such growth is absolutely necessary if poverty within these countries is to be eradicated.

A new Round provides a great opportunity. It can reinforce the movement toward true market economies, enhancing competition and promoting economic and societal transformation. At the same time, by reducing trade barriers, and thereby eliminating some of the major sources of corruption and lack of transparency, it can strengthen democratic processes. But a Round also poses great risks. If negotiations follow historical patterns – hard bargaining motivated by special interests within developed countries, with too little attention paid to the interests of the developing countries – they could strengthen the hand of those in the developing world who resist market reforms and an outward orientation. It could give confirmation and ammunition to those who see relations between the Third World and the developed countries through the prism of conflict and exploitation, rather than recognising the potential for cooperation and mutual gain. Outward-oriented policies will succeed only to the extent that there are markets in which developing countries can sell their products, as well as international rules that allow developing countries to make good use of their areas of comparative advantage.

REFERENCES

Anderson, K., B. Hoekman and A. Strutt (1999), 'Agriculture and the WTO: Next Steps' (Washington, DC: World Bank), mimeo (www.worldbank.org/trade).
Blackhurst, R., W. Lyakurwa and A. Oyejide (1999), 'Options for Improving Africa's Participation in the WTO', *The World Economy*, **23**, 491–510.
Feldstein, M. (1998), 'Refocusing the IMF', *Foreign Affairs*, **77** (March–April), 20–33.
Finger, J.M. (1998), 'GATT Experience with Safeguards: Making Economic and Political Sense of the Possibilities that the GATT Allows to Restrict Imports', World Bank Policy Research Working Paper No. 2000 (www.worldbank.org/trade).
Finger, J.M. and P. Schuler (1999), 'Implementation of Uruguay Round Commitments: The Development Challenge', *The World Economy*, **23**, 511–526.
Hertel, T.W. and W. Martin (1999), 'Liberalising Agriculture and Manufactures in a Millennium Round: Implications for Developing Countries', *The World Economy*, **23**, 455–470.
Hoekman, B. and P. Holmes (1999), 'Competition Policy, Developing Countries and the WTO', *The World Economy*, **22**, 875–93.

Ingco, M. (1996), 'Tariffication in the Uruguay Round: How Much Liberalisation?', *The World Economy*, **19**, 4, 425–46.

Mattoo, A. (1999), 'Developing Countries in the New Round of GATS Negotiations: Towards a Pro-Active Role', *The World Economy*, **23**, 471–490.

Nogués, J., A. Olechowski and L.A. Winters (1986), 'The Extent of Nontariff Barriers to Industrial Countries' Imports', *World Bank Economic Review*, **1**, 181–99.

OECD (1999), *Agricultural Policies in OECD Countries: Monitoring and Outlook* (Paris: OECD).

Stiglitz, J.E. (1998), 'Towards a New Paradigm for Development: Strategies, Policies, and Processes', Prebisch Lecture, UNCTAD (Geneva, 19 October).

Thurow, L. (1985), *The Zero-sum Solution: Building a World-class American Economy* (New York: Simon & Schuster).

Willig, R. (1998), 'Economic Effects of Antidumping Policy,' *Brookings Trade Forum 1998* (Washington, DC: The Brookings Institution).

World Bank (1999), *World Development Report 1999/2000: Entering the 21st Century* (Washington, DC: World Bank).

3

Bringing Discipline to Agricultural Policy via the WTO

Kym Anderson

1. INTRODUCTION

 ANY perceive one of the great achievements of the Uruguay Round (UR) to be the start to bringing agricultural policies under GATT discipline.[1] Following the signing of the UR accord in 1994, non-tariff barriers to agricultural imports are required to be tariffied and bound and those bound tariffs are scheduled for phased reductions. As well, farm production and export subsidies also have been reduced, mostly between 1995 and 2000 (with developing countries having an extra four or more years). That UR Agreement on Agriculture (URAA), together with the SPS Agreement (to limit the use of quarantine import restrictions to cases that can be justified scientifically) and the Dispute Settlement Agreement (which has greatly improved the process of resolving trade conflicts), ensure that agricultural trade will be less chaotic in future than prior to the formation in 1995 of the new World Trade Organisation (WTO).

Much remains to be done, however, before agricultural trade is as fully disciplined or as free as world trade in manufactures. This chapter first explains why agricultural policies need to be disciplined under the WTO (Section 2). It then examines what has been achieved through implementation of the URAA (Section 3), evaluates its impacts on developing countries (Section 4), explores what remained to be tackled as WTO members came back to the negotiating table in 2000, as was agreed in the URAA (Section 5), and reviews ways developing countries can seek to ensure that the process of reform by them and others continues into the second millennium (Section 6).

---

[1] On the long history of exceptional treatment of agriculture in the GATT, see Josling, Tangermann and Warley (1996).

2. WHY AGRICULTURAL POLICIES NEED TO BE DISCIPLINED UNDER THE GATT/WTO

The history of industrial and post-industrial development has been overlaid with a history of agricultural protection growth. Poor agrarian economies tend to tax agriculture relative to other tradables sectors, but as nations industrialise their policy regimes tend to gradually change from negatively to positively assisting farmers relative to other producers (and conversely from subsidising to taxing food consumers). The period since the 1950s has seen substantial growth in agricultural protectionism in the advanced industrial economies and its spread to newly industrialising economies, and those tendencies accelerated in the 1980s (Anderson and Hayami, 1986; Anderson, 1994 and 1995; and Lindert, 1991).

Given this history, the attempt in the Uruguay Round to reduce farm price supports was seen as both exciting and daunting: exciting, because a successful liberalisation would reduce the huge and growing waste of resources that would be associated with the continuation of past trends in farm policies; and daunting, because the history of those policy trends across many countries and over a long period suggests major counteracting of domestic political forces would be needed for a multilateral agreement to be reached and then implemented.

It seems almost incredible that the Uruguay Round could have been prolonged for years by a farm trade dispute affecting products that account for less than one-tenth of world trade and less than one-twentieth of GDP and employment in the main countries seeking exceptional treatment for agriculture. It seems all the more amazing given that the economies hurt most by these policies are those of the protecting countries themselves. The protectionist policies are wasteful in terms of raising consumer prices for food; requiring ever-larger treasury outlays to farmers; redistributing welfare with increasing inefficiency (not only because it costs consumers and taxpayers much more than one dollar for every dollar received by farmers, but also because the largest producers receive the lion's share of the benefits); making non-agricultural producers less competitive in so far as farm programmes retain resources in agriculture; and damaging the natural environment, not least because these price-support policies typically encourage excessive use of farm chemicals (Tyers and Anderson, 1992).

Why has agreement on farm trade reform been so difficult to reach? The issue involves two groups of countries. On the one hand, there are the traditionally lightly protected, food-exporting countries, involving not only the members of the Cairns Group[2] but also numerous other developing countries; and on the other

---

[2] The Cairns Group by 1999 comprised 15 members: Australia, Argentina, Brazil, Canada, Chile, Colombia, Fiji, Indonesia, Malaysia, New Zealand, Paraguay, Philippines, South Africa, Thailand and Uruguay. Originally it involved 14 countries excluding Paraguay and South Africa but including Hungary. During 1999 three more joined: Bolivia, Costa Rica and Guatemala. The group is named after the Australian city where they first met in August 1986. The Group's sole purpose was to ensure that agricultural trade liberalisation remained high on the agenda of the Uruguay Round.

hand, there are industrial countries of Western Europe, Japan and Korea that are highly protective of their farmers. Both groups have felt strongly about their positions for a long time. Indeed it is *because* those policies are so contentious that (a) the first four rounds of GATT-based multilateral trade negotiations virtually ignored them and the next three eventually had to drop them, and (b) many minilateral (regional and other preferential) trade agreements also largely exclude farm products. We should therefore not be surprised that the inclusion of farm policies in the Uruguay Round caused problems. Their inclusion was considered necessary, however, because they had become extremely distortionary by the 1980s, both absolutely and relative to non-farm trade policies, and because there was every indication that agricultural protection growth would continue to spread, cancer-like, unless explicitly checked.

The growth of agricultural protectionism in industrialising countries has contributed to the long-term downward trend in the international price of farm products relative to that for industrial products (Figure 1). What is striking about Figure 1 is not only the extent of decline of the relative price of food but also the increase in its coefficient of variation during the past two decades. That, together with the EC's provision from the latter 1970s of export subsidies to dispose of its induced surpluses, stimulated the US to defend its export markets by subsidising US farm exports as well – a move that contributed to international food prices

FIGURE 1
Real International Food Prices, 1900 to 1992 (1977–79 = 100)

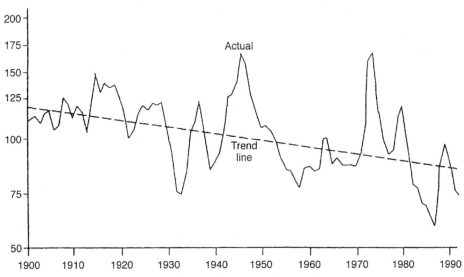

Source: Updated from Grilli and Yang (1988), showing an index of export prices in US dollars for cereals, meats, daily products and sugar, deflated by the US producer price index (primarily for industrial products), with weights based on the importance of each product in global exports in the 1977–79 base period.

falling by 1987 to their lowest level this century in real terms. The export subsidies under the US Export Enhancement Program have been very costly to the US, have added only very modestly in proportional terms to the EC budgetary cost of the Common Agricultural Policy, and have imposed large costs on other actual or would-be agricultural-exporting countries.

As a consequence of these policy developments (reasons for which are analysed in Anderson, 1995), the deadweight welfare losses in those protecting countries from distorting their food markets more than doubled over the 1980s, while the benefits to their farmers as a group increased by about 50 per cent. According to one set of estimates from a multicommodity model of world food markets, the annual benefits of these policies to farmers of Western Europe, the United States and Japan rose from $94 to $141 billion over the 1980s (in 1985 US dollars), while the cost to consumers in those countries rose from $120 to $216 billion. That study estimates the direct global loss of economic welfare because of industrial country food policies to have trebled in the 1980s, rising from $16 billion to $50 billion (Tyers and Anderson, 1992, Tables 6.5, 6.6). And that does not include the costs of lobbying for and administering the policies, nor the collection and by-product distortion costs of raising the government revenue needed to finance the subsidies, let alone the indirect cost these policies imposed in terms of holding up the Uruguay Round's conclusion.

3. THE URUGUAY ROUND ACHIEVEMENTS AFFECTING AGRICULTURE

Agriculture benefited in several important ways from the Uruguay Round. Apart from the Agreement on Agriculture itself, there were agreements relating to SPS provisions (quarantine) and to the textiles and clothing trade (which will boost net food imports of newly industrialising countries), requirements to notify and review all trade-related policy developments which will boost transparency, and major improvements in dispute settlement procedures. Each of these is considered in turn.

a. The Agreement on Agriculture

In the light of the long history of agricultural protection growth in industrial countries, even achieving a standstill in agricultural protection via the Uruguay Round could be described as progress. It would be an advance over what otherwise might have been the case in part because it would reduce the risk of newly industrialising countries following the more advanced ones down the agricultural protection growth path. As it turned out, though, only a little more than a standstill was agreed to.

The Uruguay Round's Agreement on Agriculture has three main components: reductions in farm export subsidies, increases in import market access, and cuts in domestic producer subsidies. The fact that (often discriminatory) farm export subsidies are still to be tolerated continues to distinguish agricultural from industrial goods in the GATT, a distinction that stems from the addition in 1955 of paragraphs to GATT Article XVI when the United States insisted on primary products being exempted from the new prohibition of export subsidies. Moreover, even by the year 2000 farm export subsidies need be only about one-fifth lower than they were in the late 1980s to comply with the agreement. True, the budgetary expenditure on export subsidies is to be lowered by 36 per cent from the base period, but for some commodities it may be only the agreed cut in the *volume* of subsidised exports (21 per cent for industrial countries, 14 per cent for developing countries) that bites because international food prices in the latter 1990s were higher than in the base period, so exportable surpluses have been able to be disposed of with lower subsidy outlays.

A second distinguishing feature of the agricultural agreement is that it requires non-tariff import barriers to be converted to tariffs. Those tariffs are now bound and those bindings are to be reduced over the implementation period. However, the extent of bound tariff reduction by the end of the century will be even more modest than for export subsidies: the *unweighted* average tariff cut must be 36 per cent (24 per cent for developing countries), but it could be less than one-sixth as a *weighted* average, since each tariff item need be reduced by only 15 per cent of the claimed 1986–88 tariff equivalents (10 per cent for developing countries).

Moreover, the claimed tariff equivalents for the base period 1986–88, and hence the initial tariff bindings, are in many cases far higher than the actual tariff equivalents of the time. The European Union, for example, has set them on average at about 60 per cent above the actual tariff equivalents of the CAP in recent years, while the United States has set theirs about 45 per cent above recent rates. This 'dirty' tariffication is shown in column 4 of Table 1 for the US and EU to be considerable. Nor is it confined to industrial countries. On the contrary, developing countries are even more involved in the practice. This is possible because they were allowed to convert unbound tariffs into 'ceiling bindings' unrelated to previous actual rates of protection. Many developing countries have chosen to bind their tariffs on agricultural imports at more than 50 per cent and some as high as 150 per cent – far above the tariff equivalents of restrictions actually in place in the 1980s/early 1990s (Ingco, 1996). Josling (1998, Table 1) calculates that the unweighted average bound tariffs by 2000 for a sample of 20 major countries will be between 42 and 49 per cent for each of grains, oilseeds, sugar and livestock products, and 35 per cent for fruit and vegetables.

'Dirty' tariffication has two consequences. One is that actual tariffs may provide no less protection in 2000 than did the non-tariff import barriers of the late 1980s/early 1990s. Indeed in the case of the EU the final rates for the year

TABLE 1
Uruguay Round Tariff Bindings and Actual Tariff Equivalents of Agricultural Protection, European
Union and United States, 1986 to 2000

| | Actual Tariff Equivalent (%), 1989–93 | Tariff Binding | | 'Dirty' Tariff-ication,[a] 1986–88 | Binding 2000/ Actual Tariff Equivalent, 1989–93 |
		Final Period 2000 (%)	Proportional Reduction by 2000 (%)		
European Union					
Wheat	68	109	36	1.60	1.60
Coarse grains	89	121	36	1.42	1.36
Rice	103	231	36	2.36	2.24
Beef and veal	97	87	10	1.00	0.90
Other meat	27	34	36	1.32	1.26
Dairy products	147	205	29	1.63	1.39
Sugar	144	279	6	1.27	1.94
ALL AGRIC.					
Unweighted av.	**45**	**73**		**1.61**	**1.63**
std. deviation	**57**	**96**		**1.58**	**1.68**
United States					
Wheat	20	4	36	0.30	0.20
Coarse grains	2	2	74	2.00	1.00
Rice	2	3	36	5.00	1.50
Beef and veal	2	26	15	10.33	13.00
Other meat	1	3	36	0.67	3.00
Dairy products	46	93	15	1.09	2.02
Sugar	67	91	15	1.50	1.36
ALL AGRIC.					
Unweighted av.	**13**	**23**		**1.44**	**1.77**
std. deviation	**22**	**35**		**1.20**	**1.59**

Notes:
[a] Announced base tariff rate as a ratio of actual tariff equivalent in the base period.

Source: Ingco (1995).

2000 are almost two-thirds above the actual tariff equivalent for 1989–93, and for the United States they are more than three-quarters above (final column of Table 1). The other consequence of binding tariffs at such a high level is that it allows countries to set the actual tariff below that but to vary it so as to stabilise the domestic market in much the same way as the EU has done in the past with its system of variable import levies and export subsidies. This means there will be little of the reduction in fluctuations in international food markets this decade that tariffication was expected to deliver.

It is true that some countries have agreed also to provide a minimum market access opportunity, such that the share of imports in domestic consumption for products subject to import restrictions rises to at least 5 per cent by the year 2000 under a tariff quota (less in the case of developing countries). But that access is subject to special safeguard provisions, so it only offers potential rather than actual access (another form of contingent protection). As well, there is scope to minimise the impact of those imports on the domestic market. Furthermore, market access rules formally introduce scope for discriminating in the allocation of import quotas between countries, where within-quota imports attract a much lower tariff than above-quota imports. Perhaps even more importantly, the administration of such quotas tends to legitimise a role for state trading agencies. When such agencies have selling rights on the domestic market in addition to a monopoly on imports of farm products, they can charge excessive mark-ups and thereby distort domestic prices easily and relatively covertly – just as such agencies can hide export subsidies if they are given that monopoly. There are thus elements of quantitative management of both export and import trade in farm products now legitimised under the WTO, including scope for discriminatory distortions to trade volumes as well as prices.

The third main component of the agriculture agreement is that the aggregate level of domestic support (AMS) for industrial-country farmers is to be reduced to four-fifths of its 1986–88 level by the turn of the century. That too will require only modest reform in most industrial countries because much of the decline in the AMS had already occurred by the mid-1990s. Furthermore, there are many forms of support that need not be included in the calculation of the AMS. Perhaps the most important are direct payments under production-limiting programmes of the sort adopted by the US and EU, which are classified as 'blue box' exemptions. Others such as quarantine and environmental provisions are classified as 'green box' exemptions. A risk that needs to be curtailed is that the use of such 'blue box' and 'green box' instruments may spread to other developed countries and other commodities as farm income support via trade and domestic price support measures becomes less available and in some cases eventually WTO-illegal.

In short, implementing the agricultural reforms agreed to in the Uruguay Round involved only very modest liberalisation by 2000, with plenty of room for disputes over compliance during the implementation period and for further reductions in the new millennium (see column 2 of Table 1). Only a small number of import price reductions can be expected from the Round through the implementation period, especially among developing countries. At best that will do no more than slow the decline in real prices for farm products in international markets, rather than reverse it. 'Dirty' tariffication in particular means that the real price of farm products in international markets will be barely above what it otherwise would be (see the modelling results reported in Table 2) – and it will do little this decade at least to reduce price fluctuations around that long-run trend. The Round will accelerate agriculture's relative decline and loss of farm jobs in heavily-protected industrial countries, but only slightly. And it will boost

TABLE 2
Estimated Impact of Implementing the Uruguay Round on International Prices of Farm Products
Relative to Prices of Manufactured Exports from Industrial Countries
(per cent)

	If There Had Been No 'Dirty' Tariffication	With 'Dirty' Tariffication
Wheat	10	1
Rice	4	−1
Coarse grain	5	0
Sugar	11	−1
Beef and veal	6	0
Other meat	2	−1
Dairy products	12	−1
Vegetable oils	5	−1
Coffee	−1	−2
Cocoa	0	−1
Tea	1	−2
Other foods	−1	−1
Cotton	1	−1
Other agriculture	3	−1

Source: Goldin and Mensbrugghe (1996).

gradually the competitiveness of farmers in countries where the international price rises are transmitted to the domestic market for farm products, although again the improvements will be only slight over the remainder of this decade.

But at least agriculture is now in the mainstream of the WTO (which allowed the other agreements in the Uruguay Round to be concluded), and the agreement to reopen agricultural negotiations by 2000 to continue the process of farm reform has been honoured. Moreover, the requirement to tariffy non-tariff import barriers, to quantify the Aggregate Measure of Support, and to notify all subsequent policy changes to the WTO's Committee on Agriculture are major contributions to transparency that in themselves limit the worst excesses. The new rules and obligations eventually will constrain further farm protection growth in both advanced and newly industrialised countries, thereby promising greater certainty and stability to international food markets next century. Furthermore, there has been considerable reduction in the degree of tariff escalation affecting markets for tropical export products. In the cases of rubber, jute, oilseeds, spices, tobacco and wood, for example, tariffs on the primary and semi-processed products have been lower than on the final manufactured products but the latter are to be reduced much more than the former thanks to the Uruguay Round (ESCAP, 1995, pp. 128–30). All these developments will encourage developing countries with a natural comparative advantage in farm products to exploit the new market opportunities, not least through seeking reductions in their own country's direct and indirect policy discrimination against agriculture.

b. The SPS Agreement

Because of the concern among agricultural exporters that the hard-won benefits to them from the UR agriculture agreement could be reduced by current farm protectionist measures being replaced by alternative measures such as quarantine restrictions, an agreement on Sanitary (human and animal health) and Phytosanitary (plant health) measures was also negotiated. The SPS Agreement seeks to ensure that any such SPS import restrictions are imposed only to the extent necessary to ensure food safety and animal and plant health on the basis of scientific information, and are the least trade-restrictive measures available to achieve the risk reduction desired. Although there is sufficient vagueness in the wording to ensure that the protectionist abuse of SPS measures is still possible, consultations between WTO members are leading to conflict resolution in numerous cases and, in other cases that go on to form a panel, the dispute settlement evidence to date shows that exporting countries can succeed in getting WTO panels to rule against the most excessive cases (Roberts, 1998).

c. The Agreement on Textiles and Clothing

Another major achievement of the Uruguay Round of indirect but none the less significant importance for agricultural-trading countries was the bringing of highly protected textiles and clothing back into the mainstream of GATT/WTO activities. Since the early 1960s their protection in advanced economies from import competition from newly industrialising countries had grown enormously, contrary to the policy trend for most other manufacturing industries. That had been most unfortunate for (especially densely populated) developing countries seeking to industrialise and export their way out of poverty. In turn it meant those economies' emergence as net food importers has been delayed.

When the Uruguay Round was due to be launched, developing country members of GATT made it clear they would not participate actively in the Round unless, like farm policies, textile and clothing trade policies were high on the agenda for liberalisation. That was taken seriously in the Uruguay Round, unlike in previous rounds, because advanced economies were keen to improve their access to services and capital markets, and protection of their intellectual property, in developing countries.

What was achieved in terms of commitments under the Uruguay Round to dismantle textile and clothing protection? As with agriculture, not a lot in absolute terms but a great deal relative to the past and to what might otherwise have been the case. More specifically, the MFA and its 'voluntary' export restraints (VERs) on textiles and clothing are to be dismantled so as to return textiles and clothing to the full discipline of the GATT by 2005. During the transition, quotas on trade volumes are to grow faster than in the past and eventually are to be replaced entirely by tariffs as the only restraint on trade. Those tariffs will be bound and gradually reduced. For advanced economies as a whole, the average tariff on these goods is scheduled to fall from 15.5 per cent in 1995 to 12.1 per cent by 2005. But, again as with agriculture, the devil is in the details. According to Hertel et al. (1996), by 2005 the quotas will have increased by only about half the amount necessary for them to become redundant, in which case full tariffication would require the other half of the increase to occur at the end of the ten-year transition period, which seems unlikely. It is also possible that the US and the EU will use the special safeguards and/or other forms of contingent protection such as anti-dumping duties as that time approaches.

Furthermore, while China, Taiwan and Vietnam remain outside the WTO, they are likely to enjoy little if any extra growth in their access to the EU and US textile and clothing markets as those liberalising countries are pressured to honour commitments to developing country members of WTO. Should China – the world's largest clothing exporter – be admitted to the WTO before the MFA phaseout is completed in 2005, that could add substantially to structural adjustment pressures for these declining industries in advanced economies, and reduce the quota rents to other developing country suppliers. The least-competitive firms and workers in both sets of countries are unhappy about that prospect, and may use China's accession as an excuse for not completing the phase-out of the MFA by 2005 and/or demand that China continue to restrain its exports of textile products well beyond 2005. Should that happen, a great deal of the potential economic benefits from both the Uruguay Round and China's WTO accession, particularly for food-exporting countries, would be foregone or at least postponed (Anderson et al., 1997).

In short, the bringing of textiles and clothing back into the mainstream of GATT disciplines is a major coup for newly industrialising countries and therefore to agricultural-exporting countries in so far as the former become ever-larger net food importers. But equally clearly, the implementation of this agreement will have to be monitored carefully, in the hope both of minimising any slippage (particularly if/when China joins the WTO) and of making sure further progress is made in the next round of multilateral trade negotiations as it affects this still-highly protected group of manufactures.

d. Monitoring Trade-related Policies and Providing Information

One of the reasons protectionist trade policies persist is that the losers from those policies are poorly informed about the nature and extent of their loss. In so far as they underestimate the loss, so they under-invest in lobbying against such distortionary policies. In these circumstances there is an economic return to society from supplying more information on the effects of interventionist policies. Yet many governments choose to under-supply such information, presumably at the request of those interest groups gaining from incomplete transparency (Rattigan and Carmichael, 1996).

The shortfall in national transparency agencies can be offset somewhat at least by the WTO Secretariat providing that service. It now does so, in the form both of comprehensive annual notification requirements (to the Committee on Agriculture in the case of farm policies) and of the Trade Policy Review Mechanism (TPRM). Notices of all changes in trade and trade-related policies must be published by each country and made accessible to its trading partners, as well as sent to the WTO Secretariat. The Secretariat now makes those notifications public, including through the WTO's internet website.[3] As well, the WTO's TPRM reviews each country's policies on a regular basis[4] and publishes its findings.

e. The WTO's Expanded Role in Dispute Resolution

A further Uruguay Round achievement is that the GATT's role in resolving trade disputes has been strengthened very substantially under the WTO. Each case is to be completed in less than nine months. If an appeal is lodged, the new WTO Appellate Body will hear and rule on any claim of legal error within 60 days. Rulings are automatically adopted unless the WTO membership decides by consensus not to do so, unlike under the old GATT where the party under review effectively had the power of veto. In its first two years about 100 cases have been brought, compared with a mere 300 cases in the total 48-year history of the GATT. Moreover, the panel reports are causing countries to implement significant policy changes, unlike many of the GATT dispute reports. A prominent trade law professor believes the establishment of the Dispute Settlement Body in the WTO:

> is likely to be seen in the future as one of the most important, and perhaps even watershed, developments of international economic relations in the twentieth century (Jackson, 1997, p. 176).

This development is of particular significance to agriculture because farm trade is so contentious. From the late 1940s to the mid-1990s, more than 43 per cent of GATT dispute settlement cases were agricultural (Hudec, 1998, p. 38), and ever since the WTO came into force the share has been about 30 per cent – several times agriculture's share of world trade.[5] The fact that the share has

---

[3] See the website at http://www.wto.org/wto/online/dff1.htm. WTO members' commitments under the Uruguay Round Agreement on Agriculture are available on the website of the US Department of Agriculture at http://ffas.usda.gov/scriptsw/wtopdf/wtopdf_lout.idc while applied tariffs for APEC countries can be found at the APEC website at http://www.apectariff.org

[4] Once every two years in the case of the EU, the US, Japan and Canada, every four years for the next 16 biggest traders, and every six years in the case of others except for the smallest and poorest developing countries where the interval may be longer.

[5] For a list of all the WTO Dispute Settlement cases to early 1998 involving agricultural products, see OECD (1998b, pp. 145–48).

dropped since 1994, despite there being a backlog of claims that were held over until the Round was completed, suggests the Uruguay Round's agricultural and SPS agreements may well have lessened confrontation in farm trade. And the fact that the new dispute settlement procedures are faster, more automatic, and binding once the case is finished means much more satisfactory outcomes are expected in the future than resulted pre-1995 (although the EU's inadequate responses to the banana and beef hormone cases brought against it in the late 1990s have greatly disappointed the complaining parties so far).

4. IMPACT OF THE URUGUAY ROUND AGREEMENTS ON DEVELOPING COUNTRIES

a. What Determines the Impact on a Developing Country?

The Uruguay Round was not only about agriculture of course. But it together with the many other UR agreements will boost global economic welfare substantially. Whether and to what extent a particular country shares in that welfare gain depends largely on how much (a) its trading partners lower barriers to its exports, (b) its competitors lower their trade barriers, and especially (c) how much the country concerned lowers its own trade barriers. Since the Uruguay Round involved so much more than just agriculture, and since this freeing up of global trade and the associated boost to economic growth is going to alter countries' comparative advantages, it is only possible to think about the impact of the Round on a country from a global, economy-wide perspective. In particular, will the Uruguay Round improve the country's terms of trade and, if not, will its own policy reform commitments be sufficient to ensure its citizens are none the less better off from the Round's implementation? And how will the country's agricultural sector and food security be affected? We address these questions in turn for larger economies, before focusing on the smaller and least-developed countries.

b. Overview of Recent Findings for the Larger Developing Economies

Earlier GATT Secretariat estimates put the economic benefit of the Round as a whole at between US$200 and $500 billion per year (Nordstrom, McDonald and Francois, 1994). More recent studies provide lower estimates of global welfare gains, primarily because of the more-modest agricultural reforms that are now expected thanks to 'dirty' tariffication and to the fact that agricultural protection has decreased since the Round began (the effects of which were not captured in earlier studies).[6] All such empirical studies grossly underestimate the total

---

[6] See, for example, Brown, Deardorff, Fox and Stern (1996), Francois, McDonald and Nordstrom (1996), Goldin and Mennsbrugghe (1996), Harrison, Rutherford and Tarr (1996) and Hertel et al. (1996).

benefits from the Uruguay Round, however, because they under-represent or ignore a number of important effects of the agreements that are difficult to quantify. One is in strengthening the multilateral trading system (including the bringing of services, TRIPs and TRIMs under GATT/WTO discipline) and thereby in boosting investor confidence, employment and productivity growth. Another is the encouragement that greater openness abroad gives to accelerating the unilateral reform programmes of individual (especially developing) countries beyond their Uruguay Round commitments. These studies also assume the alternative scenario is the status quo, whereas the alternative may well have involved more protectionism, higher barriers around regional blocs, and sporadic trade wars in farm products, autos, etc. with few if any winners.

Bearing those points in mind, much can still be learnt from available quantitative modelling exercises. Hertel et al. (1996) estimate a global welfare gain from agricultural and manufacturing trade liberalisation of US$260 billion per year by 2005 (in 1992 prices), or 0.4 per cent of expected global GDP. Much of that estimated benefit of the Round will accrue to developing countries, especially the more open ones and those making the largest liberalisation commitments. The estimated gain to East Asia's developing economies, for example, is a 4.7 per cent boost, primarily because of large gains from (a) textile and clothing import liberalisation by industrial countries and (b) their own reforms.

Three important implications of these results are worth stressing. One of the consequences of expanded manufacturing export opportunities is that agricultural production growth in Asian developing economies other than China and South Asia is slowed – despite farm trade liberalisation in developed countries – as more resources are attracted to textiles and clothing. This can be seen from Table 3, which shows the projected percentage changes in output between 1992 and 2005 for each sector with and without the Round, as estimated by Hertel et al. (1996).

A second important point to note from Table 3 is the absence of negative numbers in row 1. That is, even in the countries reducing their agricultural protection most (the EU, Japan and South Korea), their agricultural sectors are projected to be larger in 2005 than in 1992 – the UR reforms simply slow the expansion of their farm output.

The third point, though, is that the expansion of agriculture outside Western Europe and Northeast Asia is only slightly faster than it would have been without the Uruguay Round, because the benefits from reducing agricultural protection are so widespread and the liberalisations expected to come from the UR are very modest. And it is enough only to slow the relative decline in agriculture in middle- and upper-income countries, not to reverse it.

Francois et al. (1996) estimate the annual gain from the Round to be up to $215 billion in 1992 prices, but their model is calibrated to 1992 rather than 2005 so that gain represents up to one per cent of global GDP. That estimate assumes increasing returns to scale and imperfect competition for the industrial sector; when constant returns to scale are instead assumed, the gain is estimated to be only 0.45 per cent. The latter is close to the 0.42 per cent gain estimated by Hertel et al.'s constant returns to scale model – the difference underscoring the point that market structure assumptions are critical in such modelling work. Of that global welfare gain of $215 billion, only one-thirtieth is attributable to agriculture post-1992, compared with one-fifteenth for other primary product reform, half for textiles and clothing, and the rest for other manufactures. For Australasia, however, 60 per cent of the estimated gain is due to agriculture. Again Asian developing economies are projected to gain proportionately much more than other regions from the Uruguay Round Agreements (a GDP boost for China of

TABLE 3
Projected Percentage Change in Sectoral Output Between 1992 and 2005 Without (Upper Entry)
and With (Lower Entry) Uruguay Round Liberalisation
(per cent)

(a) East Asian Developing Countries

	S. Korea	Taiwan	China	Indonesia	Malaysia	Philippines	Thailand
Primary	65	76	121	71	102	60	95
Agriculture	43	79	125	66	69	19	77
Processed	92	94	194	111	156	73	149
Food	109	114	180	110	441	118	140
Other	134	143	246	79	119	79	104
Primary	128	142	238	73	98	67	91
Textiles	91	178	250	126	169	74	171
	221	181	262	227	217	136	205
Clothing	67	74	225	114	196	88	168
	146	89	327	639	262	285	338
Other Light	147	170	285	157	215	71	218
Manu-facturing	167	168	278	142	166	53	208
Transport,	117	89	237	146	132	33	152
Machinery and Equipment	98	83	220	130	92	30	168
Other	141	188	315	177	154	78	194
Heavy Manu-facturing	143	182	301	163	262	64	195

(*continues*)

TABLE 3 (*continued*):

(b) Industrial and Other Countries

	South Asia	Japan	North America	European Union	Latin America	Sub-Saharan Africa	Rest of World
Primary	63	30	23	12	44	76	14
Agriculture	67	13	27	5	44	75	15
Processed	94	28	21	8	48	81	24
Food	108	21	21	5	47	78	19
Other	115	60	42	24	76	43	18
Primary	103	62	43	24	78	46	18
Textiles	116	23	30	11	53	75	24
	138	25	7	3	46	58	9
Clothing	114	8	22	−12	53	111	17
	241	1	−41	−60	42	30	−11
Other Light	130	38	31	15	51	59	31
Manu-	129	40	30	15	51	63	34
facturing							
Transport,	126	30	60	46	23	13	27
Machinery	86	29	62	48	22	16	31
and Equip-							
ment							
Other Heavy	131	42	42	19	50	51	28
Manu-	102	43	41	19	50	52	29
facturing							

Source: Hertel et al. (1996, Table 14).

4.0 per cent, for other developing East Asia of 3.2 per cent, and for South Asia of 3.1 per cent per year).

What impact will the Round have on international food prices? Estimates prior to the conclusion of the Round were quite optimistic. Tyers and Anderson (1992), for example, estimated that if all industrial countries were to tariffy all their support programmes cleanly and then halve those tariffs by 2000, real international food prices would be eight per cent by the turn of the century and the volatility of those prices would be almost halved. A one-fifth reduction in protection, therefore, might lead one to expect a rise in prices of temperate foods in international markets to average perhaps 3 per cent. But that would ignore three important factors: dirty tariffication is causing the reduction in protection levels to be even less than one-fifth; tropical agricultural products trade has been liberalised even less than temperate farm trade; and non-agricultural trade also is being liberalised, so that food prices relative to manufactured goods prices can be expected to be raised even less or even to be below what they would have been without the Uruguay Round.

All the latter three influences are evident in more recent results from Goldin and Mensbrugghe's (1996) economy-wide model, summarised in Table 2. The first column shows the change in the relative price of agricultural products that could be expected if there had been no 'dirt' in the tariffication of agricultural non-tariff import barriers: temperate food prices would increase between 5 and 12 per cent, while tropical goods prices would barely change at all, relative to prices of manufactures. By comparing that first column with the second column, the impact of dirty tariffication is apparent: agricultural prices are expected to hardly change at all relative to manufactured goods prices. This result is consistent with an even more recent study by Anderson et al. (1997), which finds the Uruguay Round to raise only very slightly agricultural prices relative to prices of manufactures (less than 2 per cent) and to slightly lower the relative price of processed foods, again relative to what would have been the case without the Uruguay Round being implemented.

How can these findings be reconciled with the FAO's projection of the effect of the Round? The FAO suggested international food prices would be 5 to 10 per cent higher in the year 2000 because of the Round. The model used to generate the FAO's results does not include non-farm sectors, however, and so does not measure the change also in prices for non-farm products as a result of the Round. It is the *relative* price change that matters in terms of its effect in altering production and consumption decisions, not just the change in the absolute price of food in each country. More importantly, the FAO study effectively ignores the fact that agricultural tariffications were 'dirty'. It therefore overstates substantially the decrease in farm protection and hence the impact of the Round on international food prices (see Sharma, Konandreas and Greenfield, 1996, for a careful and balanced discussion of these reasons for the FAO's higher price projections).

In all the above-mentioned studies of the Round, the big welfare gains for Asia's developing countries are based on the assumption that China (hence Taiwan) does not join the WTO. If/when China (including Taiwan) accedes to the World Trade Organisation, global welfare will expand substantially but some developing countries competing with China in OECD markets for labour-intensive manufactures could see their benefits from the Uruguay Round diminish by China's accession. The extent of that change depends heavily on how much China would be allowed to share in the expanded access to textile and clothing markets resulting from the Uruguay Round agreement to dismantle the Multifibre Arrangement. Anderson et al. (1997) provide results under the extreme assumption that China and Taiwan are completely denied expanded market access until they join the WTO, after which they are assumed to get the same access as current WTO members

TABLE 4

Impact of the Uruguay Round on Economic Welfare and on Grain Self-sufficiency, Various Countries, 2005

(US$ billlion and per cent)

	Welfare Effects of UR		Grain Self-sufficiency (%)	
	Without China Joining WTO	*With China Joining WTO*	*Without Uruguay Round*	*With Uruguay Round (incl. China in WTO)*
China, Mainland	2.1	44.2	95	96
China, Taiwan	3.5	5.7	64	65
Hong Kong+Sing.	−0.5	3.6	–	–
Korea, Rep.	9.5	9.3	79	78
Indonesia	11.1	4.5	97	97
Malaysia	10.4	8.2	63	65
Philippines	1.4	0.1	82	89
Thailand	6.5	2.1	115	135
India	5.9	1.7	100	101
Japan	19.9	25.9	84	81
Australia+NZ	1.9	1.9	187	204
North America	31.8	37.7	132	139
Western Europe	38.6	48.8	111	99
Rest of World	20.9	19.6	92	95
WORLD	**163.0**	**213.5**	**100**	**100**

Source: Anderson et al. (1997).

without further delay. In those circumstances, global economic welfare from the Round is estimated to be $50 billion per year higher once China is allowed into the WTO, but because of China's export expansion the gain from the Round is diminished somewhat for South and Southeast Asian countries (compare columns 1 and 2 of Table 6).

How is grain self-sufficiency affected by the Round? Contrary to the many concerns expressed during the negotiations, the effects on the larger economies are likely to be quite minor – not least because the UR reforms in agriculture are now expected to be only modest. The second pair of columns of Table 4 provides one set of estimates. Malaysia and the Philippines are seen to become less import dependent and Thailand to export more rice, but otherwise the changes are no more than a percentage point or two away from what they are projected to be without the Uruguay Round being implemented.

c. What About the Smaller and Least-developed Countries?

In addition to the special and differential treatment given to developing countries in the UR Agreement on Agriculture that is noted in Section 3 above, there are additional provisions for the least-developed countries (LDCs). They include a recognition of their special interests, fewer obligations, longer implementation periods for commitments, and technical assistance provisions (see WTO, 1995, for a full list). In the case of the Agreement on Agriculture, for example, Article 15.2 exempts LDCs from having to make commitments in all three areas of domestic support, market access, and export subsidies. There is as well provision for assisting LDCs and net food-importing developing countries to cope with the effects of implementing the Round's agricultural agreement on international food prices and on reduced subsidies on exports from industrial countries. There might also be assistance provided where there has been an erosion of preference margins, as in the case of ACP countries receiving the domestic price in the European Union for their exports. Specifically, in-kind aid in the form of food, short-term financial assistance to import food, and technical assistance to improve agricultural productivity and infrastructure are provided for in this Decision.

If anything, in-kind food aid has fallen rather than increased since the Uruguay Round was completed, with the depletion of discretionary grain stocks held by governments. Assuming governments choose to hold only modest stocks in future now that there is to be less domestic price support, the cost of official food aid will be higher than under previous farm policy regimes. Hence there will be domestic political pressure for food aid to be confined more to short-term emergency and humanitarian relief and to be used less as a substitute for commercial imports by LDCs.

There is already a loan facility at the IMF to help LDCs finance cereal imports during periods of price spikes or foreign exchange shortfalls. It has been used very little in the past, perhaps because the loan carries with it conditions of the type attached to regular structural adjustment loans from the IMF and/or because of the availability up until now of food aid and subsidised exports from industrial countries. Whether it will be used more under conditions of tighter grain markets and less food aid remains to be seen.

As for technical assistance to improve LDCs' agricultural productivity and infrastructure, that too if anything declined in the 1990s. Both bilateral aid agencies and multilateral institutions, such as the international agricultural research institutes and their former key funders such as the Ford and Rockefeller Foundations, have reduced the proportions of their funds targeted at agricultural aid projects. And aid in aggregate has been growing slower as well, as industrial governments respond to demands for downsising and for providing less funding to international agencies.

Hence there is little evidence that the LDCs and net food-importing developing countries have been assisted significantly more since the implementation of the Round's Agreement on Agriculture began.

Whether this matters depends in part on whether smaller and least-developed countries are likely to suffer disproportionately from that

TABLE 5

Food Trade Specialisation of Smaller and Least-developed Economies of Asia and the Pacific, 1990–93

	Gross Food Imports as a % of all Merchandise Imports	Food Imports Net of Food Exports as a % of all Merchandise Imports
ASIA		
Afghanistan	14	7
Bangladesh	17	17
Bhutan	10	2
Cambodia	8	7
India	3	−2
Korea, DPR	11	11
Laos	6	−2
Maldives	12	12
Mongolia	10	1
Myanmar	13	−15
Nepal	10	3
Pakistan	12	6
Sri Lanka	13	10
Viet Nam	4	−14
PACIFIC		
Fiji	12	−15
Kiribati	22	16
Micronesia	15	15
New Caledonia	10	10
Papua New Guinea	13	4
Samoa	17	11
Solomon Islands	13	−4
Tonga	21	5
Tuvalu	20	20
Vanuatu	14	−0

Source: FAO (1997).

agreement. To help assess that, consider Table 5. It shows the extent to which the LDCs and smaller economies of Asia and the Pacific have been dependent on food imports. Column 1 indicates that in most cases food accounts for well below one-fifth of all merchandise imports (the unweighted average for the countries shown is one-eighth), and hence an even smaller share of all goods and services imports by these countries. But as many as one-quarter of these countries were actually net food exporters in 1990-93 (column 2) – notwithstanding the fact that some of them (India, Laos) are still classified by the United Nations as net food-importing countries. Of the other three-quarters, net food imports amount on average to only 9 per cent of all their merchandise imports. A 1 or 2 per cent change in international food prices would therefore amount to an increase of less than 0.2 per cent of these countries' import bills. This is insignificant when compared with normal year-to-year fluctuations in international food prices.

To go beyond such casual empiricism, Ingco (1996) has used the model and results reported in Table 2 to estimate more precisely the impact of the Round's effect on international prices for agricultural products for a large number of LDCs. Predictably, though, the results show the impact on both the food import bill and GDP to be extremely small, especially when it is borne in mind that the Round's implementation period is 6–10 years.[7] Certainly it would be swamped by fluctuations in their trade balances due to other economic events, and more or less offset by the normal pressures for a slight long-term decline in the real international price of food depicted in Figure 1.

Of course these policy reforms will tend to help developing countries that are net exporters of farm products and those that are so close to being food self-sufficient that they would be net exporters once food prices rise following implementation of the Round. They also are likely to help those countries that would be net food exporters but for their own distortionary policies that discriminate against farmers (Anderson and Tyers, 1993). Even in those developing countries that would remain significant food importers even after the Round is implemented, many rural households, as net sellers of food or of farm labour, would benefit from a rise in food prices.

This suggests a general conclusion that even these poor countries are unlikely to have been harmed very much by the Round's implementation, especially if they took advantage of the now-more-open markets abroad (including through reduced tariff escalation) by liberalising their own economies. However, three caveats are in order.

First, countries that enjoyed a disproportionately large share of world food aid supplied out of subsidy-generated surpluses in Western Europe or the United States may be harmed significantly in so far as they now have to purchase such imports at closer to commercial rates.

Second, countries that in the past were able to purchase a large proportion of their food imports at discounted prices financed by the export subsidies of the EU or US have found themselves less able to do so as export subsidies were cut.

And third, ACP and other developing countries benefiting from preferential or duty-free access to EU and other markets under, for example, the Lome Convention or the Generalised System of Preferences will enjoy that privilege less. This is because the domestic prices in developed countries will be closer

---

[7] This is consistent with recent results reported by the FAO (in ESCAP, 1995, pp. 267–74) which show that there would be virtually no change in food consumption or food self-sufficiency among Asia's low-income food-deficit countries as a result of the Uruguay Round. Specifically, by the year 2000 that country group's self-sufficiency in meat is projected to be lowered from 103 to 100 per cent, but its grain self-sufficiency is projected to be raised marginally from 95.7 to 96.0 per cent because of the Round.

TABLE 6
Erosion of Tariff Preferences for Agricultural Imports by Industrial Countries from the World's
Least-developed Countries
(percentage points)

	Temperate Agricultural Products	Tropical Agricultural Products
European Union		
Margin pre-UR	13.3	9.3
Margin post-UR	9.5	5.1
Margin loss	3.9	4.2
(loss in %)	(29)	(45)
Japan		
Margin pre-UR	9.4	6.5
Margin post-UR	3.5	4.2
Margin loss	5.9	2.3
(loss in %)	(63)	(35)
United States		
Margin pre-UR	3.2	5.5
Margin post-UR	1.5	3.3
Margin loss	1.7	2.2
(loss in %)	(54)	(39)

Source: UNCTAD (1995).

to international levels as their agricultural protection is reduced. However, while that reduction in the preferential margin may be large in proportional terms, it is rather minor in absolute terms. Table 6 suggests that the loss of margin in the United States amounts to about two percentage points, in the European Union to four points, and in Japan to two points for tropical products and six points for temperate farm products.

For countries adversely affected by one or more of these three phenomena (reductions in food aid, in OECD food export subsidies, and in preferential access to OECD markets), there is even more reason for them not to be seduced by the special and differential treatment clauses of the Uruguay Round but instead to reform and structurally adjust their own economies to take full advantage of the new opportunities arising from the Round.

5. LOOKING FORWARD TO THE NEXT WTO ROUND

Pathbreaking though the Uruguay Round achievements have been for agriculture, much remains to be done before world agricultural trade is as fully disciplined or as free as world trade in manufactures. Being aware of this at the end of the Uruguay Round, it was agreed that there would be a return to the negotiating table by 2000. That is unlikely to be very productive, however, unless it is part of another comprehensive round of multilateral trade negotiations whereby inter-sectoral and cross-issue tradeoffs are possible. Since services negotiations also began again in 2000, a strong case can be made for the new agricultural and services negotiations to be part of a bigger package. Among other things, that would open up the possibility for broader scrutiny of progress in reforming textiles trade which, for the reasons given above, would be especially worthwhile once China becomes a member of the WTO.

a. What Should Be on the Agenda for the Agricultural Negotiations?

In terms of farm export subsidies, nothing less than a ban is needed to bring agriculture into line with non-farm products under the GATT. They are, after all, almost exclusively a Western European phenomenon apart from sporadic US involvement: five-sixths of all export subsidies in the mid-1990s were granted by the EU, and all but 2 per cent of the rest were accounted for by the US, Norway and Switzerland (Tangermann and Josling, 1999, p. 16).

With respect to domestic subsidies, gradual reform of policies of the US and EU, in particular the further de-coupling of farm income support measures from production as with America's FAIR Act of 1996, may allow removal of the 'blue box' in the next round of talks. It was an anomaly introduced into the UR negotiations in 1992 simply to satisfy just two members so the negotiations could proceed. Also, efforts to tighten the 'green box' criteria could be made, so as to reduce the loopholes they provide for continuing output-increasing subsidies, and to further reduce the Aggregate Measure of Support.

But the most important area requiring attention has to do with import market access. Tariffication appeared to be a great step forward. However, the combination of dirty tariffication by developed economies (setting bound rates well above applied rates) and the adoption of very high ceiling bindings by developing economies allows many countries still to vary their protection as they wish in response to changes in domestic or international food markets. Reducing bound tariffs from 50–150+ per cent to the 0–15 per cent range of tariff rates for manufactures is one of the major challenges ahead. If the steady rates of reduction of the past are used, it will be several decades before that gap is closed – and some time even before many of those bound tariffs reach current applied rates.

At least three options for reducing bound tariffs present themselves. One is a large across-the-board tariff cut. Even if as much as a 50 per cent cut were to be agreed, however, many very high bound tariffs would still remain. A second option is the 'Swiss formula' used for manufactures in the Tokyo Round, whereby the rate of reduction for each item is higher the greater the item's tariff level. This has the additional economic advantage of reducing the dispersion in rates that was introduced or exacerbated during the Uruguay Round. In particular, it would reduce many of the tariff peaks and the extent of tariff escalation that bothers developing countries. And a third option is the one used successfully in the information technology negotiations, namely, the 'zero-for-zero' approach whereby, for selected products, tariffs are eliminated altogether. In contrast to the second option, this third option would increase the dispersion of tariffs across products, increasing the risk that resources will be wastefully diverted from low-cost to higher-cost activities. While that might appeal as a way of allowing attention to then focus on the politically difficult items such as dairy and sugar, the manufacturing sector experience with long-delayed reductions in protection of textiles and cars makes it difficult to view this third option optimistically as a quick solution.

The just-mentioned tariff reductions refer to above-quota imports. There is also a pressing need to focus on in-quota imports, that is, those that meet the minimum access requirements in the UR Agreement on Agriculture (generally 5 per cent of domestic sales by 2000 for developed economies). Those so-called tariff rate quotas (TRQs) were introduced ostensibly to guarantee traditional exporters a minimum level of market access, equal at least to what was available before tariffication, given that tariffs have been bound at rates greatly above applied rates. As many as 36 WTO member countries listed TRQs in their Uruguay Round schedules, of which at least half actively use them. But this system ensures that agricultural trade policies continue to be very complex. In particular, the existence of TRQs reduces the extent to which future tariff cuts will lead to actual import growth in the medium term, and it is worrying that quotas have on average been barely two-thirds filled according to the count of notifications to the WTO Committee on Agriculture during 1995 and 1996 at least (Tangermann and Josling, 1999, p. 26).

Agricultural-exporting countries are understandably reluctant to suggest TRQs be removed, because TRQs provide at least some market access at low or zero tariffs. Nor would allowing TRQs to be auctioned be seen by all as a solution, because that would be like imposing the out-of-quota tariff on quota-restricted trade that the TRQ was designed to avoid. If banning TRQs is not yet possible, the next-best alternative is to expand them, so as to simultaneously reduce their importance, increase competition, and lessen the impact of high above-quota tariffs.

One can imagine an outcome from TRQ expansion that is either optimistic or pessimistic from a reformer's viewpoint. On the one hand, optimists may say: if the TRQs were to be increased by, say, the equivalent of 1 per cent of domestic consumption per year, it would not be very long in most cases before the quota became non-binding. Expanding the TRQ could thereby be potentially much more liberalising in the medium term than reducing the very high above-quota tariffs. Such an approach may require binding within-quota tariffs at a reasonable level (such as that for manufactures).

On the other hand, negotiators familiar with the tortuous efforts to reform the quota arrangements for textiles and clothing trade see the agricultural TRQs as a way of re-cycling the acronym MFA before it disappears in 2004 when the last of the textile quota are scheduled to be removed. In this case it would stand for a 'multilateral food arrangement' (Francois, 1999). Since the first inception of textile quotas was around 1960, it looks like it will take fifty years or so before they are finally abolished. Is that the expected lifetime of agricultural TRQs?

Those with this more pessimistic view may put the case for a more radical approach to the next round of agricultural negotiations, namely to bring agriculture much more quickly into line with the treatment of non-agricultural goods in the WTO. For example, they might call for the total elimination of agricultural TRQs (along with export subsidies and export credits) and a major reduction in bound (out-of-quota) tariffs. To soften the blow of that request, their quid pro quo could be to put less emphasis on trying to discipline farm domestic measures other than direct output-increasing subsidies. As Sumner (2000) has shown, many forms of domestic support are infra-marginal and contribute little to net exports. The almost infinite scope for re-instrumentation of domestic price-support measures makes disciplining them very difficult anyway. And, as Snape (1987) has pointed out, tightening constraints on border measures would ensure an increasing proportion of the cost of support programmes would be exposed via the budget and thereby subjected to regular domestic political scrutiny.

b. Agriculture and 'New' Trade Issues

Inclusion of new trade agenda issues in the next round is considered by some developing country negotiators as undesirable because it would distract attention from the market access issues that are deemed to be of greater importance to them. However, their inclusion could have the advantage that more OECD non-agricultural groups would take part in the round which, depending on the issue, could counter-balance forces favouring agricultural (and other sectoral) protection. As well, better rules on some of those new issues would reduce the risk of farm trade measures being replaced or made ineffective by domestic agricultural measures and technical barriers to trade that may be almost as trade-distorting – a risk that has grown considerably in the past year or so.

Such issues as competition policy and investment policy are as relevant for developing country agriculture as for other groups. However, since they may not be included in the millennium round, and their implications for agriculture are in any case discussed well elsewhere (e.g., Tangermann and Josling, 1999), attention in the rest of this section is focused on the interests of developing countries in two emerging issues that very directly affect agriculture. They are the issues surrounding (a) technical standards, including SPS and food safety in the wake of the new biotechnologies, and (b) agriculture's so-called multifunctionality.

c. Technical Standards, Including SPS and Food Safety Measures

The inability of the Standards Code that came out of the Tokyo Round to adequately address sanitary and phytosanitary (SPS) issues, plus the desire to reduce the risk of re-instrumentation of agricultural support to SPS measures in response to the reforms committed to under the URAA, gave birth to the SPS Agreement during the UR. That agreement defined new criteria that had to be met if a country chose to impose regulations more onerous than those agreed in international standards-setting bodies. It, together with the UR's strengthening of the dispute settlement procedures at the WTO, was bound to raise the profile of SPS matters. That profile has been raised even more dramatically, especially in Europe, with the emergence of several food safety issues: 'mad-cow' disease, beef hormones, and transgenic food products or genetically modified organisms (GMOs).

Developing countries have a complex set of interests in these developments. One is that the SPS Agreement requires a WTO member to provide scientific justification for any measure that is more trade-restrictive than the appropriate international standard would be, and to assess formally the risks involved. At least some technical assistance to help developing countries meet these requirements has been provided, but more may be needed.

A second interest is in maintaining and increasing access to other members' markets that are protected by SPS measures. Again some technical assistance in meeting those importers' standards is helpful. However, numerous countries use very blunt quarantine instruments that excessively restrict imports well beyond what is necessary for protecting the health of their plants and animals, or their citizens in the case of food safety concerns. For example, there are outright bans on imports of many products, including into agricultural-exporting countries seeking to preserve a disease-free image. The levels of protection involved are in some cases equivalent to tariffs of more than 100 per cent. Without some form of notification requirement on WTO members that forces members to disclose the degree to which trade is restricted by such measures, reform in this area is likely to be confined to the very small proportion of those cases that are brought before the WTO's dispute settlement body (DSB). The resource requirements of such legal proceedings ensures the pace of reform by that means alone would be glacial, and would be skewed towards concerns of those richer WTO members able to afford to bring such cases to the DSB.

Who gains and who loses from an SPS measure varies from case to case, depending on how widespread are the externalities affecting production and/or consumption. In the straightforward situation where the import restriction is aimed simply to prevent the rise in the cost of disease control for domestic farmers, the latter group gains at the expense of domestic consumers and overseas producers. James and Anderson (1998) provide an example where the cost to consumers is likely to have outweighed any possible benefit to producers, resulting in a net national loss (not to mention the loss to potential overseas suppliers) from apparently excessive protection in that case where broader externalities appeared to be absent.

Those domestic consumers are unlikely to be a source of pressure for liberalisation of quarantine barriers, however, and not just for the usual reasons (poor information, high costs of collective action because of free riding, etc.). As well, citizens are often concerned about possible risks to the natural environment from importing exotic diseases and/or about the safety of imported food. And their demands for higher quality, safer food and for environmental protection are going to continue to rise with their per capita incomes.

However, perceptions about the safety of different foods and food production and processing methods, and conformity assessment procedures, differ greatly – even between countries with similar income levels. The WTO Dispute Settlement case, brought by the US/Canada against the EU over its ban on imports of beef that had been produced with the help of growth hormones, shows that standards differences across countries are difficult to resolve even with a great deal of scientific advice. So too does the controversy over the banning of intra-EU beef trade over the 'mad-cow' disease scare. How much more, then, are trade disputes likely to arise over issues in which the scientific evidence is far less complete? Thus not having consumers' concerns represented in the SPS Agreement has been a two-edged sword: on the one hand it has meant the absence of a voice arguing that domestic consumers should have better access to lower-priced imported food currently excluded by excessive quarantine regulations; but on the other hand it has kept out of the SPS debate such issues as the consumers' 'right to know' via, for example, labelling. That latter concern is not going to disappear though. On the contrary, it is likely to show up in dispute settlement cases under the WTO's Agreement on Technical Barriers to Trade (TBT).[8]

Whether or not wealthy consumers are irrational and hyper risk averse when it comes to food safety issues is not really the point. Providing them with more scientific information, and improving the reputation of national, regional and international standards-setting bodies, may be valuable initiatives but they may

---

[8] Indeed one paper has already been posted on the Internet advocating activists to argue under the TBT Agreement for the right of WTO member governments to require compulsory labelling of products containing GMOs sold in their markets (Stillwell and Van Dyke, 1999).

do little to alter consumer opinions in the medium term, and in any case such information is scarce on new issues (Mahe and Ortalo-Magne, 1998; Henson, 1998).

In the case of policy dialogues surrounding GMOs, far more heat than light has been generated so far. Attempts to promote science-based assessment of the risks involved have met with extreme versions of the precautionary principle, manifest in the form of compete bans on their production, importation and/or sale in numerous markets. Proposed solutions such as segregating GMO products and identifying them via labels on affected food items have been rejected by many consumer groups; they have also been resisted by the major producing countries in North and Latin America, who claim that 'like' products are involved and so no costly GMO labelling is warranted. The fact that the production of some GMO products is less damaging to the environment than is the production of traditional farm products has done little to dissuade civil society groups of their opposition to GMOs.

How are developing countries affected by this issue? Two ways in particular are worth noting: one is via the impact of the new technology in so far as it is lowering costs of food production; the other is via any food trade barriers that may be erected in response to consumer concerns in (mostly OECD) countries. The former would benefit those food-exporting developing countries able to attract the new technology, which places a premium on their having in place sound intellectual property law and enforcement (because seed companies would otherwise be wary of selling into or producing in such countries). If they cannot make productive use of the new biotechnologies, however, their competitiveness on international markets may be eroded as international food prices come down. Net food-importing developing countries could benefit from that price fall, and perhaps even more so if OECD countries ban imports of GMO products. The likely impact is clouded, however, by the fact that a premium might be attached to GMO-free products in international trade. This is clearly an area requiring more empirical economic research.[9]

While such agricultural issues will arise increasingly under the Uruguay Round's SPS and TBT agreements, they will also arise in other, non agricultural-related contexts. As with state-trading, subsidies, and competition policies, there is a strong case for developing common disciplines for all types of products, whether agricultural or not. In the case of TBT, there is nothing special about food as compared with, say, dangerous chemicals or heavy metals involved in the production or disposal of manufactured goods. A key advantage of having a common set of rules for risk analysis and risk management is that inconsistencies in current arrangements, and the problems that will keep causing for dispute settlement, would be reduced.

---

[9] Early attempts to examine this GMO issue empirically are reported in Nelson et al. (1999) and Nielsen and Anderson (2000).

d. Agriculture's So-called Multifunctionality

Considerable attention has been given in some OECD countries to the term 'non-trade concerns', which appears in Article 20(c) of the URAA. WTO members agreed that, in negotiating the continuation of the agricultural policy reform process after 1999, 'non-trade concerns' would be taken into account. While not spelt out in any detail, the preamble to the URAA defines those concerns to include security of food supplies and protection of the environment. A third concern is the viability of rural areas. The governments discussing these three items are characterising them as positive externalities and in some cases public goods that are jointly produced along with food and fibre. Hence their use of the word 'multifunctionality' to describe these features of agricultural production.

So-called 'non-trade' concerns are becoming an issue in the WTO in numerous areas, not just with respect to agriculture. They are a direct consequence of the lowering or outlawing of trade barriers: with less natural and governmental protection from import competition, domestic policies are becoming relatively more important as determinants of the international competitiveness of certain industries. Despite their 'non-trade' adjective, these concerns need to be dealt with in the WTO because they certainly can affect trade. Ideally they should be handled in the same way for all sectors (for example, under an expanded Agreement on Subsidies and Countervailing Measures), but until that is done they cannot be ignored in the up-coming agricultural negotiations.

These concerns are not really new, but they are being packaged a little differently than in the past. A key question is: do they require exceptional treatment, or are WTO provisions sufficient to cater for them, for example via the URAA's 'green box'? The short answer appears to be that WTO provisions are adequate (Anderson, 1998). The answers to more-specific questions also seem to suggest no special case for trade measures. For example, does agriculture deserve more price support and import protection than other sectors because of the non-marketed externalities/public goods it produces jointly in the process of producing marketable food and fibre? That is, do these unrewarded positive externalities exceed the negative externalities from farming by more than the net positive externalities produced by other sectors? And even if they did, to what extent if any, are those farmer-produced externalities under-supplied? The current farm support programmes may more than adequately encourage their supply. And where there is under-provision, what are the most efficient ways to boost their production to the socially optimal levels? Certainly trade measures are a long way from first-best.

6. CONCLUSIONS AND OPTIONS FOR DEVELOPING COUNTRIES

The WTO's millennium round offers probably the best prospects ever for developing countries in general – and their rural communities in particular – to secure growth-enhancing reforms. Traditional agricultural market access liberalisation should be the key priority issue in the next WTO round of multilateral trade negotiations, given the enormous potential for global and developing country welfare gains from reducing agricultural protection. Assurances are also needed that the EU and US will honour fully the spirit of their commitment to gradually expand market access for textiles and clothing, and not simply replace the remaining half of the quantitative restraints on trade in those products, expected to be still there at the end of 2001, with 'safeguard' measures by the end of the phaseout scheme three years later. Substantial progress in freeing up more trade in both these sectors is essential if the next round is to be a genuine development round.

Such reform could boost enormously the earnings of the world's poor, the vast majority of whom are in rural households of developing countries. Rural households would benefit even in newly industrialising economies that take advantage of expanding opportunities to export textile products, for example through some of their household members moving to new jobs in nearby clothing factories.

From an agricultural development perspective, attention should focus also on reducing protection granted to other manufacturing and services industries. Protection in those sectors still bestows a significant anti-agricultural bias in many developing countries, making it more difficult for them to benefit from the agricultural and textile trade reforms of OECD countries. Those reforms can be done unilaterally, but the next WTO round offers an opportunity to obtain a quid pro quo, and can be a useful instrument through which to lock in such reforms domestically.

This next round will, however, be conducted in an environment in which globalisation forces (including ever-faster development and international transfers of information, ideas, capital, skills and new technologies) will, by having ever-stronger impacts on domestic markets, simultaneously trigger insulationist policy reactions. For example, further reductions in traditional measures of farm protection will meet significant resistance in numerous OECD countries, as farm groups join with food safety and environmental groups to argue for new forms of agricultural protection. In these circumstances the mercantilist nature of trade negotiations may require that the agenda of the next WTO round include not only other sectors but also some 'new trade agenda' items so as to provide the potential for beneficial issue linkages and tradeoffs.

Given the apparent goodwill towards making this next WTO round a development round, and given that many developing countries have embraced major reforms unilaterally during the past decade or so (Michalopoulos, 1999), perhaps developing countries should adopt a quite different approach from the past this time. Consideration might be given, for example, to exchanging more MFN market access with OECD countries rather than seeking special and differential (S&D) treatment and tariff preferences. S&D simply allows developing country governments to continue to keep shooting their economies in the foot by delaying beneficial reforms; and tariff preferences tend to divide developing countries into sub-groups, thereby weakening their individual and collective bargaining strength.

A striking example of the latter has been exposed in the prolonged and extremely costly dispute over access to the EU market for bananas. The EU policy regime involves layers of preferences that have divided developing countries into 'we' and 'they' groups and thereby weakened their chances of securing a better deal for all.

Another illustration of how preferential treatment has reduced the resolve of developing countries to push for OECD farm policy reform has to do with their food imports from the protectionist countries. Food export subsidies, export credits and non-emergency food aid all are by-products of OECD farm support programmes. Without those programmes most developing countries would be better off through expanded trade opportunities, and those that would not could be compensated with expanded access to OECD markets for tropical products and/or direct financial aid (which would be a far more efficient way of transferring resources to developing countries than doing it in kind as a way of disposing of surpluses).

With these examples in mind, would developing countries' interests be served by the proposal for OECD countries to provide preferential access to exports of least-developed countries? If the things that matter (such as agricultural and textile products) were to be effectively excluded from such a deal, little of substance would be gained by the least-developed countries, and yet those countries would then feel less able to join other developing countries in seeking lower MFN tariffs on products of export interest to all developing countries. Meanwhile, OECD countries could use this initiative as an excuse for not reforming as much in the key areas.

All this suggests a potentially high payoff for developing countries acting collectively to push hard for greater market access for farm and textile products, and for technical and economic assistance to aid their reform processes, in return for providing more access to developing country markets for goods and services. The political price of the latter offer is, after all, now much lower than it used to be: the forces of globalisation are such that economies are now rewarded more, via inflows of foreign capital, for good domestic economic governance, but they are also penalised more if poor policy choices are not corrected. Two such corrections that would at the same time help the cause of reducing agricultural protection abroad would be for developing countries to commit to not using taxes or other restraints on agricultural exports, and to reduce their (often very high) ceiling bindings on their own import tariffs on farm products.

Finally, what else should developing countries do to help their own reform processes complement those abroad? One obvious thing is to direct new economic and technical assistance funds towards reducing the under-investments in rural infrastructure (human as well as physical), agricultural research and development, and agricultural technology transfer. Liberalising foreign investment rules and improving intellectual property law enforcement would enhance the prospects for both transfers of new biotechnologies and their further development locally. And removing domestic disincentives to farmers in the form of agricultural export taxes, manufacturing protection, and over-valued exchange rates remain essential.

REFERENCES

Anderson, K. (1994), 'Food Price Policy in East Asia', *Asian-Pacific Economic Literature* **8**, 2, 15–30.

Anderson, K. (1995), 'Lobbying Incentives and the Pattern of Protection in Rich and Poor Countries', *Economic Development and Cultural Change*, **43**, 2, 401–23.

Anderson, K. (1998), 'Domestic Agricultural Policy Objectives and Trade Liberalization: Synergies and Trade-offs', COM/AGR/CA/TD/WS(98)101, in Proceedings of the OECD Workshop on Emerging Trade Issues in Agriculture (Paris, 25–26 October, published on the internet at http://www.oecd.org/agr/trade/). (A revised version is to appear in the *Australian Journal of Agricultural and Resource Economics*, **44**, 3, September 2000.)

Anderson, K. and R. Tyers (1993), 'More on Welfare Gains to Developing Countries from Liberalizing World Food Markets', *Journal of Agricultural Economics*, **44**, 2, 189–204.

Anderson, K., B. Dimaranan, T. Hertel and W. Martin (1997), 'Asia-Pacific Food Markets and Trade in 2005: A Global, Economy-Wide Perspective', *Australian Journal of Agricultural and Resource Economics*, **41**, 1, 19–44.

Anderson, K., Y. Hayami and Others (1986), *The Political Economy of Agricultural Protection* (Boston, London and Sydney: Allen and Unwin).

Brown, D.K., A.V. Deardorff, A.K. Fox and R.M. Stern (1996), 'Computational Analysis of Goods and Services Liberalization in the Uruguay Round', in W. Martin and L.A. Winters (eds.), *The Uruguay Round and the Developing Countries* (Cambridge and New York: Cambridge University Press, ch 11).

ESCAP (1995), *Benefits and Challenges Facing Asia-Pacific Agricultural Trading Countries in the Post-Uruguay Round Period*, Studies in Trade and Investment 11 (Bangkok: United Nations).

FAO (1997), *FAOSTAT Files* (Rome: Food and Agriculture Organisation).

Francois, J.F. (1999), 'Market Access Liberalization in the WTO 2000 Negotiations', paper to be presented at the WTO/World Bank Conference on Agriculture and the New Trade Agenda from a Development Perspective (Geneva, 1–2 October).

Francois, J.F., B. McDonald and H. Nordstrom (1996), 'Assessing the Uruguay Round', in W. Martin and L.A. Winters (eds.), *The Uruguay Round and the Developing Countries* (Cambridge and New York: Cambridge University Press, ch 6).

Goldin, I. and D. van der Mennsbrugghe (1996), 'The Uruguay Round: An Assessment of Economywide and Agricultural Reforms', in W. Martin and L.A. Winters (eds.), *The Uruguay Round and the Developing Countries* (Cambridge and New York: Cambridge University Press, ch 2).

Grilli, E.R. and M.C. Yang (1988), 'Primary Commodity Prices, Manufactured Goods Prices, and the Terms of Trade of Developing Countries: What the Long Run Shows', *World Bank Economic Review*, **2**, 1, 1–48.

Harrison, G.W., T.F. Rutherford and D.G. Tarr (1995), 'Quantifying the Uruguay Round', in W. Martin and L.A. Winters (eds.), *The Uruguay Round and the Developing Countries* (Cambridge and New York: Cambridge University Press, ch 7).

Henson, S. (1998), 'Regulating the Trade Effects of National Food Safety Standards', COM/AGR/CA/TD/TC/WS(98)123, in Proceedings of the OECD Workshop on Emerging Trade Issues in Agriculture (Paris, 25–26 October, published on the internet at http://www.oecd.org/agr/trade/).

Hertel, T.W., W. Martin, K. Yanagishima and B. Dimaranan (1996), 'Liberalizing Manufactures Trade in a Changing World Economy', in W. Martin and L.A. Winters (eds.), *The Uruguay Round and the Developing Countries* (Cambridge and New York: Cambridge University Press, ch 7).

Hudec, R.E. (1998), 'Does the Agreement on Agriculture Work? Agricultural Disputes After the Uruguay Round', IATRC Working Paper No. 98-2 (Department of Applied Economics, University of Minnesota, April).

Ingco, M. (1995), 'Agricultural Trade Liberalization in the Uruguay Round: One Step Forward, One Step Back?', supplementary paper prepared for a World Bank Conference on *The Uruguay Round and the Developing Countries* (Washington, DC, 26–27 January).

Ingco, M. (1996), 'The Uruguay Round and the Least-Developed Low-Income Food-Deficit Countries', paper presented to the Inter-Agency Meeting of the World Food Situation and Net Food-Importing Countries (The World Bank, Washington, DC, 18–19 December).

Jackson, J.H. (1997), *The World Trading System: Law and Policy of International Economic Relations* (2nd ed., Cambridge MA: MIT Press).

James, S. and K. Anderson (1998), 'On the Need for More Economic Assessment of Quarantine Policies', *Australian Journal of Agricultural and Resource Economics*, **41**, 4, 525–44.

Josling, T. (1998), 'The Uruguay Round Agreement on Agriculture: A Forward Looking Assessment', COM/AGR/CA/TD/WS(98)100, in Proceedings of the OECD Workshop on Emerging Trade Issues in Agriculture (Paris, 25–26 October, published on the internet at http://www.oecd.org/agr/trade/).

Josling, T., S. Tangermann and T.K. Warley (1996), *Agriculture in the GATT* (London and New York: Houndmills).

Lindert, P.H. (1991), 'Historical Patterns of Agricultural Policy', in C.P. Timmer (ed.), *Agriculture and the State: Growth, Employment and Poverty* (Ithaca: Cornell University Press).

Mahe, L.P. and F. Ortalo-Magne (1998), 'International Co-operation in the Regulation of Food Quality and Safety Attributes', COM/AGR/CA/TD/TC/WS(98)102, in Proceedings of the OECD Workshop on Emerging Trade Issues in Agriculture (Paris, 25–26 October, published on the internet at http://www.oecd.org/agr/trade/).

Michalopoulos, C. (1999), 'The Integration of Developing Countries into the Multilateral Trading System' (mimeo, World Bank and WTO Secretariat).

Neilsen, C.P. and K. Anderson (2000), 'GMOs, Trade Policy, and Welfare in Rich and Poor Countries', paper prepared for the World Bank Workshjop on Standards, Regulation and Trade (Washington, DC, 27 April).

Nelson, G.C., T. Josling, D. Bullock, L. Unnevehr, M. Rosegrant and L. Hill (1999), *The Economics and Politics of Genetically Modified Organisms: Implications for WTO 2000*, with J. Babinard, C. Cunningham, A. De Pinto and E.I. Nitsi, 'Bulletin 809' (College of Agricultural, Consumer and Environmental Sciences, University of Illinois at Urbana-Champaign, November).

Nordstrom, H., B. McDonald and J.F. Francois (1994), 'The Uruguay Round: A Global General Equilibrium Assessment', CEPR Discussion Paper No. 1067 (London: Centre for Economic Policy Research, November).

Rattingan, G.A. and W.B. Carmichael (1996), *Trade Liberalization: A Domestic Challenge for Industrial Nations* (Canberra: National Centre for Development Studies, ANU).

Roberts, D. (1998), 'Implementation of the WTO Agreement on the Application of Sanitary and Phytosanitary Measures: The First Two Years', Working Paper No. 98-4 (Department of Applied Economics, University of Minnesota, May).

Sharma, R., P. Konandreas and J. Greenfield (1996), 'An Overview of the Impact of the Uruguay Round on Agricultural Prices and Incomes', *Food Policy*, **21**, 4.

Snape, R.H. (1987), 'The Importance of Frontier Barriers', in H. Kierzkowski (ed.), *Protection and Competition in International Trade: Essays in Honour of W. M. Corden* (Oxford: Basil Blackwell, ch 15).

Stillwell, M. and B. Van Dyke (1999), 'An Activist's Handbook on Genetically Modified Organisms and the WTO' (Center for International Environmental Law, Washington, DC and Geneva, March, www.consumerscouncil/org/ccc/policyhandbk399.htm).

Sumner, D. (2000), 'Domestic Support and the WTO Negotiations', *Australian Journal of Agricultural and Resource Economics*, **44**, 3, (forthcoming).

Tangermann, S. and T. Josling (1999), 'The Interests of Developing Countries in the Next Round of WTO Agricultural Negotiations', paper presented at the UNCTAD workshop on Developing a Proactive and Coherent Agenda for African Countries in Support of their Participation in International Trade Negotiations (Pretoria, 29 June to 2 July).

Tyers, R. and K. Anderson (1992), *Disarray in World Food Markets: A Quantitative Assessment* (Cambridge and New York: Cambridge University Press).

UNCTAD (1995), 'Translating Uruguay Round Special Provisions for Least-Developed Countries into Concrete Action: Issues and Policy Requirements' TD/B/WG.8/3 (Geneva: UNCTAD, 21 June).

WTO (1995), 'Provisions Related to Least-Developed Countries in the Uruguay Round Agreements, Legal Instruments and Ministerial Decisions', paper presented by the WTO Secretariat to a brain-storming meeting (UNCTAD, Geneva, 18–19 May).

4

Liberalising Agriculture and Manufactures in a Millennium Round: Implications for Developing Countries

Thomas W. Hertel and Will Martin

1. INTRODUCTION

L IBERALISATION of trade in agricultural and industrial products was at the centre of all GATT Rounds, and will likely be an important part of any millennium round of negotiations. Research to date has provided a number of interesting and important findings on the implications of liberalising these commodities, and the delay resulting from the failure of the Seattle Ministerial provides more time for them to be digested and incorporated in the structure of future negotiations.

Agricultural trade liberalisation is part of the built-in agenda of negotiations laid down in the Uruguay Round. It is a high priority for a number of countries, especially the Cairns Group members, but firmly resisted by others. Clearly, there will be a strong focus not only on the potential for gains in this area, but also on the implications of different approaches. Thus, the modalities of agricultural liberalisation need to be examined particularly carefully. Trade in industrial products is not included in the built-in agenda, and so the initial question to be addressed is whether it should be included. Most commentators seem to regard liberalisation of industrial products primarily a subject of interest to developed countries. Thus, a key question from a developing country perspective is to assess whether liberalisation of these products is of interest to developing countries.

This chapter examines the two questions outlined above. It does this by drawing on a range of the currently available studies for agriculture. For industrial products, it draws heavily on a study by the authors (Hertel and Martin,

1999), which is one of the few that focuses on the implications of including liberalisation of industrial products.

2. IMPLICATIONS OF AGRICULTURAL LIBERALISATION

A very broad indication of the potential implications of agricultural liberalisation in the Millennium Round is provided by Hertel, Anderson, Francois and Martin (1999). This analysis is based on a model of the world economy updated to 2005, when the Uruguay Round (UR) tariff reductions have been fully phased in and the MFA quotas abolished. These authors estimate that a 40 per cent reduction in post-UR agricultural tariffs and export subsidies will cause an increase in global real income of about $60 billion per year. This figure increases by $10 billion if domestic support is also reduced by 40 per cent, although the uncertainty in the degree to which such producer payments are linked to production decisions makes such analysis difficult (ABARE, 1999).

While the largest dollar amounts of gain accrue to the developed countries, the percentage real income gains (first set of bars in Figure 1) are largest in developing countries, such as South Asia (other than India) and Southeast Asia (other than Indonesia). The gains from liberalisation are widely distributed amongst developing countries, with virtually all regions except the heavily food

FIGURE 1

Implications of a 40 Per Cent Reduction in Agricultural Trade Barriers

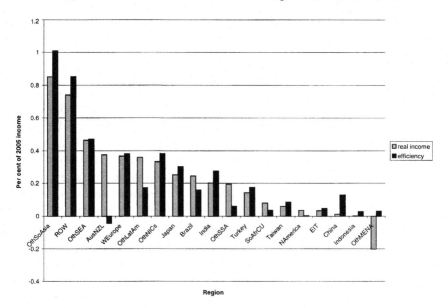

importing Other Middle East region experiencing overall gains. Most of these gains arise from the efficiency gains from reducing countries' own liberalisation (second set of bars in Figure 1), although some food exporting regions, such as Australia and New Zealand, realise important gains from terms of trade improvements. Impacts of this liberalisation on agricultural trade volumes are mixed – while reducing tariffs tends to increase import volumes, reductions in production and export subsidies tend to reduce them.

Modalities for Agricultural Negotiations

The precise outcome of the agricultural negotiations will depend heavily on the specific modalities used in the negotiations. In contrast with industrial products, agriculture is assured a place on the negotiating agenda and considerable attention has been focused on the specific approaches that might be used to bring about liberalisation in this sector. Unfortunately, the Uruguay Round agreement that brought agriculture back under multilateral disciplines introduced more complexity into the set of measures affecting market access than is present in industrial products. The system of tariff rate quotas designed to ensure continued access by traditional exporters following tariffication is a source of particular complexity.

Anderson, Hoekman and Strutt (1999) identify the priorities in further progress on agriculture as: reducing import barriers; disciplining domestic support; and elimination of export subsidies. As they make clear, substantial reductions in import barriers would be required to even begin to approach parity with the treatment of manufactures trade. Nothing short of elimination of export subsidies would be sufficient to do so. Interestingly, however, the agricultural disciplines on domestic support go beyond, at least in principle, those prevailing for industrial products.

One legacy of the Uruguay Round agreement on agriculture was (virtually) complete coverage of bindings on agricultural commodities. Unfortunately, the process that achieved this included a wide range of loopholes, such as the selection of a period with high support base and 'dirty tariffication' in developed countries; and ceiling bindings in developing countries. These weaknesses in the agreement allowed many tariff bindings to be substantially above the previously applied average tariff rates (Hathaway and Ingco, 1995).

This gap between applied tariff rates and tariff bindings in agriculture is particularly large in many developing countries (Abbott and Morse, 1999). As Francois (1999) notes, this means that quite substantial reductions in tariff bindings will be required if any liberalisation in applied rates is to be achieved. However, this does not imply that reductions in bindings are irrelevant. If it is recognised that in practice protection is stochastic, even tariff bindings above current rates have value (Francois and Martin, 1998). In this situation, a tariff binding maps all applied tariff rates above the binding onto the bound value, and hence reduces both the mean and the variance of the distribution of protection.

One superficially appealing approach to dealing with the gap between bound and applied rates is to focus on the applied rates, and to make them the basis for future negotiations. In a one-shot game, this would clearly be the optimal approach to achieving liberalisation. However, it is worth remembering that the GATT took eight Rounds of negotiations to bring tariffs on industrial products in the high income countries down to their present low levels, and that it is unlikely that agricultural liberalisation will prove any easier than liberalisation of industrial products. Such an approach would create incentives for countries to keep applied tariff rates high in order to conserve bargaining chips for future negotiations – a seriously perverse incentive effect.

In this situation, there appears to be merit in approaches that focus on tariff bindings seeking the largest reductions in the highest tariff bindings. Approaches such as the Swiss formula used in the Tokyo Round, or some of the other formulas considered at the time, might be useful in achieving sharp top-down reductions in tariff bindings in a way that would increase efficiency and provide more market access without creating perverse incentive effects.[1] Josling and Rae (1999) suggest the use of a 'cocktail' approach in which the very highest tariffs, which are likely to contain a good deal of 'water', are reduced using a formula approach; moderate tariffs are subject to a uniform percentage cut; and nuisance tariffs are abolished.

A particular complication in the market access component of the agricultural negotiations is created by the system of tariff rate quotas (TRQs) introduced in the Uruguay Round. These have been heavily used by OECD countries since that agreement (Boughner and DeGorter, 1999; and Elbeheri et al., 1999). While many developing countries have reported TRQs to the WTO, their practical impact on trade has been very limited, with one or two exceptions (Abbott and Morse, 1999). In order to understand the implications of TRQs for trade liberalisation under a new WTO round, we refer to Figure 2 which considers the three alternative regimes that may prevail.

Under a tariff rate quota, there is an out-of-quota tariff, t_{out}, that applies to imports above a specified quantity, Q. Imports are assumed to be in perfectly elastic supply, and volumes below the quantity limit Q must pay only the in-quota tariff, t_{in}. In Case (1), the volume of imports is determined by the out-of-quota tariff and the net import demand curve. Because the in-quota imports are subject to a lower tariff rate, they generate a rent to those fortunate enough to receive the quota allocations. The level of the in-quota tariff is important in Case (1) only because it determines the per-unit rent. The total rent transfer is represented by

---

[1] See Hoekman and Kostecki (1995) for a description of the alternative formulas that have been considered in negotiations.

FIGURE 2
Tariff Rate Quotas: Three Important Cases

Case (1) Imports exceed TRQ

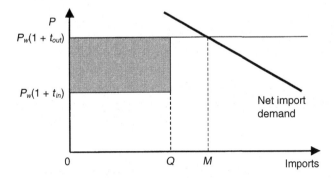

Case (2) Imports at TRQ

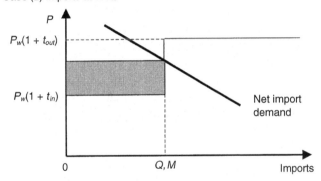

Case (3) Imports in quota

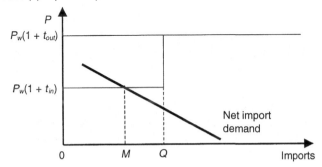

Source: Elbeheri et al. (1999).

the shaded area and it may accrue to either importing firms, the domestic government (in the case whereby licences are auctioned), or foreigners in those cases whereby the licences are allocated to exporters. In practice, the estimated quota rents are often less than this amount due to economic waste stemming from the allocation of import licences to high cost exporters as well as transactions costs associated with obtaining and filling the quota (Anderson, 1999; and Boughner and DeGorter, 1999).

In Case (2), imports are not profitable at the out-of-quota tariff, but are profitable at the in-quota tariff. In this case, import volume, and hence domestic price, are determined by the quota. This price, in turn, determines the value of the quota rent as the amount by which import values exceed their values at world market prices. In Case (3), imports are only profitable at the in-quota tariff. The volume of imports is now determined by this tariff and there are no quota rents.

Elbeheri et al. (1999, p. 22) provide very useful indicators of the extent to which countries fall in Cases (1), (2) and (3) on a number of their sensitive agricultural commodities included as sugar, dairy, meats and grains. For the US, EU, Canada and Japan, their results suggest that imports exceeded the quota volume in 13 cases out of 16. Only for US imports of meats and Canadian imports of wheat and other grains did 1996 imports appear to be consistent with Case (3). They also provide estimates of the distribution of quota rents between importers and exporters. In these industrial countries, the allocation of quota rents is uneven, with many countries allocating a substantial share of the quota rents to exporters. By contrast, in the Philippines and Korea, the two developing countries where Abbott and Morse find evidence of binding TRQ regimes, it appears that quota rents are retained by importers.

Understanding these different regimes is critical to predicting the outcome of attempts to liberalise trade. Consider first the impact of reducing out-of-quota tariffs. In Case (1), reductions in t_{out} will tend to increase imports. In Case (2), reductions in out-of-quota tariffs will only expand exports to the extent that they cause a shift in regime to Case (1). In Case (3), reductions in out-of-quota tariffs will be ineffective as long as t_{out} exceeds t_{in}.

Expansions of tariff rate quotas, on the other hand, will be ineffective in expanding imports in Case (1). In this situation, their only effect will be to increase the volume of imports on which scarcity rents are earned. In Case (2) increases in the quota will expand imports, and increase the volume on which rents accrue. In Case (3) increases in quota volumes will be ineffective and only reductions in in-quota tariffs will stimulate the volume of imports.

Given the evidence on the TRQ mechanisms in use and the regions in which they are operating, it seems likely that reductions in out-of-quota tariffs would be the most effective instrument for achieving market liberalisation in the majority of cases. Since most markets appear to be best represented by Case (1), expansions in quota volumes would appear to be a very uncertain approach to liberalisation since, in many cases, they would simply not result in any expansion of exports. This problem with the quota expansion approach to liberalisation is in addition to the political problems that appear to be associated with achieving liberalisation in this way.[2] However, this does not necessarily mean that expansion of quota volumes should be ruled out. When Elbeheri et al. examined the consequences of reducing over-quota tariffs on sugar imported into the US and the EU, they found that almost half of the exporting countries would lose as a consequence of the reductions in quota rents associated with a 33 per cent cut in out-of-quota tariffs (a reduction in the shaded area in Case (1) as t_{out} declines). When the same reduction in out-of-quota tariffs was paired with a 50 per cent increase in tariff rate quota volumes, all but two of the countries experienced gains, and the remaining losses fell to negligible levels. Thus there may be some grounds for liberalising on both price and quantity margins simultaneously in order to secure acceptance of the overall liberalisation programme by importing and exporting nations alike.

3. THE IMPORTANCE OF INCLUDING INDUSTRIAL TARIFFS IN THE NEGOTIATIONS

Hertel and Martin (1999) have examined the implications of including industrial products in the Millennium Round. Under a widely held North-South view of the world economy, the inclusion of industrial products in the negotiations would be primarily of interest to industrial countries, since developing countries[3] are assumed to be primarily exporters of commodities. While it is still true that developing countries have a (small) positive balance of trade in commodities and a (small) negative balance in manufactures, there has been a sweeping change in the structure of developing country economies in the past two decades. According to Figure 3, in the mid-1960s, manufactures exports accounted for only around a quarter of developing country exports. By the early 1980s, during the preparatory period for the Uruguay Round, this share was still around a third. However, by the mid-1990s, this share had risen to around three-quarters, and projections undertaken by Hertel and Martin (1999) suggest it will go on rising.

Interestingly, much of the increase in the exports of developing countries during the past three decades has not followed the traditional north–south pattern.

---

[2] The Multifibre Arrangement was established in 1973 to replace a series of earlier quota regimes on cotton textiles – all of which had as their ostensible objective the progressive *liberalization* of textiles and clothing.

[3] Since the context of their analysis is the WTO negotiations, the set of developing countries considered by Hertel and Martin is those countries that would likely self-elect developing country status in the WTO – a wider set of countries than the World Bank would designate low and middle income countries. See the paper for comprehensive definitions of the classification of countries and commodities. All of the data in this study were drawn from the Global Trade Analysis Project database (see www.agecon.purdue.edu/gtap).

FIGURE 3

The Increasing Share of Manufactures in Developing Country Exports

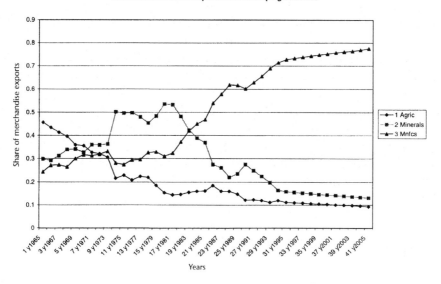

Share of merchandise exports from developing countries

FIGURE 4

The Increasing Importance of South–South Trade

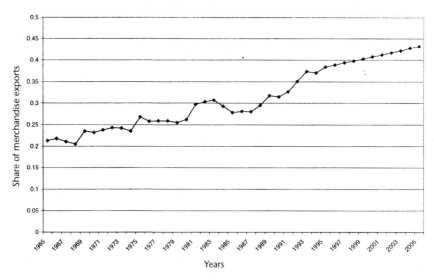

Share of Developing Country Exports to other Developing Countries

Source: Hertel and Martin (1999).

The share of exports of developing countries going to other developing countries has risen sharply as the importance of developing countries in the world economy has risen, and barriers to trade in these countries have declined. Figure 4 shows close to a doubling of the share of developing country exports going to other developing countries since the mid-1960s, and this share is projected to increase further by the year 2005.

The rise in the importance of manufactures exports shown in Figure 3 is not just an artefact of the importance of labour-intensive exports in the high growth economies of East Asia. This is clear from Figure 5, which shows that, except for Sub-Saharan Africa and Middle East and North Africa, the share of manufactures in total merchandise exports was over 40 per cent in 1995.

Another important influence on the consequences of including industrial products in the negotiations is the initial pattern of protection. An extremely aggregated, but informative, perspective on these patterns is provided by Table 1, which highlights some important systematic differences. The industrial countries impose very low average tariffs on their imports of manufactures from other high-income countries. The average tariffs that they impose on manufactures exports from developing countries are, on average, four times as

FIGURE 5

The Share of Manufactures Exports is Substantial in Almost All Regions

Manufactures' share in merchandise exports: 1995

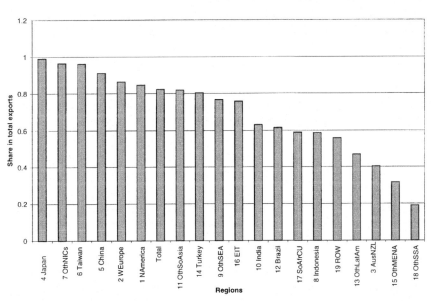

Source: Hertel and Martin (1999).

high. This is primarily because of the relatively high tariffs on products such as textiles and clothing, in which developing countries have a strong comparative advantage.

Table 1 also highlights the severity of the barriers that developing countries face in other developing countries. The average tariff faced by developing countries on their exports of manufactures to these markets, at 12.8 per cent, is almost four times as high as they face in industrial country markets. Given the increasing importance of developing country markets for their exports of manufactures, this suggests that these barriers are of considerable importance, and that reductions in these barriers are likely to be of particular importance in the future.

Barriers faced by developing countries on their exports of agricultural products are also high. These tariffs are estimated to average 15.6 per cent in high income countries, and 20.1 in developing countries. The rates for the industrial countries are much lower than are indicated by the well-known OECD estimates (OECD, 1999) for the industrial countries. This is because the OECD estimates of assistance to agriculture include all domestic support as well as border protection, and because the OECD numbers focus on raw agricultural products, rather than the broader set of agricultural and food commodities covered by WTO negotiations on agriculture (GATT, 1994, p. 56).

The importance for manufactures trade of the tariffs levied by developing countries is further highlighted by Table 2, which presents estimates of the implied tariffs paid. These are constructed by multiplying the marginal tariffs levied on the relevant trade flows by the value of the corresponding trade flow. From this table, it appears that the barriers that developing countries face in other developing countries account for over 70 per cent of the total tariffs levied on their exports of industrial products. This contrasts sharply with agriculture where

TABLE 1
Patterns of Protection, 1995

| Exporting Region | Importing Region | |
	High Income %	Developing %
Manufactures		
High Income	0.8	10.9
Developing	3.4	12.8
World	1.5	11.5
Agriculture		
High Income	15.9	21.5
Developing	15.1	18.3
World	15.6	20.1

Source: Hertel and Martin (1999).

TABLE 2
Implied Tariffs Paid, by Commodity, Source and Destination, 1995

	Importing Region	
Exporting Region	High Income $bn	Developing $bn
Manufactures		
High Income	16	93
Developing	23	57
World	40	150
Agriculture		
High Income	37	20
Developing	16	14
World	53	34

Source: Hertel and Martin (1999).

more than half of the levies charged on developing country exports are associated with their exports to industrial countries.

To obtain a very broad impression of the consequences of liberalising manufactures trade, Hertel and Martin (1999) perform a very simple experiment in which applied tariffs on industrial products are reduced by 40 per cent in all countries. This generates an increase in global trade volume of more than $380 billion – or about 4.7 per cent of projected merchandise and non-factor service trade in 2005. This increase is reflected in almost all products, including non-manufactures. The largest increase is for wearing apparel. Even after the Uruguay Round phase-out of the Multifibre Arrangement quotas, trade volume in this sector rises by more than 20 per cent. This politically sensitive sector remains heavily protected, even in the high income countries. Textiles and autos follow in importance.

The real income impacts of these manufacturing tariff cuts are more complex to analyse. Welfare gains from such multilateral liberalisation are fundamentally determined by two factors: the change in the efficiency with which any given economy utilises its resources, and changes in a country's terms of trade (TOT). The first bar in Figure 6 reports the real income gains, by region, as a share of 2005 income, while the second reports the efficiency gains. The difference between these two is accounted for by the terms of trade effect. If the real income gain exceeds the efficiency gain, then the terms of trade effect are positive, and vice versa. The efficiency gains are closely related to the degree to which a country liberalises its markets. Sharp tariff cuts, giving rise to increased access to cheaper imported goods, generate gains in consumption as well as improvements in the efficiency with which domestic resources are used.

It is perhaps not surprising to see that the largest efficiency gains (as a share of income) are in the developing economies where tariffs are highest in the 2005

FIGURE 6

The Implications of a 40 Per Cent Tariff Cut on Industrial Products for Real Income (Left Bar) and Efficiency (Right Bar)

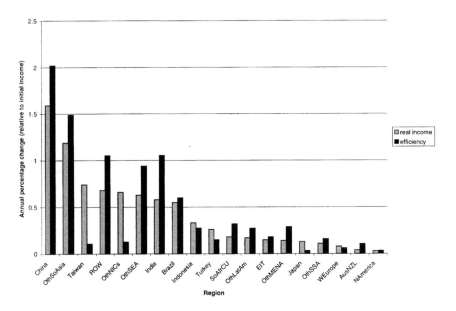

Source: Hertel and Martin (1999).

base (second set of bars in Figure 6). China's gains are the largest, followed by Other South Asia and India. These are the regions with the highest initial tariffs. China's greater gains, relative to India (which is projected to have higher protection levels in 2005), are due to the fact that the manufacturing sector in China is larger and more trade-oriented in the 2005 projections underlying this analysis. In the far right-hand side of Figure 6, it is clear that the tariff cuts in the industrialised economies of Japan, Western Europe, Australia/New Zealand and North America, generate almost no efficiency gains, because tariffs are already extremely low and there is little left to be gained from cuts. While their real income gains are somewhat larger due to positive terms of trade effects, following increased exports from developing countries, the bulk of the gains appear to go to the developing countries themselves. Indeed, the latter are estimated to receive three-quarters of the total gains from liberalising manufactures trade (Hertel and Martin, 1999).

Clearly, these results suggest that there are strong economic and political-economic reasons for developing countries to support the inclusion of industrial products in the forthcoming negotiations. From a political perspective, industrial products make up a very large share of exports, and frequently these products are produced by a relatively small number of producers who can provide active support for the politically difficult reforms required by a trade negotiation. From an economic perspective, the substantial static welfare gains outlined above are a good reason to support their inclusion, as are the potential dynamic gains associated with moving to a more outward-looking manufacturing sector.

The potential dynamic gains from tariff liberalisation are the subject of considerable debate and empirical research. In a recent OECD study (Dessus et al., 1999), the authors estimate the relationship between trade intensity and total factor productivity (TFP). They find that for every 10 per cent rise in trade intensity (exports plus imports, divided by GDP), total factor productivity rises by 0.9 per cent. The authors proceed to apply this TFP growth factor to the increased trade stimulated by tariff elimination for industrial and agricultural products, and they find that their estimated 'dynamic' gains are fully 15 times as large as their static gains! Of course, their estimated relationship is merely indicative of the correlation between – not the causality from – openness and productivity. While Dessus et al. (1999) suggest that imported technology and stiffer competition from imports are the likely vehicle for these TFP gains, the authors do not explicitly model the mechanism by which the improved productivity comes about. Furthermore, there are likely to be other prerequisites for attaining the higher TFP observed in more open economies, including favourable institutions and macro-economic stability. In summary, much more work is required before these 'dynamic' gains from trade liberalisation can be deemed reliable.

Overall, the quantitative analysis to date of industrial product liberalisation is highly stylised and simplified. The use of a uniform percentage cut in applied rates of protection is traditional in *ex ante* modelling applications and provides a rough guide to the potential benefits from a broad-based liberalisation. However, it does assume that such a broad-based liberalisation can be brought about through the WTO process. In practice, policy instruments in this area are tariff bindings, and the actual outcome may depend heavily on the precise approach to liberalisation chosen. From theory we know that the gains are likely to be larger than those indicated if negotiators choose a top-down approach that reduces the variance of protection more than a uniform cut. Equally clearly, the gains will be less if a methodology is used that brings about less reduction in the variance of protection – perhaps by preserving the politically sensitive tariff peaks. Further work that takes these potential differences into account is necessary. Such work should flush out the implications of choices within the relatively broad approach to liberalisation that is likely to emerge from the preparatory process.

4. CONCLUSIONS

This chapter brings together the available evidence regarding the impact of future, multilateral liberalisation in agricultural and manufacturing trade on developing countries. In agriculture, the biggest barriers to trade reside in industrialised countries. Accordingly, they command a large share of the gains from trade reforms. However, when measured relative to projected GDP in 2005, the largest percentage gains from liberalisation accrue to developing countries in South and Southeast Asia where the agricultural sector is itself quite large and rather distorted by current policies. The same is true of the East Asian NICs. Developing country exporters in Latin America are also big gainers, but about half of their increased income derives from improved terms of trade stemming from increased demand for their products overseas.

The modalities of liberalisation in a Millennium Round will be particularly important in the agricultural sector, particularly in light of the TRQs that were installed to protect market access under the Uruguay Round Agreement on Agriculture. Unfortunately, these TRQs reduce transparency. They also have served to create (or in some cases preserve) substantial quota rents. The presence of these rents increases the risk that some countries will lose from further liberalisation, particularly when liberalisation takes the form of reductions in out-of-quota tariff rates. Fortunately, it appears that these risks can be greatly diminished by policies that combine reductions in out-of-quota tariffs with increases in the volumes allowed under the quotas. The combination of these measures will also ensure a more rapid move towards free trade in agricultural products.

While further reforms to agricultural trade are already part of the built-in agenda for the next Round of WTO negotiations, industrial products are notably absent. The conventional wisdom is that tariff cuts on industrial products are primarily in the interest of the so-called industrial countries. Yet industrial country manufacturing tariffs are now quite low – outside of a few sensitive sectors – and interest in this area of liberalisation has accordingly diminished. Should the developing countries take up the banner of manufacturing tariff cuts? The findings of Hertel and Martin (1999) suggest that the world has changed fundamentally from that depicted in traditional North–South models. Far from being indifferent to the inclusion of industrial products, as traditional models would suggest, developing countries should be the strongest advocates of their inclusion in a future WTO round. The average developing country depends on manufactures for about three-quarters of its merchandise exports. There are potentially substantial gains to developing countries in this area from reductions in tariff peaks in industrial countries, from increased market access in other developing countries, and from efficiency gains resulting from lowering their own barriers.

REFERENCES

ABARE (1999), *Reforming Agricultural Trade Policies*, Research Report No. 99–12 (Canberra, Australia).

Abbott, P. and A. Morse (1999), 'TRQ Implementation in Developing Countries', Paper presented at the Conference on Agriculture and the New Trade Agenda in the WTO 2000 Negotiations (WTO, Geneva, 1–2 October).

Anderson, K. (1999), 'Agriculture, Developing Countries and the WTO's Millennium Round', Paper presented at the Conference on Agriculture and the New Trade Agenda in the WTO 2000 Negotiations (WTO, Geneva, 1–2 October).

Anderson, K., B. Hoekman and A. Strutt (1999), 'Agriculture and the WTO: Next Steps', Paper presented to the Second Annual Conference on Global Economic Analysis (Avernaes Conference Centre, Denmark, 20–22 June).

Dessus, S., K. Fukasaku and R. Safadi (1999), *Multilateral Tariff Liberalization and the Developing Countries*, Policy Brief No. 18 (Paris: OECD).

Elbeheri, A., M. Ingco, T. Hertel and K. Pearson (1999), 'Agriculture and WTO 2000: Quantitative Assessment of Multilateral Liberalization of Agricultural Policies', Paper presented at the Conference on Agriculture and the New Trade Agenda in the WTO 2000 Negotiations (WTO, Geneva, 1–2 October).

Francois, J. (1999), 'The Ghost of Rounds Past: The Uruguay Round and the Shape of the Next Multilateral Trade Round', Paper presented at the Conference on Agriculture and the New Trade Agenda in the WTO 2000 Negotiations (WTO, Geneva, 1–2 October).

Francois, J. and W. Martin (1998), 'Commercial Policy Uncertainty, the Expected Cost of Protection, and Market Access', Tinbergen Institute Discussion Paper (Rotterdam).

GATT (1994), *The Results of the Uruguay Round of Trade Negotiations: The Legal Texts* (Geneva: GATT Secretariat).

Hathaway, D. and M. Ingco (1995), 'Agricultural Liberalization and the Uruguay Round', in W. Martin and L.A. Winters (eds.), *The Uruguay Round and the Developing Countries* (Cambridge: Cambridge University Press).

Hertel, T. and W. Martin (1999), 'Would Developing Countries Gain From Inclusion of Manufactures Trade in the WTO 2000 Negotiations?' World Bank Paper presented at the Conference on the Millennium Round, WTO (Geneva, 20–21 September).

Hertel, T., K. Anderson, J. Francois and W. Martin (1999), 'Agriculture and Non-agricultural Liberalization in the Millennium Round', Paper presented at the Conference on Agriculture and the New Trade Agenda in the WTO 2000 Negotiations (WTO, Geneva, 1–2 October).

Hoekman, B. and M. Kostecki (1995), *The Political Economy of the World Trading System: From GATT to WTO* (Oxford: Oxford University Press).

Josling, T. and A. Rae (1999), 'Multilateral Approaches to Market Access Negotiations in Agriculture', Paper presented at the Conference on Agriculture and the New Trade Agenda in the WTO 2000 Negotiations (WTO, Geneva, 1–2 October).

OECD (1999), *Agricultural Policies in OECD Countries: Monitoring and Outlook, 1999* (Paris: OECD).

5

Developing Countries in the New Round of GATS Negotiations: Towards a Pro-Active Role

Aaditya Mattoo

1. INTRODUCTION

DEVELOPING countries need to ensure that multilateral rules and commitments on trade in services contribute to economically rational policy-making at the national and international levels. Their reluctant participation in past negotiations has not been conducive to the achievement of this goal. The next round of services negotiations requires a change in negotiating strategies. Rather than resist the liberalisation of domestic markets and seek a dilution of multilateral rules, they need to push aggressively for the liberalisation of both domestic and foreign services markets and to promote the development of improved rules. If developed countries rise to the challenge of eliminating the barriers they maintain to exports from developing countries, we may well witness a virtuous cycle of mutually beneficial liberalisation.

A number of basic themes emerge from this chapter and related research on services trade liberalisation. There are substantial gains both from liberalisation within developing countries, especially in key infrastructure services like telecommunications, transport and financial services, and from the elimination of barriers to their exports. Successful domestic liberalisation requires greater emphasis on introducing competition than changing ownership; regulation to remedy market failure and pursue legitimate social goals with economic efficiency; and credibility of policy reform programmes. Effective access to foreign markets requires the elimination of explicit restrictions as well as disciplines on implicit regulatory barriers. A central question in preparing for the next round of services negotiations is how the GATS can help achieve these objectives.

This chapter discusses why liberalisation of trade in services should lead to improved economic performance; argues that certain policy choices developing countries made in key services sectors, often under negotiating pressure, were not socially desirable; discusses the substantial gains that could arise from the elimination of the barriers to developing country service exports; proposes a possible formula for breaking the stalemate on the movement of individual service providers; and demonstrates how appropriately designed GATS rules on domestic regulations can help both to promote reform at the national level and meaningful market access at the international level. Table 1 provides a summary of the issues discussed in this chapter, their current status and what seem to be the desirable outcomes.

2. THE BENEFITS OF LIBERALISING TRADE IN SERVICES

Restrictions on trade in services, as on trade in goods, reduce the level of real GDP which is equivalent to a loss in welfare.[1] In the case of services, there is an additional twist in that many services are inputs into production and inefficient production of such services act as a tax on production. Thus, goods trade liberalisation in the absence of services trade liberalisation could well result in negative effective protection for goods, highlighting the need for the latter to keep pace with the former.[2]

Well functioning service industries contribute to growth in different ways. An efficient financial sector allows resources to be deployed where they have the highest returns. King and Levine (1993) demonstrate that efficient financial services contribute to and precede faster economic growth. Improved telecom efficiency generates economy-wide benefits as telecommunications are a vital intermediate input and are crucial to the diffusion of knowledge. Similarly, transport services contribute to the efficient distribution of goods within a country, and greatly influence a country's ability to participate in global trade. Business services such as accounting and legal services are important in reducing transaction costs; education and health services are necessary in building up the stock of human capital, a key ingredient in long-run growth performance.

Services and goods liberalisation differ in some key respects. In services, attaining efficiency is not just a matter of liberalising trade barriers, but also of instituting an appropriate domestic regulatory framework. Services liberalisation also entails, in most instances, movement of factors of production. A country that liberalises its services sector is likely to augment its stock of capital (through

---

[1] The restriction creates a wedge between domestic and foreign prices, leading to a loss in consumer surplus that is greater than the gain in producer surplus arising from higher domestic production.

[2] See, e.g., Hoekman and Braga (1997), Findlay and Warren (1999) and Hoekman and Djankov (1997).

increased FDI) and crucially the stock of human capital and technology that is embodied in or associated with such FDI. The impact of this on long-run growth is unambiguously positive. Furthermore, there is evidence that FDI is more productive than domestic investment (e.g., Borensztein et al., 1998), indicating the presence of positive technology spillovers. This is as true for developing country capital importers as for developed country importers of skilled labour services. The contribution of imported skilled labour to the high-technology sectors in the US is now widely recognised.

Studies examining the link between liberalisation of trade in goods and growth are as profuse as those on the services–growth link are sparse. This reflects in part the complexity of services sectors, especially the difficulty in encapsulating the multiplicity of restrictions in easily quantifiable and comprehensible indices. An important research priority is to replicate the trade in goods-growth studies for services, while controlling for other determinants of growth. As a first step in filling this gap, Mattoo, Rathindran and Subramanian (1999) have constructed openness indices for two services sectors – telecommunications and financial services – and introduced these in standard cross-country growth regressions. Although preliminary, the results suggest the partial correlations between financial services liberalisation and growth found by, e.g., Claessens and Glaessner (1998) and Francois and Schuknecht (1999) are robust: liberalisation contributes meaningfully to explaining cross-country growth performance.

3. CHOOSING THE PATTERN OF LIBERALISATION

a. Entry and Ownership

Restrictions on foreign commercial presence assume particular significance in the case of services where cross-border delivery is not possible, so that consumer prices depend completely on the domestic market structure. Restrictions on new entry and on the participation of foreign capital are the most common, particularly in communications and financial services (Table 2). A basic conclusion from the literature on privatisation is that larger welfare gains arise from an increase in competition than from simply a change in ownership from public to private hands. In the GATS context countries have often conceded increased 'market access' under pressure from trading partners in the form of increased foreign ownership of existing domestic firms, rather than by allowing new entry. Considerable negotiating energy was also devoted to maintaining existing foreign ownership (Mattoo, 1999). This trend was particularly visible in the financial services negotiations, where the so-called 'grandfather provisions' guaranteed ownership and branching rights of incumbent foreign firms while far

TABLE 1

Summary of Selected GATS Negotiating and Domestic Policy Issues, Current Status and Desirable Outcomes

Issue	Current Status	Desirable Outcome
Market access commitments under Article XVI of GATS	Numerous restrictions, particularly on entry and foreign equity; in some cases more emphasis on allowing increased foreign ownership and protecting foreign incumbents than on allowing new entry.	Further liberalisation, with greater emphasis on eliminating restrictions on entry and promoting increased competition.
	Limited use of the GATS, except in basic telecom, to precommit to future liberalisation.	Wider use of the GATS to lend credibility to future liberalisation programmes.
	Extremely limited market opening commitments on the presence of natural persons.	Enhanced scope for the temporary, contract-related presence of natural persons.
Pro-competitive regulation (Articles VIII and IX, and the Telecom Reference Paper)	Weak basic provisions with limited scope (Article VIII) and limited bite (Article IX), but commitment to desirable principles in the Reference Paper should contribute to enhanced competition.	Generalise the pro-competitive principles in the Reference Paper to other network-based sectors. Strengthen disciplines to deal with international cartels (e.g. in transport).
		Strengthen domestic pro-competitive regulation to protect interests also of consumers.
Domestic regulation (Article VI)	Weak current disciplines (Article VI:5), allow 'grandfathering' of protection through certain regulatory instruments; some success in accountancy negotiations in instituting a 'necessity test' but disappointing elaboration of disciplines on measures such as qualification requirements.	Generalise the application of a necessity test to regulatory instruments in all sectors, especially where they impede developing country exports.
		Strengthen domestic regulations to remedy asymmetric information-related problems in financial, professional, and other services.
		And choose economically efficiency instruments to achieve universal service objectives.

Mutual Recognition Agreements (Article VII)	Delicate balance (in Article VII): MRAs are allowed provided recognition is not used as a means of discrimination and third countries have the opportunity to accede or to demonstrate equivalence.	Ensure that MRAs do not become a means of discrimination. Improve quality and uniformity of domestic regulation where socially desirable, to strengthen case for foreign recognition.
Safeguards (Article X)	Limited progress in current negotiations; no agreement on whether such a mechanism is necessary, desirable and/or feasible.	Create an avenue for temporary adjustment-related demands for protection, provided it is subject to strong, enforceable disciplines that prevent protectionist abuse.
Government procurement (Article XIII)	Limited progress in current negotiations; general reluctance to assume strong disciplines.	Promote transparency and non-discrimination disciplines, but link to the elimination of barriers to mobility of natural persons to fulfil procurement contracts in construction and other services.
Subsidies (Article XV)	Subject to non-discrimination requirements where national treatment commitments exist. Little progress in current negotiations.	Ensure freedom for the use of subsidies where they are the best instrument to achieve legitimate economic or social objectives.
Electronic commerce	Decision not to impose customs duties, which has little meaning since quotas and discriminatory internal taxation are still permitted in many cases.	Widen and deepen scope of cross-border supply commitments on market access (prohibiting quotas) and national treatment (prohibiting discriminatory taxation) to ensure current openness continues.

TABLE 2
Types of Market Access Restrictions on Commercial Presence in Services Sectors (All Countries)

Sector	Number of Members with Commitments	Restrictions Per Commitment On						
		Number of Suppliers	Value of Transactions or Assets	Number of Operations	Number of Natural Persons	Types of Legal Entity	Participation of Foreign Capital
1 Business services	89	0.2	3.4	0.0	0.8	4.0	3.6
2 Communication services	85	3.9	2.1	0.2	0.5	4.3	3.8
3 Construction and related engineering services	60	0.1	0.9	0.0	0.2	0.9	0.9
4 Distribution services	38	0.2	0.7	0.0	0.1	0.4	0.4
5 Educational services	32	0.1	0.3	0.0	0.0	0.9	0.5
6 Environmental services	40	0.2	0.7	0.0	0.1	0.7	0.6
7 Financial services	91	4.6	4.3	1.4	0.9	8.6	4.4
8 Health and related social services	34	0.2	0.3	0.1	0.2	0.6	0.4
9 Tourism and travel related services	114	0.2	0.4	0.1	0.1	0.5	0.4
10 Recreational, cultural and sporting services	49	0.1	0.3	0.0	0.1	0.5	0.2
11 Transport services	70	0.3	0.9	0.0	0.1	1.9	1.4

Note: Restrictions per commitment are calculated by dividing the total number of restrictions in a sector by the number of Members with commitments.

Source: Adlung, Carzeniga and Mattoo (1999).

more limited rights were assured for potential entrants, potentially placing them at a competitive disadvantage.

Foreign investment clearly brings benefits even in situations where it does not lead to enhanced competition (i.e., there are entry restrictions). Foreign equity may relax a capital constraint, can help ensure that weak domestic firms are bolstered (e.g. via recapitalising financial institutions), and serve as a vehicle for transferring technology and know-how, including improved management. However, if FDI comes simply because the returns to investment are artificially raised by restrictions on competition, the net returns to the host country may be negative (returns to the investor may exceed the true social productivity of the investment – Hindley and Smith, 1984). To some extent the rent appropriation may be prevented by profit taxation or by holding competitive auctions of licences or equity, but the static and dynamic inefficiencies from lack of competition would still exist.[3]

Given the existence of rent-generating restrictions on competition, it is possible to rationalise the observed limitations on foreign ownership as seeking to balance the efficiency-enhancing and the rent-appropriation aspects of foreign investment. However, this still leaves the question why we observe such widespread restrictions on entry. While it is possible to construct special models of market and/or regulatory failure where entry barriers enhance welfare,[4] restrictions generally aim to protect the incumbent suppliers (not necessarily national) from immediate competition for infant industry type reasons, to facilitate 'orderly exit' or simply because of political economy pressures. Monopolistic or oligopolistic rents may also be seen as a means to allow firms to fulfil universal service obligations. Both of these arguments are considered further below. In some cases a form of 'investment pessimism' exists, leading to the belief that promises of oligopoly rents are necessary to attract new investment. However, it is not clear why the market structure needs to be determined by policy, unless there are some initial investments the benefits of which may be appropriated by rivals. Finally, governments may seek to raise revenue (or rents for politicians/bureaucrats) by auctioning monopoly or oligopoly rights. This amounts to indirect appropriation of consumers' surplus. But the static and dynamic inefficiencies consequent upon lack of competition would still exist.

Entry restrictions are becoming harder to justify in the face of growing evidence of the benefits of competition. In Latin America, for example, countries that granted monopoly privileges of six to ten years to the privatised state telecommunications enterprises saw connections grow at 1.5 times the rate

---

[3] And, neither addresses appropriation by existing foreign share owners. In this context, grandfathering commitments assume particular significance.
[4] One example is excessive entry by firms that are ignorant of each other's costs; the social benefits of competition between firms may then outweigh the social costs of duplication of investment.

achieved under state monopolies but only half the rate in Chile, where the government retained the right to issue competing licences at any time (Wellenius, 1997). Mattoo (1999) finds a significant negative relationship between performance (measured by price and quality indicators) in the telecom sector and the number of firms and the existence of an independent regulator, and generally a weaker relationship with the share of public and foreign ownership. These results support the view that the consumer benefits arise more from increased competition and effective regulation than from a change in ownership.

b. Precommitment to Future Liberalisation

One reason governments may be reluctant to liberalise immediately is a perceived need to protect the incumbent suppliers from competition – either because of infant industry type arguments or to facilitate 'orderly exit.' One reason for the failure of infant industry policies in the past, and the innumerable examples of perpetual infancy, was the inability of a government to commit itself credibly to liberalise at some future date. The GATS offers a valuable mechanism to overcome the credibility difficulty. Governments can make binding commitments to provide market access and national treatment at a future date. Failure to honour these commitments would create an obligation to compensate those who are deprived of benefits, making the commitment more credible than a mere announcement of liberalising intent in the national context. A precommitment to liberalise can also instil a sense of urgency in domestic reform, and in efforts to develop the necessary regulatory and supervision mechanisms.

Several governments have taken advantage of the GATS to strike a balance between their reluctance to unleash competition immediately on protected national suppliers and their desire not to be held hostage in perpetuity either to the weakness of domestic industry or to pressure from vested interests. The most striking examples are in basic telecommunications, where a number of developing countries have bound themselves to introduce competition at precise future dates. The use of the GATS as a mechanism for lending credibility to liberalisation programmes has been disappointing in other sectors.

4. SERVICES EXPORTS OF DEVELOPING COUNTRIES

a. Potential Gains and Current Barriers

There are likely to be significant gains world-wide if restrictions on services exports from developing countries are eliminated. With greater liberalisation, particularly in mode 4 – movement of natural persons – many more developing countries could 'export' at least the significant labour component of services such as construction, distribution, environmental and transport.

One of the most striking recent examples of a developing country service export success story is the Indian software industry, which has emerged as a significant supplier to developed country markets. Indian software exports grew from US$225 million in 1992–93 to US$1.75 billion in 1997–98 (at a compound annual growth rate of approximately 50 per cent).[5] Some elements of this story are noteworthy.

First, despite the growing importance of cross-border electronic delivery of software services, the movement of natural persons remains a crucial mode of delivery. Even though the share of on-shore services in total Indian software exports has been in continuous decline (in 1988, the percentage of on-site development was almost as high as 90 per cent), about 60 per cent of Indian exports are still supplied through the temporary movement of programmers, i.e. services are delivered on-shore, at the client's site overseas.[6]

Secondly, it cannot be assumed that other countries' trade policies will become progressively more liberal, particularly with regard to movement of persons. In the early 1990s, the US government introduced rules that obliged foreign workers to acquire temporary work visas (H1-B visas), and limited the number of visas issued during a year to 65,000. This contributed to the relative decline of on-shore services by Indian firms (Heeks, 1998). In 1998, in response to mounting labour shortages experienced in the US IT sector, the annual visa cap was raised to 115,000 for both 1999 and 2000. This quota increase is likely to lead to a boost in US on-site imports of software services, especially as they relate to 'Year 2000' work. The question is whether liberalisation will continue after the 'Year 2000' problem has been resolved.

Third, significant gains can be had from further liberalisation. There are wide differences in the cost of software development and support: the average cost per line of code in Switzerland (the most expensive country) exceeds by more than five times that of India (the cheapest country); average salaries are more than eleven times higher in Switzerland (Mattoo, 1999). Even though differences in labour productivity imply that a lower average salary of programmers may not necessarily translate into a lower average cost per line of software code, by outsourcing programming activities firms in developed countries can significantly save on development and support costs. Against the background of a total market for software services worth about US$58 billion in the United States, US$42 billion in Europe and US$10 billion in Japan, such cost savings could well be substantial.[7] Other gains from trade liberalisation for importing countries

---

[5] See the National Association of Software and Service Companies (NASSCOM) website <http://www.nasscom.org>. These exports consist mainly of standardised coding and testing services.

[6] See http://www.nasscom.org. The dominance of on-shore delivery is due to inter alia a reduction in information asymmetries with regard to the performance of programmers, need for continuous client-developer interaction, and demands by Indian programmers to be sent abroad, in part to improve their skills and expose themselves to international markets (see Heeks, 1998).

[7] These figures were computed from WTO (1998, Table 3). Data refer to 1997.

include a more competitive market structure for software services, increased
choice, as countries may develop a special expertise for certain development or
support services, and greater diffusion of knowledge.

Health services are another area in which developing countries could become
major exporters, either by attracting foreign patients to domestic hospitals and
doctors, or by temporarily sending their health personnel abroad. In Cuba, the
government's strategy is to convert Cuba into a world medical power.
SERVIMED, a trading company created by the government, prepares health/
tourism packages. During 1995/96 25,000 patients and 1,500 students went to
Cuba for treatment and training respectively, and income earned from sales to
health services to foreigners was US$25 million. Again, cost savings for patients
and health insurers can be significant. For instance, the cost of coronary bypass
surgery could be as low as Rs70,000 to 100,000 in India, about five per cent of
the cost in developed countries. Similarly, the cost of a liver transplant is one-
tenth of that in the United States (United Nations and WHO, 1998).

A major barrier to consumption abroad of medical services is the lack of
portability of health insurance. For instance, US federal or state government
reimbursement of medical expenses is limited to licensed, certified facilities in
the United States or in a specific American state. The lack of long-term
portability of health coverage for retirees from OECD countries is also one of the
major constraints to trade. In the United States, for instance, Medicare covers
virtually no services delivered abroad. Other nations may extend coverage
abroad, but only for limited periods such as two or three months. This constraint
is significant because it tends to deter some elderly persons from travelling or
retiring abroad. And those who do retire abroad are often forced to return home to
obtain affordable medical care. The potential impact of permitting portability
could be substantial. If only three per cent of the 100 million elderly persons
living in OECD countries retired to developing countries, they would bring with
them possibly US$30 to 50 billion annually in personal consumption and US$10
to 15 billion in medical expenditures (United Nations and WHO, 1998).

Many different barriers constrain the movement of natural persons. The many
formalities alone (e.g. to obtain a visa) make red tape related to FDI seem trivial
by comparison. The most obvious barriers are explicit quotas and/or economic
needs tests, e.g., requirements that employers take timely and significant steps to
recruit and retain sufficient national workers in the speciality occupation and that
no worker has been laid off for a certain period preceding and following the filing
of any work permit or visa application.[8] Qualification and licensing requirements
and the regulations of professional bodies are major barriers as well. The entry of

---

[8] Other barriers to movement of natural persons include double taxation, wage-matching
requirements (wages paid to foreign workers should be similar to those paid to nationals in that
profession, eliminating the cost advantage for foreigners), and local training requirements (to
replace foreign with national labour within a certain time frame).

foreigners can be impeded by non-recognition of their professional qualifications, burdensome licensing requirements or by the imposition of discriminatory standards on them. The requirement of registration with, or membership of, professional organisations can also constitute an obstacle for a person wishing to provide the service on a temporary basis.

b. Using the GATS Negotiations to Enhance Market Access

There is no doubt that the Uruguay Round outcome in services was unbalanced. The much-touted trade-off between modes of delivery simply did not take place. Although antipathy to commitments on labour mobility in partner countries was a major contributing factor, an unwillingness on the part of developing countries to open up domestic services markets made their demands for labour mobility difficult to sustain. With developing countries opening up their markets, the prospects for serious inter-modal trade-offs are greater now – e.g., liberalisation of labour movement in return for allowing greater commercial presence for foreign service providers. Severe shortages of skilled labour in the US and the powerful constituency of high-technology companies lobbying for relaxation of visa limits also makes this a propitious time to put labour mobility squarely on the negotiating agenda.[9]

It would seem to be in the interest of all countries to separate clearly temporary movement from migration, and to push for liberalisation only with respect to the former. For exporting countries, it is clear that both the financial and knowledge benefits would be greatest if service suppliers (particularly those who have benefited from a subsidised education) return home after a certain period abroad.[10] And for importing countries, such temporary movement should create fewer social and political problems than immigration.

One option to extract meaningful mode 4 commitments would be to require a country to provide increased 'foreign labour content entitlements' to their domestic firms in relation to the country's increased exports of services.[11] The requirement would be internationally symmetric: all countries would be obliged

---

[9] The notions of the US as the unrivalled centre of technology and the role of technological progress in motoring the recent US economic expansion resonate deeply with the US public. They would therefore be loath to countenance any obstacles to this march of progress even if it involves greater imports of labour-related services.

[10] Over 50 per cent of all migrating physicians come from developing countries. In Ethiopia, for example, during 1984–94, 55.6 per cent of the pathology graduates from the Addis Ababa Faculty of Medicine left the country. In Ghana, of the 65 who graduated from the Medical School in 1985, only 22 remained in the country by 1997. If these countries had adequate medical staff at home, these figures would be less cause for concern.

[11] Mattoo and Olarreaga (2000). In a way Bill Gates' recent testimony before Congress arguing for the need to allow more software engineers to enter to maintain international competitiveness is not far-removed from the suggested scheme.

to create such entitlements, though how much they are used would be determined by sound economic considerations of modal comparative advantage. Entitlements would not be bilateral, but international. This approach is also based on a balance of concessions, an appealing principle in trade negotiations. Exporters of labour services would receive benefits commensurate with efforts to open up their domestic services markets. The scheme would also generate a desirable liberalising momentum. Conventional mercantilist negotiations on trade barriers create a holdback problem: I would rather give less to get more from you. By linking my export possibilities to your actual exports, the proposed scheme induces me to be more open.

c. Ensuring Barrier-free Electronic Commerce

Electronic commerce offers an increasingly viable alternative to the movement of individuals. WTO Members have decided that for the moment electronic delivery of products will continue to be free from customs duties. There are proposals to make this permanent. Fortunately most electronic commerce is already free of barriers (except of course those created by differences in standards), and so the objective is really to preclude the introduction of new barriers. But is duty-free electronic commerce the appropriate route?

Liberating e-commerce from duties is either superfluous or virtually devoid of value. Since the bulk of such commerce concerns services, the relevant regime is that established by the GATS regime on cross-border trade. The GATS allows countries to decide whether to commit to market access, i.e. not to impose quotas, and to national treatment, i.e. not to discriminate in any way against foreign services and suppliers. If a country has already made such a commitment, then any further promise not to impose duties is superfluous because customs duties inherently discriminate against foreign services. If a country has not made such a commitment, then the promise not to impose customs duties is worth little, because a country remains free to impede access through discriminatory internal taxation – which has been carefully excluded from the scope of the decision. Worse, the prohibition of such duties may induce recourse to quotas which are ironically still permissible in spite of being economically inferior instruments. Hence, the focus on duty-free treatment is misplaced. The objective should rather be to push trading partners into making deeper and wider commitments under the GATS on cross-border trade regarding market access (which would preclude quantitative restrictions) and national treatment (which would preclude all forms of discriminatory taxation).

Table 3 summarises the current state of commitments on cross-border supply in some of the areas in which developing countries have an export interest. In software implementation and data processing, of the total WTO Membership of over 130, only 56 and 54 Members, respectively, have made commitments; and

TABLE 3
GATS Commitments on Mode 1 in Selected Service Sectors

Sector/Subsector	Number of Countries	Market Access Cross-Border Supply (%)			National Treatment Cross-Border Supply (%)		
		Full[a]	Part[a]	No[a]	Full[a]	Part[a]	No[a]
Professional Services	74	19	17	64	14	10	76
Computer and Related Services							
a. Consultancy service related to the installation of computer hardware	51	57	20	24	51	22	27
b. Software implementation	56	54	27	20	48	29	23
c. Data processing	54	54	26	20	46	31	22

Notes: Percentage may not add up to 100 due to rounding.

[a] Full: full commitment; Part: partial commitment; No: no commitment.

only around half of these commitments guarantee unrestricted market access, and a similar proportion guarantee unqualified national treatment. In all professional services, there are commitments from 74 Members, but less than a fifth assure unrestricted market access and national treatment, respectively. There clearly remains considerable scope for widening and deepening commitments.

5. DEALING WITH DOMESTIC REGULATIONS

Developing countries have much to gain from strengthened multilateral disciplines on domestic regulations. The development of such disciplines can play a significant role in promoting and consolidating domestic regulatory reform. The telecommunications experience is a powerful example of this possibility. Such disciplines can also equip developing country exporters to address regulatory barriers to their exports in foreign markets.[12] For instance, unless disciplines are developed to deal with licensing and qualification requirements for professionals, market access commitments on mode 4 will have only notional value. However, there are limits to what can be achieved at the multilateral level, and some of the key regulatory challenges must still be addressed at the national level. This is because multilateral trade rules are designed to ensure market access, and not directly to promote economic efficiency or social welfare.

One of the ironies of the GATS is that among its weakest provisions are those dealing with domestic regulations, which have such an obviously powerful

---

[12] These gains, of course, imply a cost: giving up domestic regulatory discretion. But if multilateral disciplines are desirable then this cost is no different from the first benefit identified above.

influence on international trade in services. The reason is not difficult to see: it is extremely difficult to develop effective multilateral disciplines in this area without seeming to encroach upon national sovereignty and unduly limiting regulatory freedom. Nevertheless, it is desirable and feasible to develop horizontal disciplines for domestic regulations.[13] The diversity of services sectors, and the difficulty in making certain policy-relevant generalisations, has tended to favour a sector-specific approach. However, even though services sectors differ greatly, the underlying economic and social reasons for regulatory intervention do not. And focusing on these reasons provides the basis for the creation of meaningful horizontal disciplines.

Such a generic approach is to be preferred to a purely sectoral approach for at least three reasons: it economises on negotiating effort, leads to the creation of disciplines for all services sectors rather than only the politically important ones, and reduces the likelihood of negotiations being captured by sectoral interest groups. It is now widely recognised that the most dramatic progress in the EU single-market programme came from willingness to take certain broad cross-sectoral initiatives. In the WTO context, the experience of the accountancy negotiations shows the propensity for single sectoral negotiations on domestic regulations to produce a weak outcome.

Even if a horizontal approach is desirable, is it feasible? The economic case for regulation in all services sectors arises essentially from market failure attributable primarily to three kinds of problems, natural monopoly or oligopoly, asymmetric information, and externalities. Market failure due to natural monopoly or oligopoly may create trade problems because incumbents can impede access to markets in the absence of appropriate regulation. Because of its direct impact on trade, this is the only form of market failure that needs to be addressed directly by multilateral disciplines. The relevant GATS provision, Article VIII dealing with monopolies, is limited in scope. As a consequence, in the context of the telecom negotiations, the reference paper with its competition principles was developed in order to ensure that monopolistic suppliers would not undermine market access commitments (Tuthill, 1997). These principles should be generalised to a variety of other network services, including transport (terminals and infrastructure), environmental services (sewage) and energy services (distribution networks), by ensuring that any major supplier of essential facilities provides access to all suppliers, national and foreign, at cost-based rates.

In all other cases of market failure, multilateral disciplines do not need to address the problem per se, but rather to ensure that domestic measures to deal with the problem do not serve unduly to restrict trade. (The same is true for measures designed to achieve social objectives.) Such trade-restrictive effects can arise from a variety of technical standards, prudential regulations, and

---

[13] What follows draws upon Gamberale and Mattoo (1999).

qualification requirements in professional, financial and numerous other services; as well as from the granting of monopoly rights to complement universal service obligations in services like transport and telecommunications. The trade-inhibiting effect of this entire class of regulations is best disciplined by complementing the national treatment obligation with a generalisation of the so-called 'necessity' test. This test leaves governments free to deal with economic and social problems provided that any measures taken are not more trade restrictive than necessary to achieve the relevant objective. This test is already part of the recently established disciplines in the accountancy sector. It is desirable to use it to create a presumption in favour of economically efficient choice of policy in remedying market failure and in pursuing non-economic objectives (Mattoo and Subramanian, 1998). For instance, in the case of professionals like doctors, a requirement to re-qualify would be judged unnecessary, since the basic problem, inadequate information about whether they possess the required skills, could be remedied by a less burdensome test of competence. In sum, the telecommunications and accountancy models, suitably developed and generalised, can together ensure that domestic regulations achieve their objectives without sacrificing economic efficiency.

This is not to say that there is no need for sector-specific disciplines. For instance, there is valuable work that could be done to establish how best to deal with asymmetric information and differences in standards between countries. But we can make a useful beginning by taking a cross-sectoral approach. Such a route is particularly desirable because at the multilateral level, harmonisation and mutual recognition are not meaningful alternatives to the application of a necessity test – even though they can play a role at the regional or plurilateral level. The pessimism with regard to harmonisation is based on the absence of widely accepted international standards in services.[14] With regard to mutual recognition agreements (MRAs), it would seem that even in strongly integrationist Europe, despite a significant level of prior harmonisation, the effect of MRAs may have been limited by the unwillingness of host country regulators to concede complete control (Nicolaidis and Trachtman, 1999). In any case, MRAs are like sector-specific preferential arrangements, and can have similar trade-creating trade-diverting effects. Multilateral disciplines must be used to ensure that MRAs are not used as a means of discrimination and exclusion.[15] Otherwise, their result may well be to create trade according to patterns of mutual trust rather than the pattern of comparative advantage.

---

[14] Where such standards exist, as in banking or maritime transport, meeting them is seen as a first step towards acceptability, rather than as a sufficient condition for market access.

[15] These disciplines operate at two levels: the general rules on preferential arrangements and the specific rules for MRAs. Article V on integration agreements does not explicitly preclude MRAs, and several countries have chosen to notify their MRAs under this provision. However, Article VII of the GATS dealing specifically with recognition, strikes a delicate balance by allowing such

The development of multilateral disciplines is in no way a substitute for strengthening domestic regulatory mechanisms and institutions. At least three areas are of considerable importance.

(i) Dealing with monopolies

The telecom Reference Paper illustrates both the strengths and the limitations of the multilateral approach. The primary concern of the paper, as of WTO rules in general, is to ensure effective market access, and hence the focus on the terms of interconnection. Wider concerns about consumer interests and how they may be affected by monopolistic behaviour are not addressed by the Paper. While there can be little doubt that price determination is ideally left to competitive markets, and regulatory price setting is fraught with difficulties, yet regulatory authorities in developing countries where competition is slow to develop need to equip themselves, legally and technically, with the ability to regulate prices.[16] This would seem particularly desirable in countries like some of those in the Caribbean, which have locked themselves into exclusive supply contracts with a single telecom provider well into the next century. Importantly, while nothing in the GATS prevents a country from pursuing any form of pro-competitive regulation provided it is not discriminatory, the capacity of most developing countries to exercise such regulation is limited.

(ii) Dealing with asymmetric information

The need for effective regulation of financial services needs no elaboration, particularly in light of the recent experiences of many countries. Again it is incumbent on the countries themselves to create adequate mechanisms for such regulation. And such regulation is clearly necessary to benefit fully from liberalisation. Other areas where the inadequacy of regulatory mechanisms to deal with asymmetric information is a problem have received relatively less attention. For instance, in professional services, low standards and disparities in domestic training and examinations can become a major impediment to obtaining foreign recognition. Thus inadequacies in domestic regulation can legitimise external barriers to trade. A further twist is that domestic consumers may actually prefer cheap, low quality products. The question of how best to achieve the needs of export markets given domestic preferences for quality is clearly an area where much more research is needed.

---

agreements, provided they are not used as a means of discrimination and third countries have the opportunity to accede or demonstrate equivalence. It should be clarified that this provision, with its desirable non-discriminatory and open-ended nature, overrides Article V of the GATS as far as MRAs are concerned.

[16] In many developed country markets where fully competitive conditions have not been established, such as the telecommunications sector in the United Kingdom, the final price itself has been regulated.

(iii) Achieving universal service and non-economic objectives

Attaining social objectives in an economically efficient manner is a major challenge for national policy-makers. The manner in which they pursue this objective can have a profound impact on trade in a variety of areas, ranging from financial, transport, telecommunications, health and education services. Interestingly, the telecom Reference Paper acknowledges the right of a country to define universal service obligations provided they are administered in a transparent, non-discriminatory and not excessively burdensome manner. But it does not prescribe the appropriate means to achieve this objective – this is left to national governments.

Historically, governments frequently relied on public monopolies to pursue (often unsuccessfully) universal services objectives, either through cross-subsidisation across different segments of the market, or through transfers from the government or government-controlled banks. In addition to the inefficiencies created by monopolistic market structures, the burdens imposed by these obligations on existing national suppliers are even now a major impediment to liberalisation in many countries. For instance, domestic banks saddled with bad debts because of past directed-lending programmes are not well equipped to deal with foreign competition.

Nevertheless, the current handicap of universal service obligations can in principle also be imposed on new entrants. Thus, such obligations were part of the licence conditions for new entrants into fixed network telephony and transport in several countries. But as in many other cases, recourse to fiscal instruments has proved more successful than direct regulation. For instance, in Chile, government subsidies equivalent to less than 0.5 per cent of total telecommunications revenue, allocated through competitive bidding in 1995, mobilised 20 times as much private investment to extend basic telephone services to rural areas (Wellenius, 1997).

A third instrument is to fund the consumer rather than the provider (Cowhey and Klimenko, 1999). Governments have experimented with various forms of vouchers, from education to energy services. This last instrument has at least three advantages: it can be targeted directly at those who need the service and cannot afford it; it avoids the distortions that arise from artificially low pricing of services to ensure access; and finally, it does not discriminate in any way between providers.

6. CONCLUSION

Although the most important services policy reforms need to be taken at the domestic level, there is substantial scope for constructive use of the multilateral trading system both in realising credible domestic liberalisation and securing market access abroad. This chapter has discussed some of the major issues confronting developing countries – a more comprehensive treatment can be found in Mattoo (1999). Major recommendations are summarised in Table 1.

Certain policy choices made by developing countries, often under negotiating pressure, are not likely to maximise domestic welfare. Examples emphasised in this chapter were 'market access' concessions that allow increased foreign ownership of existing firms rather than new entry, and guarantee the privileged status of foreign incumbents. Furthermore, where the immediate introduction of competition was not feasible, too little advantage has been taken of the GATS to lend credibility to future liberalisation plans.

Persistent barriers to services exports of developing countries are depriving the world of substantial welfare gains. These barriers include explicit quotas whose elimination or relaxation must be negotiated directly, and implicit regulatory hurdles that must be dealt with by strengthening GATS rules on domestic regulations. In particular, efforts must be made to break the stalemate on the movement of individual service providers – creating 'foreign labour content entitlements' is one possibility. It is also desirable to enhance the security of market access for electronic delivery of services. This is best accomplished by widening and deepening the scope of GATS commitments on cross-border delivery, rather than by perpetuating the current WTO decision on duty-free treatment for electronically delivered products.

One of the ironies of the GATS is that provisions dealing with domestic regulations are among its weakest, even though they have an obviously powerful influence on international trade in services. Appropriately designed GATS rules on domestic regulations (on which negotiations have already begun) can serve a valuable dual purpose, helping both to promote reform at the national level and meaningful market access at the international level.

REFERENCES

Adlung, R., A. Carzeniga and A. Mattoo (1999), 'The Pattern of Restrictions in GATS Schedules' WTO (mimeo).
Borensztein, E., J.D. Grigorio and J.W. Lee (1998), 'How Does Foreign Direct Investment Affect Economic Growth?' (Washington, DC: IMF).
Claessens, S. and T. Glaessner (1998), 'Internationalization of Financial Services in Asia' (World Bank, mimeo).
Cowhey, P. and M.M. Klimenko (1999), 'The WTO Agreement and Telecommunication Policy Reforms' (World Bank, www.worldbank.org/trade).
Findlay, C. and T. Warren (1999), 'How Significant are the Barriers? Measuring Impediments to Trade in Services', in P. Sauve and R. Stern (eds.), *Services 2000: New Directions in Services Trade Liberalization* (Washington, DC: Brookings).
Francois, J.F. and L. Schuknecht (1999), 'Trade in Financial Services: Procompetitive Effects and Growth Performance' (Tinbergen Institute, mimeo).
Gamberale, C. and A. Mattoo (1999), 'Domestic Regulation and the GATS', World Bank (mimeo).

Heeks, R. (1998), 'The Uneven Profile of Indian Software Exports,' Development Informatics Working Paper No. 3 (Institute for Development Policy and Management, University of Manchester, http://www.man.ac.uk/idpm/diwpf3.htm).

Hindley, B. and A. Smith (1984), 'Comparative Advantage and Trade in Services', *The World Economy*, **7**, 369–90.

Hoekman, B. and S. Djankov (1997), 'Effective Protection and Investment Incentives in Egypt and Jordan: Implications of Free Trade with Europe', *World Development*, **25**, 281–91.

Hoekman, B. and C. Primo Braga (1997), 'Protection and Trade in Services: A Survey', *Open Economies Review*, **8**, 285–308.

King, R.G. and R. Levine (1993), 'Finance, Entrepreneurship and Growth: Theory and Evidence', *Journal of Monetary Economics*, **32**, 513–42.

Mattoo, A. (1999), 'Developing Countries and the New Round of GATS Negotiations: From a Defensive to a Pro-active Role' (World Bank, www.worldbank.org/trade).

Mattoo, A. and M. Olarreaga (2000), 'Liberalizing Mode 4 Under the GATS: A Proposed Solution' (World Bank, mimeo).

Mattoo, A. and A. Subramanian (1998), 'Regulatory Autonomy and Multilateral Disciplines', *Journal of International Economic Law*, **1**, 303–22.

Mattoo, A., R. Rathindran and A. Subramanian (1999), 'The Impact of Services Trade Liberalization on Growth: A Cross-Country Analysis' (World Bank, mimeo).

Nicolaidis, K. and J.P. Trachtman (1999), 'From Policed Regulation to Managed Recognition: Mapping the Boundary in GATS', in P. Sauve and R. Stern (eds.), *Services 2000: New Directions in Services Trade Liberalization* (Washington, DC: Brookings).

Tuthill, L. (1997), 'The GATS and New Rules for Regulators', *Telecommunications Policy* (November).

United Nations and WHO (1998), 'International Trade in Health Service – A Development Perspective,' in S. Zarrilli and C. Kinnon (eds.), *United Nations Conference on Trade and Development* (Geneva).

Wellenius, B. (1997), 'Telecommunications Reform – How to Succeed', *Public Policy for the Private Sector* (The World Bank: Note 130, October).

World Trade Organisation (1998), 'Computer and Related Services', Background Note by the Secretariat, S/C/W/45 (98–2805) (July).

6

Options for Improving Africa's Participation in the WTO

Richard Blackhurst, Bill Lyakurwa and Ademola Oyejide

1. INTRODUCTION

INCREASING globalisation of the world economy, particularly relating to trade and investment flows, is accompanied with continuing marginalisation of many countries in Africa. Sub-Saharan Africa (SSA) in particular stands out as a region of the world which is being largely by-passed in the rapidly unfolding process of global integration. Many efforts to reverse SSA's marginalisation are based on a belief that fuller integration into the global economy, on appropriate terms, could enhance the conditions for more rapid economic growth by providing more favourable and secure market access for the region's exports, and by fostering the expansion and diversification of those exports.

The World Trade Organisation (WTO) has emerged as a key institutional mechanism that shapes the global economy. This imposes new and challenging demands on SSA countries, in particular as the WTO is the international institution in which the SSA voice is, perhaps, least heard. Full-fledged integration of SSA countries into the global trading system requires building the requisite capacity to enable them to contribute to shaping and designing the rules and regulations for its management by active participation in WTO activities, backed up by active and informed support from home-based analysts and policy makers.

2. PARTICIPATION IN THE WTO

There are several dimensions to participation in WTO activities. Active involvement in designing rules governing trade-related policies is by no means the only one. There is the give-and-take involved in multilateral trade negotiations, when countries seek more favourable and secure market access

95

for their exports in exchange for granting similar 'concessions' to their trading partners. Another dimension is the use of the rules and procedures to ensure that each country's rights are enforced and its obligations met.

When considering the benefits of enhanced participation in the WTO, it is important to keep in mind that the WTO occupies an unusual niche in the effort to assist the SSA countries: first, it has no money to lend or give away; and second, access to foreign markets for SSA exports – the issue most people think of when asking how the WTO can help – is *not* anywhere near the top of the list of explanations for SSA's poor economic performance. Most if not all SSA governments – and especially the technocrats and the private sectors in those countries – now accept that the key problem *at this point in time* is not a lack of market access, but rather the inadequate domestic supply response to *existing* market access opportunities. Where does that leave the WTO?

• *New market access.* Part of the answer is that the WTO should continue to press for improved *and bound* market access for the exports – potential as well as traditional – of lower-income developing countries, because once these countries solve the domestic supply response problem, better access to foreign markets will become important. This effort will require a greatly enhanced participation of SSA countries in the work of the WTO. The efforts of international secretariats or trading partners are no substitute for active participation of SSA countries themselves in the design of the market access parts of the next round and subsequent negotiations.

• *Protecting existing market access.* A second part of the answer, which also involves a greatly enhanced participation of the SSA countries in the WTO, is the role WTO rules and procedures can play in protecting *existing* market access. The very large increase in dispute settlement cases since the establishment of the WTO is not only a testimony to the effectiveness of those procedures and their credibility in the eyes of the member countries, but also pragmatic evidence that countries cannot rely exclusively on the 'good citizenship' of trading partners to ensure compliance with WTO obligations (the new Advisory Centre on WTO Law, discussed briefly below, will be very helpful here).

• *Improving the domestic supply response.* A third role for the WTO, one we believe is the most important at this point in time, is to help the SSA countries deal successfully with their principal current economic challenge – improving their domestic supply response. Because of the high ratios of trade to GDP in SSA countries, substantially enhanced participation in the WTO would help to improve the supply responses in those countries in at least three important ways:

• Contribute to a better and more timely implementation of the country's Uruguay Round commitments, and to a more careful observance of WTO obligations. These would bring an important additional degree of stability and predictability to the country's trade-related policies, which is very good for economic efficiency and investor confidence, domestic as well as foreign. WTO rules and obligations, by reducing policy discretion, also help to insulate public officials from the inevitable pressure from powerful special interest groups to introduce or maintain policies that allow them to gain at the expense of the general population. Frequent policy reversals in SSA countries have generated serious credibility problems (Oyejide, 1996). Given the traditionally weak policy commitment mechanisms in SSA countries (Collier and Gunning, 1997), effective participation in the WTO could be of tremendous significance. This weakness of the domestic 'agencies of restraint' in the typical SSA country is traceable to weak administrative structures, poor political legitimacy of ruling regimes, frequent changes in governments and political regimes, and lack of an autonomous, independent, fair-minded and competent judiciary (Collier, 1996). This suggests a role for the WTO as a guarantor of stable and rational trade policy regimes in SSA (to take an example which SSA countries have almost totally ignored, a country could greatly increase the credibility of trade reforms by 'binding' those reforms in its WTO schedules).

• Increase the likelihood that the SSA countries would play a full and active role in the next round. They will have many opportunities, in the course of negotiating for better access to foreign markets, to reduce their own tariffs and increase their tariff bindings. Trade negotiating rounds offer economic reformers in SSA countries an important opportunity to use *external* pressure – from trading partners – to counter protectionist pressures from domestic special interest groups. This would contribute importantly to avoiding a repeat of their Uruguay Round experience, when the SSA countries did very little in the way of reducing and binding their tariffs (there is absolutely no doubt that this failure to liberalise, along with their inadequate supply response, explains why the SSA countries gained relatively little from the Uruguay Round).

• Raise the profile of trade policy in the domestic economic debate. Together with better trade policies, this higher profile can lead to better economic policies outside the trade area, as the issue of economic efficiency in general gets more attention and moves up the public policy agenda.

Effective participation in the WTO is typically channelled through three mechanisms (Blackhurst, 1999). A country's resident delegation in Geneva serves as the arrowhead for the country's pursuit of its national interests in the WTO. Because the WTO is 'member-driven,' there are a large number of delegate meetings – averaging about 46 meetings a week in Geneva in 1996, not counting informal consultations (Blackhurst, 1998). This places a considerable premium on a country's capacity to maintain in Geneva a skilled, versatile and relatively large delegation which can engage in the daily meetings and consultations that drive the WTO process. Key staff in home capitals with analytical and policy-making skills provide direct operational support and guidance to the resident Geneva delegation. Finally, there are the professionals with the technical, legal, political and legislative skills, distributed among various institutions in the capital, who contribute to effective participation in the WTO process by implementing the country's commitments.

In assessing the constraints on effective SSA participation in previous multilateral trade negotiations, Oyejide (1990 and 1998), Ohiorhenuan (1998) and Yeo (1998) identify two factors in particular. First the perception that the processes and mechanisms associated with these negotiations were 'unbalanced' and weighted against developing countries, and second, the inherent inadequacies of the SSA participants. Many SSA countries were overwhelmed by the complexity of the negotiations and the technical nature of many issues being discussed and/or negotiated.

On the positive side, SSA participation in negotiations and related WTO activities has witnessed a gradual and evolutionary build-up (Oyejide, 1990, 1998 and 1999). It is generally agreed that SSA countries participated more actively in the Uruguay Round than in any of the earlier negotiations. SSA countries are moving away from the practice of subsuming their interests under those of the broader group of developing countries – and hence taking no real direct and active interest in the negotiating process – and are now more actively involved in WTO activities (Oyejide, 1990).

3. THE VIEW FROM CAPITALS

Establishing an adequate and skilled professional home-based support staff has turned out to be quite difficult in many SSA countries, primarily because of the diffused nature of the trade policy-making process and lack of coordination among the institutions involved in the design and implementation of trade policy. In the typical SSA country, trade policy making involves a number of government ministries, departments and related institutions. At the centre is the Cabinet, usually the highest policy-making body, chaired by the President and in which all ministries are represented. Material presented to the Cabinet on trade policy issues normally involves not only the ministries (such as Finance, Trade and Industry, Agriculture, and Foreign Affairs) which are directly represented in the Cabinet but also institutions such as the Central Bank, the Revenue Authority and similar ancillary public sector agencies. While major trade policy decisions are taken by the Cabinet, the key policy implementation roles are performed by the Ministry of Finance (trade taxes and revenue), the Ministry of Trade and Industry (trade and industrial policy), and the Ministry of Foreign Affairs (commercial diplomacy and international agreements).

As the expanding mandate of the WTO has drawn more domestic institutions into the process of designing and implementing trade and trade-related policies, coordination within and among ministries and other governmental agencies has become a major problem in many SSA countries, where institutional rigidities and bureaucratic struggles over 'turf' are endemic. One result is that there are significant differences among SSA countries regarding the location of real compared to nominal authority with respect to the articulation and implementation of trade policy. Another element of the coordination problem arises from the split in responsibility between (a) trade policy formulation and (b) authority to negotiate and sign trade agreements. This implies not just a simple division of labour between different agencies, but rather fundamental differences in perspectives. As Ohiorhenuan (1998) suggests, in SSA countries where the Ministry of Foreign Affairs has responsibility for negotiating and signing trade agreements, not only would the country's participation be driven by foreign policy rather than economic considerations, but the lead agency in multilateral trade negotiations could be considerably weakened by its limited understanding of economic issues and its limited interaction with major domestic trade policy stakeholders.

Staffing of the various ministries and other government agencies involved with trade-related policy making in many SSA countries is another cause for concern. Oyejide (1999) notes several problems, including inadequate capacity for monitoring and analysing the trade policies of key trading partners and limited personnel with requisite knowledge of international trade law. National consultation and coordination on WTO activities involve functions that are largely technical, requiring the specialised knowledge and skills of trade analysts, lawyers, economists, and so forth, as well as rigorous analysis, that are beyond the capacity of many members of the inter-ministerial committees. Technical support teams are therefore critical, but the few SSA countries (such as Nigeria) that have created support teams (the Tariff Board in Nigeria) have not succeeded in staffing them adequately. Hence, many SSA countries have been unable to effectively use these consultative and coordination mechanisms for the intended purpose.

The problems of poor capacity for articulating, coordinating and implementing trade policy at the national level in SSA have been recognised and have attracted suggestions for reform. Among the most promising is the idea of an executive trade policy agency (Hoekman, 1995; Winters, 1995; and Yeo, 1998) which would report directly to the president/prime minister. The agency would gather data, carry out analyses of the costs and benefits of existing and proposed trade policies and make public the results of its analyses. While this could assist in encouraging public debate on trade policy in SSA it does not appear to directly address the staffing inadequacies and institutional weaknesses that currently inhibit SSA's effective participation in the WTO process.

a. Regional Coordination on SSA Trade Policy

The lack of the human and institutional capacity in individual SSA countries needed for fuller and more effective participation in the WTO process poses a significant problem that is not amenable to 'quick-fix' solutions. An alternative mechanism for achieving more effective participation in the short term is regional coordination of SSA trade policy, particularly in the WTO context (Kennes, 1998; Michalopoulos, 1999; Yeo, 1998; and Oyejide, 1999). For the small and poorer countries, Michalopoulos (1999) argues that it may not necessarily be an optimal use of their scarce resources to seek individual representation in the context of the WTO process. These countries should instead establish a process of consultation with 'like-minded' countries in the context of which their interests can be pursued in the WTO. Along similar lines, Kennes (1998) suggests that regional organisations could play an important role in enhancing SSA capacity to participate effectively in the WTO process. Through pooling resources, these organisations may be able to provide services to their member states in a more cost effective way than when the member states act on their own.

Efforts could include cooperation in information gathering, policy analysis and participation in WTO committees and other activities. Joint actions could ensure that issues of importance are studied and understood, brought to the attention of individual countries and appropriate decisions taken. This could extend to the harmonisation and coordination of negotiating strategies and agendas, which could enhance the status and bargaining position of SSA countries. Finally, the various forms of joint action could provide a more cost effective and quicker way of building the human and institutional capacity required to enable SSA countries to substantially enhance their participation in the WTO process.

Several analysts (Oyejide, 1998; and Yeo, 1998) suggest that the failure of SSA countries to act in a coordinated fashion during the Uruguay Round can be attributed, at least in part, to the failure to harmonise their negotiating agendas and strategies. But this view has not gone unchallenged. Wang and Winters (1997) argue that greater SSA unity during the negotiations may not have improved the outcome for SSA since, acting as a group, SSA countries probably had little more clout than when they act individually. In a study of the trade liberalisation experiences of ten SSA countries from the early 1970s to the mid-1990s, Oyejide (1996) found that 'the least significant stimulus for trade liberalization among the case study countries is membership of a regional integration arrangement'.

Following the inauguration of the African Economic Community (AEC) at the June 1997 summit meeting of the Organisation of African Unity (OAU), the urgent need for a permanent institutional mechanism to coordinate, support, and prepare African governments for WTO negotiations was affirmed. At the first AEC meeting of African Ministers of Trade in April 1998, it was agreed that the AEC Technical Committee on Trade, Customs and Immigration would serve as the main forum for discussion and coordination of trade policy in Africa and the central body to which all African institutions would report on trade-related matters. Mindful of the fact that other regions have been coordinating their positions in multilateral negotiations, Ministers also mandated the General

Secretariat of the OAU/AEC to utilise existing inter-governmental machinery for the purpose of helping African governments to harmonise and coordinate their negotiating positions in the WTO framework.

At the sub-regional level, a similar process of coordination is under way. The most active sub-regional group appears to be the Southern African Development Community (SADC). The fourth special meeting of the SADC Industry and Trade Committee of Ministers was held in April 1998 to 'draw up a SADC common position' as an input into preparing a common African position for the WTO Ministerial Conference in May 1998. This meeting explicitly recognised that, in the past, African participation in the WTO process was marginal because they were involved individually and without a coordinated common position. It affirmed that the new focus on harmonisation and coordination of positions constitutes a strategic approach for strengthening participation of member countries in the WTO process and that the common African position would be based on national and regional considerations (we return to this point below).

4. THE VIEW FROM GENEVA

Table 1 lists the 38 SSA countries in the WTO and provides data on the size of the delegations resident in Geneva, Brussels and New York.[1] These figures give only a rough approximation of the number of officials actually available to work directly on the various international relations activities in the three cities, and in most instances they overstate the number available because (a) several delegations list as delegates people whose principal functions involve support activities (accounting, communications) but who are called on occasionally to cover meetings during busy periods, and (b) in the case of the WTO, the vast majority of the officials listed in the WTO *Directory* also have to cover other international organisations in Geneva (and often Vienna), and thus frequently spend only a small part of their time working on WTO activities.

The figures in the first column of Table 1 paint a bleak picture, the most depressing aspect being the fact that 15 of the 38 countries had no resident delegate (to *any* international organisation) in Geneva as of April 1999, and four had only one. In other words, 19 SSA countries – one-half of the SSA WTO membership – have no delegate resident in Geneva and available to focus more or less full-time on WTO activities. True, many are countries with small populations, but seven of the 19 have populations ranging from 7 to 45 million.

---

[1] Eleven SSA countries are not in the WTO: Cape Verde (1995 population 386,000 according to the UN), Comoros (612,000), Eritrea (3.2 million), Ethiopia (56.4 million), Equatorial Guinea (400,000), Liberia (2.1 million), Reunion (655,000), Sao Tome and Principe (133,000), Seychelles (73,000), Somalia (9.5 million) and Sudan (26.7 million). As of August 1999, accession working parties have been established for two of the eleven – Seychelles and Sudan.

TABLE 1

SSA WTO Members: Number of Delegates Resident in Geneva, Brussels and New York (first half of 1999)

Country	Geneva WTO		Geneva UN	EC Brussels	UN New York	Pop. Millions
Nigeria	6	(5)	10	8	26	115
Congo, Dem. Rep.	1		2	4	5	45
South Africa	5		17	16	19	38
Tanzania	5	(1)	4	6	8	30
Kenya	3		10	11	14	27
Uganda	5		5	4	7	20
Ghana	3	(1)	9	7	10	18
Mozambique	0		0	4	5	18
Cameroon	3	(1)	4	12	8	14
Cote d'Ivoire	2		8	11	9	14
Madagascar	3		8	5	9	14
Angola	3	(1)	6	8	8	11
Burkina Faso	0		0	6	6	11
Zimbabwe	4	(2)	9	9	14	11
Malawi	0		0	4	6	10
Mali	0		0	4	5	10
Niger	0		0	4	2	9
Senegal	2		9	6	11	9
Zambia	4		7	7	8	9
Chad	0		0	1	3	7
Guinea	2		3	5	10	7
Rwanda	3	(2)	1	3	3	7
Benin	0		0	10	10	6
Burundi	2		2	3	3	6
Sierra Leone	0		0	3	6	5
Togo	0		0	8	6	4
Central African Rep.	0		0	3	3	3
Congo	2		2	6	7	3
Lesotho	1		3	5	6	2
Mauritania	1		1	4	4	2
Namibia	0		0	6	11	2
Botswana	0		0	7	7	1
Djibouti	1		0	2	3	1
Gabon	2		5	10	6	1
Gambia	0		0	5	8	1
Guinea-Bissau	0		0	5	4	1
Swaziland	0		0	5	7	1
Mauritius	5	(2)	6	6	5	1

Notes:
Parentheses indicate the number of delegates that appear in the WTO *Directory* but *not* in the UN Geneva *Directory*. Country name in italics indicates a least developed country. Vacant positions were not counted.

Sources: WTO (1999), UN (1999a and 1999b), Commission Europeenne (1999), and World Bank (1998).

Nor is size necessarily a crucial variable. Of the 18 WTO members with a separate mission in Geneva devoted exclusively to the WTO, five have populations *under* 7 million: Costa Rica (3 million), Honduras (6 million), Hong Kong (6 million), Norway (4 million) and Panama (3 million).[2] And of course from Table 1 there is Mauritius, with a population of just over 1 million and five delegates listed in the WTO *Directory*.

Is the size of the delegation in Geneva and the support staff in capital dealing with WTO issues important for a country which accounts for only a tiny share of world trade? One response is to note that the WTO relies primarily on consensus decision-making and that when voting is necessary it is on a one-country one-vote basis, in contrast to the weighted voting used in the World Bank and IMF. More fundamentally, what matters for a country's economy is not the country's share of world trade, but rather the share of trade in the country's total output – in other words, the ratio of trade to GDP. In fact, the trade-to-GDP ratios for many SSA countries are not only high, but also *higher* than the corresponding ratios for many OECD countries.

a. Questionnaire Results

Of the 23 SSA delegations with at least one official resident in Geneva, 11 completed and returned a questionnaire prepared for this chapter (some questions received fewer than 11 replies).

(i) Resources and workloads

In one delegation, four people spend 100 per cent of their time on WTO work, and in two delegations there were two delegates which spend between 95 and 100 per cent of their time on the WTO. For five delegations, the number of 'full-time-equivalent' officials working on WTO activities ranged from 0.75 to 2.1, and two delegations reported only one-quarter of a 'full-time-equivalent' person working on WTO matters. These results confirm the earlier point that the already very small numbers in column one of Table 1 overstate – often substantially – the number of SSA delegates resident in Geneva and working more or less full-time on WTO-related matters.

Virtually all of the SSA delegations in Geneva are staffed by officials from the Ministry of Foreign Affairs rather than the Ministry of Commerce/Trade – that is, by people who have little or nothing to do with WTO matters when they are back home. This means not only that they know very little about WTO work when they arrive, but that the WTO experience they gain while in Geneva is not put to use

---

[2] The other 13 are Australia, Chile, Colombia, Ecuador, Guatemala, Hungary, India, Mexico, Switzerland, Thailand, Turkey, and the United States, plus Nigeria, which has a *de facto* separate delegation to the WTO.

when they return home. *Any meaningful effort to improve the participation of SSA countries in the WTO must deal with this problem.*

(ii) Cooperation with other delegations in Geneva

Eight of the 11 delegations reported they cooperate, with varying degrees of success, with other SSA delegations on WTO matters. The most commonly mentioned groups were SADC,[3] the informal WTO African Group, and the African, Caribbean and Pacific (ACP) group of countries (on Lomé Convention issues). However, it was clear that cooperation of the type described below for the Nordic Group and the Association of South East Asian Nations (ASEAN) does not currently exist among SSA countries. Two principal obstacles/difficulties to improving cooperation among SSA countries on WTO were stressed by nearly all delegations: diverging interests and priorities, often associated with differing levels of development; and shortage of staff, especially staff with the necessary technical expertise.

(iii) Support from capital

Six delegations indicated 'very little' and four indicated 'moderate' when describing support from capital. Asked about the degree of effective coordination on WTO issues among the different ministries in capital, seven answered 'poor' and three answered 'adequate'. Coordination appears to be handicapped both by a low level of representation from the various ministries and by a high turnover among the representatives.

(iv) Preparations for the next round

Asked if the government had made reasonable progress in identifying potential agenda items of particular importance to the country, four delegations replied 'yes' and five replied 'no'. (Population size was a good predictor – the four delegations which replied 'yes' ranked one, two, three and six among the nine which replied to the question.) Ten delegations replied in the affirmative when asked if cooperation with a group of 'like minded' countries on particular agenda items – such as fish and fish products or agriculture – was feasible (note that, in this instance, the reference is to an issue-specific group along the lines of the Cairns Group).

b. Other Countries' Experience with Cooperation in the WTO

Other than the European Union (and the Central European Free Trade Area (CEFTA) Group, which is relatively new), there are two important examples of moderately small groups of countries cooperating in the GATT/WTO to (a) share the responsibility for coordinating and covering the various activities, and (b)

---

[3] Only six of SADC's 14 members have a resident delegation in Geneva.

speak with one voice whenever possible. One is the Nordic Group – which ceased to function when Finland and Sweden joined the EU – and the other is the ASEAN Group.[4] The following brief overview of the experiences of the two groups is based on interviews with officials based in Geneva.

(i) Motivation for cooperation

Both groups agreed there are two motivations: to raise the political profile and political strength of the participants (make them more interesting to deal with), and to economise on the use of the limited number of delegates resident in Geneva and available to work on GATT/WTO activities.

(ii) Cooperation on 'non-binding' versus 'potentially binding' issues

Cooperation is easier on non-binding issues which involve 'general positioning' and on which the group can take a position without there being a risk that one or more members would eventually have to change national laws/practices in some trade-related area. Potentially binding issues are those which could progress to the point that national laws/practices would have to be changed to bring them into line with GATT/WTO rules/procedures. The Nordics report achieving considerable success in cooperation/coordination on both non-binding and binding issues, the high degree of homogeneity in economic outlook being an important factor behind this success. The ASEANs believe that on non-binding issues they have achieved a good degree of cooperation/coordination, but that success on binding issues has been, to date, rather modest.

(iii) Principal factors contributing to successful cooperation

The following factors were mentioned as having contributed to the success of the two groups: collective political need and will to cooperate based on *national* interests; parallel economic and trade interests; relatively open economies; geographic proximity; a catalyst event (see below); historical political/cultural affinity; cultural values which contribute to less confrontational relations, especially values that stress tolerance; a tradition of cooperation in the region on a range of issues, based on like-mindedness and mutual trust; a cooperative

---

[4] The *Nordic Group*, which functioned from the Kennedy Round through the Uruguay Round, originally was composed of Denmark, Finland, Iceland, Norway and Sweden. After joining the EC in 1973, Denmark did not actively participate in Nordic activities in the GATT (but continued until recently to participate in Nordic cooperation in the UN). With the entry of Finland and Sweden into the EU on 1 January, 1995 (the same day the WTO came into being), formal Nordic cooperation in Geneva on trade issues ceased. The *ASEAN Group* was created by the Bangkok Declaration (1967). The founding members were Indonesia, Malaysia, Philippines, Singapore and Thailand, and the original goals included economic, technical, scientific and political cooperation. The ASEAN Free Trade Area (AFTA) was agreed to in 1992, and in 1994 it was agreed to reduce the transition period from 15 to ten years. Current membership includes the original five countries plus Brunei, Cambodia, Laos, Myanmar and Vietnam. Seven of the ten countries are WTO members, and accession working parties have been established for Laos and Vietnam.

institutional structure that links the capitals and encourages and supports cooperation on a range of issues that extends beyond trade-related policies (cooperation among the Nordics and within ASEAN is *not* limited to cooperation on GATT/WTO activities); and a shared perception that trade and trade policy are important for the pace of economic development, and that by acting collectively the members will have more political clout in the GATT/WTO.

(iv) Catalyst for cooperation

In both instances, negotiating rounds were a catalyst for cooperation. For the Nordics it was the Kennedy Round, and for ASEAN it was the Uruguay Round, plus the preparations for the 1996 Singapore Ministerial. Clearly the message here is that groups of SSA countries should try very hard to use the preparations for the next round as the catalyst for increased cooperation not only on the negotiations, but also on regular WTO activities. In this respect, the failure of WTO ministers in Seattle to agree on an agenda for a new round – by giving SSA countries more time to organise cooperative arrangements – is a blessing in disguise.

(v) How cooperation on covering GATT/WTO meetings worked/works

During the Uruguay Round, the Nordics divided up responsibility for covering the various negotiating committees, and this division of work remained virtually unchanged over the course of the round. In contrast, they rotated responsibility for meetings of the Council, the contracting parties, and the Uruguay Round's Trade Negotiations Committee. Coordination work (meetings of officials) was divided about evenly between Geneva and capitals.

In Geneva the ASEAN countries divide assignments for coordinating WTO issues/committees. When there is a collective ASEAN view, the coordinating country conveys it. Either one or two countries is assigned to an issue/committee (it divides about evenly), for a minimum of one year. Responsibility for coordinating work of the General Council, in contrast, is rotated each six months. There is an ASEAN Geneva Committee which meets formally at least twice a year, and holds informal weekly meetings (at ambassador level), supplemented by frequent ad hoc coordination meetings to discuss particular issues. A substantial proportion of the coordination activities occur in Geneva.

For the Nordic Group, procedures to accommodate 'publicly' differences among the members were not a major issue because situations in which the group could not arrive at a consensus occurred so rarely. When it did exceptionally occur, a member of the group could still intervene in a GATT discussion on behalf of the group, indicating, without necessarily going into details, that there were still different views within the group. While ASEAN members are expected to be 'flexible' *vis-à-vis* their individual positions, respect for the different views of other members takes precedence over the desire for consensus. This extends to the nature of the interventions in GATT/WTO meetings when there is not a consensus; if a sub-set of four ASEAN members, for example, agrees on a common position, one of the four intervenes on behalf of itself and the other three (mentioned individually), but with no mention of their ASEAN affiliation.

5. ENHANCING SSA PARTICIPATION IN THE WTO

There are two principal options available to SSA governments: devote additional resources to WTO activities in Geneva and the capital, and cooperate with other countries to share the WTO workload.

a. Increasing or Re-deploying Existing Resources

The 'classic' solution, often viewed as the principal option for lower-income developing countries, is to attempt to obtain additional funds from foreign donors. Another option involves increasing expenditures on WTO activities, without reducing expenditures on other government budget items. Third, the government can shift funds from other parts of the government's budget to the category of 'international relations', and use those funds to enhance capacity to participate in WTO activities.

A fourth option – which gains considerable credibility from the fact that for much of the half-century after the GATT was created, relations between virtually all of the SSA countries and the GATT were characterised by benign neglect on both sides – is to reallocate spending priorities *within* the international relations area. The situation is improving, but the legacy from the benign neglect period is still evident today in the allocation of government posts – both in capitals and overseas – between WTO-related work on the one hand, and work related to other international organisations and diplomatic missions on the other.

The overseas part of that legacy is evident from Table 1: every SSA country except Mauritius has a larger delegation in either Brussels or New York than in Geneva, while 29 have a larger delegation in *both* Brussels and New York (recall, moreover, that the responses to the questionnaire made it clear that only a *very* small proportion of the Geneva-based delegates work on WTO activities).

We believe all SSA countries should (a) give serious consideration to taking between two and five posts (depending on the size of the delegation) from the country's delegation to the UN General Assembly in New York, and shifting those posts to Geneva to work full-time on WTO matters; (b) give serious consideration to assigning more of their Geneva-based delegates to full-time work on WTO matters; and (c) also examine whether it would be possible to shift some posts from their EU delegation in Brussels to Geneva to work full-time on the WTO, without interfering with activities in Brussels that have proven to be important for the country's economic development. The expanded WTO delegation should be de-linked from the Ambassador to the UN organisations in Geneva – as, for example, Costa Rica, Honduras and Panama have done – and its staff should report to the Minister of Trade/Commerce.

It is not that we believe the work being done in New York and Geneva (or Brussels) is unimportant, but rather that in the future a sizeable proportion of that work almost certainly will have a lower priority – *contribute less to the country's economic development* – than WTO-related work in Geneva.

b. Options for Groups of SSA Countries to Cooperate on WTO Activities

Among the factors the Nordics and ASEANs say contributed to successful cooperation, the four most relevant for the SSA countries at this point are: geographic proximity; history of political/cultural affinity; a tradition of cooperation in the region on a range of issues, based on like-mindedness and mutual trust; and a cooperative institutional structure that links the capitals and encourages and supports cooperation on a range of issues that extend beyond trade-related policies.

In our view, two sub-regional groupings offer the most promise for getting together to cooperate on WTO activities. One is UEMOA (the West African Economic and Monetary Union), which through its common external tariff policy already has experience cooperating on trade policy issues. Because of its dominant role, cooperation is likely to revolve around the interests of Cote d'Ivoire, but since those interests are largely shared by other UEMOA members, this is not likely to be a major problem.

The other is the East African Cooperation countries. The number of countries involved is small, and they are located in close proximity to one another. Because the four factors identified above are definitely present, they should be well placed to cooperate effectively on WTO matters, including the next trade round. A prior step, however, is to ratify and implement the East African Cooperation Treaty, and to establish the common external tariff, thereby signifying a degree of common internal trade and macroeconomic policy.[5]

---

[5] In *SADC*, where South Africa plays a leading role and the number of countries involved is rather large and diverse, cooperation would most likely revolve around South Africa, which may not necessarily represent the interests of the majority. This is not to say that the SADC countries have not started cooperating on WTO matters, but judging from the Nordic/ASEAN experiences, it seems unlikely that SADC will become an effective institution for detailed cooperation on WTO matters any time soon. The experience of the Nordics and the ASEANs also suggests that SSA *as a whole* does not have the characteristics needed for successful, detailed, day-to-day cooperation on WTO activities.

6. THE WTO'S ROLE IN ENHANCING SSA PARTICIPATION

Since the launch of the Uruguay Round in 1986, the number of non-OECD members has increased by more than half, from 67 to 103. If the countries in the process of acceding to the WTO – nearly all of which request technical assistance – are included, there is a doubling to 134. Two other developments have also increased the demand for technical assistance: (a) many non-OECD countries which were GATT contracting parties all along, but in name only – that is, GATT members but with little or no interest in participating in GATT activities or rounds – have decided that active participation in the WTO is important for their economic development (this describes many of the SSA countries);[6] and (b) the accession process has become a much more complicated exercise, both because the members toughened up the requirements and because the policy coverage of the WTO is considerably greater than that of the GATT. Comparing 1999 with 1986, it seems to us it is not unreasonable to assume, as a rough 'rule of thumb', that the demand (need) for WTO technical assistance and training from *members* has increased by 50 per cent, and that if acceding countries are included, there has been an overall 100 per cent increase.

What about GATT/WTO funding for technical cooperation activities? Since 1986, the Technical Cooperation and Training Division's staff has increased, but only enough to keep the Division's share of the Secretariat staff constant (at just over five per cent), while the *nominal* budget for technical cooperation missions and the commercial policy training courses has increased, but not by enough to avoid a decline in their share of the overall budget from 2.2 to 1.9 per cent. In other words, the entire Secretariat was getting more staff and funds to cope with a greatly expanded agenda in the post-Uruguay Round era (services, intellectual property, dispute settlement and so forth), and the increases for technical cooperation activities only allowed the Division to cope with the increased workload associated with this greatly expanded agenda. This is totally distinct from the increase in the workload stemming from the increase in the number of countries needing technical assistance. The bottom line is that there was no increase in WTO staff or in budgeted funding for technical cooperation in response to a doubling of the number of countries needing technical assistance.

---

[6] Virtually all of the 38 SSA countries in the WTO joined the GATT 1947 under the provisions of Article XXVI:5(c). All a country had to do was certify that it had 'full autonomy in the conduct of its external commercial relations and of the other matters provided for in the [General Agreement].' Because there was no accession working party, a country could become a full GATT contracting party without knowing or learning anything of substance about the GATT, and without the other GATT members knowing anything about its trade regime. This route to membership is not available under the WTO.

To a *limited* degree, the resulting huge gap between needs and resources has been filled in recent years by ad hoc donations (trust funds) by a few WTO members. Such ad hoc funds, however, are a poor substitute for funds provided through the regular budget, for two reasons: they make planning technical cooperation activities very difficult and bias it toward the short-term; and, more seriously, ad hoc funds do not allow the Secretariat to hire additional regular staff, which creates serious problems because many kinds of technical assistance can only be competently provided by professionals with direct experience working in the Secretariat.[7]

Why have the member countries refused to provide even minimally adequate levels of technical cooperation funding through the regular WTO budget? Money cannot be the real issue, since the amount involved is so trivial. One way of putting the money question in perspective is to consider the figures in Table 2, which show that in 1996 there were 15 international *economic* organisations with larger staffs than the WTO and 14 with larger budgets. If the member countries had agreed to shift *one-quarter of one per cent* of the budgets of those 14 organisations to the WTO budget, it would have provided an additional $17 million (26 million Swiss francs) a year – which is roughly three times the size of the current WTO technical assistance budget, including the 80 per cent that comes in the form of ad hoc contributions – *without any increase in their overall contributions to the international economic organisations.*

If it is not the money, what is it that explains the state of the WTO's technical cooperation budget? It's hard not to be suspicious that one factor (the principal factor?) is a desire by many WTO members to avoid increasing the capacity of the lower-income countries to play an active and effective role in the WTO. Certainly the attitude of many of the larger traders to the new Advisory Centre on WTO Law, whose purpose is to help developing countries defend their legal rights in the WTO, points in that direction. The one success at the Seattle Ministerial was the signing of the Agreement establishing the Centre as a new international organisation. Only nine developed countries – which commit themselves to provide financial support to the Centre – were among the 29 founding signatories. A number of big traders which are firm believers in the rule of law at home and in a rules-based trading system – the European Commission (which strongly opposed the Centre's establishment), the United States, Germany, France and Japan – did not sign the Agreement.[8]

---

[7] One of the casualties of the Seattle Ministerial meeting was the failure of the ministers to approve Norway's proposal, supported by a large number of WTO members, to increase the budget for technical cooperation and training by 10 million Swiss francs over three years.

[8] Regarding the European Commission's position, see the *Financial Times* editorial of 18 February, 1999. The nine developed countries which signed the Agreement in Seattle are Canada, Denmark, Finland, Ireland, Italy, Netherlands, Norway, Sweden and the United Kingdom. Further details on the Centre are available on the WTO web site <http://www.wto.org> in the section on the Trade and Development Centre.

TABLE 2
Staff and Annual Budget of Selected International Economic Organisations

Organisation	Number of Staff in 1996	Annual Budget in 1996 (millions of US dollars)
World Bank	6,781[a]	1,375
UN Food and Agriculture Organisation (FAO)	5,100	600[b]
UN Development Programme (UNDP)	4,914[c]	1,400[c]
International Monetary Fund (IMF)	2,577[d]	475
Organisation for Economic Coop. and Development (OECD)	2,322[e]	330
International Labour Organisation	2,286	290
World Food Programme	2,069[f]	1,200
UN Industrial Development Organisation (UNIDO)	1,758	193
UN Office for Project Services	941[g]	403[h]
UN Population Fund	919	305
International Civil Aviation Organisation (ICAO)	759	60
European Bank for Reconstruction and Development (EBRD)	753	213
UN Environment Programme	745	99[i]
International Telecommunication Union (ITU)	726[g]	139[g]
World Intellectual Property Organisation (WIPO)	630	121
World Trade Organisation (WTO)	513	94[j]
UN Conference on Trade and Development (UNCTAD)	443	78

Notes:
[a] The staff figure includes an estimated 1,100 long-term consultants.
[b] Sum of regular budget ($325 million) and field programme expenditure (mainly technical asistance).
[c] 1995; the budget figure incorporates the core programme, support budget, and extra-budgetary items.
[d] In terms of effective staff years.
[e] Includes 350 consultants, experts, fellows and temporary staff.
[f] Plus 2,178 temporary staff employed mainly in emergency operations.
[g] 1995.
[h] 1994.
[i] Includes contributions to Environment Fund, Trust Fund, Counterpart Fund and regular budget.
[j] Includes $3.7 million for the Appellate Body. The figure of 513 for the staff includes the staff servicing the Appellate Body, but not the seven members of the Body.

Sources: The figures in this table were compiled from a variety of sources, including WTO budget documents, *Yearbook of International Organizations 1996/1997* (K.G. Saur, Munich), descriptive material published by the organisations, web sites and personal communications.

WTO's Role in Providing Technical Assistance

Allocating responsibility for technical assistance between the WTO Secretariat and other institutions can be a subjective exercise. Space considerations preclude any attempt to pursue the issue here, but we would like to point out that if the examination of which institutions are best placed to provide which type(s) of assistance starts from the assumption that only a limited amount of technical assistance money (including staff) will be provided to the WTO, the answer to the question 'Who should do what?' will be biased. There is absolutely no doubt that in recent years the debate has suffered from such a bias.

The total failure to consider the possibility of reaching out to countries in need of technical assistance by opening WTO regional offices is a case in point. While the principal function would be to provide demand-driven technical assistance in a more effective (and probably cheaper) way, WTO regional offices could also help overcome the general indifference on the part of many SSA governments and private sectors to the potential gains from enhanced participation.[9] The importance of the latter function is evident from the point, stressed by many SSA delegates, that while low per capita incomes clearly are a factor behind the grossly inadequate resources available for participation in the WTO, the most serious culprit in virtually every SSA country is a lack of knowledge, on the part of both government officials and the private sector, of what the WTO can offer.

7. SUMMARY

The fundamental challenge, for both the SSA countries and for the other WTO members, involves not money but knowledge and priorities. Participation in the WTO could be substantially enhanced without any increase in the external relations budgets of the SSA countries. The WTO's technical assistance budget could be substantially increased without raising overall contributions for international economic organisations.

Table 1 indicates the allocation of delegates between the WTO, UN Geneva, the EC in Brussels and UN New York with which the 38 SSA countries in the WTO began the new century. Table 2 indicates the 'team' of international economic institutions, and the allocation of staff and funding among them, with which the world community began the new century.[10] Both tables reflect

---

[9] What would regional offices cost? A large number of 'variables' would have to be specified before this could be answered with any precision, but a very rough calculation, based on a staff of three officials and three secretaries, suggests that an amount of money equal to three per cent of the Secretariat's 1999 budget would be enough to set up, on an experimental trial basis, four regional offices in 2000.

[10] The figures refer to 1996, and there obviously have been some changes, but the general picture one gets from Table 2 certainly is relevant today.

decisions made 20 or 30 or more years ago, when the world economy and the perceived policy options were very different from today. Common sense suggests that the allocations in both tables need to be re-examined in light of the new global economy that has emerged since the mid-1980s:

A change in the priorities of the SSA governments, to reflect the fact that commercial diplomacy has replaced political diplomacy as the critical area for countries pursuing economic development, would allow at least two-thirds of the 38 SSA countries to put a very respectable size team to work full-time on WTO activities in Geneva, and to make a corresponding increase in support staff in capital, without any net increase in government expenditure.

Even a *tiny* shift in the priorities of the major trading nations *vis-à-vis* the allocation of resources among the 17 international economic organisations in Table 2 would be sufficient to provide all the additional funding the WTO would need – not only to supply the needed technical assistance, but also to play an active role in persuading the governments and private sectors in the SSA countries of the benefits of increased participation in the WTO – without any net increase in government expenditure.

A final remark concerning the latter point. The major delegations never tire of reminding the WTO Secretariat staff – and anyone else who will listen – that the WTO is a 'member driven' organisation. This is correct and almost certainly accounts for the exceptional success of the GATT/WTO system. The major delegations now have an opportunity to show – if it's true – that they mean it should be driven not just by them, but by all its members.

REFERENCES

Blackhurst, R. (1998), 'The Capacity of the WTO to Fulfill its Mandate', in A.O. Krueger (ed.), *The WTO as an International Organization* (Chicago: University of Chicago Press).
Blackhurst, R. (1999), 'Capacity Building in Africa for Enhanced Participation in the WTO', Paper prepared for the Dissemination Conference of the AERC Collaborative Research Project on Africa and the World Trading System (Yaounde, 17–18 April, Nairobi: AERC, mimeo).
Collier, P. (1996), 'The Role of the African State in Building Agencies of Restraint', in M. Lundahl and B. Ndulu (eds.), *New Directions in Development Economics: Growth, Environmental Concerns and Government in the 1990s* (London: Routledge).
Collier, P., P. Guillaument, S. Guillaumont and J. Gunning (1997), 'The Future of Lomé: Europe's Role in African Growth,' *The World Economy*, **20**, 285–305.
Commission Europeenne (1999), *Corps diplomatique: accredite aupres des Communautes europeennes et representations aupres de la Commission* (Janvier).
Hoekman, B. (1995), 'Trade Laws and Institutions: Good Practices and the World Trade Organization', *World Bank Discussion Paper No. 282* (Washington, DC: World Bank).
Kennes, W. (1998), 'African Regional Integration Institutions and Enhanced African Participation in the Global Trading System', Note prepared for the AERC Workshop on Africa and the World Trading System (Mombasa, 26–29 April).
Michalopoulos, C. (1999), 'The Developing Countries in the WTO', *The World Economy*, **22**, 1.
Ohiorhenuan, J.F.E. (1998), 'Capacity Building Implications of Enhanced African Participation in

Global Trade Rules-Making and Arrangements', Paper prepared for the AERC collaborative research project on Africa and the World Trading System (Nairobi: AERC, mimeo).

Oyejide, T.A. (1990), 'The Participation of Developing Countries in the Uruguay Round', *The World Economy*, **13**, 3, 427–44.

Oyejide, T.A. (1996), 'Regional Integration and Trade Liberalization in Sub-Saharan Africa: An AERC Collaboration Research Project Summary Report', *AERC Special Paper*, No. 28 (Nairobi: AERC).

Oyejide, T.A. (1998), 'Global Economic Governance Through Multilateral Negotiations: Africa in the World Trade Organization', Draft Research Project Proposal (Nairobi: AERC, mimeo).

Oyejide, T.A. (1999) 'Perspectives and Modalities of African Participation in the WTO Process', Paper prepared for the Dissemination Workshop of the AERC collaborative research project on Africa and the World System, (Yaounde, 17–18 April, Nairobi: AERC).

United Nations (1999a), *Missions permanentes aupres des Nations Unies a Geneve, No. 84* (Avril).

United Nations (1999b), *Permanent Missions to the United Nations*, No. 282 (May).

Wang, Z.K. and L.A. Winters (1997), 'Africa's Role in Multilateral Trade Negotiations', *Policy Research Working Paper No. 1846* (Washington, DC: World Bank).

Winters, L.A. (1995), 'Who Should Run Trade Policy in Eastern Europe and How?', in L.A. Winters (ed.), *Foundations of an Open Economy: Trade Laws and Institutions for Eastern Europe* (London: CEPR).

World Bank (1998), *World Development Indicators* (Washington, DC: World Bank).

World Trade Organisation (1999), *Directory* (April).

Yeo, S. (1998), 'Trade Policy in Sub-Saharan Africa: Lessons from the Uruguay Round Experience', Paper prepared for the AERC collaboration research project on Africa and the World Trading System (Nairobi: AERC) (mimeo).

7

Implementation of Uruguay Round Commitments: The Development Challenge

J. Michael Finger and Philip Schuler

1. INTRODUCTION

𝔄T the Uruguay Round, developing countries took on unprecedented obligations not only to reduce trade barriers, but to implement significant reforms both on trade procedures (e.g., import licensing procedures, customs valuation) and on many areas of regulation that establish the basic business environment in the domestic economy (e.g., technical, sanitary and phytosanitary standards, intellectual property law).

This chapter is about the latter commitments. They are more than policy commitments, they are investment decisions. Implementation will require purchasing of equipment, training of people, establishment of systems of checks and balances, etc. This will cost money and the amounts of money involved are substantial. Based on Bank project experience in the areas covered by the agreements, an entire year's development budget is at stake in many of the least developed countries.

Would such money be well spent? Least developed country institutions in these areas are weak, and might benefit from strengthening and reform. However, our analysis indicates that WTO regulations reflect little awareness of development problems and little appreciation of the capacities of the least developed countries to carry out the functions that SPS, customs valuation, intellectual property, etc. regulations address. For most of the developing and transition economies – some 100 countries – money spent to implement the WTO rules in these areas would be money unproductively invested.

We touch also on another point. Because of their limited capacity to participate in the Uruguay Round negotiations, the WTO process has generated no sense of 'ownership' of the reforms to which WTO membership obligates them. From their perspective, the implementation exercise has been imposed in an imperial way, with little concern for what it will cost, how it will be done, or if it will support their development efforts. Thus the developing countries have neither economic incentive nor political will to implement these obligations.

Our analysis is based on World Bank project experience in customs reform, SPS, and intellectual property regulation. In each of these areas we reviewed Bank experience with four questions in mind:

1. How much will implementation cost?
2. What are the development problems in this area?
3. Does the WTO agreement correctly diagnose the development problems?
4. Does the WTO agreement prescribe an appropriate remedy?

'Appropriate' in the fourth question refers both to correct identification of the problem and to recognition of the capacities (resource constraints) of the least developed countries. To provide specificity to the scope and cost of investments that may be involved in implementing Uruguay Round commitments, the core of this chapter is a review of (primarily) World Bank experience with customs reform, with application of sanitary and phytosanitary standards, and with installation of systems of intellectual property rights. In each area we outline basic WTO obligations and we examine how implementation might be managed so that it best helps the least developed countries to use trade as a vehicle for development. We start with a brief look at least developed countries' participation in the Uruguay Round negotiations. This participation, or lack thereof, has left these countries with no sense of ownership of the commitments they have undertaken.

2. NO LEAST DEVELOPED COUNTRY 'OWNERSHIP' OF THE RULES

'Ownership' of the rules is an important element in the functioning of any system of rules; particularly important in systems such as the WTO, where the central organisation has limited power to enforce. Building among members a solid sense of ownership of such rules begins with participation in establishing them – for WTO rules, with effective participation in the WTO negotiations in which the rules were agreed.

The African Economic Research Consortium's (AERC) evaluation of sub-Saharan African countries' participation in the Uruguay Round found that it had been minimal. These countries lacked the capacity to engage substantively on the wide range of issues that the Uruguay Round embraced. An indicator: of all the written proposals, comments, etc. circulated at the WTO during the Uruguay Round negotiations, less than three per cent were submitted by sub-Saharan countries (Ogunkola, 1999, p. 3). The AERC evaluation identified weaknesses at three levels:

1.   Geneva delegations were small and lacked persons with the technical backgrounds needed to participate effectively. A competent diplomat without the backing of a technical staff was not an effective delegation.[1]
2.   Links between WTO delegations and the government at home were not developed. There was a lack of established process to involve the relevant ministries with issues that were being negotiated in Geneva, e.g., health and agriculture ministries with negotiations on sanitary and phytosanitary standards, the customs agency with the customs valuation negotiations.
3.   Stakeholders, e.g., the business community, were minimally involved.

But all of the African members of the GATT chose to accept the new obligations of the WTO. Ogunkola (1999) concludes that

> [w]hile the participation of Africa has been limited by the capacity to negotiate, the ratification of the agreement and the single undertaking clause made the implementation of the agreement almost non-negotiable.[2]

Result: there came forward in these countries no sense of ownership of the implied reforms. To them, the reforms were imposed by the major trading countries.[3] Given these attitudes, it is difficult to rally support for implementation, and attempts to force implementation through the WTO dispute settlement mechanism would likely reinforce the impression that the WTO rules are imperially imposed from the outside, for the benefit of the outside.

---

[1] Of 65 developing country GATT/WTO members when the Uruguay Round began, 20 did not have delegations in Geneva. Of the 20, 15 were represented from embassies in other European cities, and 5 by delegations based in their national capitals. Furthermore, developing country delegations were notably smaller than those of the industrial countries. In 1987, when the Uruguay Round began, the EU had in Geneva a delegation of 10, EU Member States' delegations included an additional 57 persons. The US delegation numbered 10, the Japanese, 15. Only 12 developing countries had delegations of more than three persons. The larger ones: Korea, Mexico and Tanzania, 7 each; Brazil and Indonesia, 6 each; Thailand, Hong Kong and Egypt, 5 each. Of the 48 least developed countries, 29 are WTO members, but only 11 of these maintain delegations in Geneva. As of January 1999, 6 least developed countries were negotiating accession to the WTO, another 6 were observers, not negotiating accession. Data are from Michalopoulos (1998).
[2] 'Single undertaking' here means that each member was expected to take on all obligations, that the codes approach of the Tokyo Round, in which each member could opt to sign some codes and not sign others, was not available. John Croome, who served in the GATT/WTO Secretariat throughout the Tokyo and Uruguay Rounds, has pointed out in correspondence that 'single undertaking' initially referred to the members voting on all parts of the agreement as a whole, i.e., that the outcome of the tariff negotiations would not be put up for approval separately from the outcome of the subsidies negotiations. As the negotiations progressed, the meaning of 'single undertaking' expanded to include the 'no country can opt out of any part' meaning.
[3] An African food scientist remarked to us in conversation, 'They want us to adopt the SPS agreement so that we will import more chickens from them.'

TRIPs, the customs valuation agreement, the SPS agreement and several others suggest that developed country members furnish technical assistance to developing country members that so request it. This provision however is not a binding commitment. Thus, the developing countries took on *bound* commitments to implement in exchange for *unbound* commitments of assistance.

3. CUSTOMS VALUATION

The WTO agreement addresses only customs *valuation* – only one part of the customs process. In addition to providing information on how much customs reform might cost, we will argue in this section that given the initial situation in many developing countries (which we will briefly characterise) changing the valuation process without overall customs reform is not likely to improve the predictability of the customs process. Likewise, changing the customs valuation process would not lessen significantly the possibility of using the customs process as a non-tariff barrier.

Scope and content of the Customs Valuation Agreement. The Uruguay Round Customs Valuation Agreement establishes the *transactions value* of the shipment in question as the primary basis for customs value and prescribes a hierarchy of methods for determining that value. The first, and basic, option is that customs value will be the transaction value of *the* imported merchandise – the price actually paid or payable for *the* specific shipment. The agreement provides a list of items (add-ins) that must be included in the price actually paid or payable, e.g., packing costs, cost of tools, dies and moulds provided by the buyer. The second alternative is the transaction value of *identical* merchandise – sold for export to the same country of importation at or about the same time – for which a transaction value can be determined. The third, fourth and fifth are likewise attempts to come as close as operationally possible to the transactions value of the specific shipment. The agreement also provides a rogue's gallery of methods that *may not* be used, such as the selling price of competing domestic products, or the selling price on the market of the exporting country or on another export market.

Presumed administrative environment. The valuation process the Uruguay Round agreement imposes is one that complements customs systems in place in most of the advanced trading nations (including both developing and industrial countries). That system is based on generalised use of electronic information management and built-in incentives for self-compliance. Trade in these countries takes place in large-scale lots and duty rates are generally low. In this context, departure from routine business practice is costly, e.g., retrieving additional information in response to a valuation inquiry. Importers normally conduct the valuation process themselves, including application of the add-ins and take-outs needed to comply with the rules. In Norway, a paperless customs declaration system operates around-the-clock, average clearance takes 15 minutes and is almost always completed well before the goods arrive. About 85 per cent of declarations pass through the system without being stopped for further investigation (WCO, 1999). Questioning and verification of the importer-submitted customs value does not normally cause physical delay of the shipment. Instead, the importer posts a customs bond sufficient to cover the amount in question. Financial institutions in many least developed countries do not offer such bonds.

a. Developing Countries' Customs Practices and Problems

Customs practices in many least developed countries differ significantly from those in place in the more advanced trading nations. The differences are often differences in basic concept, not just differences of detail or efficiency.

Physical control.   Effective customs administration has both *physical* and *administrative* dimensions. Physical control is about keeping track of what passes into and out of the country. In many poorer countries, traditional smuggling – goods sneaked across the border away from recognised ports – is a significant problem. At a duty rate of 50 per cent, the duty on the number of televisions one person can transport on a bicycle-journey can come, in a poor country, to a year's wages. Where physical control systems are poor, smuggling need not involve clandestine overland trails or secret moonlit beaches. Goods often move through ports without coming under the supervision of customs authorities.

Administrative processes.   Customs processes in poorer countries exhibit many interacting weaknesses – excessive procedures that are not codified – often not even a published schedule of current tariff rates is available – poorly trained officials, a civil service system that does not pay a living wage and depends on officials receiving side-payments for performing their functions, and ineffective provision for appeal. Cunningham (1996), in an assessment of several least developed countries considering customs reform, observed that systems and procedures appeared to have evolved to maximise the number of steps and approvals – to create as many opportunities as possible for negotiation between traders and customs officials. It should be evident from this introduction to customs problems in poorer countries that valuation is only an inch in the whole yard of customs operations that need improvement.

b. Reform Experience in Developing and Transition Economies

We present in this section a brief digest of our review of customs reform projects in several countries. A brief tabulation of the cost of customs reform projects in several countries is reported in Table 1.

TABLE 1
Costs of Customs Reform Projects, Selected Countries

Country	Major Elements	Cost
Armenia, 1993–1997	Draft new customs law, train staff, and computerise procedures – component of an institution building project	$1.604 million
Lebanon, 1994–2001	Train staff, introduce new tariff classification, computerise procedures – component of a revenue enhancement and fiscal management project	$3.82 million
Tunisia, 1999–2004	Computerise and simplify procedures	$16.21 million
Tanzania	Buildings, equipment, new processes, training	$10 million

Scope. Reform projects have included the following elements, few projects covered all the elements.

- *Computerisation* – including computerised customs systems, systems for warehouse inventory control and for statistical reporting.
- *Valuation procedures.*
- *Cargo controls* – speed up processing and eliminate fraudulent or incorrect valuation.
- *Building refurbishment* – refurbish customs buildings necessary to house ASYCUDA.
- *Administrative reforms* – establish a new division responsible for customs valuation and tariff classification, recruit and train staff, establish appeals tribunal, reduce discretion exercised by customs officers.
- *Anti-smuggling equipment* – provide laboratory and detection equipment for drug interdiction and other anti-smuggling efforts. Equipment ranges from x-ray equipment and gas chromatographs to communications equipment.
- *Management and staff training* – train staff in basic management, customs procedures and computer operations; establish staff training schools.
- *Screenings for drug interdiction.*
- *Legislative reforms* – rewrite laws, formally accede to the Harmonised System Convention, increase transparency.

To sum up this section, the reforms we have reviewed cover some 16 major categories of activities ranging from rewriting legislation through training in auditing procedures, physical security in customs warehouses, to policing of smuggling and of traffic in illicit drugs. Various of these components involve a cost in the neighbourhood of $10 million per country.

4. SANITARY AND PHYTOSANITARY STANDARDS

The SPS agreement recognises the right of governments to restrict trade when necessary to protect human, animal or plant life or health, but limits exercise of that right to the measures that do not unjustifiably discriminate between countries with the same conditions and are not disguised restrictions on trade. The SPS agreement further constrains a Member to impose such restrictions:

- only to the extent necessary to protect life or health,
- based on scientific principles,
- not maintained if scientific evidence is lacking.

The latter bullet implies that SPS measures can be put in place only on the basis of careful laboratory testing and analysis and if science-based concerns about food safety or serious threats to animal or plant health have been identified.

The WTO SPS agreement requires that the process of developing and enforcing SPS regulations be transparent. Governments must publish proposed regulations in advance and allow public comment, including from foreign exporters. Governments must notify the relevant international body of any changes to SPS rules and must establish Enquiry Points so that traders can determine a country's present and planned SPS regulations and processes.

Clout for exporters.   Before the SPS agreement was in force, an exporter had, in effect, to comply with the importing country's SPS measures. With the agreement in force, the exporter must still comply with the importing country's SPS measures, but the importing country is, by the agreement, required to demonstrate that its SPS measures are in fact based on science and are applied equally to domestic and foreign producers. The Uruguay Round agreement puts the WTO on the side of those exporters who do comply – the exporter now has clearer grounds for challenging an import restriction.

In use, a heavier burden for developing countries.   While the SPS agreement does not require that a country's *domestic* standards meet the agreement's requirements, it does require that the standards the country applies *at the border* meet those requirements. In this regard, the agreement likely places a heavier burden on developing than on industrial countries – this resulting from the standards already in place in the industrial countries more-or-less being established as the standard to which the developing countries must comply.

Article 3 of the SPS agreement specifies that SPS measures in conformity with relevant international conventions are to be *deemed* necessary to protect human, animal or plant health, and *presumed* consistent with the agreement. A country may adopt other standards or methods, but to apply them at the border the WTO agreement places on the country the burden of demonstrating their scientific merit and appropriateness. Industrial countries have been leaders in establishing these international conventions, the resulting conventions being in significant part generalisations of industrial country practices and standards. This does not imply that such standards are bad standards in a scientific sense, it does however imply that the SPS agreement provides for a more effective assault against current developing countries' use of SPS measures against imports than against industrial countries' use.

Application requires investment.   For a developing country to effectively use the WTO agreement to defend its export rights or to justify its import restrictions, it will have to upgrade its SPS system to international standards. Effective use of the WTO agreement depends on extensive investments, it is not a matter of applying *existing systems* of standards to international trade, it is a much broader matter of installing world-class systems.

a. Lessons Learned from World Bank Experience

The World Bank has assisted several countries to implement sanitary and phytosanitary regulations. Bank projects supporting SPS systems have typically placed these measures in a general development context of ensuring food security, increasing agricultural productivity and protecting health, rather than focusing on the narrower objective of meeting stringent requirements in export markets.

Scope.   One SPS-related project that the Bank has supported, an export reform project in Argentina, did however have as its objective to improve trade performance. The principal objective of the programme was to gain international recognition of certain zones as disease free or pest free. Argentina's meat, fruit and vegetable exports have been limited by other countries' concerns over the presence particularly of foot and mouth disease and citrus canker. In addition, the programme recognised that diversification into higher value-added exports such as processed meats, seeds, and horticultural products required producers to meet more stringent quality control standards. Some of the components of the programme that related directly to implementation of SPS standards were: upgrading veterinary services, central and field; laboratories; quarantine stations; disease and pest eradication programmes; certification of disease-free and pest-free zones; training, facilities and equipment for seed certification and registration, for quality control, and for certification to ensure the absence of chemical residues in exported meat; a laboratory to bring wool certification up to international standards; and staff and equipment for research aimed at reducing chemical residues.

Cost.   The costs of several SPS-related projects that the World Bank has supported are reported in Table 2. In addition to such costs to the government, producers in the private sector bear other costs of complying with SPS regulations: vaccinating livestock, eliminating pesticide residues, guaranteeing sanitary food processing conditions, etc.

TABLE 2
Costs of SPS-related World Bank Projects

Country	Project Description	Cost
Argentina, 1991–1996	General agricultural export reform project	$82.7 million
Brazil, 1987–1994	Livestock disease control project	$108 million
Algeria, 1988–1990	Locust Control project	$112 million
Vietnam, 1994–1997	Pest management component of Agricultural Rehabilitation project	$3.5 million
Madagascar, 1980–1988	Livestock vaccination component of Rural Development project	$11.8 million
Hungary, 1985–1991	Slaughterhouse modernisation component of Integrated Livestock Industry project	$41.2 million
Russia, 1992–1995	Improve food processing facilities, disease control – component of Rehabilitation Loan	$150 million
Poland, 1990–1995	Food processing facilities modernisation component of Agro-industries Export Development project	$71 million
China, 1993–2000	Animal and plant quarantine component of Agricultural Support Service project	$10 million
Turkey, 1992–1999	Modernise laboratories for residue control – component of Agricultural Research project	$3.3 million

5. INTELLECTUAL PROPERTY RIGHTS

The WTO TRIPs agreement covers the *seven* main areas of intellectual property: copyright, trademarks, geographical indications, industrial designs, patents, layout designs of integrated circuits, and undisclosed information including trade secrets. In each area, the agreement specifies minimum standards of protection that governments must provide,[4] requires governments to provide procedures to enforce, and provides means of dispute settlement. The minimum standards are similar for each of the seven areas; they cover, in the instance of patents (WTO, 1999, pp. 214f):

---

[4] One critic however argues that 'these [are] not "minimum" standards of intellectual property protection in the classical sense of the term; rather, they collectively expressed most of the standards of protection on which the developed countries could agree among themselves' (Reichman, 1998, p. 586).

- What is patentable.
- What rights flow to the owner of a patent – government is obligated to prevent unauthorised persons from using, selling or importing the patent, the patented process, the patented product or the product or products directly made from the patented process.
- What exceptions to those rights are permissible – e.g., compulsory licensing may be required.
- How long the protection lasts.[5]

The TRIPs agreement, like the SPS agreement, builds on standards expressed in relevant international conventions such as the Paris Convention for the Protection of Industrial Property (1967) and the Washington Treaty – the Treaty on Intellectual Property in Respect of Integrated Circuits, sometimes labelled the ICIP Treaty (1989).

Extension of IPR obligations. The TRIPs Agreement requires each WTO member to adhere to the provisions (with a few provisions excepted) of these international IPR conventions, whether or not the member is party to those conventions. This, of itself, is a major extension for many countries. For example, the coverage of integrated circuits is an extension for many countries, including industrial countries.[6] Under TRIPs, WTO members must consider unlawful – if not authorised by the right-holder – the import, sale, or other commercial distribution of the integrated circuit design, of integrated circuits containing that design, and of articles that contain such integrated circuits.

Another example, the Rome Convention that establishes rights of performers, producers of sound recordings, and broadcasters has few signatories, particularly among developing countries. The TRIPs agreement creates the obligations on governments that allow recording companies from one country to attack unauthorised reproduction and sale of its products within another country. In addition, the TRIPs agreement in some areas has broader coverage than the relevant international convention. It goes beyond, for example, the Berne Convention to obligate copyright protection for certain computer programs and computerised data bases, and it provides the first multilateral obligations on industrial designs (e.g., textile designs).

---

[5] The TRIPs agreement provided the following transition periods: developed countries, until 1 January, 1996; developing countries and transition economies, up to 1 January, 2000; least developed countries, up to 1 January, 2006 – and may be extended on 'duly motivated' request by a least developed country. Developing countries that at present provide patent protection to processes and not to products, for example in the food, chemical and pharmaceutical sectors, can delay up to 1 January, 2005, the application of the obligation to protect products. Even here, governments must provide that inventions made between 1995 and 2004 will be able to gain patent protection after 1 January, 2005.

[6] This treaty is not yet in force; having thus far only nine signatories, of which only one has ratified.

The enforcement provisions of TRIPs require that a member provide civil as well as criminal remedies for infringement of intellectual property rights. They also obligate members to provide means by which right-holders can obtain the cooperation of customs authorities to prevent imports of infringing goods.

Wiggle room. While it is impossible to predict how the process of application and interpretation through the WTO dispute settlement mechanism will play out, a number of legal experts[7] see sufficient 'wiggle room' in the agreement so that developing countries could – within a good faith implementation of their obligations – strike a balance between the interests of second-comers and the need to promote innovation and investment. This would however require a considerable departure from the balance that has been institutionalised in the industrial countries' intellectual property rights law. That balance, many experts argue, is tipped toward the interests of commercialised producers of knowledge – tipped past the point of optimality even for the community of interests that make up industrial country societies.[8]

The tendency of the WTO is however to give the benefit of the doubt to established standards. Finding grounds for moving away from established standards is particularly difficult in the area of intellectual property rights. They are, after all, an existential matter of legal definition, not a scientific matter of empirical estimation.

How to do it. Even for an individual country, it would be nigh on impossible to provide objective guidelines as to how to strike the optimal balance between legal incentives to create, and the costs that are thereby incurred by users and potential second-comers. Systems in place must be defended as the outcome of accepted (e.g., democratic) political processes, not of scientific calibration. It would be even more difficult to scale this balance to different levels of economic development. Analysts have so far built up little knowledge of the impacts of various forms of intellectual property rights on economic development, even less about different degrees of any form.[9]

Our review of case studies in support of IPR again shows a considerable range of needed reforms; drafting new legislation (e.g., to extend IPR protection to plant varieties), augmenting administrative structures (e.g., capacity to review applications, including computerised information systems and extensive training for staff) and buttressing enforcement. Some information on costs is reported in Table 3.

---

[7] Reichman (1998), and references cited there.

[8] Reichman (1998, p. 589) for example urges that 'the logical course of action for the developing countries in implementing their obligations under the TRIPs Agreement is to shoulder the pro-competitive mantle that the developed countries have increasingly abandoned. Templeman (1998) argues that there is no public justification for the level of intellectual property rights defined by industrial countries' laws.'

[9] Abbott (1998, p. 501) in his introduction and summing-up to an issue of the *Journal of International Economic Law* devoted to TRIPs, notes this lack of understanding of the impact of IPR on economic development.

TABLE 3
World Bank Projects Related to Intellectual Property Rights

Country	Project Description	Cost
Brazil, 1997–2002	Train staff administering IPR laws – component of Science and Technology Reform project	$4.0 million
Indonesia, 1997–2003	Improve IPR regulatory framework – component of Information Infrastructure Development project	$14.7 million
Mexico, 1992–1996	Established agency to implement industrial property laws – component of Science and Technology Infrastructure project	$32.1 million

6. CONCLUSIONS

We draw the following major lessons from our review.

Reform is needed. In the areas we have covered, customs administration, sanitary and phytosanitary standards and intellectual property rights, we found no shortage of projects to review. Developing countries are willing to borrow money to finance improvements in these areas; hence it is evident that they, themselves, see a need for reform.

Delay is not an asset. We should be careful not to be lulled into the mercantilist ethic of a reciprocal negotiation in which delay, of itself, is a victory. Where reform is needed, to delay the improvements is to lengthen the time that the people in these countries remain poor. Time will, of course, be needed for implementation, but implementation periods should be based on the engineering requirements to accomplish the required construction, not handed out as second prize in a tough negotiation.

Do it my way. The content of the obligations imposed by the WTO agreements on customs valuation, intellectual property rights and SPS can be characterised as the advanced countries saying to the others, *Do it my way!* The customs valuation agreement imposes a system in use in the leading industrial countries on all TRIPs and the SPS agreement is explicit in establishing international conventions developed in large part by the industrial countries as the WTO standard.

While the SPS agreement appears to allow the retention of an indigenous system, doing so is not a real alternative. In defending trade-related actions, the systems recognised by international conventions have the legal benefit of the doubt, an indigenous system must prove itself. The least developed countries do not have the resources needed to do that; hence the only effective option for a country that retains an indigenous system of standards is *not to apply* standards at the border.[10] The WTO's *free* rider problem has not gone away, it has been swapped for a *forced* rider problem, its burden shifted from the industrial countries to the least developed countries.

Heavier obligations on developing countries.   For the advanced countries whose systems are compatible with international conventions (or vice versa) the WTO brings no more than an obligation to apply their *domestic regulations* fairly at the border. This includes not discriminating among transactions involving different countries and not unnecessarily impeding international transactions. Countries that at present apply their own indigenous standards, have the additional – and far larger – obligation to apply the internationally sanctioned standards in their domestic economies. Though new WTO areas, e.g., SPS, intellectual property rights, aim at the trade-related aspects of their subject matter, for the least developed countries they require first the establishment of such systems, or the conversion of indigenous systems to the system recognised by international conventions.

A related lesson is that the scope of what the WTO regulates is narrower than the scope of what must be done to make development sense out of implementation. For example, customs valuation versus customs reform – it helps little to change customs *valuation* procedures if containers still stay on the dock for 60 days.

Inappropriate diagnosis and inappropriate remedy.   One effect of this 'Do it my way!' nature of the agreements is to intensify the ownership problem, discussed below. In addition, this characteristic brings back our initial questions. From a development perspective:

- Do the WTO agreements appropriately identify the problems faced by developing countries?
- Given the least developed countries' needs and their resource bases, do the agreements provide the most effective remedy?

The customs valuation agreement, we have argued above, provides neither appropriate diagnosis nor appropriate remedy. It addresses only a small part of least developed countries' problems with customs administration and of course provides no remedy over other parts. Over the small part of the problem it covers, it provides an inappropriate remedy, one incompatible with the resources they have at their disposal.

Our conclusions on the intellectual property rights agreement are similar. As to diagnosis, its focus is not on encouraging innovation or protecting endogenous technology in developing countries, it is on industrial country enterprises' collecting for intellectual property on which least developed countries now

---

[10] We are not arguing here that the iron fist imposes the wrong standards. Our concern is to remove the velvet glove of comforting rhetoric from that fist.

recognise no obligation to pay. The default remedy is to copy industrial country intellectual property law. While legal scholars point out that the intellectual property agreement allows for the possibility of adopting intellectual property law that is friendly to users and to second-comers, they point out that the benefit of the doubt is on the side of copying present industrial country approaches. A major cost of standardising on the current industrial country example is to cut off experimentation – the process of developing more appropriate legal approaches in developing countries.[11]

Effective implementation and compliance involves investment-development projects, but WTO negotiations have not supported examination from this perspective. The dynamic behind the WTO process has been the export interests of major enterprises in the advanced trading countries. Development ministries in the advanced countries frequently complain how hard it is to get their trade ministries to pay attention to development issues. In the advanced countries, development ministries are junior partners in making trade policy; at the WTO, the least developed countries have little capacity to organise and to advance their own interests.

No ownership of the reforms in least developed countries. The lack of instinctive ownership of the reforms needed to comply with WTO obligations will make implementation very difficult, and will likely push governments to superficial adjustments aimed at avoiding clashes with trading partners. Private and social sector shareholders were not involved in the creation of these obligations – nor even the government agencies that will ultimately be responsible for implementation. How the least developed countries organise their participation in WTO affairs needs modification; perhaps the WTO process also.

Allowing for alternatives vs. providing alternatives. Each of the three Uruguay Round agreements we have reviewed includes a promise of assistance to implement. In addition, each provides for delayed implementation, and provides also a way for a least developed country to request an extension beyond the agreement's deadlines. The latter provision might be interpreted as recognition that the prescribed or default technology included in the agreements might not be the most suitable for the least developed countries. Though the agreements allow for the possibility that alternative approaches might be developed and recognised, they provide no such alternative. As to developing alternatives, the WTO negotiations are a self-interest propelled process. Narrowly interpreted, that places the burden of developing alternatives that are appropriate to least developed countries' needs and their resources on the least developed countries themselves.

---

[11] Matthew Stillwell of the Centre for International Environmental Law pointed this out to us.

It costs money.   The project costs we have presented here provide a first approximation to the investments needed to implement WTO obligations on SPS, IPR and customs reform. To gain acceptance for its meat, vegetables and fruits in industrial country markets, Argentina spent over $80 million to achieve higher levels of plant and animal sanitation. Hungary spent over $40 million to upgrade the level of sanitation of its slaughterhouses alone. Mexico spent over $30 million to upgrade intellectual property laws and enforcement that began at a higher level than are in place in most least developed countries. We identified some 16 elements, in customs reform, each of which can cost more than $2.5 million to implement. The figures, for just three of the six Uruguay Round Agreements that involve restructuring of domestic regulations, come to $150 million.[12] One hundred and fifty million dollars is more than the annual development budget for eight of the twelve least developed countries for which we could find a figure for that part of the budget.

REFERENCES

Abbott, F.M. (1998), 'The Enduring Enigma of TRIPS: A Challenge for the World Economic System', *Journal of International Economic Law*, **1**, 4 (Oxford: Oxford University Press), 497–52.

Cunningham, B. (1996), *Tanzania: Strategy and Action Plan to Reform Customs Administration* (Tanzania Revenue Authority, June).

Michalopoulos, C. (1998), *Developing Countries' Participation in the World Trade Organization*, Policy Research Working Paper No. 1906 (Washington DC: The World Bank, March).

Ogunkola, E.O. (1999), 'African Capacity for Compliance and Defense of WTO Rights', Conference Paper for AERC Sponsored Africa and the World Trading System (Yaounde, Cameroon, 17–18 April).

Reichman, J.H. (1998), 'Securing Compliance with the TRIPS Agreement After US v India', *Journal of International Economic Law*, **1**, 4 (Oxford: Oxford University Press), 603–6.

Templeman, L.S. (1998), 'Intellectual Property', *Journal of International Economic Law*, **1**, 4 (Oxford: Oxford University Press), 585–602.

World Customs Organisation (1999), 'Survey of Customs Reform and Modernization: Trends and Best Practices', on WCO Website at www.wcoomd.org/frmpublic.htm.

WTO Secretariat (1999), *Guide to the Uruguay Round Agreements* (The Hague, Kluwer Law International).

---

[12] The experiences we have reviewed were in the more advanced developing countries, the costs could be higher in the least developed countries who will begin further from the required standards.

8

WTO Dispute Settlement, Transparency and Surveillance

Bernard M. Hoekman and Petros C. Mavroidis

1. INTRODUCTION

𝕴 T is frequently argued that one of the major results of the Uruguay Round –
especially for developing countries – was the strengthening of GATT
dispute settlement procedures (DSP) and surveillance mechanisms. DSP became
a more automatic process, with greatly reduced opportunities for participants in
disputes to block the creation of panels and the adoption of reports. The Trade
Policy Review Mechanism (TPRM) became a central part of the WTO, and was
expected to result in significantly greater transparency of national policies. Many
observers were of the view that as a result of these innovations developing
countries would be more able to identify potential violations of WTO
commitments and have disputes settled in their favour (e.g., Whalley, 1996;
Schott and Buurman, 1994; and Croome, 1999).

The use of DSP in the first five years of the WTO would appear to support the
optimistic expectations. Over 160 requests for consultations were brought to the
WTO in its first five years of operation; three times more on a per annum basis
than under the GATT. Developing countries are more often involved than in the
past – about 25 per cent of all cases were brought by or against developing
countries. Some developing countries have successfully contested actions by
large players (e.g., Costa Rica – US restrictions on cotton textiles; and Venezuela
and Brazil – US gasoline regulations). However, least developed countries are not
involved in the DSP at all: there have been no cases involving sub-Saharan
countries (Table 1). As argued below, this may reflect an unwillingness to bring
cases, as well as resource constraints. The costs of DSP are disproportionately
heavy for developing countries.

Most observers believe that while certainly not perfect, the experience
to date suggests the WTO dispute settlement system is working quite well.
Most suggestions for reform are therefore incremental and relatively

TABLE 1
Participation in WTO Dispute Settlement Cases
(April 1994–March 1999)

No. of Appearances as Complainant		No. of Appearances as Respondent	
Member	No. of Disputes	Member	No. of Disputes
United States	54	United States	30
EC	43	EC	26
Canada	13	Japan	12
India	8	India	12
Mexico	7	Korea	10
Japan	7	Canada	9
Brazil	6	Brazil	8
Thailand	4	Argentina	8
New Zealand	4	Australia	6
Honduras	3	Indonesia	4
Guatemala	3	Turkey	4
Switzerland	3	Mexico	3
Argentina	2	Chile	3
Hungary	2	Ireland	3
Australia	2	Guatemala	2
Chile	2	Slovak Republic	2
Philippines	2	Belgium	2
Panama	2	Hungary	2
Korea	2	Greece	2
Uruguay	1	Pakistan	2
Sri Lanka	1	Philippines	2
Singapore	1	Sweden	1
Poland	1	Peru	1
Colombia	1	Thailand	1
Costa Rica	1	United Kingdom	1
Indonesia	1	Denmark	1
Ecuador	1	Czech Republic	1
Peru	1	Venezuela	1
Hong Kong	1	Poland	1
Pakistan	1	Portugal	1
Malaysia	1	Malaysia	1
Venezuela	1	Netherlands	1
Czech Republic	1	France	1
Memo items:			
G4	118	G4	90
Other OECD	22	Other OECD	27
Developing/Transition	43	Developing/Transition	47
Least Developed	0	Least Developed	0

Note:
Excludes third parties.

Source: Horn, Mavroidis and Nordström (1999).

specific.[1] We take a somewhat more systemic view in this chapter and argue that notwithstanding the overall satisfaction with the system, there is a need to enhance the ability of – and incentives for – developing countries to use WTO mechanisms to enforce market access rights. To some extent this can be done through changing the rules of the dispute settlement game. As, if not more important, are efforts to enhance transparency. Although much has been done to bolster the surveillance role of the WTO – e.g., the TPRM – we argue in this chapter that consideration should be given to developing transparency mechanisms that are parallel to and independent of the WTO. These could involve the private sector and non-governmental organisations (NGOs) that have a major stake in the functioning of the trading system. The focus of such mechanisms should be on analysis as much as on surveillance – including the identification of the costs and benefits of alternative methods of implementing WTO agreements. Greater transparency regarding the likely economic effects of alternative policy and rule-making proposals for countries at different levels of development could be a valuable mechanism to increase the relevance and 'ownership' of WTO agreements.

2. ENFORCEMENT – SYSTEMIC ISSUES AND DEVELOPING COUNTRY CONCERNS

WTO dispute settlement procedures have a number of characteristics, four of which are worth highlighting: (i) only governments have standing; (ii) compensation for damages is customarily not requested and awarded; (iii) the ability to enforce rulings is very asymmetric; and (iv) the costs of the process are significant.

a. Governments as Filters

Export industries must petition their governments to bring cases to the WTO – first bilaterally through consultations, then to a panel. Only governments have legal standing to bring cases to the WTO DSP. Thus, export interests must operate through a government filter. This affects the incentives for the private sector to bring cases forward. If there is a substantial probability that the government will not be willing to bring the case to the WTO, cases may not be brought forward. Governments may engage in 'tacit collusion' by refraining from contesting measures through fear of stimulating counter claims (the 'glass house' syndrome). More generally, developing country governments may be unwilling to bring cases if they fear this will have detrimental consequences in non-trade

---

[1] For recent analyses and proposals for improvement by legal experts, see Davey (1999), Hudec (1999) and Jackson (1999).

areas (e.g., continued aid flows or defence cooperation). While it is the role of government to determine priorities and to make the tradeoffs it deems most beneficial for the nation as a whole, concerns that bringing a case would 'disturb' a country's relationship with a major trading partner to some extent nullifies the raison d'être of the WTO – the establishment of a rule-based as opposed to a power-based system of trade relations.

One option to address this problem is to give exporters direct access to the WTO, i.e., 'privatise' DSP. Levy and Srinivasan (1996) develop a simple model that explores the possible consequences of such privatisation, and conclude that this is a bad idea. They show that: if a government maximises national welfare it may have good reasons not to pursue a trade case because the expected national return is negative (due to issue linkage by the partner); removing a government's discretion to decide whether or not to prosecute a case can make it more difficult to make commitments in trade negotiations; and that there is therefore a good case for permitting only governments to bring cases to the WTO. The Levy and Srinivasan analysis illustrates the importance of full information – governments must be able to determine as accurately as possible what the cost to the economy is of not taking action. Domestic consultation and 'transparency' mechanisms may need to be strengthened to ensure that the 'right' calculation or tradeoffs are indeed being made. Their analysis also suggests there is value in seeking to create multilateral mechanisms that reduce the burden on individual countries of identifying and contesting WTO violations.[2] These issues are discussed further below.

b. Remedies

A government found to be in violation of the WTO is generally told to bring its measures into compliance with the rules. How this is to be done is usually left to the discretion of the losing party. The most panels can do is to make specific suggestions regarding the way a losing party can bring its measures into conformity. The recent *Bananas* case illustrates that plaintiffs are well advised to request specific suggestions to prevent strategies of 'implementation avoidance' (Hoekman and Mavroidis, 1996). If panels limit themselves to standard recommendations to bring measures into compliance, disagreement between the parties as to the adequacy of the implementing measures taken by the losing party may preclude the complainant from obtaining authorisation to take countermeasures. Another panel will first have to rule on the adequacy of the implementing measures.

---

[2] Hoekman and Mavroidis (1999) suggest that strengthening enforcement mechanisms at the national level could also help alleviate the problem, as this channel does not allow threats to be exercised in non-trade areas.

The standard remedies generally obtained in the WTO context do not provide great incentives to the private sector to invoke DSP. The length of time it can take for the DSP to run its course is substantial – up to 2½ years. This is a long time for exporters to be subject to a measure that may be a violation of the WTO, especially for countries that do not have a diversified export base. More importantly, standard remedies that require a member to bring its measures into compliance with WTO obligations do not involve any compensation for damages incurred or financial penalties. This reduces the attractiveness of using the system. If damages or financial compensation could be obtained, the 'time cost' as well as the resource costs associated with DSP (see below) would become much less important. In principle, there is nothing to prevent countries from seeking compensation – the fact that complainants do not customarily request compensation is rooted in the history of the GATT. Many WTO members, including developing countries, have been unwilling to go down this track, perhaps in part due to uncertainty regarding possible repercussions (e.g., regarding potential liability). Some countries have also argued that their legal systems prohibit compensation.[3]

c. Enforcement Threats

Economists often note that there are asymmetric incentives for countries to deviate from the WTO, as the ultimate threat that can be made against a member that does not comply with a panel recommendation is retaliation. Small countries cannot credibly threaten this because raising import barriers will have little impact on the target market while being costly in welfare terms. Thus, pressure to comply with panel rulings is largely moral in nature. In practice the system has worked rather well, in that recourse to retaliation has rarely been required to enforce multilateral dispute settlement decisions (Hudec, 1993). This is largely a reflection of the repeated nature of the WTO 'game' and the resulting value that governments attach to maintaining a (reasonably) good reputation. Nonetheless, asymmetry in enforcement ability can affect the incentives to use the system. The classic recommendation by economists to address the problem is to change the rules so that non-implementation of panel recommendations would be punished by withdrawal of market access commitments by *all* WTO members. Suggestions to this effect have always been resisted (Hudec, 1987). A basic problem with retaliation is that it involves raising barriers to trade, which is generally detrimental to the interests of the country that does so, and to world welfare more generally. Much better from an economic perspective would be to encourage use

---

[3] Although it can be pointed out that a basic principle of public international law holds that domestic law cannot be invoked to deviate from an international obligation (Art. 26 Vienna Convention on the Law of Treaties).

of the provisions in the WTO for re-negotiating concessions. This would ensure that the net impact of dispute resolution would lead towards more liberal trade, rather than create mechanisms through which trade barriers are raised, as re-negotiation involves compensating members affected by a withdrawal of a concession by reducing other trade barriers.

d. Resource Costs

An issue that is frequently raised by developing countries is that rich countries such as the US, the EU or Canada – the major players in terms of dispute settlement activity (Table 1) – are well equipped with legal talent, are well briefed by export interests, and have a worldwide network of commercial and diplomatic representation that feeds their systems with relevant data. Developing countries, in contrast, have limited national expertise available and find it difficult to collect the type of information that is required to bring or defend WTO cases. The cost of bringing cases to the WTO is substantial and prevents many developing countries from using the system to their full advantage (ACWL, 1999). Although to some extent countries can buy legal expertise,[4] scarcity of national administrative resources to identify and prepare cases is a major constraint. Developing countries also find it more difficult to supply panellists – the opportunity costs of seconding delegates for panels is much greater than for OECD countries with larger missions in Geneva and more expertise in capitals.

In considering possible options for improving WTO DSP, it is useful to distinguish between 'upstream' and 'downstream' stages. The former revolves around identification and preparation of potential cases; the latter revolves around the Geneva panel process. From the perspective of many firms it may not be worth the time and effort required at the 'upstream' stage to convince the government that a case is worth pursuing. Violations of the WTO often will not be contested because firms and industry associations either do not know that a government is 'breaking the law' or lack the incentive to blow the whistle. Frequently there is a collective action problem, and under-provision of the public good (DSP) is likely to result. Solutions require increasing the benefits to firms of collecting data on potentially WTO illegal policies; and reducing the costs of doing so. The former can be pursued by establishing mechanisms to facilitate private sector cooperation, within and across countries to compile information; the latter can be pursued by devising mechanisms to facilitate identification of

---

[4] Until *Bananas III* countries were impeded from bringing non-government, private legal counsel before the panel, but an Appellate Body decision to allow representation by private lawyers removed this constraint as far as the Appellate Body was concerned. A subsequent panel then decided there were no provisions in the WTO or the DSU that prevented a WTO member from determining the composition of its delegation to panel meetings (Palmeter and Mavroidis, 1999).

potential violations and reducing the need to involve governments in the enforcement of WTO commitments.

3. STRENGTHENING THE UPSTREAM DIMENSIONS OF ENFORCEMENT

Enforcement requires that violations of WTO commitments are identified. Information is therefore a critical factor. Frequently this is under-supplied – the government is not told of foreign trade practices that restrict national exports; or conversely, is not confronted with complaints on the part of foreign exporters regarding policies that impede their access to the domestic market. This may be because the affected market is too small to make it worth bringing a case (Hoekman and Mavroidis, 1999), or because traders are unaware that the WTO applies.

One option to deal with the information problem is to create mechanisms through which data on trade and investment barriers is collected and analysed by a specialised, independent body. Such an approach would reduce the burden on individual enterprises to have expertise on WTO matters, and reduce the cost of collecting, aggregating and analysing information. Data could be collected through periodic surveys of a representative cross-section of companies that are actively involved in importing and exporting, multi-nationals, trade and industry associations, and consumer organisations. The information that is compiled by the surveying agency would be used to assess the status quo on export markets, as well as policies maintained by the government that have an effect on imports, and help identify potential WTO cases. Firms and other stakeholders (consumer groups, NGOs) have an interest in cooperating across countries as well.

Cooperation among the private and voluntary sector to monitor government policies would help complement the TPRM mechanism. The TPRM process is arguably too infrequent to be very useful for enforcement, as most countries are reviewed only once every six years or more. Resources are centred primarily on the larger traders, who are reviewed every 2 or 4 years depending on size. It can be argued that the frequency of surveillance is the inverse of what is required, given that export interests have the greatest incentives to monitor the policies that are applied by the largest trading countries. However, a counter argument is that high-income nations obtain relevant information from their commercial attachés around the world and their private sector, whereas developing country networks of commercial attachés are much more limited, and their private sector export interests will tend to be concentrated in fewer markets. Thus, the payoff to multilateral surveillance of major markets may be more important for them. A major limitation of the TPRM is that WTO staff do not have a mandate to identify whether policies violate the WTO. Nor does the process centre on specific cases or issues that are of concern to the private sector and might become the subject of future negotiations or disputes.

A private cooperative effort to collect information could be a good complement to the TPRM by identifying not only potential violations of WTO commitments but also the costs to business of status quo policies that are WTO consistent. It would not involve direct access by firms and NGOs to DSP – only national governments would have legal standing in the WTO. But more and better information could assist in overcoming unwillingness on the part of governments to pursue cases motivated by foreign policy reasons or by concerns about possible repercussions in other areas of cooperation (e.g., development aid flows). If firms from a large number of nationalities are involved in the information collection and analysis effort and a number of governments are petitioned to take (joint) action, an individual government's incentive not to take up a complaint may be reduced. Full exploitation of the potential benefits of timely and comprehensive information and analysis requires complementary changes in the 'downstream' WTO process. This is discussed below.

To be useful for advocacy and enforcement purposes, the information that is compiled must be analysed. The economic effects of policies must be ascertained, and the legality of observed measures with WTO rules assessed. Advisory centres to do the latter could be independent from the information collection effort, or be an integrated dimension of the process. Public-private partnerships with a regional dimension could be envisaged – e.g., by building on the institutions that are created in the context of creating and implementing regional integration agreements (Weston and Delich, 1999).

Many fora already exist through which business cooperates and coordinates policy/lobbying positions *vis-à-vis* governments. The most prominent international body is the International Chamber of Commerce (ICC) located in Paris. The ICC has consultative status in the United Nations system, and is the most visible avenue for international business to express its views on international policy matters. Mention can also be made of the Business and Industry Advisory Committee, which provides business input into the deliberations of OECD bodies, and the Alliance for Global Business. In many countries there are similar institutions, as well as numerous industry-specific bodies. They are primarily focused on lobbying for changes in regulations or policies. Although business associations have become more aware of the potential payoff of investing resources to influence international negotiations, they have done less to compile the type of information and undertake the analysis that would help policymakers identify the key constraints to competition and provide an input into better enforcement of WTO agreements.

4. POSSIBLE REFORMS AT THE DOWNSTREAM (WTO) STAGE

A major concern of developing countries regarding the WTO process is the cost-benefit ratio associated with DSP. Costs – both financial and in terms of human resources – are significant, while benefits are generally perceived to be limited due to the relative weakness of the available remedies.

a. Resource Constraints

Resource constraints reduce the ability of a developing country government to participate in the multilateral dispute settlement process. Least developed countries in particular are at a disadvantage in bringing cases and defending their rights because of the absence of representation in Geneva and a severe scarcity of both financial resources and relevant expertise (South Centre, 1999). Article 27:2 DSU provides for technical assistance to be given to developing countries by the WTO Secretariat. The WTO's ability to satisfy this mandate is very limited – legal technical assistance services are provided by two academic experts on a part-time basis. The adequacy of the assistance on offer is further reduced by the DSU requirement that such assistance can only be provided *after* a Member has decided to submit a dispute to the WTO. Thus, assistance in evaluating whether practices are inconsistent and determining what might be 'winning' cases cannot be given, so that technical assistance is mostly used when developing countries are respondents. The consensus among developing countries is that the available assistance is inadequate.

A number of options can be identified to 'level the playing field.' One that has been actively pursued by a group of WTO members is to establish an Advisory Centre on WTO Law (ACWL). This entity would be given resources by participating countries to be used to finance technical (legal) assistance for dispute settlement cases on a cost-sharing basis (ACWL, 1999). Prior to the Seattle Ministerial, major OECD players such as the US and the EU had not indicated a willingness to support (and help fund) an ACWL, and large developing countries such as Argentina, Brazil and India were also lukewarm. However, one of the few achievements of the Ministerial meeting in Seattle was the signing of an agreement to establish an ACWL. Analogous to the role a 'public defender' can play in domestic legal systems to ensure that all citizens are able to defend themselves, an international mechanism to subsidise the ability of poor nations to bring and defend cases may help to 'level the playing field' to some extent.[5] For such a mechanism to be most effective, it is important that the

---

[5] There are two models possible here. One is the ACWL model which would involve permanent staffing. Another is to provide financing (subsidies) to developing countries, which can be used to hire whatever representation they deem most suited to the task. From an efficiency point of view some combination is preferable, allowing for country preferences and choices to be expressed.

'upstream' part of the DSP chain be strengthened concurrently, as this is crucial in identifying potential cases.

Another dimension of the resource constraint concerns participation in panels by developing country officials. Panels tend to comprise officials. While this cuts costs – officials continue to be paid by their governments – the opportunity costs for developing countries are high given limited representation in Geneva, and limited trade expertise generally. One way of addressing this constraint would be to establish a permanent roster of panellists who would be committed to being available for DSP work, and would be compensated for their time through the WTO budget. Greater professionalisation of panels could have a number of additional benefits, including reducing the burden on the WTO Secretariat associated with DSP, more rapid conclusion of cases, and greater consistency in outcomes (Davey, 1999; and Hudec, 1999). Moving away from diplomatic representation would also facilitate granting access to panel hearings by NGOs and interest groups, as the scope for such entities to put pressure on panellists would be reduced (because panellists would not be beholden to particular governments). Professionalisation will of course have implications for the WTO budget, so there must be a willingness among WTO members to raise the funding required.

Many cases that involve developing countries will generally pertain to relatively small trade volumes. Another way of recognising resource constraints is to consider adopting 'light' dispute settlement procedures for 'small' cases brought by developing countries (e.g., where the exports constitute less than one per cent of apparent consumption in the importing market). In such cases, a single panellist could be appointed and the judicial review process be required to be completed within three months. This would be beneficial to developing countries by lowering the cost of litigation (indeed, no lawyers may be needed). A related possibility would be to allow 'light' procedures to be used in cases where affected exports are large in relative terms for the country or countries bringing the case (e.g., account for more than five per cent of total exports). For developing countries a small absolute trade flow in dollar terms may represent a large proportion of its total exports, making it particularly important that rapid review is available.

b. More Effective Remedies

Two remedies-related issues were discussed previously: the problem of ensuring that a losing party effectively brings its measures into compliance with its obligations, and the type of remedies that panels are permitted (encouraged) to suggest. Requesting specific recommendations by the panel can help reduce the scope for 'implementation avoidance' disputes of the type that occurred in *Bananas*. If the panel's specific suggestions are followed by the respondent, this should automatically create an irrefutable presumption of legality/adequacy as far as implementing measures are concerned. Moving in this direction should be relatively straightforward. Changing the type of remedies will be more difficult. Developing countries can make a strong case that violations of the WTO are disproportionately burdensome for them given the fragility of many of their export industries and the fact that their export base is generally much less diversified than in high income countries. Obtaining compensation for damages can therefore be argued to be more important for developing countries. Provision for granting of compensation for damages could also help offset prevailing resource constraints – legal expertise should be easier to attract, and developing country firms should have a greater incentive to monitor policies and bring cases forward.

Of course, financial compensation for damages incurred will be controversial and opposed by many WTO members. One way to limit the implications might be to restrict the right to demand compensation to countries with a low level of per capita income (such as $1,000). Even then, serious questions will need to be addressed regarding the determination of the appropriate level of compensation. It seems clear that this could easily become a highly contentious matter in itself. It may therefore be preferable not to attempt to mainstream compensation as a remedy. A more practical and less contentious approach to the problem would be to create mechanisms that reduce the need for compensation by: (i) identifying potential violations rapidly; (ii) allowing these to be addressed in a timely fashion; and (iii) at lower cost than is currently the case. One possibility discussed below to achieve these objectives is to outsource and strengthen surveillance and to delegate some of the enforcement task to an independent 'special prosecutor' that has the mandate to defend developing country interests.

c. Outsourcing and Delegating Enforcement

As noted above, the fact that only governments have standing in the WTO may limit the number of cases that are brought, and imposes a relatively greater burden on developing countries. Political realities – asymmetric distribution of power; threats of cross-issue linkages – will always be a powerful force constraining the ability (willingness) of governments to assist national firms defend their rights. This suggests that dispute settlement should be a collective (multilateral) endeavour not only for the reasons emphasised by economists (to increase the power of enforcement threats), but also to reduce the incidence of 'self-censorship.' Although governments cannot be obliged to cooperate to bring joint cases, business and NGOs can play a role in lobbying for joint actions to be brought. The international information collection and analysis body proposed above could help provide a focal point for such efforts.

A more effective mechanism that could be considered to 'multilateralise' DSP would be the creation of an independent 'Special Prosecutor'. This office would be granted the mandate to identify and contest potential WTO violations on behalf of developing countries, using information drawn from private sources – including the information collection mechanism described earlier if this is created – the TPRM, the business and financial press, etc. Such outsourcing of enforcement could help address both the resource constraints and the incentive problems (fear of cross-issue linkage) that may impede developing country governments from pursuing cases. Seeking to move in this direction deserves serious consideration by developing countries as it could substantially increase the probability that developing country interests will be defended. Although cases brought by the special prosecutor could not be backed by the threat of retaliation (as they are not brought by or on behalf of a government), findings against a WTO member would lead to moral pressure to bring measures into conformity. The history of GATT and WTO DSP suggests that this is an important factor in inducing WTO members to abide by the rules of the game.

d. Towards Greater Transparency

Although many NGOs argue that one of the major failings of the WTO is inadequate transparency of its operations, great progress has been made on this front in recent years. The best illustration is the WTO internet home page, which provides access to much of the documentation that is prepared by and submitted to the WTO – documents that under GATT procedures were 'restricted' and not made available to the public. But much more can be done. Much of the data generated by the WTO is not freely available, significantly reducing the transparency role of the WTO. Examples include the Integrated Database (IDB) of protection and trade flows and the reports of the TPRM, neither of which are freely available for downloading through the web. Such outputs are best regarded as public goods that should be distributed free of charge. Attempts at cost recovery by the Secretariat in this area are counterproductive as they greatly restrict the use and dissemination of very useful information (Francois, 1999). Policies that restrict access to data on trade policies and trade flows are also counterproductive, as they impede the ability of think tanks and NGOs to analyse policies.

But there is a need to go beyond greater transparency of WTO processes and outputs. A complementary option that might be considered is the creation of an international public interest body that would act as a forum to explore the likely WTO consistency of contested measures in a process. By making this independent of the WTO, it would allow for direct access by non-governmental bodies. Such a 'parallel track' would allow all interested parties to explore the facts of a case, determine the economic impact of a given situation, and identify more efficient policy options. A parallel transparency body that is independent of the WTO could also help address demands by NGOs that the WTO should be opened up to greater participation by voluntary organisations and the private sector. Most attention in this regard has centred on DSP, with arguments that panel hearings should be open to the public, and that briefs by the parties be made publicly available. Greater transparency of WTO dispute settlement processes would be beneficial, although as noted above, a necessary condition may be professionalisation of panels. But the need for greater transparency extends beyond the downstream dispute settlement process.

A transparency body might help shed light and build consensus by identifying whether there are cross-border spillovers, their size, the economic or environmental impact of policies, including their distributional effects within and across countries, and whether alternative instruments exist that could attain governmental or societal objectives (more) efficiently. Such an entity could be used as a discovery mechanism through which greater understanding could be obtained regarding the effects of national policies on various constituencies and stakeholders, both within and across economies.[6] It could play a constructive role by acting as a focal point for exploring the pros and cons of potential multilateral rules in new areas, and a forum to analyse the economic and development impact of specific policy measures that have been taken by governments, or which are being proposed by WTO members, NGOs, or other stakeholders. The role of such an international entity could extend to being a forum to determine the scientific basis – or lack thereof – of regulatory policies (standards, bio-tech, SPS, etc.). Such policies are rapidly becoming a major source of tension and controversy, and developing countries in particular could benefit from a neutral and objective forum in which standards-related policies and issues are analysed.

In short, a transparency entity could help ensure that the development dimension of current and proposed multilateral rules be considered. As noted by Finger and Schuler (1999), creating mechanisms to assess the relevance of WTO agreements for the process of economic development is urgently needed, and is something that to date has not been done by the WTO. Clearly careful thought needs to be given to the appropriate design and governance of a transparency body. In principle it could be a public-private partnership, including industry associations, the International Chamber of Commerce and NGOs among its members, with part of the funding being generated by public institutions. Of great importance is that it have sufficient funding to perform quality work, and be independent of governments and the WTO. Independence and separation will

---

[6] Hoekman and Mavroidis (1994) have argued that such 'discovery' is perhaps the most useful dimension of GATT non-violation procedures. Although the recent *Fuji-Kodak* case illustrated that the process is valuable in getting the facts on the table for discussion, a stand-alone transparency mechanism that is not directly tied to DSP would be a better approach to achieve this goal.

minimise the extent to which discussions and analysis is influenced by strategic negotiating considerations.

5. CONCLUDING REMARKS

The incentive for governments to negotiate and abide by international trade agreements depends in part on the effectiveness of enforcement provisions. Enforcement is particularly important for developing countries, which will rarely be able to exert credible threats against large trading entities that do not abide by the negotiated rules of the game. In this chapter we have discussed some of the systemic aspects of the enforcement problem. Since the WTO rests on decentralised enforcement of international obligations (the ultimate remedy being an authorisation to adopt bilateral countermeasures), it inherits all of the asymmetries that arise when there are substantial differences in bargaining power. Standard solutions suggested in the economic literature to address this problem include multilateralisation of sanctions and the adoption of remedies that deter transgressions (e.g., compensation). Moving in this direction would benefit developing countries, who are mostly 'small' in terms of the leverage they can exert. However, moves towards multilateral enforcement or compensation are unlikely to prove politically feasible. Progress may be easier in the two other areas discussed in this chapter: enhancing transparency and information, and adopting more efficient and effective DSP procedures. A combination of efforts that focus on these two dimensions of enforcement could significantly improve the incentives for developing countries to participate in WTO DSP and increase their sense of 'ownership' of the institution.

Even in the context of the limited 'traditional' WTO remedies, reputation costs are often an effective mechanism to induce WTO-compatible behaviour. Large traders, if brought to 'court' more frequently by developing countries, may therefore be induced to behave in a more WTO-consistent manner. Increased transparency plays a major role in this connection: better and more timely information about applied policies and the merits of a particular case is a precondition for enforcement. In our view the private sector and voluntary organisations must play a much greater role in collecting and transmitting information on the policies that are applied by WTO members. In part this can be achieved through cooperative mechanisms at the national level that reduce the costs of monitoring. Such national efforts could also be coordinated internationally to identify measures that affect groups of countries.

Efforts can usefully also be made to reduce the costs for developing countries of using WTO DSP. Developing countries are at a disadvantage, given their limited resource base. The introduction of less costly 'light' procedures in cases where the object of the dispute is below a certain threshold may act as an incentive for developing countries to submit more cases by bringing the cost of litigation down and increasing the likelihood of more rapid redress. Providing legal assistance along the lines proposed by a number of WTO members would also be beneficial to developing countries, and the agreement in Seattle to create an ACWL was one of the few positive results to emerge from the meeting. Finally, consideration might be given to the creation of an independent 'Special Prosecutor' that is given the mandate to identify potential violations of WTO commitments by members that are detrimental to developing countries and to initiate dispute settlement proceedings.

A major problem with WTO DSP is that only governments have standing. Although there are compelling reasons why governments should continue to have sole access to DSP – with the exception of the proposed 'special prosecutor' – consideration could be given to establishing mechanisms through which stakeholders can express their voice and explore the economic and social (distributional) implications of policy proposals. One possibility would be for the private sector and NGOs to cooperate in the establishment of a transparency body that would operate in *parallel* to the WTO process. Such an entity might not only help defuse specific disputes through a process of analysis of the facts and the economic development dimensions of cases – outside of the regular WTO mechanisms, thereby allowing non-governmental entities to participate – but also be a forum for discussion and analysis of issues that are not (yet) subject to multilateral disciplines.

REFERENCES

Advisory Centre on WTO Law (1999), Final Proposal Document (www.itd.org).

Croome, J. (1999), *Reshaping the World Trading System: A History of the Uruguay Round* (The Hague: Kluwer Law International).

Davey, W. (1999), 'Improving WTO Dispute Settlement', in J. Bhagwati (ed.), *The Next Trade Negotiating Round: Examining the Agenda for Seattle* (New York: Columbia University Press).

Finger, J.M. and P. Schuler (1999), 'Implementation of Uruguay Round Commitments: The Development Challenge' (mimeo, World Bank, www.worldbank.org/trade).

Francois, J. (1999), 'Maximizing the Benefits of the Trade Policy Review Mechanism for Developing Countries' (mimeo, World Bank www.worldbank.org/trade).

Hoekman, B. and P.C. Mavroidis (1994), 'Competition, Competition Policy and the GATT', *The World Economy*, **17**, 121–50.

Hoekman, B. and P.C. Mavroidis (1996), 'Policy Externalities and High-Tech Rivalry: Competition and Multilateral Cooperation Beyond the WTO', *Leiden Journal of International Law*, **9**, 273–318.

Hoekman, B. and P.C. Mavroidis (1999), 'Enforcing WTO Commitments: Dispute Settlement and Developing Countries' (mimeo).

Horn, H., P.C. Mavroidis and H. Nordström (1999), 'Equity in the WTO Dispute Settlement System: Participation' (mimeo).

Hudec, R. (1987), *Developing Countries in the GATT Legal System* (Aldershot: Gower Press for the Trade Policy Research Centre).

Hudec, R. (1993), *Enforcing International Trade Law* (New Hampshire: Butterworth).

Hudec, R. (1999), 'The Agenda for Reform of the Dispute Settlement Procedure', in J. Bhagwati (ed.), *The Next Trade Negotiating Round: Examining the Agenda for Seattle* (New York: Columbia University Press).

Jackson, J.H. (1999), 'Dispute Settlement and the WTO: Emerging Problems', in J. Bhagwati (ed.), *The Next Trade Negotiating Round: Examining the Agenda for Seattle* (New York: Columbia University Press).

Levy, P. and T.N. Srinivasan (1996), 'Regionalism and the (Dis)advantage of Dispute Settlement Access', *American Economic Review* (Papers and Proceedings, May).

Palmeter, D. and P.C. Mavroidis (1999), *Dispute Settlement in the World Trade Organization: Practice and Procedure* (The Hague: Kluwer Law International).

Schott, J. and J. Buurman (1994), *The Uruguay Round* (Washington DC: Institute of International Economics).

South Centre (1999), 'Issues Regarding the Review of the WTO Dispute Settlement Mechanism', Working Paper No. 1 (February).

Weston, A. and V. Delich (1999), 'Settling Trade Disputes After the Uruguay Round: Options for the Western Hemisphere', Latin American Trade Network Discussion Paper (June, downloadable from 'other WTO 2000 links' on www.worldbank.org/trade).

Whalley, J. (1996), 'Developing Countries and System Strengthening in the Uruguay Round', in W. Martin and L.A. Winters (eds.), *The Uruguay Round and the Developing Countries* (Cambridge: Cambridge University Press).

9

Maximising the Benefits of the Trade Policy Review Mechanism for Developing Countries

Joseph F. Francois

The purpose of the Trade Policy Review Mechanism ('TPRM') is to contribute to improved adherence by all Members to rules, disciplines and commitments made under the Multilateral Trade Agreements and, where applicable, the Plurilateral Trade Agreements, and hence to the smoother functioning of the multilateral trading system, by achieving greater transparency in, and understanding of, the trade policies and practices of Members. (*Marrakesh Agreement Establishing the WTO*, Annex III(A))

There are no statesmen in this business. Trade theory is about identifying whose hand is in whose pocket and trade policy is about who should take it out. (Finger, 1981, n1)

1. INTRODUCTION

THE rights and obligations embodied in the WTO are not limited to tariffs. They also include a set of agreements that limit the scope of non-tariff actions. Adherence to these obligations is also reinforced by procedures for the settlement of disputes and for the regular monitoring of the policies of World Trade Organisation (WTO) Members through the Trade Policy Review Mechanism (TPRM). The TPRM was established (on a provisional basis) in 1989 as a part of the GATT following the December 1988 Montreal Mid-Term Review of the Uruguay Round. It was made a permanent part of the World Trade Organisation (WTO) through Annex 3 of the 1995 Marrakesh Agreement establishing the World Trade Organisation. The stated purpose of the TPRM is enhancement of the transparency and understanding of WTO Members' trade policies (see the quote above). This chapter is concerned with the value of the TPRM, and particularly its promotion of transparency, for developing countries.

When considering the gains from increased stability and transparency of policy regimes under WTO rules (*vis-à-vis* the GATT 1947 system), it is helpful to recall that for much of the postwar period a common characteristic of most developing country trade regimes was their ingenuity in combining policy instability with opacity. In this context, policy bindings can limit the scope for arbitrary increases in protection, and hence have the potential to boost the credibility of policy reforms. The domestic and foreign credibility of trade reforms may also be enhanced by periodic monitoring, such as that undertaken through the TPRM.

This chapter is organised along the following lines – What? Why? and What Next? Section 2 focuses on what the TPRM is. It briefly describes the TPRM mechanism itself. Section 3 then elaborates on why the TPRM may be relevant for developing countries. In particular, what are the benefits of enhanced policy credibility? This is followed, in Section 4, by a discussion of ways in which the TPRM and its byproducts might be made more useful for the design and enhanced credibility of trade policy in developing countries. A summary is contained in Section 5.

2. WHAT IS THE TPRM?

The TPRM was introduced on an interim basis in 1989. It was motivated by concerns that the only available review of global trade policies at the time was one produced by the Office of the US Trade Representative. Logically, this report was viewed as one that was biased towards US interests (see Keesing, 1998, for discussion). Being a US report, it also steered clear of US trade barriers. In its first years, the TPRM was limited to a review of policies affecting trade in goods. However, with the creation of the WTO, which also includes services and intellectual policy commitments, the TPRM was expanded to cover new areas like trade in services and intellectual property rights. The TPRM was moved from interim to permanent status with the creation of the WTO.

The frequency of reviews varies across WTO Members. There are technically three review cycles: every two years for the four largest trading entities (the United States, the European Union, Japan, and Canada); every four years for the next 16 countries; and every six years for other Members. There is nothing sacred in the two-year cycle, and one frequent option raised for stretching the resources devoted to the TPRM is to stretch the review time out for the big 4. Even under the existing schedule, in practice not all Members are reviewed on this cycle. There are provisions for a longer interval for least-developed countries, and the practice has been to review the smaller trading countries only when they request a review. Table 1 provides a list of reviews conducted since 1995.

TABLE 1
TPRM Reports 1995–1999 (including scheduled 1999 reviews)

1999	1997
Argentina	Malaysia
Togo	European Union
Guinea	Mexico
Egypt	Chile
United States of America	Benin
Bolivia	Paraguay
Israel	Cyprus
Philippines	Fiji
Romania	
Nicaragua	**1996**
Papua New Guinea	El Salvador
Thailand	Canada
Togo	United States
Argentina	Brazil
	New Zealand
1998	Korea
Canada	Colombia
Hong Kong, China	Zambia
Indonesia	Norway
Uruguay	Singapore
Burkina Faso and Mali	Switzerland
Trinidad and Tobago	Czech Republic
Jamaica	Dominican Republic
Turkey	Venezuela
The Solomon Islands	Morocco
Hungary	
Australia	**1995**
Nigeria	Thailand
South African Customs Union	Slovak Republic
India	Sri Lanka
Japan	Mauritius
	Uganda
	European Union
	Côte d'Ivoire
	Costa Rica
	Japan
	Pakistan
	Cameroon

The TPRM reports are prepared by the WTO's Trade Policies Review Division (the TPRD). This Division, at full strength, consists of only one Director, 16 professional and 11 support staff. The approach of the TPRM is therefore very different from country monitoring by the World Bank and the IMF. Where the Bank and IMF, comparatively speaking, have armies of analysts following national policy developments, the WTO works on a relative shoe-string budget. Yet even these resources are under constant pressure, as the mission of the WTO has expanded greatly *vis-à-vis* the old GATT 1947 without a comparable expansion of resources.

There is a constant struggle within the WTO Secretariat to move scarce staffing positions across divisions. Hence, though the TPRM seems understaffed given its mission, the TPRM is actually the largest division in the small WTO Secretariat, and there is a constant and real danger that economist slots within the division will be liquidated to make way for more lawyers within the organisation. For this reason, any discussion of changes to the TPRM, even cosmetic ones, immediately raise questions about resources and the possibility of outside assistance.

The TPRD writes its reports on the basis of Member replies to a questionnaire, discussions with officials during mission visits, and information collected from other (unofficial) sources. The entire process usually takes about ten months. While the TPRM reports draw on academic research, they have also generated occasional reviews of national policy within the academic press. This includes 'reviews' of the reviews published in the journal *World Economy*. (See for example Anderson, 1995; Balasubramanyam, 1995; Fane, 1996; Gunning, 1996; Holden, 1995; Kehoe, 1995; Krenin, 1996; Krueger, 1995; Pelkmans and Carzaninga, 1996; Qureshi, 1995; Togan, 1995; and Wonnacott, 1996.)

3. WHY THE TPRM?

a. Policy Credibility in Developing Countries

What are the benefits of the TPRM for developing countries? Two sets of potential benefits are emphasised in this section. Both involve reduction in policy uncertainty. The first relates to improved monitoring of trading partner commitments under the various WTO agreements. In particular, this involves added insurance that the larger export markets (i.e. the OECD) will meet their commitments regarding market access for developing countries. The second set of reasons relates to the credibility of domestic policy reform and to how such reform is viewed by domestic and international investors.

For the reasons outlined in this section, we should view a truly effective TPRM as one that, when applied to trading partners, contributes to political support for trade reform at home, to the general orientation of the economy toward tradable activities, and to investor confidence. However, for developing countries to benefit, they must actively engage themselves in the TPRM process, pressing their own interests not just with regard to OECD markets, but also with regard to the trade policies of other developing countries. An effective TPRM should also serve to reinforce the credibility and rationality of home policies regarding the domestic and international economy. Improvements that may move us closer to such a regime are discussed in Section 4.

b. Market Access in Export Markets

As trade economists, we often emphasise import protection when writing on trade policy However, political emphasis during negotiations is not placed on home protection. Rather it is placed on protection in export markets. Improved market access, which to exporters means more restrictive bindings on protection in export markets, is the price demanded by governments for own-liberalisation. This follows, in part, from the willingness of individual exporters to back initiatives that involve improved access to their export markets.[1]

While improved market access is an important precondition for political support for liberalisation at home, there are other effects that follow from improved market access conditions in export markets. Reduced uncertainty about trading conditions in export markets has significant welfare implications for the economy as a whole. Francois and Martin (1997) offer a formalisation of this point. Uncertainty about the terms-of-trade depresses the expected level of national income. Such uncertainty can follow directly from trade policy in export markets. Beyond this, such uncertainty also provides incentives for investors to shy away from tradable sectors. Wincoop (1992) for example, offers econometric evidence that increased terms-of-trade uncertainty leads to a higher fraction of national resources (employment and capital) being placed in the non-tradables sector. In effect, uncertainty about the general conditions of market access (i.e. the terms-of-trade) acts as a tax on the tradables sector of the economy. It hits both import competing and export sectors. It also serves to dampen investment. Mendoza (1997) for example offers both theoretical arguments and econometric evidence supporting the assertion that terms-of-trade uncertainty implies significant macroeconomic costs, manifested as lower investment and growth rates.

A very real source of market access uncertainty involves contingent protection. Uncertainty (and hence intertemporal variability) in the rate of protection can be particularly marked in import monitoring and administered protection regimes such as those imposed where dumping is alleged. In this regard, Winters (1994) finds that import surveillance, in the case of the European Union, has a significant dampening effect on trade. Tollefsen (1994) notes that, as a group, VERs and monitoring mechanisms are the most common form of non-tariff barrier (NTB) protection applied in the industrial countries. Both are a common outcome of threatened or suspended anti-dumping and countervailing duty actions. Boltuck et al. (1990) make a similar point with regard to the US anti-dumping mechanism,

---

[1] If one believes that own-liberalisation is an important source of welfare gains, then the GATT/WTO can be viewed as a very successful trick. By pressing for mutual liberalisation in export markets, Member countries are actually, on net, acting as if they were jointly pursuing import liberalisation (as one's imports are another's exports). Therefore, own liberalisation is pressed by the harnessing of mercantilist interests.

where the system of posted duty bonds, estimated duties, and administrative reviews adds considerable price uncertainty to importers of good subject to anti-dumping reviews. With the spread of anti-dumping regimes to the developing countries themselves (a spread aided by technical assistance from the WTO, World Bank, and European Union), developing countries will encounter difficulties in this area in coming years as they try to gain access to other developing country markets.

The TPRM, by subjecting the largest OECD markets to periodic review, shifts the balance of power in the WTO, ever so slightly, in favour of the developing countries. It ensures that the trade policy practices of the industrial countries are subjected to periodic, public peer review. While the TPRM is not charged with passing judgement on the compliance of Members with WTO obligations, it plays an important transparency role. For example, it makes it easier for the developing countries to point collectively to the use of dumping duties by the European Union and the United States against developing countries. Perhaps equally important, the TPRM also subjects the developing countries themselves to a review of market access conditions. Since some of the most dynamic export markets (recent crises notwithstanding) over the next two decades will be found outside the OECD, reduced uncertainty about market access in developing country markets is going to be increasingly important for developing countries themselves. (See Blackhurst et al., 1995, for a discussion of the importance of developing country market access to other developing country markets.)

c. The TPRM and the Credibility of Domestic Reform

The movement, starting in the mid 1980s, to market based policies in developing countries has served to highlight the importance of political economy constraints in the economic reform process. As North (1990) has emphasised, not all stable policy regimes are characterised by good practice. In fact, through most of history, and across most of the world, regimes conducive to stagnation and decline have been remarkably tenacious and even robust. The recent experiences with capital market crises in Brazil and Russia have served to remind us of this reality. Politics can conspire (often with apparent ease) to stymie well-intentioned reform efforts.

Membership in the WTO involves commercial policy commitments (technically called commercial policy 'bindings'). Because policy reform undertaken in the context of binding external commitments involves restraints on backsliding, it may carry more credibility than otherwise (Francois, 1997). Periodic reviews under the TPR mechanism can serve to remind capital markets of this fact, enhancing the expected durability of domestic reforms and the extent to which such reforms are 'locked-in' under external obligations.

The net result under such a situation would be a reduction in policy uncertainty. As recent research (discussed above) suggests, the reduction of policy uncertainty in this way may have important positive implications for investor confidence.

d. The Advantages of Boosting Investor Confidence

From a developing country perspective, an effective TPRM should have two outcomes. The first is that it should boost the security of market access in export markets. At the same time, it should also boost credibility of domestic policy and policy reform. Taken together, both in turn should serve to boost investor confidence and reduce country risk.

What are the likely investment-related benefits of a fall in country risk? They relate to dynamic mechanisms that have been examined in the context of simulation analysis by Kehoe (1998) and Young and Romero (1994) for Mexico, and Baldwin et al. (1997) for the Central and East European Countries (CEECs). Francois (1997) and Francois and Martin (1998) focus more broadly on developing countries.

In general, the conditions for international capital lending reflect a number of factors, including risk of nationalisation, and the security provided by outside obligations (i.e. the Mexican GATT accession in 1986 and the NAFTA, or CEEC obligations as part of their efforts to join the EU). As elements are added to the climate that reduce the underlying risk premium, investors are willing to accept projects that yield lower returns. The result is an increase in investment levels, and hence a national income gain from the reduced risk premium. This is related to expanded production and rising labour productivity and wages. Arguably, this effect may be one of the most important medium- to long-run effects of anchoring investment-related external policy reforms.

How important are such effects? First, we know from Wincoop (1992) and Mendoza (1997) that trade-related uncertainty is associated with lower investment and growth rates and with a shift in resources toward non-tradables. In addition, we also know that riskier policy regimes are directly associated with higher capital costs. As a result, rates of return on capital differ sharply across nations. Such differences can be very persistent. Put simply, investors demand a risk premium on funds invested in nations with economic and/or political environments that are perceived as unstable.

One view on these costs, offered by Baldwin et al. (1997), involves the cross-country comparison of international lending terms. Such a comparison is provided in Figure 1. The figure plots, on the horizontal axis, World Bank estimates of the basis point spread charged to emerging economies for dollar-denominated fixed rate issues in 1994–95 (World Debt Tables, 1996 Extracts, World Bank 1996). The vertical axis plots country risk indexes (from the

FIGURE 1
Risk and Return in Emerging Markets 1994–95

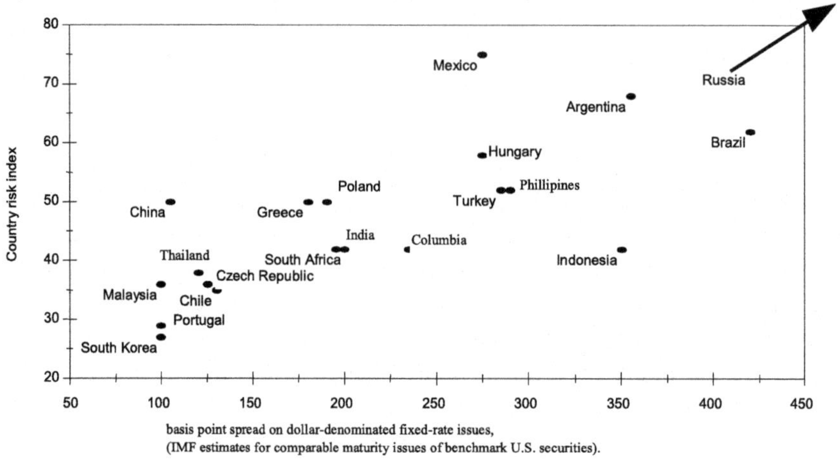

basis point spread on dollar-denominated fixed-rate issues,
(IMF estimates for comparable maturity issues of benchmark U.S. securities).

Economist Intelligence Unit) for 1995. (Russia is off the charts on both axes.) It can be seen that country risk does correlate closely with rates of return. 'Safe' markets, from the point of view of investors, enjoy a significant advantage in capital markets.

4. SOME RECOMMENDATIONS

Since the inception of the TPRM, several authors have examined the process itself and made recommendations for improvement. One of the more detailed overviews is provided by Keesing (1998). Keesing makes several sets of recommendations. One general recommendation relates to improved dissemination of the existing reports through the economics and business press. However, this is tied to a comment that:

the (WTO) External Relations Division ... does not yet try to use the TPRs systematically to influence policymakers in the member countries and beyond (Keesing, 1998, p. 46).

This leads us to a second set of recommendations made by Keesing (and other authors), that the TPRM should be used as a more proactive mechanism by the WTO. This includes the targeting of opinion leaders in Member countries, and the use of the mechanism to highlight the cost of protection. It also includes subjective comments on policy credibility and sustainability as well.

The view of this author is that the TPRM plays a very important role, but one misunderstood by those who recommend that the TPRM be more proscriptive.[2] In particular, the TPRM is at its heart a vehicle for providing information. It was not meant to be used for policy recommendations. The WTO Members said as much when stating, in Annex 3 of the Uruguay Round Agreements defining the TPRM (see the Appendix) that the TPRM 'is not ... intended to serve as a basis for the enforcement of specific obligations under the Agreements or for dispute settlement procedures, or to impose new policy commitments on Members.'

The value of the TPRM reporting process lies in the strong (and correct) belief that the report is purely positive, rather than normative. It focuses on accurate information valuable to the global trade policy community. This alone is an important task. The information that results is taken seriously precisely because the TPRD does not expressly set out to make pronouncements on the merits of the policies they describe. TPRM reports describe the policy landscape, exposing it to the daylight for the Members, their leaders, the business press, academia, and the electorate themselves to inspect, evaluate, and discuss. In the process, they also summarise external views on these policies.

The information role of the TPR is important, for the reasons outlined above. The availability of comparable data across countries places the developing countries on a more equal footing during trade negotiations. It also serves to keep trade policy a relatively open process, important for the democratic setting of policy. In the poorer countries, it provides an otherwise impossible chance to examine the overall trade policy implications of otherwise disjoint policy decisions. Within this pure informational role, there is indeed scope for improving the value of the TPRM to developing countries. Potential improvements are listed in Table 2. They are discussed below. They are grouped into three broad categories: (1) data extension; (2) data dissemination; and (3) follow-up.

a. Data Issues

A substantial amount of useful data is collected as part of the TPR process. This includes current tariff schedules, recent changes in tariff schedules, other price and quantity measures affecting exports, and information on the structure of the economy itself.[3] This is all tied into a discussion of the recent evolution of trade policy in the country, and the general national policy context in which these changes have taken place. Without substantially changing the data collection requirements, some changes could be introduced that would enhance the information value of these efforts. These are discussed below. They are tied to a related recommendation (further below) that the resulting information be disseminated more widely.

---

[2] In all fairness to the authors cited, they were writing before the debacle in Seattle. We should emphasise the role of the TPRM as a source of information. Using it to make the WTO Secretariat more proscriptive would only fuel the suspicions of Seattle men about the organisation.
[3] Keesing (1998) provides a good discussion of the process.

TABLE 2
Recommendations for Improving the Value of the TRPM

---

1. Data Issues

  1.1   Add the tariff data collected as part of the TPRM to the integrated database.
  1.2   Maintain a detailed, TPRM-based time-series database of protection data, linked to trade
        and production data.
  1.3   Use the periodic TPRM reports as an opportunity to construct a 'quantitative' database
        that draws on other notifications under various WTO bodies.

2. Dissemination

  2.1   Distribute the full TRPM reports, at no cost, on the WTO WWW site.
  2.2   Distribute detailed protection data, at no cost, on the WTO WWW site.

3. Follow-up

  3.1   Integrate detailed TPRM data into TRAINS and SMART.
  3.2   Integrate protection data collected during the TPRM into the GTAP database.
  3.3   Provide follow-up technical assistance to local stake-holders.

- *Add the tariff data collected as part of the TPR to the integrated database.*
  The integrated database (IDB) is a computerised database of applied and
  bound tariff rates, maintained by the WTO Secretariat and available to
  participating Members for consultation during negotiations. The participation by the least developing countries in the IDB is limited by the resource
  constraints they face. (Developing countries must first supply the data that is
  then placed into the IDB.) The IDB was critical to quantitative assessment
  of the Uruguay Round (see, for example, the studies in Martin and Winters,
  1995), and will play a similar role in the next Round. In theory, the tariff
  data relevant for the IDB are also collected as part of the TPRM process.
  Especially for the least developed countries, this seems like an ideal
  opportunity to kill two birds with one stone. Unfortunately this is not
  feasible given current against resource constraints within the TPRM
  Division itself. However, one could easily justify spending some of the
  development assistance funds provided by developed WTO Members to this
  integration of the TPRM with efforts to augment the IDB.[4]
- *Maintain a detailed, TPRM-based time series database of protection data,
  linked to trade and production data.* The TPRM provides a unique
  opportunity to build a global time series on levels of protection in Member
  countries. National tariff schedules must be processed anyway so that
  descriptive statistics can be produced. There has been some effort within the
  WTO Secretariat to produce a limited amount of time series data from past
  TPRM reports. However, because the detailed data on individual TPRM

---

[4] This has been done on occasion in the recent past. A general policy in this direction would serve to
keep the developing country coverage in the IDB relatively broad and current.

reports are not joined into a detailed *collective* database, and in fact are often set aside and eventually 'lost' as analysts move on to the next review, a tremendous opportunity is lost. At the moment, historic series can only be produced based on the summary data published in tabular form in the reports. More effort should go into producing a time series out of the raw data. Such data could be used not just for more detailed discussion of individual countries across time, but also for more detailed sectoral discussion across countries. Obviously, there is scope to integrate such an effort with enhancement of the IDB, as discussed above. Such data (perhaps using GTAP or comparable data) should also be linked within the database to available information on the structure of production.

- *Use the periodic TPRM reports as an opportunity to construct a 'quantitative' database that draws on other notifications under various WTO bodies.* There are a number of bodies within the WTO that have reporting requirements. For example, members are required to report on implementation of Uruguay Round Agreements, anti-dumping and counter-vailing actions. Relational databases of these notifications are in some cases maintained within the WTO Secretariat. However, these are generally legal in nature (as are the notifications themselves). For the delegations from the least developed countries, there is no hope of wading through these notifications to find the big picture. The resources simply are not available.[5] The closest they come is background material prepared by the WTO Secretariat. The periodic TPRM reviews provide an opportunity to marry these notifications with economic data, and to integrate them into a general database on protection measures.[6] This should not be controversial. In theory, Member notifications are made precisely to promote transparency across Members (and presumably to generally promote the transparency of the whole WTO *vis-à-vis* non-governmental organisations and citizens in Member states). Such an approach would simply make the notifications more accessible. Those Members that never submit notifications could continue to do so. This would simply show up as holes in the data that might, on occasion, be filled during a TPR.

---

[5] In fact, many of the least developing countries do not even have a WTO Mission, or else have a small mission tasked with covering all international organisations in Geneva. This disparity with developed countries can be particularly striking. For example, during the Uruguay Round the US steel industry had better representation than many of the least developing countries (combined).

[6] As an example, governments notify their dumping and countervailing duty actions every six months. These notifications can be downloaded from the WTO web site (with a time lag). Unfortunately, the notifications are very aggregated. Hence, they may tell you that flat-rolled steel from Korea is subject to a US dumping duty. They do not tell you the information needed to assess the economic impact and the implications for market access (matching duties with affected trade flows, for example), or the fact that these duties replaced voluntary export restraints.

b. Dissemination

The next area where the process can be improved is through dissemination. The TPRM reports are a basic tool for promoting transparency in the global trading system. Unfortunately, there is an emphasis on cost recovery for what should be viewed as a public good. This cost-recovery model should be replaced by one targeting low-cost but broad dissemination.

- *Distribute the full TPRM reports, at no cost, on the WTO WWW site.* The Members should recognise the reports for what they are (public goods), and move toward full free electronic dissemination. The IMF has taken a similar tack on its web site with many of its reports. National government agencies, like the US International Trade Commission, follow a similar tack as well. The WTO recovers only limited costs (and perhaps none on net) from charging for these reports. The policy of only making current reports available in hard copy limits public access. (Keesing reports that typical production runs for the English version of a report are 900 to 1000 copies. Most of these remain in Geneva.) Certainly, this limits access by potential users in academia, local research institutions, and the local press within developing countries. This in turn limits penetration into the community of local stake-holders. The WTO has itself taken a step to correct this problem. Several years of past TPRM reports are now available on CD-ROM. While distribution of CDs and hard copies should perhaps continue on a commercial basis, the historic reports from the CD, and new ones as they are made available, should be posted publicly on the internet as well. This is an obvious low-cost form of general distribution. If some Members object to a departure from 'cost-recovery,' then technical assistance money should be devoted to underwriting this effort.
- *Distribute detailed protection data, at no cost, on the WTO WWW site.* Electronic dissemination should extend beyond the current report. The underlying data, enhanced as described above, should also be disseminated on the internet. This would allow for public interest groups in Member countries to access protection information directly. Unfortunately, there are Members who do not want the public to have access to their tariff schedules. This has so far effectively blocked public access to the IDB.[7] However, at least for Members who have undergone a TPR, the cat is already out of the bag and in print. In addition, some regional organisations have already published tariff rates for their members. For example, one can find tariff rates for MERCOSUR members and APEC members on the internet. The

---

[7] Efforts to assess the Uruguay Round were caught in an elaborate dance between Members who, on the one hand wanted an assessment, and on the other hand did not want the public to know the exact terms of what was being assessed.

European Commission also makes tariff rates for selected trading partners available on the internet. The TPR is a logical mechanism for collecting such information globally, and making it available to the citizens of the global village. This should be combined with information on bindings, so that the public (especially the business and financial communities) can make more informed assessments of the scope for commercial policy backsliding in various areas. Ideally, such a public access database would include:

- tariff rates
- tariff bindings
- current and past anti-dumping and countervailing duty actions and suspension agreements
- affected trade flows under these various measures
- notifications by members of preferential arrangements
- commitments made under the GATS.

Such a database should allow for the wholesale download of relevant data (rather than the tariff-line-by-tariff-line approach of the legally-focused relational databases). Such an approach is consistent with the electronic distribution of data by some national governments, like price and wage data published electronically by the US Bureau of Labor Statistics on the internet. Like the TPRM reports, governments need to recognise the public good aspect of such a data product. For many developing countries, this may be the most cost effective way to consistently make available the information needed for active participation in trade negotiations with industrial countries. It is also an effective way to subsidise research on the trade policies of developing countries.

c. Follow-up

Finally the value of the process would be greatly enhanced if there was a more explicit link between the final product of the TPRM and work by related international agencies and consortiums.

- *Integrate detailed TPRM data into TRAINS and SMART.* UNCTAD produces a CD-ROM that provides a detailed overview of protection and trade. There is obvious scope for the UNCTAD TRAINS team to work directly with the detailed information produced by the TPR Division *after the report has been completed* (cost-sharing might even be worked out) to ensure that the detailed information collected during the TPRM process is included in the TRAINS dataset. Similarly, there may be scope for a formal arrangement for incorporating the same data in the World Bank's WITS system for trade policy analysis. (Past cooperation efforts between the World Bank and the WTO on the IDB have been problematic.)

- *Integrate protection data collected during the TPRM into the GTAP database.* In addition to TRAINS and the World Bank WITS system, there is the GTAP consortium. The GTAP consortium includes the WTO, the World Bank, the European Commission, and the OECD. Its purpose is to produce a globally consistent database on trade, production, and protection data. This dataset has emerged in recent years as a functional core for quantitative modelling of regional and multilateral trade agreements. Especially on the developing country side, the detailed TPRM-related data on protection should be made available to the GTAP consortium. This would help ensure that the GTAP dataset has adequate *accurate* coverage of developing WTO Members.

- *Provide follow-up technical assistance to local stake-holders.* As a follow-up to the entire TPRM process, development assistance should be directed toward working with the less developed WTO Members after a TPRM report has been completed. This would not be part of the TPRM itself. Rather, a formal institutional mechanism should be established, whereby technical assistance should be provided to Member governments through the WTO (perhaps jointly with similar efforts by UNCTAD) *upon request* to help them use the detailed data produced to make their own assessment based on the data collected. On one extreme, this may simply involve help in simply disseminating the economic content of the report across the local research and policy community. Alternatively, it may involve formal quantitative research. Obviously, this is beyond the scope of the TPRM itself. At the same time, it is a logical next step with the information produced.

5. SUMMARY

This chapter is concerned with the Trade Policy Review Mechanism (TPRM), the policy review function of the World Trade Organisation (WTO). The TPRM was established (on a provisional basis) in 1989 as a part of the GATT following the December 1988 Montreal Mid-Term Review of the Uruguay Round. It was made a permanent part of the World Trade Organisation (WTO) through Annex 3 of the 1995 Marrakesh Agreement establishing the World Trade Organisation. The stated purpose of the TPRM is enhancement of the transparency and understanding of WTO Members' trade policies.

From a developing country perspective, a truly effective TPRM should accomplish several interrelated goals. By promoting transparency of trading partner policies (developed and developing) it should contribute to political support for trade reform at home and to the general orientation of the economy toward tradable activities. It should also serve to reinforce the credibility and rationality of home policies regarding the domestic and international economy. Taken together, all these should add up to a boost to investor confidence in developing country markets.

Several improvements that may move us closer to such a regime are discussed. These include better organisation and retention of the data already collected as part of the TPRM process, better dissemination of the information collected as part of the TPRM process, and technical assistance in the use of this information. Such technical assistance should target local stake-holders, and promote their use of the information collected to inform and guide the local policy process.

APPENDIX

Annex 3 to the Marrakesh Agreements

TRADE POLICY REVIEW MECHANISM

Members hereby *agree* as follows:

A. *Objectives*

(i) The purpose of the Trade Policy Review Mechanism ('TPRM') is to contribute to improved adherence by all Members to rules, disciplines and commitments made under the Multilateral Trade Agreements and, where applicable, the Plurilateral Trade Agreements, and hence to the smoother functioning of the multilateral trading system, by achieving greater transparency in, and under-standing of, the trade policies and practices of Members. Accordingly, the review mechanism enables the regular collective appreciation and evaluation of the full range of individual Members' trade policies and practices and their impact on the functioning of the multilateral trading system. It is not, however, intended to serve as a basis for the enforcement of specific obligations under the Agreements or for dispute settlement procedures, or to impose new policy commitments on Members.

(ii) The assessment carried out under the review mechanism takes place, to the extent relevant, against the background of the wider economic and developmental needs, policies and objectives of the Member concerned, as well as of its external environment. However, the function of the review mechanism is to examine the impact of a Member's trade policies and practices on the multilateral trading system.

B. *Domestic Transparency*

Members recognise the inherent value of domestic transparency of government decision-making on trade policy matters for both Members' economies and the multilateral trading system, and agree to encourage and promote greater transparency within their own systems, acknowledging that the implementation of domestic transparency must be on a voluntary basis and take account of each Member's legal and political systems.

C. *Procedures for Review*

(i) The Trade Policy Review Body (referred to herein as the 'TPRB') is hereby established to carry out trade policy reviews.

(ii) The trade policies and practices of all Members shall be subject to periodic review. The impact of individual Members on the functioning of the multilateral trading system, defined in terms of their share of world trade in a recent representative period, will be the determining factor in deciding on the frequency of reviews. The first four trading entities so identified (counting the European Communities as one) shall be subject to review every two years. The next 16 shall be reviewed every four years. Other Members shall be reviewed every six years, except that a longer period may be fixed for least-developed country Members. It is understood that the review of entities having a common external policy covering more than one Member shall cover all components of policy affecting trade including relevant policies and practices of the individual Members. Exceptionally, in the event of changes in a Member's trade policies or practices that may have a significant impact on its trading partners, the Member concerned may be requested by the TPRB, after consultation, to bring forward its next review.

(iii) Discussions in the meetings of the TPRB shall be governed by the objectives set forth in paragraph A. The focus of these discussions shall be on the Member's trade policies and practices, which are the subject of the assessment under the review mechanism.

(iv) The TPRB shall establish a basic plan for the conduct of the reviews. It may also discuss and take note of update reports from Members. The TPRB shall establish a programme of reviews for each year in consultation with the Members directly concerned. In consultation with the Member or Members under review, the Chairman may choose discussants who, acting in their personal capacity, shall introduce the discussions in the TPRB.

(v) The TPRB shall base its work on the following documentation:

(a) a full report, referred to in paragraph D, supplied by the Member or Members under review;

(b) a report, to be drawn up by the Secretariat on its own responsibility, based on the information available to it and that provided by the Member or Members concerned. The Secretariat should seek clarification from the Member or Members concerned of their trade policies and practices.

(vi) The reports by the Member under review and by the Secretariat, together with the minutes of the respective meeting of the TPRB, shall be published promptly after the review.

(vii) These documents will be forwarded to the Ministerial Conference, which shall take note of them.

D. *Reporting*

In order to achieve the fullest possible degree of transparency, each Member shall report regularly to the TPRB. Full reports shall describe the trade policies and practices pursued by the Member or Members concerned, based on an agreed format to be decided upon by the TPRB. This format shall initially be based on the Outline Format for Country Reports established by the Decision of 19 July, 1989 (BISD 36S/406-409), amended as necessary to extend the coverage of reports to all aspects of trade policies covered by the Multilateral Trade Agreements in Annex 1 and, where applicable, the Plurilateral Trade Agreements. This format may be revised by the TPRB in the light of experience. Between reviews, Members shall provide brief reports when there are any significant changes in their trade policies; an annual update of statistical information will be provided according to the agreed format. Particular account shall be taken of difficulties presented to least-developed country Members in compiling their reports. The Secretariat shall make available technical assistance on request to developing country Members, and in particular to the least-developed country Members. Information contained in reports should to the greatest extent possible be coordinated with notifications made under provisions of the Multilateral Trade Agreements and, where applicable, the Plurilateral Trade Agreements.

E. *Relationship with the Balance-of-Payments Provisions of GATT 1994 and GATS*

Members recognise the need to minimise the burden for governments also subject to full consultations under the balance-of-payments provisions of GATT 1994 or GATS. To this end, the Chairman of the TPRB shall, in consultation with the

Member or Members concerned, and with the Chairman of the Committee on Balance-of-Payments Restrictions, devise administrative arrangements that harmonise the normal rhythm of the trade policy reviews with the timetable for balance-of-payments consultations but do not postpone the trade policy review by more than 12 months.

F. *Appraisal of the Mechanism*

The TPRB shall undertake an appraisal of the operation of the TPRM not more than five years after the entry into force of the Agreement Establishing the WTO. The results of the appraisal will be presented to the Ministerial Conference. It may subsequently undertake appraisals of the TPRM at intervals to be determined by it or as requested by the Ministerial Conference.

G. *Overview of Developments in the International Trading Environment*

An annual overview of developments in the international trading environment which are having an impact on the multilateral trading system shall also be undertaken by the TPRB. The overview is to be assisted by an annual report by the Director-General setting out major activities of the WTO and highlighting significant policy issues affecting the trading system.

REFERENCES

Anderson, K. (1995), 'The GATT's Review of Australian Trade Policy,' *The World Economy: Global Trade Policy 1995*.

Balasubramanyam, V.N. (1995), 'India's Trade Policy Review,' *The World Economy: Global Trade Policy 1995*.

Baldwin, R.E., J.F. Francois and R. Portes (1997), 'The Costs and Benefits of Eastern Enlargement: The Impact on the EU and Central Europe,' *Economic Policy: A European Forum*; 0, 24, (April), 125–70.

Blackhurst, R., A. Enders and J.F. Francois, (1996) 'The Uruguay Round and Market Access: Opportunities and Challenges for Developing Countries,' in W. Martin and A Winters, (eds.), *The Uruguay Round and Developing Countries* (Cambridge University Press).

Boltuck, R., J.F. Francois and Kaplan, S. (1990), 'The Economic Implications of the Administration of the U.S. Unfair Trade Laws.' in R. Boltuck and R. Litan (eds.), *Down in the Dumps*, (Brookings: Washington DC).

Fane, G. (1996), 'Indonesia', *The World Economy: Global Trade Policy 1996*.

Finger, J.M. (1981), 'Policy Research,' *Journal of Political Economy*, 89, 1270–72.

Francois, J.F. (1997), 'External Bindings and the Credibility of Reform,' in A. Galal and B. Hoekman (eds.), *Regional Partners in Global Markets* (London: Centre for Economic Policy Research).

Francois, J.F. and W. Martin (1998), 'Commercial Policy Uncertainty, the Expected Cost of Protection, and Market Access,' Tinbergen Institute working paper (May).

Gunning, J. (1996), 'Zimbabwe', *The World Economy: Global Trade Policy 1996*.

Holden, M. (1995), 'GATT Trade Policy Review – South Africa: 1993,' *The World Economy:*

Global Trade Policy 1995.

Keesing, D.B. (1998), *Improving Trade Policy Reviews in the World Trade Organization* (Institute for International Economics: Washington).

Kehoe, T. (1995), 'A Review of Mexico's Trade Policy from 1982 to 1994,' *The World Economy: Global Trade Policy 1995.*

Kehoe, T. (1998), 'Capital Flows and North American Economic Integration,' in J. Francois and R. Baldwin (eds.), *Dynamic Issues in Commercial Policy Analysis* (CEPR and Cambridge University Press, Cambridge).

Krenin, M. (1996), 'Israel', *The World Economy: Global Trade Policy 1996.*

Krueger, A. (1995), 'U.S. Trade Policy and the GATT Review,' *The World Economy: Global Trade Policy 1995.*

Mendoza, E.G. (1997), 'Terms-of-Trade Uncertainty and Economic Growth,' *Journal of Development Economics*, **54**, 2, 323–56.

North, D. (1990), *Institutions, Institutional Change, and Economic Performance* (Cambridge: Cambridge University Press).

Pelkmans, J. and A. Carzaniga (1996) 'The European Community', *The World Economy: Global Trade Policy 1996.*

Qureshi, A.H. (1995), 'Some Lessons from 'Developing' Countries' Trade Policy Reviews in the GATT Framework: An Enforcement Perspective', *The World Economy*, **18**, 3, 489–503.

Togan, S. (1995), 'Trade Policy Review of the Republic of Turkey,' *The World Economy: Global Trade Policy 1995.*

Tollefsen, T.C. (1994), 'An Analysis of Barriers to Trade and Implementation of NTBs in the Haaland/Norman CGE Model,' Working Paper no. 13/1994 (Foundation for Research in Economics and Business Administration, Norwegian School of Economics and Business Administration, January).

van-Wincoop, E. (1992), 'Terms of Trade Uncertainty, Savings, and the Production Structure,' *Journal of International Economics*, **33**, 3–4, 305–25.

Winters, L.A. (1994), 'Import Surveillance as a Strategic Trade Policy.' in P. Krugman and A. Smith (eds.), *Empirical Studies of Strategic Trade Policy* (University of Chicago Press: Chicago).

Wonnacott, R. (1996), 'Canada', *The World Economy: Global Trade Policy 1996.*

Young, L. and R. Romero (1994), 'A Dynamic Dual Model of the North American Free Trade Agreement,' in J. Francois and C. Shiells (eds.), *Modeling Trade Policy: Applied General Equilibrium Assessments of North American Free Trade* (Cambridge: Cambridge University Press).

10

Industrial Policy and the WTO

Bijit Bora, Peter J. Lloyd and Mari Pangestu

1. INTRODUCTION

𝕬 PPROACHES and thinking on how to achieve rapid structural change and economic growth have ranged from inward-looking, import substitution industrialisation behind high protection to outward-oriented, export promotion strategies considered to be part of the success story of East Asia. Although results on the value of interventions and their outcomes are mixed, a plethora of studies show that industrialisation behind protective walls often extends beyond reasonable periods of 'infancy,' have led to efficiency and welfare losses, and entrenched vested interests. Despite the strong theoretical case against activist industrial policy, it is still pursued widely in a number of countries.[1]

In the 1990s, however, rapid technological change, shorter product cycles, and developments in information technology have combined with privatisation, trade and foreign investment liberalisation to produce a distinctly different global economy. In this context, developing countries are striving to ensure that their industries are competitive by using industrial policy to promote particular sectors to their perceived advantage. The term industrial policy is not well-defined. A useful working definition is 'government efforts to alter industrial structure to promote productivity based growth,'[2] suggesting the objective should be economy-wide factor productivity growth rather than merely changing the structure of industrial outputs. However, in most cases industrial policy has multiple objectives, including short-term employment, increased output, better

---

[1] Korea, Taiwan Province of China and Japan are three examples where government intervention in the form of activist policies was important for the pace and direction of development (Lall, 1994; Asian Development Bank, 1999, pp. 208–10). This intervention, however, was not confined to protection. It included aspects of targeted technological promotion and skill development. In an effort to replicate this success many developing countries have taken the position that they too should be allowed to pursue such policies and not be restricted by multilateral rules.
[2] World Bank (1992). Martin and Mitra (forthcoming) show that the productivity growth rate in agriculture is higher than in manufacturing both on average and for groups of countries at different stages of development.

distribution and enhancing technological capacity. There are often also, rightly or wrongly, non-economic objectives of national pride and prestige, as well as the perceived need to promote 'strategic' domestic industries. These objectives are further confused to the extent that many developing countries take the view that foreign ownership may not always fit in with broader development objectives including enhancing domestic capabilities (UNCTAD, 1999a). That is, growth in per capita GDP based on domestic assets seems to be preferred to growth based on foreign assets. Some countries may be prepared to trade off a lower growth rate with lower foreign ownership against a higher rate of growth with more foreign ownership.

The focus of 'industries' almost invariably seems to be on the manufacturing sector. This leaves out agriculture and mining, and services. Restricting the discussion to manufacturing industries alone discriminates against non-manufacturing industries and leads to inefficiencies in the production allocation of the economy. In this chapter, industrial policy is not restricted by sector.

The traditional instruments of industrial policy have been tariffs and subsidies to industries, aimed at rectifying alleged market failures (Lall, 1994) and directing resources into certain sectors considered more conducive to development. Recently, more attention has been devoted to factor markets, especially foreign direct investments (FDI). Here the belief is that FDI is a bundle of assets which can contribute to growth, but that the use of these assets by affiliates of transnational corporations (TNCs) can also hinder a country's development efforts. Government intervention is then called for to control the negative effects of operations of foreign affiliates (UNCTAD, 1999b).

This chapter reviews the objectives and instruments of industrial policy in the context of a changing global environment and multilateral disciplines. We start with an analytical review of the justification for industrial policy to provide a benchmark against which objectives, instruments and outcomes can be measured. The focus then turns to the theoretical and applied aspects of industrial policy, followed by a survey of the extent to which WTO rules affect a member's ability to pursue industrial policy objectives and the possibilities and implications of revising these rules.

2. THEORY OF INDUSTRIAL POLICY

The traditional infant industry argument, based on the existence of some dynamic externality, continues to lurk behind most advocacy of industrial policy. Kemp (1964) provides the first careful statement of the argument. He identified learning processes such as worker learning by doing or on-the-job training as the source of the cost saving and distinguished between learning processes which are internal to the firm and those which are external. The former is appropriable by the firm. Only those that are external to the firm warrant assistance and then only if the reductions in cost over time compensate for the higher costs during the period of assistance,[3] with all flows appropriately discounted. The tax-subsidy to be provided is temporary. This is now the standard basic story.

This argument immediately raises a number of policy difficulties. It never provides a justification for blanket assistance to all firms in an industry or even a sub-industry; the existence of an externality and the required cost saving must be demonstrated in every case. Baldwin (1969) raised a second difficulty. He pointed out that a tariff (or subsidy) provides no incentive per se for a firm to acquire more knowledge. Because the intervention is output-based, a firm will increase output by the least costly method, not necessarily by acquiring more technology. The correct policy implied by the argument, supposing it is demonstrated, calls for a subsidy related to knowledge creation; e.g., a subsidy on the particular workers who learn by doing. Most knowledge or skill acquisition is process- or job- or product-specific, so that the corrective subsidy will be confined to the process or job or product or whatever and based on the variable with which the externality is associated. Thus, there are severe qualifications to the infant industry argument.

These qualifications are examples of a much more general theme in the literature on government intervention. Each externality or market failure calls for a tax-subsidy whose base is the variable which generates the externality or failure, and the tax-subsidy rate will be that rate which gives the optimal effect. Bhagwati (1971) gives an early statement of the rule. Any tax-subsidy other than the optimal tax-subsidy causes by-product effects (Corden, 1974) that impose costs on the economy. Moreover, the tax-subsidy rate varies across firms in an industry if the strength of the effect justifying intervention varies across firms. Even when an intervention is called for, a choice of a sub-optimal instrument with by-product effects reduces the net benefits obtainable from the optimal instrument and may in fact be welfare-reducing.

a. Second-best Arguments for Industry Protection

A number of variants of the infant industry argument are based on the presence of policy distortions in the economy, such as tariffs or commodity taxes, which are considered unremovable and therefore permanent. These are applications of the theory of the second-best. In their famous article, Lipsey and Lancaster (1956) showed that if an optimisation problem is modified by the addition of new

---

[3] If the instrument of assistance is a subsidy rather than a tariff, one should add the costs imposed by the tax which funds the subsidy costs.

constraints, the first-order conditions that characterised the first-best optimisation are in general violated. In the context of international trade, this means that free trade may not be the best policy for a small competitive economy. For example, if a subset of importable goods is subject to unremovable distortions in the form of tariffs, the second-best optimum calls for tariffs or trade subsidies on some or all of the remaining goods whose prices are not fixed. The nature of the second-best set of taxes-subsidies can be characterised in terms of the relationships of substitutability and complementarity between the two sets of goods (see Lloyd, 1974; and Hatta, 1977).[4]

These models also pose major difficulties for policy makers. It is not clear why some policies are permanently unchangeable and others are freely changeable. Moreover, determining the second-best policy requires perfect knowledge of all aspects of the economy, including all supply and demand parameters, in fact the determinants of the behaviour of all agents in the economy. This is grossly unrealistic. Third-best interventions made in ignorance of the true values of some behavioural parameters may be welfare-reducing.

Numerous second-best theory models purport to show that trade-related investment measures (TRIMs) are welfare improving for developing countries.[5] These models introduce additional constraints due to the presence of unemployed factors due to a fixed minimum wage or to a tariff on the final good. The arguments made are subject to the same objections as to the infant industry argument: the cause of policy-induced distortions should be addressed at the source. Such first-best reform avoids the by-product loss of welfare due to the increase in the price to consumers of the output of the protected sector and the distortions of the production structure of the industry. Performance requirements have negative effects if they are pushed too far. As in the infant industry case, a content plan provides no incentive for upstream firms to acquire more knowledge. The incentive is merely to increase their outputs. The arguments for TRIMs have an old-fashioned ring. They ignore the benefits of technology and management from foreign investments, and belong to an era when there was no pressure on developing countries to liberalise trade.

---

[4] As with the infant industry argument, the optimal government intervention and the associated rates of tax-subsidy depends on the exact nature of the constraints. Usually a tariff is called for on the outputs of some industries, because in the models that were used, each industry produces only one good. If there are many-good industries, the second-best taxes-subsidies will vary across the goods in an industry.

[5] See Chao and Yu (1993), Yu and Chao (1998), Greenaway (1992), Moran (1998), Morissey and Rai (1995), Richardson (1993) and Rodrik (1987). An older literature which makes a similar case for export subsidies on the grounds that tariffs and other policies which promote import substitution have discriminated against exports is reviewed by Harris and Schmitt (1999).

b. Technology Development

Some writers have advocated border assistance on the grounds of technology development.[6] However, the previous section makes it clear that government interventions to develop technology should be technology-based, not output-based. With few exceptions, the technologies used by producers in developing countries are not the latest or most advanced in the world. Generally speaking, when new industries or products are established they will, in most cases, use a technology already developed in some other more advanced or industrialised country. In this context, FDI will be an important vehicle for technology transfer. Such transfers occur in two ways:

- foreign technology has a higher total factor productivity which is transferred initially to the enterprise with foreign investment in the host economy;
- knowledge of the enterprises with foreign investment spills over to other firms in the same industries.

Each of these effects occurs within industries (appropriately defined), that is, they are intra-industry effects. The first will be called the direct technology transfer effect and the second the spillover effect. The direct technology transfer effect assumes foreign investors have a superior technology which is transferable to foreign affiliates. In recent years this effect has been incorporated in a number of models of technology catch-up or technology ladders. Technology differences are viewed as given across nations, the result of past R&D or other processes of technology acquisition. No attempt is usually made to explain these differences (see, e.g., Barro and Sala-i-Martin, 1995, ch. 6). These models are simplistic, with no international trade in goods and only one sector, but they introduce two key ideas. The first is a relationship between the variety of the capital inputs and output, and the second is a complementarity effect between FDI and human capital accumulation in the host economy. With international trade, the composite capital input adds new varieties through the importation of new capital goods as the foreign varieties can only be supplied by foreign producers. This is one vehicle of technology improvement.

The notion that knowledge spills over from one firm to others has become popular in recent years. Blomstrom (1989) provides an early and influential statement, though the idea was put forward much earlier by Findlay (1978), who called it 'contagion'. This notion has an intuitive appeal but has been modelled in different ways. In the spillover models, where improvements in total factor productivity are associated with learning by doing, there is a kind of externality. However, the host country government has little possibility of capturing these

---

[6] For example, Balasubramanyam (1991) bases his argument for content plans on the incentives provided to multinational companies to develop technology in the materials sector of the host economy.

benefits if they are associated with the aggregate industry output in the rest of the world or of the whole world. If there are spillovers associated instead with FDI in some industries, this is an added benefit of FDI but such benefits will be industry-specific and the government would have to know the mechanism by which the technology is transferred in order to capture them. FDI incentives will be a crude and generally ineffective way of capturing benefits of FDI as they are firm- or process-specific, where they exist. R&D subsidies are not warranted unless there is some general uniform externality associated with R&D. The best way to maximise the benefits of technology transfers associated with FDI is through the adoption of generic measures aimed at improving the overall regulatory and economic environment by enhancing competition, improving human capital skills and technological capacity.

The critical question in this debate is the nature of the technology transfer. In concluding their survey of technology and trade, Grossman and Helpman (1995, p. 1334) note that to answer the question:

> ... what can the South do to encourage technology transfer to indigenous agents without causing the Northern innovators to take their business elsewhere ... we will need models that pay closer attention to how knowledge is transmitted within and between firms.

c. Strategic Trade Policy

Strategic trade policy is a set of cases developed in the 1980s that supposedly justify government interventions on the basis of strategic interdependence among a small number of firms. Brander (1995) surveys the theory. A standard example is a model of two duopolists, each from a different country, competing in a third country market. If there are no home market effects, an export subsidy granted by the government of one of them may improve national welfare by allowing the domestic producer to earn additional profits in the export market that exceed the amount of the subsidy payment. This outcome is extraordinarily fragile as it is conditional on firms' decision variables being strategic substitutes (i.e., greater output by the subsidised firm reduces its competitors' profits). It is not robust: if the conditions of entry or the choice of decision variable (Cournot or Bertrand competition or whatever) or the presence of economies of scale or other features of the model change, the nature of the optimal intervention changes. Selecting the optimal level of the (optimal) instrument imposes high information requirements on the intervening government. This kind of intervention also lends itself to political manipulation with the possibility that the subsidies will go to producers that seek to protect themselves from foreign competitive pressures rather than the producers who can shift profits. Finally, such strategic policy interventions may be in the interests of one country intervening alone but if the second country retaliates, there is a prisoners' dilemma – both lose. This is because the result stems from profit-shifting between markets. From a world welfare point of view it is not efficient to have any intervention.

Other strategic policy cases with different assumptions about the nature of competition are subject to the same objections (Brander, 1995). There is, therefore, nothing in strategic trade theory to recommend it to developing countries. In most markets, these countries are price-takers. If the market conditions should conform to some model of strategic trade policy intervention, developing countries do not satisfy the informational and political economy requirements for successful intervention. They would do better to take action to increase competition in such markets.

There is another even more powerful objection to the theory. It ignores completely the rules of the WTO. These rule out export subsidies on manufactures and severely constrain the levels of tariff rates as most industrial tariffs are now bound. These rules have evolved over 50 years precisely in order to constrain national beggar-thy-neighbour policies. Moreover, as with the second-best argument for tariffs, one should not take the conditions of imperfect competition as given. The WTO has become more concerned with competition in world markets in recent years. Most small-number competition markets are the result of government-sanctioned restraints on entry (such as the tolerance of export cartels) rather than natural monopoly. Action in the WTO and other inter-governmental fora such as the OECD should be to remove barriers to entry and cross-border competition and thereby make markets competitive.

d. The Case of East Asia

Whether government intervention, ranging from credit and export subsidies, protection, and export promotion measures were effective in the spectacular growth experienced by East Asia is a longstanding question. Some interventions were successful, in part because they were performance- or contest-based (World Bank, 1992). The evidence on the effectiveness of export subsidies and promotion is not conclusive, although East Asia is often used as an example where it worked. Export promotion that uses incentives to encourage exports works in the same way as import protection and can be subject to the same abuses. Export subsidies can be abused through over invoicing, false shipments, and ad hoc subsidies that do not necessarily go to the most competitive exporters. The relative success of export promotion interventions in East Asia is because with exports, the criteria for performance was much easier to measure and could be used as a performance criteria or contest-based mechanism to ensure that it was effectively used (World Bank, 1992). In studies that look at what determines exports, export subsidies showed little change in the years prior to the boom of East Asian exports, as quoted in Mody, 1999. Furthermore, some East Asian economies, such as Indonesia, had in fact moved away from using export subsidies since the mid-1980s.

Obviously there are also other factors that influence exports. Supporting measures that complement export subsidies could be important. In Korea, for instance, detailed sectoral and firm-specific export targets were identified and given access to export credits. There were also benefits associated with agencies that developed new markets, standards and certification mechanisms.

Many of the instruments that East Asian countries have used that fall under export promotion and import restrictions would not now be allowed under multilateral rules, and some other policies would violate the new WTO agreements, especially those on Trade Related Investment Measures (TRIMs), Subsidies and Countervailing Measures (SCM) and Trade-Related Aspects of Intellectual Property Rights (TRIPS). Only instruments such as government provision of information to exporters and changes in the exchange rate would still be allowed under the present rule structure. Export promotion agencies such as the Japan External Trade Organisation (JETRO) are still allowed, as long as their task is only to provide information and not to provide export guarantees or insurance elements.

An examination of WTO rules and the East Asian experience to date would indicate that many instruments are no longer permitted. However, there are still instruments that could be used, and the usual caveats about specificity of policy to the objective or target applies. Furthermore, instruments must be implemented in a transparent way, have built-in performance requirements and have a clear exit point. Prior to the crisis there were many derogations from such basic concepts. These were also compounded by a close relationship between business and government to channel capital and credit to specific sectors.[7]

3. IMPLICATIONS FOR DEVELOPING COUNTRIES IN THE MILLENNIUM ROUND

WTO rules restrict the industrial policy instruments available to members. In this section we examine some of the issues arising from the possible revision of WTO rules as they relate to the pursuit of industrial policy objectives by developing countries. A number of policies that distort trade are still allowed under existing rules. However, the added discipline imposed by the WTO has reduced the flexibility of national governments to pursue development objectives. Different countries have different objectives and hence require different sets of policy tools. The impact of WTO rules on countries differs accordingly.

---

[7] In the post-crisis era a number of issues regarding corporate governance and restructuring are emerging as being critical for a sustainable recovery. See Bora et al. (1999) for a more detailed discussion of local content policies pursued in East Asia, as well as recent dispute settlement cases in the WTO in the area of TRIMs.

Nevertheless, there are some common features of the agreements, which deserve to be highlighted (Bora et al., 1999).

- First, since MFN and national treatment are the cornerstones of the rules-based system, any non-border policy that has an effect on goods and services trade is under discipline, or has been negotiated an exemption.
- Second, the rules are ownership neutral. Policies such as subsidies and local content protection do not distinguish between foreign affiliates and domestic enterprises. What is important in the WTO is the 'trade effect' of the instrument. Thus, countries seeking to apply a particular policy to foreign-owned firms must first find a provision in the agreement that allows the use of the policy. Then they can apply it to a foreign firm as long as there is no 'trade effect'.
- Third, the promotion of industries for investment and export growth is being narrowed to generic instead of specific policy instruments. This levels the playing field for international trade and does little to allow countries to develop specific industries through specific policy instruments.
- Fourth, 'special and differential' (S&D) treatment for developing countries has typically been in the form of transition arrangements providing a certain length of time in which to bring policies into conformity with WTO rules. In some cases members are exempt from these responsibilities.

a. Import Protection

The scope for import protection continues to diminish. Tariffs are declining, local content protection is on the verge of being prohibited and contingent protection is now somewhat more disciplined. The issue related to industrial policy that we wish to address here concerns local content protection. Local content policies are prevalent primarily in large-scale industries where there is scope for significant linkages with domestic industries. There is evidence that this policy has been successful in establishing some industries in some countries. Australia, for example, used local content policies in the establishment of its automotive manufacturing industry. However, it was an inefficient industry. The policy has recently been abandoned and tariff rates reduced (Bora and Pomfret, 1996). The end result is an industry that is more competitive, albeit after some structural adjustment, vindicating those who argue that local content policies are not required for an efficient competitive industry (Pursell, 1999). However, it is arguable that a content-protected industry would not exist at all if the local content policies had not been used in the first place. This appears to be the developing country view, i.e., as newly industrialising economies they have not had the 40-year grace period that, say, the Australian automotive period had, nor did they have the degree of protection and market access afforded to Canada through the Canada-US Autopact.

Given these considerations, what is the best way to proceed? If developing countries have as their objective efficient national production, content plans distort the production within an industry and thereby lead to inefficiencies, as noted above. If there is a dynamic learning or cost reduction process, a tariff or subsidy assisting temporarily the processes in which the cost reduction occurs is much preferable to a continuation of content plans for the whole industry. If developing countries have as their development objective something other than efficiency, as in the Indonesian autos case (Bora et al., 1999, annex 1), there will be an inconsistency with the fundamental rules of the trading system. In the automobile case when a completely built-up unit is imported for assembly it will usually be feasible to source at least 20 per cent of the products locally.[8] This means that in order to increase local content further imports will have to be displaced. Here, one must question whether the development objective is compatible with efficient long-run allocation of resources, or whether it favours some group at the expense of national development.

b. Export Promotion

Direct intervention by governments to boost exports is being increasingly restricted by WTO rules. This leaves little room to manoeuvre for developing countries in the area of export subsidies for industrial products. Nevertheless, there is a wide range of alternatives that are still pursued by governments, including export credit and insurance below market rates, concessional tax and duty provisions and export processing zones. While some of these remain WTO-consistent, developing countries need to reassess the extent to which other policies which discriminate in favour of particular producers are in their national interest. This will determine the extent to which they should negotiate further restrictions to export subsidies in the next round. Their focus, encouraged by the existing set of rules, should be on reducing fiscal and procedural constraints to exports (Laird, 1997), trade facilitation, and generic policies to make the country more competitive such as infrastructure development, an appropriate exchange rate policy, human capital formation, innovation policies, and joint venture agreements. All are important for determining export competitiveness, and all are still unconstrained within the framework of the WTO.

c. Competition Policy

One area of generic producer-neutral policies that promote efficient production is that of competition policy. Competition policy is the set of policies which promote competition among producers in markets. Increasingly, as markets

---

[8] These would be generic components for which transport costs are high such as tyres and oil.

become globalised, competition is international and the aim should be to make markets internationally contestable.

It has been suggested that the WTO could be the location of internationally enforceable multilateral competition law that could address anti-competitive behaviour which affected persons in other countries. Given the diversity of views, it is unlikely that binding multilateral competition laws will develop in the foreseeable future. However, the WTO still plays an important role in promoting competition. One of the most important determinants of competition in markets is the freedom of movement of goods across borders and, especially in the service industries, the freedom of movement of FDI. These are subject to WTO rules and discipline. One merit of the WTO rules in this context is that they are neutral between foreign and domestic producers (except to the extent that exceptions to national treatment are inscribed by members in their GATS schedules). This helps to ensure that domestic and foreign producers are able to compete on equal terms.

Developing countries are sometimes concerned over restrictive business practices of multinational corporations that establish affiliates in their economies; for example, price fixing and market allocation. This has led some to introduce requirements relating to domestic and export performance in an attempt to counter these practices. However, performance requirements are an inappropriate response as they apply to foreign investors irrespective of their market power and practices and they require the government of the host country to estimate the second-best level of the performance requirement. Foreign investors are subject to the laws of the host economy. When, therefore, the anti-competitive practices occur in the host economy, the appropriate response is the application, and if necessary the development, of national competition laws. This addresses the source of the problem directly and without by-product effects.

d. Market Access for Foreign Investors

Despite the progress made on extending multilateral disciplines into new areas, policies relating to foreign direct investment were not included in the Uruguay Round Agreements.[9] The substantial growth in FDI during the past 15 years makes it an important component of the global economy. In the context of industrial policy the inclusion of foreign direct investment rules, or a General Agreement on Investment (GAI) would have major implications for developing countries.[10]

The precise impact would, of course, depend on the nature of the agreement; its architecture, scope and provisions. Currently there is no broad political support

---

[9] Apart from those in GATS dealing with FDI in services and some aspects of other agreements that impact on FDI. WTO (1996, ch. 4) surveys WTO investment-related rules and disciplines.

[10] Another possible name could be a General Agreement on Foreign Investment (GAFI).

for a full and comprehensive multilateral agreement. However, in the context of restrictions placed on industrial policy that were reviewed in the previous section, it may be in developing countries' interests to consider the possibility of a modest achievement in this area. The reason is that with reduced government intervention, developing countries will have to rely more heavily on TNCs for the skills and inputs required to assist in restructuring (UNCTAD, 1995). This is not to say that they are not capable of developing competitiveness themselves. But experience has shown, especially in East Asia, that TNCs can allow a quick and easy entry into world markets.

There is scepticism on the part of many host national governments about putting in place rules on investment. This does not mean that efforts should simply be stalled. Instead, this means investigating avenues that simultaneously allow the achievement of rules and the advancement of developing country interests. One way to tackle this problem is to split the contentious issue of market access for foreign investors from performance requirements. Issues related to performance requirements could be confined to the revision of the TRIMs agreement and market access for foreign firms could be negotiated separately. In fact, this is the current WTO architecture: the GATS deals with market access for foreign service firms, while the TRIMs agreement deals with certain performance requirements. A GAI could extend this concept to other sectors thereby expanding the rules on commercial presence. Such an initiative would also allow developing countries to argue strongly that the GAI framework could be based on the positive list approach as in the GATS to avoid renegotiating commitments. Within the context of industrial policy initiatives a GAI would leave the GATT rules on goods intact and provide an opportunity for developing countries to develop rules on specific foreign investment issues including: incentives to attract foreign investors, mandatory licensing and joint-venture arrangements, equity restrictions and perhaps even other elements of TNC practices. GATT rules simply do not allow such possibilities.

e. Performance Requirements for Foreign Investors

Many developing countries feel aggrieved over the Uruguay Round TRIMs agreement. There are three issues: the extent to which these instruments are related to foreign ownership; extending the list of covered policies; and whether developing countries should have special and differential treatment.

Although some developing countries argue that TRIMs are a foreign investment issue (Youseff, 1999) a recent WTO dispute panel concluded that:

> contrary to India's argument, we find that nothing in the TRIMs Agreement suggests that the nationality of the ownership of enterprises subject to a particular measure is an element in deciding whether that measure is covered by the Agreement. We therefore find without textual

support in the TRIMs Agreement the argument that since the TRIMs Agreement is basically designed to govern and provide a level playing field for foreign investment, measures relating to internal taxes or subsidies cannot be construed to be a trade-related investment measure (WTO, 1999, p. 339, para. 14.73).

Thus, there is no scope to implement a performance requirement (based on the existing illustrative list) in a discriminatory fashion. Measures that are prohibited are prohibited regardless of ownership. If developing countries perceive that measures on the illustrative list are required to meet other objectives and must be implemented on foreign firms this will need to be negotiated. Chances of succeeding are likely very low given that a measure will be prohibited because it distorts trade.

Extending the illustrative list of TRIMs will involve intensive negotiations. The current list is very much a compromise. The investment provisions of the North American Free Trade Agreement and the draft OECD Multilateral Agreement on Investment (MAI) contained longer lists. Some developed countries will seek to extend the list in the next round, while developing countries will likely oppose this. The most contentious area is expansion of the list to policies that relate to technology transfer beyond straightforward equity restrictions. Joint-venture laws, licensing requirements and patent requirements are all typically implemented within the context of expanding local capacity through technology transfer. These policies have an effect on the location decision of transnationals. The extent to which they are trade related and fall within the framework of the current TRIMs agreement is questionable. If members want the TRIMs list to include these measures, clear evidence on their trade effect will have to be provided. At the same time, developing countries should not be complacent about the success of these policies. There is some evidence to suggest that they can achieve certain development objectives, but at the same time there is also evidence to suggest that alternative policies, namely liberalisation, may result in a more efficient outcome.

Performance requirements for services should also not be ignored. Article XVI GATS lists six measures that members are not allowed to maintain for sectors they schedule unless they list a derogation. For the forthcoming negotiations developing countries may want to consider to what extent they wish to delink this connection; that is, to have a standalone provision not allowing these measures.

Responding to developing country concerns within the context of TRIMs will not be easy. Some members have already flagged performance requirements as an important component of their development strategy. Furthermore, it is likely that some members that have notified TRIMs to the WTO will take advantage of Article 5.3 of the Agreement and seek an extension of the transition period. While these are predictable and negotiable elements, the real difficulty will be attempts to allow a specific carve-out for some policies. For example, the 'traffic light approach' used in the subsidies agreement could be followed in the TRIMs agreement. Measures that directly affect trade could be prohibited (red light), those that are critical for development, even though they affect trade directly could be included in a permissible category (green light). The actionable category (yellow light) could include policies where members cannot agree on their precise effect on trade.[11]

f. Special and Differential Treatment

The preamble to Article VIII of GATT recognises both the possibility for developing countries to protect infant industries and a mechanism for allowing such protection. This provision was complemented subsequently by various other provisions. A crucial negotiating issue will be the extent to which policies that are prohibited under WTO rules will be allowed for developing countries.

Consider again the case of local content protection. A WTO panel (Bora et al., 1999, annex 1) has concluded unambiguously that Indonesian policy contravenes Article III of GATT (national treatment). Nevertheless, some members will take the position that such policy is critical for development. If this is the case, the only way to handle the issue is to examine what the optimal length of time is for a developing country to achieve its objectives with the policy.[12] A similar issue arises with respect to export subsidies. Developing countries maintain that, despite their disadvantage in competing with developed countries on a budget basis, export subsidies are needed to develop new markets.

Two other aspects of S&D treatment that need to be examined are how to determine qualification for S&D treatment and the optimal transition period.

- Qualification. The current method of identifying members that qualify for S&D treatment is to use the UN classification of Least Developed Countries. In the subsidies agreement, a GNP per capita criterion is used. Given the ad hoc nature of some of these measures and the specific nature of industrial policy, the new negotiations may want to consider using performance-based measures. These can be either export or import measures.
- Extensions of transition periods. The issue here is the appropriate length. For industrial policy exemption from obligations, it may be useful to examine specific exemptions that fit the problems of developing countries. For example, the five-year period adopted in the TRIMs agreement does not seem to have been derived from any empirical work. The same is true of the gap of two years in the transition period granted developing and least developing countries.

---

[11] This format follows the proposal by Switzerland during the TRIMs negotiations. See Gibbs and Mashayeki (1998) for an account of the Uruguay Round TRIMs negotiations.
[12] Or to conclude that it is a failure.

A final area of negotiation is the possibility of snap-back of protection. For example, Article XVIIIc GATT allows for members to implement tariffs to develop certain industries. This could be another issue for the next round, but should be reviewed carefully. Article XVIIIc has certain conditions attached to it, which have limited its use. The effect of these conditions has been to force developing countries to think strongly about the rationale for protection. Indeed, tariff bindings is one of the central and critical features of GATT rules. Our view is that to raise protection once it has been bound should be avoided. The focus should be on the criteria for determining eligibility for S&D treatment and its duration.

4. CONCLUSIONS

Many developing countries are attempting to boost their competitiveness by supporting industries and products with the potential for high growth and high value added. The debate on the role of the government in achieving this objective continues. The theoretical literature shows that a case for government intervention is weak. On the other hand the empirical evidence shows that governments have had a role in the export and growth success of some countries.

WTO disciplines on subsidies, local content protection, export restrictions and TRIPS reduce the flexibility of governments to pursue policies in these areas. However, they do so in an ownership-neutral manner – they apply to both foreign and domestic firms. They are also not country neutral in that some WTO members are exempted from obligations. This is an acceptable way to account for the needs of developing countries, but clearly more needs to be done. The rules themselves are quite consistent with the large body of theoretical and applied work on trade and industrial policy. Only those policies that directly affect international trade by favouring domestic products over imported products are included. Even then there are a number of areas where government policies that directly affect trade are not included – such as export subsidies in agriculture and services and export performance requirements. These should be a priority for the forthcoming negotiations, either through existing agreements, or as suggested, within an investment rules framework.

The effect of WTO disciplines is not so much to rule out the role of government, but rather shift its emphasis to the supply side. Policies that relate to infrastructure, human capital formation, innovation and diffusion of technology, capacity building and competition policies are now critical for export competitiveness. These policies also need to be complemented with a stable exchange rate that does not penalise (or favour) exports. These are generic pro-development policies, that is, they are not confined to and do not favour particular industries or producers. Efforts to challenge WTO rules that require ownership neutrality should not be pursued within the context of applying GATT rules, but within a General Agreement on Investment. This way, specific issues relating to foreign affiliates such as market access, and their performance and behaviour, can be addressed with specific policies.

The empirical evidence, with strong theoretical support, shows that selective industrial policies result in more losers than winners. Nevertheless, the political economy of trade policy makes it difficult for developing countries to agree to bind policies within multilateral rules. The way to handle this problem is to examine ways in which S&D treatment can account for the diversity of developing countries, both in terms of their income levels and their objectives. Clearly, a uniform five-year transition period for all policies does not take into account the different speeds at which developing countries can adjust to a new regime. Instead, this differential should be examined further within the context of an 'appropriate' transition period, or perhaps a performance-based measure. At the same time, clogging the WTO mechanism with S&D provisions that will never be implemented is not the way to go. Those making a case for further S&D provisions may want to consider an omnibus approach to this issue. As with a GAI, such an approach would target the specific nature of the problem, which is the difficulty that developing countries are having with respect to their implementing WTO obligations.

REFERENCES

Asian Development Bank (1999), *Asian Development Outlook 1999* (ADB: Manila).

Balasubramanyam, V.N. (1991), 'Putting TRIMs to Good Use', *World Development*, **19**, 1215–24.

Baldwin, R.E. (1969), 'The Case Against Infant Industry Protection', *Journal of Political Economy*, **77**, 295–305.

Barro, R.J. and X. Sala-i-Martin (1995), *Economic Growth* (New York: McGraw-Hill).

Bhagwati, J.N. (1971), 'The Generalized Theory of Distortions and Welfare', in J.N. Bhagwati et al. (eds.), *Trade, Balance of Payments and Growth: Papers in Honor of Charles P. Kindleberger* (North-Holland: Amsterdam).

Blomstrom, M. (1989), *Foreign Investment and Spillovers* (London: Routledge).

Bora, B. and R. Pomfret (1996), 'Manufacturing Policies', in R. Pomfret (ed.), *Australia's Trade Policies* (Melbourne: Oxford University Press).

Bora, B., P. Lloyd and M. Pangestu (1999), 'Industrial Policy and the WTO' (UNCTAD, mimeo).

Brander, J.A. (1995), 'Strategic Trade Policy', in G.N. Grossman and K. Rogoff (eds.), *Handbook of International Economics*, Vol. 3 (Amsterdam: North Holland).

Chao, C.C. and E.S.H. Yu (1993), 'Content Protection, Urban Unemployment and Welfare', *Canadian Journal of Economics*, **26**, 481–92.

Corden, W.M. (1974), *Trade Policy and Economic Welfare* (Oxford: Clarendon Press).

Findlay, R. (1978), 'Relative Backwardness, Direct Foreign Investment and the Transfer of Technology: A Simple Dynamic Model', *Quarterly Journal of Economics*, **92**, 1–16.

Gibbs, M. and M. Mashayekhi (1998), 'The Uruguay Round Negotiations on Investment: Lessons for the Future', Division on Trade in Goods and Services and Commodities (UNCTAD, mimeo).

Greenaway, D. (1992), 'Trade Related Investment Measures and Development Strategies', *Kyklos*, **45**, 139–59.

Grossman, G.N. and E. Helpman (1995), 'Technology and Trade', in G.N. Grossman and K. Rogoff (eds.), *Handbook of International Economics*, Vol. 3 (Amsterdam: North Holland).

Harris, R.G. and N. Schmitt (1999), 'Do Two Wrongs Make a Right? Export Incentives and Bias in Trade Policy', in J. Piggott and A.D. Wodland (eds.), *International Trade Policy and the Pacific Rim* (Basingstoke: Macmillan).

Hatta, T. (1977), 'A Theory of Piecemeal Policy Recommendations', *Review of Economic Studies*, **44**, 1–22.

Kemp, M.C. (1964), *The Pure Theory of International Trade* (Englewood Cliffs, NJ: Prentice-Hall).

Laird, S. (1997), 'WTO Rules and Good Practice on Export Policy', Staff Working Paper TPRD9701 (Geneva: WTO).

Lall, S. (1994), 'The East Asian Miracle Study': Does the Bell Toll for Industrial Strategy?', *World Development*, **22**.

Lipsey, R. and K. Lancaster (1956), 'The General Theory of Second Best', *Review of Economic Studies*, **25**, 11–32.

Lloyd, P.J. (1974), 'A More General Theory of Price Distortions in Open Economies', *Journal of International Economics*, **4**, 365–86.

Martin, W. and D. Mitra (forthcoming), 'Productivity Growth and Convergence in Agriculture and Manufacturing', *Economic Development and Cultural Change*. Also released as Policy Research Working Paper 2171 (Washington, DC: World Bank).

Mody, A. (1999), 'Industrial Policy After the East Asian Crisis', World Bank Policy Research Working Paper 2112 (May).

Moran, T. (1998), *Foreign Direct Investment and Development* (Washington, DC: Institute for International Economics).

Morissey, O. and Y. Rai (1995), 'The GATT Agreement on Trade-related Investment Measures: Implications for Developing Countries and their Relationship with Transnational Corporations', *Journal of Development Studies*, **31**, 702–24.

Pursell, G. (1999), 'The Australian Experience with FDI and Local Content Programs in the Auto Industry', Paper presented at the Conference on WTO, Technology Transfer and Globalisation of Firms, Institute of Economic Growth (New Delhi, 25–26 March).

Richardson, M. (1993), 'Content Protection with Foreign Capital', *Oxford Economic Papers*, **45**, 103–17.

Rodrik, D. (1987), 'The Economics of Export Performance Requirements', *Quarterly Journal of Economics*, **102**, 633–50.

UNCTAD (1995), *World Investment Report: Transnational Corporations and International Competitiveness* (Geneva: United Nations).

UNCTAD (1999a), *World Investment Report 1999: FDI and the Challenge of Development* (Geneva: United Nations).

UNCTAD (1999b), *Preparing for Future Multilateral Trade Negotiations: Issues and Research Needs from a Development Perspective* (Geneva: UNCTAD) Sales No. E.99.II.D.17.

World Bank (1992), *The East Asian Miracle: Economic Growth and Public Policy*, (Washington, DC: World Bank).

World Trade Organisation (1996), *Annual Report 1996*, Vol. I (Geneva: WTO).

World Trade Organisation (1999), *Indonesia – Certain Measures Affecting the Automobile Industry: Report of the Panel* (Geneva: WTO). Document number WT/DS54/R, WT/DS55/R, WT/DS59/R, WT/DS64/R.

Youssef, H. (1999), 'Special and Differential Treatment for Developing Countries in the WTO', TRADE Working Paper No. 2 (South Centre, Geneva).

Yu, E.S.H. and C.-C. Chao (1998), 'On Investment Measures and Trade', *The World Economy*, Global Trade Policy, **21**, 4, 549–61.

11

Subsidiarity and Governance Challenges for the WTO: Environmental and Labour Standards

Jim Rollo and L. Alan Winters

1. INTRODUCTION

T HE failure of December 1999's WTO Ministerial Meeting in Seattle to launch a new round of global trade negotiations had much to do with bad process. But underlying it were apparently unbridgeable gulfs over regulation: between the EU and the US on investment and competition, and between developed and developing countries on trade and labour standards and, to a lesser degree, on trade and environmental standards. These failures were symptomatic of the fundamental challenge facing the members of the WTO: how far should global trading rules intrude inside the border?

The GATT was a treaty of provisional application and its signatories were reticent about moving beyond either the border or a consensus-driven agenda. But, perhaps more in tune with the plans for the original International Trade Organisation, the WTO is more ambitious. It has a clear regulatory agenda in intellectual property and sanitary and phytosanitary barriers to trade, and a dispute settlement procedure which has moved away from consultation and consensus towards legal process and definitive judgements handed down by a permanent Appellate Body. These extensions in the direct effect of WTO rules have concerned many member governments and raised the ire of much of civil society, both of which saw them as intrusions into domestic policy making. At the same time, and not wholly consistently, parts of civil society have also seen the dispute settlement procedure as a potential mechanism for pursuing their international agenda in countries.

This paper asks whether environmental and labour standards should be brought under the WTO, and answers, pretty definitively, 'no'. The case for standards in these areas is indisputable, but the case for internationalising them is not. Where there is such a case, it is one for international cooperation directly in these areas, rather than for seeking to enforce standards on unwilling partners through the use of trade sanctions. Using trade sanctions threatens to embroil the WTO in these issues in which it has neither the technical ability nor the political legitimacy to act effectively. The danger of this is that not only will labour and environmental standards be maladministered, but that we could well also lose the benefits that have traditionally flowed from the GATT in terms of economic growth via trade liberalisation. If, ultimately, labour and the environment do figure in WTO law, we urge that multilateral agreement be required before any action is permitted under these rubrics. The GATT's traditional enforcement mechanism of allowing individual members to act against imports from another member held to be in violation of some norm is too intrusive and subject to abuse to be trusted in cases where such deep issues of sovereignty and taste are at stake.

We develop this argument in the following sections. First, we consider the principles of sound regulation in general. We then examine EU experience in the labour and environmental fields and find it an inappropriate model for global co-operation. Section 4 considers general arguments surrounding the intersection of trade and environmental/social policies, while Section 5 examines two cases in greater detail – global externalities and child labour. Finally, Section 6 concludes.

2. REGULATORY PRINCIPLES

The economic literature on regulation is largely about market failure. This may arise because of excluded markets, e.g. the environment, because of imperfect information/information asymmetries, e.g. food safety and the provision of professional or financial services, or because of imperfect competition and misuse of market power. But market failure is not by itself a sufficient reason for regulation: the benefits of intervention need to be compared with the costs. Costs include not only compliance costs incurred by the regulated entities, but also monitoring costs, possible spillovers in related areas and costs that might arise if inappropriate regulation undermines the legitimacy of other necessary rules.

The more prescriptive regulation is in instructing producers or consumers how to produce or what to consume, the more likely it is to be inefficient. Inefficiencies arise from stifling innovation on the supply side and reducing choice on the demand side of the market as well as raising direct costs in terms of inspection. This suggests the use of regulatory instruments which use the market to encourage flexibility and choice both of products and production techniques: for example, taxes or tradable quotas to deal with environmental externalities, labelling to deal with information asymmetries including risk, and liability insurance to encourage product safety.

At a more general level the economic analysis of regulation puts a premium on transparency, predictability and non-discrimination both in objectives and in application to prevent corruption or capture by interest groups. Predictability requires that responsibilities for ensuring the desired outcomes should be clearly assigned. An example of this from the environmental field is the 'polluter-pays principle'.

Turning to international regulation, we must add the commonplace that countries have different tastes, cultures, governmental and legal systems, educational and physical endowments. All of these suggest that social choices will differ from country to country. Efficiency criteria based on individual utility maximisation suggest that regulatory regimes should apply to the largest feasible communities, but only subject to their achieving a reasonable homogeneity of views. This suggests that regulatory regimes should be determined as closely as possible by the communities to which they apply unless there are spillovers to other communities, in which case they too should be consulted. Among such spillovers, we would count cross-border externalities, economies of scale and public goods.

Thus regulation that meets locally defined needs is likely to be more efficient and legitimate than regulation imposed from afar which violates local tastes and reduces local comparative advantage. This is essentially the case for subsidiarity: unless there are significant spillovers there is no efficiency case for imposing one set of standards across different regulatory domains. If a society is content with its regulatory framework there is no case for imposing a different one on it.

From this arise two supposed challenges to open trade. First, absent externalities, the low cost/high cost argument is not a case for discrimination in trade. Regulatory standards with purely local effects generate purely local benefits, which presumably outweigh the costs in the local domain. If local producers are economically harmed by the regulatory regime when open to foreign competition, then in economic terms, that is an efficient outcome.

Second, goods produced under different regulatory regimes may be materially different, but in ways that are not immediately evident to purchasers. This problem can be met by the use of labels rather than trade controls. Even if foreign goods are viewed as unsafe, the most that is required is that they be required to meet the same standards as home products. As long as foreign products are not discriminated against actually or potentially by the design of local regulation, there is no inefficiency in this.

In an international context therefore as well as meeting the domestic tests set out above, regulation:

- should be non-discriminatory with respect to international trade (and investment);

- relate to closely defined cross-border spillovers;
- be restricted in geographical coverage to the extent of those spillovers; and
- be implemented locally and in line with local circumstances and tastes.

These last three principles imply that the regulatory agency should be accountable to the relevant communities. Only in this way is it likely to command confidence about appropriateness of the chosen method of regulation and compliance. In other words the closer to the regulated the regulator is, the more likely it is to be trusted and hence legitimate.

3. REGULATION, LIBERALISATION AND SUBSIDIARITY IN THE EUROPEAN UNION[1]

In this section we examine the EU experience with liberalisation and its relevance to the challenges facing the WTO. The EU's progress on regulatory barriers has been slow and has required the development of notions such as mutual recognition and subsidiarity to reconcile central regulation with the continuing exercise of members' national sovereignty. Given its manifest differences from the community of all nations, the EU is not an appropriate model for global regulation.

a. The European Approach to Liberalisation

The Treaty of Rome envisaged not just a customs union but also a common market. While the customs union was put in place without significant difficulty, the common market was harder to implement. Barriers to internal trade remained both at the border and inside it via regulatory differences including some specifically permitted by the Treaty of Rome. The initial approach to these regulatory barriers was to attempt harmonisation. This either failed outright or went extremely slowly, because the reluctance to give up national standards was buttressed by the need for unanimity in the relevant decision processes.

Key to a changed approach were two judgments by the European Court of Justice (ECJ). First in 1974, the Court held (the Dassonville judgment) that regulatory barriers to trade were to be considered as measures with equivalent effect to quantitative barriers to trade and which were prohibited under Article 30 of the Treaty. This effectively allowed freedom of intra-Community trade to prevail over regulatory barriers. Second, in 1979 the ECJ judged (in the Cassis de Dijon case) that the German authorities could not exclude a product that was in free circulation in France and apparently safe in use, from the German market because it did not meet German standards. As long as regulatory objectives were

---

[1] There are a large number of texts which trace the history of the integration process in Europe of which Pelkmans (1997) most closely links the process with economic analysis.

equivalent, harmonisation was not necessary because all members could be assumed to be pursuing those objectives efficiently. Thus consumers could safely be left to choose between regulatory regimes. In its purest form, this implied competition among rules and *de facto* mutual recognition.

Where safety (or other fundamental issues) were at stake, member states decided it was not enough to leave it to the consumer to decide. Mutual recognition had to be combined with agreement on minimum standards, which, in turn, after 1987 could generally be agreed by (qualified) majority vote rather than unanimity. Majority voting also applied to policies that were traditionally the responsibilities of the nation state, such as employee and environmental protection, both of which are of relevance in the WTO context.

In practice social harmonisation has proceeded extremely slowly in the EU. Even before the Treaty of Rome was signed, differential costs of employment rights legislation had been seen as a potential source of competitive advantage (see Bean et al., 1998, ch. 1 and for references). Initial concern focused on the possibility that differential application of national policies across sectors would give unfair advantage to home producers (see, in particular, the Spaak Report of 1956), and the French worried that their generous social provision would represent a competitive disadvantage and allow 'social dumping' on their market – Sapir (1996). Despite the inclusion of social clauses in the Treaty of Rome, effective harmonisation only made serious progress with the Social Protocol of the Maastricht Treaty of 1991. This gave treaty backing for minimum standards on issues such as working time, worker consultation, rights of migrant workers to social security, equal opportunities, health and safety at work. But the implementation of these directives is left largely to the member states.

Proponents of the social chapter did not deny the social dumping argument, but they also appealed to equity and efficiency arguments. The former took the form that EU citizens should all have the same rights – just as do citizens of any particular member state – and the latter that common rights are necessary to operationalise the free movement of labour (Pelkmans, 1997, p. 37).

Equity was also held to require common environmental standards, such that EU citizens enjoy, e.g. the same drinking water/air quality even where these are not cross-border pollutants. However, one can also detect trade motivations in EU environmental policy. For example, the fear that pollution-intensive firms will move to countries with lower standards seems implicit in EU demands for environmental harmonisation with Eastern candidate members even where it imposes significant costs on those countries (Mayhew and Orlowski, 1999). Also, EU members are allowed to have more stringent environmental standards than the EU minimum, and to impose them on imported goods, so long as the rules are not unnecessarily discriminatory.

b. Subsidiarity

The increasing importance of the regulatory function of the EU – perhaps most obviously on social and environmental issues but also on monetary and financial policies – led to increased tension between member states and the central institutions. This was raised in the 1980s by Germany and Holland in the context of environmental standards. In the German case this unease about whether it was legitimate to legislate at the European level on subjects which had largely local effect drew on a tradition of the social doctrine of subsidiarity which deals with the relationship between the state and the individual and also on that between different levels of government. Definitions of subsidiarity are complex but in the context of this paper it holds that intervention by the state should be undertaken by the level of government closest to the task in hand (Tietmeyer, 1999, p. 29). The debate within the European Community culminated in Article 130r of the Single European Act on the environment which included elements of subsidiarity language, if not the term.

The economic implications of subsidiarity were developed in the Padoa-Schioppa Report (Padoa-Schioppa, 1987). This concluded that the level of regulation should be determined by whether there are positive or negative cross-border externalities or economies of scale which justify collective action, beyond intergovernmental cooperation by the member states. Such tests are recognised in Article 3b of the Treaty on European Union 1993 which states inter alia:

> The Community shall take action ... only if ... the objectives of the proposed action cannot be achieved ... by the member states and can therefore, by reason of scale or effects of the proposed action, be better achieved by the Community.

As a result of the commitment to subsidiarity, proposals for EU-level regulation now receive much greater scrutiny than in the past. The treaty tests apply not just to the case in principle for EU-level regulation but also to the compliance costs involved and whether and to what degree implementation can be left to member states. EU environmental regulation is increasingly of a framework nature, while standards-setting is tending towards benchmarking rather than prescription (Sbragia, 2000).

c. The EU, Regulation and Lessons for the WTO

For a group of sovereign states, the EU has clearly achieved a remarkable degree of market integration. But it is not a suitable role model for the global community. The EU has strong central institutions notably the Commission (which is independent of the member states and has the sole right of formal legislative proposal), and the European Court of Justice (which is superior to all national courts in matters of EU law) and, increasingly, the European Parliament. While the Council of Ministers (the EU's intergovernmental arm) searches for consensus, greater use of the qualified majority voting rule ensures that the general will cannot be held back by one or two dissident member states. Furthermore, the 15 EU member states are relatively homogenous culturally, historically, economically and socially. The WTO, on the other hand, comprises sovereign states at widely different levels of economic and social development, has a small and weak secretariat, and works very largely by consensus. Although the WTO dispute settlement system, in particular the Appellate Body, arguably has a similar role as the ECJ, its mandate is not wholly clear (Jackson, 1998) and its enforcement powers far weaker. If regulatory harmonisation cannot be achieved among 15 relatively homogenous member states (and the more so if it is remembered that progress was difficult even when there were only six members) how likely is it among 134 members of the WTO?

Although the EU does not provide a template for global regulation and liberalisation, it does offer some 'how not to' lessons. First, legitimacy is a live issue in the EU and the development of the principle of subsidiarity indicates a need to keep regulators close to the regulated to ensure that local tastes are respected. Second, the principle of mutual recognition is hard to implement because it requires so much mutual trust and commonality of objectives; it probably has only restricted applicability at a global level. Third, it is hard to avoid the conclusion that some elements of EU environmental and social regulation aim at 'levelling the playing field' by increasing the costs of some partners; it is hence deliberately, if not wholly, protectionist in intent. Fourth, EU harmonisation at least partly arises from and is legitimised by objectives of political integration, which will not cut much ice in the WTO.

4. THE INTERSECTION BETWEEN TRADE POLICY AND ENVIRONMENTAL AND SOCIAL ISSUES

Environmental and labour issues are on the WTO agenda for essentially three reasons. First, trade and the environment do sometimes overlap and there may be at least a second-best argument for linking their policy instruments. Second, environmental and social groups wish to ensure that WTO law does not block their preferred domestic policies. Third, these groups also wish to co-opt the WTO dispute settlement procedure, with its apparently powerful sanctions, to enforce their preferred policies elsewhere. We argue that the WTO is ill-designed for these other objectives and that pursuing them could undermine its proven value in boosting material welfare by liberalising trade. Whether such pursuit nonetheless makes sense depends on the trade-off between different objectives and the effectiveness of the WTO in achieving them.

The environment is the classic externality, and if environmental effects flow across borders, efficiency requires international policy cooperation. However, since international trade is rarely the direct cause of environmental degradation, trade interventions will rarely be the first-best solution, and international co-operation will ideally only rarely involve the WTO directly. However, if it is impossible to manage a problem directly and if the problem is strongly affected by trade, trade instruments may offer some benefit either directly or as enforcement mechanisms for non-trade aims, as possibly with the Montreal Protocol on CFCs.

A second kind of problem reflects coordination failure, as, for example, in a race to the bottom if countries compete to reduce standards to attract investment. First best would be just to coordinate standards, but if that is impossible, trade intervention could again in theory provide a second-best enforcement mechanism. However, since the standards involved generally pertain to purely national concerns, the need is for minimum, not uniform, standards. Moreover, unless there are very clear procedures for defining international standards and for identifying violations, the use of trade sanctions for this purpose would very probably embroil the WTO in substantive issues for which it is ill-equipped technically or politically to deal.

Trade and standards also intersect if 'tastes' become internationalised. Differences in taste (including the ability to bear or carry pollution, or to work in unpleasant conditions) provide a classical reason for international trade – those best able to cope should produce the dirty/unpleasant goods. But if citizens of country A have preferences about what happens to those in country B, they will seek international action, including, potentially, trade interventions. This is a political statement, not an economic or environmental one, and while we recognise the legitimacy of intervention in other countries' affairs under some circumstances, notions of sovereignty and self-determination suggest that it should be made extraordinarily difficult to legitimise such intervention. Righting the right of unilateral intervention into the GATT seems to us to place the bar far too low. The GATT rules that require like goods to receive like treatment and that define 'like' in terms of goods' observable characteristics regardless of their process of production is a useful bulwark against interference here. While the latter definition may need to be relaxed eventually, as voluntary process standards become common commercial ways to guarantee quality (e.g. the use of ISO 9000), by far the best solution to specific process issues such as labour standards is for appropriate specialist institutions to monitor them.

A further aspect of taste that could provide a basis for international trade is attitude towards risk, which economists recognise as being just as legitimately part of the utility function as is, say, liking oranges. The WTO's Sanitary and Phytosanitary Agreement uses scientific risk assessments as the criterion for permitting restrictive standards, but implicitly presumes that everyone has the same attitude to risk. But a country which is more risk-averse may wish to be more restrictive about certain activities or goods.[2] So long as they accord imports national treatment, such restrictions are no less legitimate than trade measures stemming from other differences in taste, such as tariffs. Combining such sensitive issues with the WTO's demanding dispute settlement procedure has already produced great strains in the EU-US case of beef hormones, and eventually runs the risk of so reducing the legitimacy of the GATT-WTO system that we lose the benefits it has already generated.[3] Discipline is clearly required to prevent standards from becoming protectionist instruments, but equally sovereignty must also have a role to play when the uncertainties are great.[4]

The WTO's apparently uniquely effective enforcement mechanism is hugely attractive to those with other agendas. But trade sanctions have not been particularly successful at achieving broad political ends – Hufbauer, Schott and Elliot (1990) – and if we see environmental and social enforcement in unilateral terms, with one partner empowered to reject a specific import from another, it will need to be clothed in an administrative procedure like those used for safeguards or anti-dumping. Experience with the latter explains developing countries' worries that any WTO social/environmental clause would be captured by industrial country protectionists. Esty (1994) advocates such 'multilateral unilateralism' – unilateral action sanctioned conditionally by multilateral rules – and it is indeed the GATT's traditional enforcement mechanism. In our view, however, its unsuitability for cases dealing with issues of deep sovereignty, differences of taste, and process method is a further reason for keeping social and environmental policy out of the WTO. Finally, of course, there is a limit to the number of objectives that a single instrument can be used for. Using trade sanctions and WTO DSP to enforce labour standards etc. will inevitably reduce its punch on issues such as non-discrimination and trade liberalisation.

The final interface between trade policy and environmental and social policy is 'good ol' protectionism'. It is widely recognised that any excuse for interfering with trade will attract the attention of those who want protection, and, indeed, many of the WTO's and individual countries' procedures are designed to try to separate these claims from others residing more firmly in public policy. There is no point believing that environmental and social regulations will be different. This is not to say that all advocates of intervention are protectionists, far from it,

---

[2] Once we recognise the fallibility of science, similar issues arise with uncertainties in the areas of the risk assessments themselves. Recall, for example, the UK establishment's tarnished record on public information in areas such as BSE and thalidomide.

[3] The EU has rejected imports of US beef on the grounds that the growth hormones used in its production may be harmful. It has produced no evidence for this but claims, that in European eyes, the risks are large enough to warrant intervention. The Appellate Body has ruled them in breach of the requirements of the SPS agreement.

[4] This is not an easy balance to strike. One can certainly detect an element of protectionism in the EU position on beef: if EU producers used hormones to match the efficiency levels of the Americans, the budgetary strain of the extra output could strain the CAP.

but some certainly are. It may seem invidious to question anyone's motives for seeking such obvious virtues as a clean environment and a decent wage for all of humanity, but it is worth asking of all advocates what they are actually doing to achieve those goals in addition to lobbying for trade restrictions.

5. TWO EXAMPLES

a. *Global Externalities*

Global externalities are a case in which collective action at the global level is required, but this need not necessarily be action by the WTO. The Montreal Convention on Ozone Depletion defines responsibilities for reducing CFC emissions and calls on member countries not to trade with non-members in prohibited substances (and products made with them). Similarly, CITES requires a ban on international trade in ivory as a means to preserving elephant stocks.[5] These cases potentially involve the WTO if a member country facing trade restrictions under one of these agreements chose to bring a trade policy dispute to a DSP.

If the complainant is a member of the convention in question, the case seems quite easy for the WTO to deal with. As things stand, sanctions would probably be in violation of WTO obligations. There may be cover for trade restrictions under Article XX on grounds of protection of natural resources but not outside your own territory and not for unnecessary discrimination. However, given the large membership of these conventions and the collective nature of the imposition of sanctions, not only would there be little sympathy for the transgressor, but other countries would almost certainly have enough votes to grant themselves a waiver for the action anyway. It would be a messy business, but it would pose no insurmountable problems.

The more complex case occurs when members of a nearly global convention wish to sanction a country that does not belong to the convention but is a member of the WTO. The waiver strategy is also available here, but seems less legitimate since the 'transgressors' would have made no commitment to abide by the terms of the convention. Pursuing it would be very corrosive.

To forestall such problems, it may be wise for the WTO membership to start planning how they might cooperate with other multilateral bodies to achieve collective goals. For example, they might usefully set out the conditions under which they would permit trade sanctions. We suggest the following necessary conditions as means both to give the process legitimacy and reduce the chances of protectionist capture:

---

[5] We treat the elephant population as a global resource here, as perhaps the dolphin population should also be treated.

- sanctions be genuinely a last resort;
- decisions to sanction a transgressor should be collective, with a very substantial majority;
- provision be made for frequent review to see if sanctions need to be continued;
- sanctions should be applied by all members of the convention; and
- individual countries should have no discretion about what products are restricted nor how.

One might also suggest that the WTO assure itself that sanctions were likely to be effective and that no less trade-distorting measures were available. While reasonable in technical terms, these last provisions would immediately raise the spectre of the conflict between the WTO and environmental conventions. This would create uncertainty and international friction, and leave the WTO in the position of assessing substantive questions in areas in which it had no expertise.[6] It could thus potentially undermine the WTO's political legitimacy. Thus we propose that the issues of effectiveness, necessity and efficiency of trade sanctions be tackled when the WTO decides which conventions to recognise and that, thereafter, it accepts any trade restrictions that approved conventions imposed through due process.

Conventions which the WTO might 'recognise' for this purpose should:

- contain analysis showing that trade sanctions were necessary, likely to be effective, and least-cost means of enforcement;
- have membership by a substantial proportion of those affected, increasing to a very substantial proportion if the convention seeks to impose upon non-members;
- have treaty status in countries' domestic legislative processes; and
- have provision for periodic reviews of its effectiveness and its enforcement mechanisms.

These rules seem to separate out cases in which genuine cross-border issues arise, without opening up the protectionist floodgates. They use a multilateral approach to a multilateral problem and so, hopefully, head off any slippage into unilateralism.

b. Child Labour

Developing countries' use of child labour has negligible material effects on industrial countries, either directly or indirectly via policy spillovers. Industries

---

[6] This is not a trivial point – see, for instance, the debate on the ivory trade ban, which, according to commentators such as Swanson (1993), merely increases the chances of extinction by reducing the economic value of elephants.

and labour in industrial countries just do not compete with the sectors most affected by child labour (Basu, 1999). For example, the USA produces no soccer balls and any attempt to discipline its current major suppliers – Pakistan, China, Indonesia, India and Thailand – is likely to generate trade diversion, not new jobs in America. Similarly, no-one argues that industrial countries will reduce their own child labour standards in response to third-world competition.[7] Thus the case for industrial country intervention rests solely on altruism – a concern for children in poor countries. We do not dispute the undesirability of child labour, nor that concern for children in developing countries is legitimate. 'Just do something' is an understandable human response to horrifying stories, but is not a sound basis for intervention, especially in another country. We consider two strands of the argument.

First, is there a need for child labour standards, and if so, what should they be and should they be harmonised across countries? Given the choice, responsible parents (the vast majority) would prefer to see their young children in school rather than working. Child labour is mainly a response to poverty or poor schooling, and while legislation may be required for pathological cases, any supposed endemic problem must be tackled in these dimensions. In some cases, part-time work is the only means by which families can afford part-time school, so blanket bans on working could be quite counter-productive. It is far better to think in terms of conditioning work on participation in education. A legal ban will make child labour more difficult to manage, as it will be driven underground.

Since conditions vary between countries, so too will views on the correct education/working trade-off. Standards are essentially national affairs, and while international bodies such as UNICEF and the World Bank may bring the case for them and advice on administering them to governments' attention, they do not seem to be the stuff of international compulsion.

The second issue is, if countries have standards for child labour, is there a case for international enforcement, and should this include trade sanctions? We argue not. Restricting purchases of goods made by children is likely to create more not less hardship. As children lose jobs in developing country export sectors, their families will fall further into poverty. It is very unlikely that children will suddenly switch to schooling as the alternative occupation. Rather, child input will be shifted back in the production chain, where its direct effect on exports is less clear and where industrial country trade policy cannot reach it. Children may be diverted into less desirable and worse-paid occupations, such as garbage sorting and prostitution. Thus trade sanctions are more likely to hide the problem than solve it.

---

[7] There is, in fact, a possibility that developing countries could be involved in a race to the bottom – none can risk raising its standards unilaterally for fear of losing markets to those that have not – Basu (1999). But so far this argument has not figured at all in the debate.

Even 'ethical' trade, whereby industrial country companies seek to guarantee that their products are free of child labour (and other 'undesirable' features), can have perverse effects. The complexity of policing such guarantees is leading companies to concentrate their purchases on large companies, preventing economic activity from trickling down to small scale, local entrepreneurs and home workers. Thus it is likely to hurt the poor, and hence the families most likely to resort to child labour.

Despite the (possibly) best efforts of governments, import restrictions are always in danger of capture by protectionist groups. Basu (1999) notes that among the first use of the USA's Hawkins-Sanders Amendment on forced and indentured child labour was to criticise Brazil's largest orange juice producer. But the trigger for action was not new evidence of child abuse but that this firm had recently bought a US firm and cut back its work force.

If, despite these arguments, activists still feel compelled to tackle developing country child labour internationally, it is important to ensure that they do so multilaterally – as we argued above with environmental regulation. The WTO does not have the expertise to develop or even assess labour standards and so is not the body to manage any such system. This job falls naturally to the ILO, which has been doing it for many years. With today's instant communications, the ILO's sanction of naming and shaming transgressors is increasing in effectiveness and is likely to be able to induce a good deal of compliance by itself. If it were felt that this issue was sufficiently important to warrant a more coercive approach and trade sanctions were sought, these would need to be approved by the WTO. As above, we would suggest that they be so only if they are agreed multilaterally by a large majority and offer no discretion to individual countries on which products to sanction. Moreover, it is important that the determination of child labour abuses be based on the whole economy rather than just in the export sector. There is no virtue in international action just forcing child labour inland.

Finally, to meet Basu's point that child labour standards are essentially a question for developing countries, industrial countries should assist developing countries to collude among themselves to raise standards. This would be real philanthropy for, as Brown, Deardorff and Stern (1996) note, successful collusion will raise the prices of child-intensive exports and hence turn the terms of trade in favour of developing countries. Whether developing countries wish to avail themselves of such help is for them to determine in the ILO.

6. CONCLUSION

There are many good reasons for regulation but this does not make the WTO a good place for doing it. The GATT and the WTO have done an excellent job in fostering growth through trade liberalisation, but they are poorly placed to deal with issues surrounding environmental and labour standards. Forcing these regulatory issues into the GATT mould risks breaking it altogether.

Regulation is necessary to internalise externalities, resolve coordination failures and pursue various other so-called non-economic objectives. To be effective it must be legitimate, which, in turn, requires that it have several technical and political characteristics outlined in Section 2 above. The EU has found it difficult to meet these criteria, and it will be even more difficult for the WTO to do so, with its disparate membership and reliance on consensus. Without legitimacy, regulation, and eventually regulators, fall into disrepute and disuse, and with them even those parts of their mandates that they can carry out effectively.

The EU is a poor role model for the globalisation of environmental and social standards. It has greater cultural and economic homogeneity, far deeper and more powerful institutions and stronger links to local democracy than could possibly occur in a global body. Nonetheless, it has made very slow progress in these areas. It has been forced to formulate the doctrine of subsidiarity to balance centrality with national sovereignty. This requires regulation to be conducted at the 'appropriate' level, and positive proof that the benefits of centralisation outweigh both the compliance costs and the benefits of intergovernmental co-operation to achieve the same objective.

The attraction of the WTO for environmental and social policy activists lies not in its substantive ability, which is low in both areas, nor in the direct effects of trade on these objectives, which is rarely large. Rather it lies in the WTO's enforcement mechanisms and dispute settlement procedure. But, as we have shown, these are not well-suited to cases where taste may vary, deep issues of sovereignty are at stake or the offence lies in production process rather than in an observable characteristic of the good concerned. The traditional GATT approach of allowing countries to restrict imports subject to certain criteria is too vulnerable to capture and too readily permits the interference of one country in another's affairs to be satisfactory in these sensitive cases. We argue that if, nonetheless, any of these issues do end up in the WTO, the decisions and sanctions should be multilateral. In this way, egregiously anti-social behaviour can be punished without the risk of a stream of day-to-day frictions undermining the trading system.

We illustrated this analysis with two examples that figured in Seattle – global externalities and child labour standards. These led to several conclusions that we believe are of broader relevance:

- whenever the WTO is used for the enforcement of something other than trade policy, both the determination to act and the action should be multilateral; unilateralism – even of a multilateral variety – is just too dangerous in sensitive cases.

- if sanctions imposed for social reasons are directed at the goods where violations are held to have occurred, they will probably harm the very people they are supposed to help – e.g. child labourers or workers with no right of association thrown out of work as demand for their output is constrained;
- labelling may not be the answer if guaranteeing the truth of the labels is costly or it is discriminatory; and
- given that we do not *know* how economies will react to new regulations we must be cautious. It is difficult to claw back powers once they are internationalised and impossible to do so without weakening the organisation which had overseen them.

Thus to borrow a principle from environmental economics, we advocate:

- the virtues of regulo-diversity, which, in parallel with bio-diversity, suggests keeping several models of regulations alive, just because one might prove to be useful in ways that we cannot foresee at present; and
- a regulatory version of the precautionary principle – don't legislate at a higher level unless you are sure the benefits will outweigh the costs.

The points made above are free-standing arguments for not permitting environmental or social trade restrictions under the WTO. The GATT and now the WTO have been a force for good in the world economy, but their traditional agenda is far from exhausted – e.g. continuing agricultural and textile protection – and work under the GATS has barely started. Environmental and social issues not only distract from these issues, but can actively undermine the process of negotiation, compromise and ultimate balance as we saw in Seattle. To risk the chance of achieving concrete good with a very high probability for the chance of progress in areas where the returns are uncertain and the probability of success low does not seem to be sound or responsible governance.

REFERENCES

Basu, K. (1999), 'International Labour Standards and Child Labour', *Challenge* (September).

Bean, C. et al. (1998), 'Social Europe: One For All?', *Monitoring European Integration*, **8** (CEPR: London).

Brown, D., A. Deardorff and R. Stern (1996), 'International Labour Standards and Trade: A Theoretical Analysis', ch. 5 of J. Bhagwati and R. Hudec (eds.), *Fair Trade and Harmonization: Prerequisites for Free Trade?* (Cambridge, Mass.: MIT Press).

Esty, D. (1994), 'Greening the GATT', Institute for International Economics (Washington, DC).

Hufbauer, G.C., G. Schott and K.A. Elliot (1990), 'Economic Sanctions Reconsidered: History and Current Policy', Institute for International Economics (Washington, DC).

Jackson, J.H. (1998), *The World Trading System: Law and Policy of International Economic Relations*, 2nd ed. (Cambridge, Mass.: MIT Press).

Mayhew, A. and W. Orlowski (1999), 'The Impact of EU Accession on Enterprise Adaptation and

Institutional Development in the EU-Associated Countries in Central and Eastern Europe', EBRD Working Papers (London: EBRD, forthcoming).

Padoa-Schioppa, T. (1987), *Efficiency, Stability and Equity* (Oxford: OUP).

Pelkmans, J. (1997), *European Integration: Methods and Economic Analysis* (Netherlands, Open University, Longman, Harlow, Essex).

Sapir, A. (1996), 'Trade Liberalisation and the Harmonisation of Social Policy: Lessons from European Integration', in J. Bhagwati and R. Hudec (eds.), *Fair Trade and Harmonization. Prerequisites for Free Trade?* (Cambridge, Mass.: MIT Press).

Sbragia, A. (2000), 'Environmental Policy: Economic Constraints and External Pressures', in H. Wallace and W. Wallace (eds.), *Policy Making in the European Union* (Oxford: OUP).

Swanson, T. (1993), 'Regulating Endangered Species', *Economic Policy*, **16** (April), 183–205.

Tietmeyer, H. (1999), *The Social Market and Monetary Stability* (London: Economica).

12

From TRIMs to a WTO Agreement on Investment?

Bernard Hoekman and Kamal Saggi

1. INTRODUCTION

𝕴 N the last fifty years, countries have negotiated increasingly stringent disciplines on trade policies under the auspices of the General Agreement on Tariff and Trade (GATT) and more recently, the World Trade Organisation (WTO). Much less has been done to discipline policies that affect factor movement. With the exception of the General Agreement on Trade in Services (GATS), there are no disciplines in the WTO regarding policies pertaining to labour and capital movement. Some WTO members have argued that there is a need to negotiate multilateral rules for investment policies, such as the right of establishment and national treatment for foreign investors. These arguments largely revolve around market access objectives. For example, in many sectors the preferred mode of supplying a market may be through foreign direct investment (FDI), not exports. However, if FDI is restricted by the host country, foreign firms have an interest in lobbying for rules that guarantee them market access. Other lines of argument emphasise the potential payoffs to developing countries of signing on to multilateral rules as a commitment device (Markusen, 1998; and Moran, 1998) and the need to ensure that investment policies do not distort the mode of supply choice of foreign firms (Feketekuty, 2000; and Low and Mattoo, 2000).

The value of sales by foreign affiliates of multinationals has been growing rapidly, driven by falling communication and transportation costs, and liberalisation of FDI regimes in many countries. The eagerness to attract FDI is reflected in the use of fiscal and financial incentives to investors as well as the proliferation of bilateral investment treaties (BITs). As of 1999, over 1,600 BITs have been negotiated, compared to some 400 at the beginning of 1990 (UNCTAD, 1997). At the same time, many countries continue to subject multinationals to investment measures such as licensing and local content requirements, export performance and/

or technology transfer commitments. In fact, it is not unusual to find investment incentives being offered in conjunction with performance requirements, perhaps in order to partially offset the negative impact of the latter. The two-faced nature of the global policy environment reflects the guarded optimism with which many countries view multinational firms.

In the Uruguay Round an agreement on trade-related investment measures (TRIMs) was negotiated. Certain OECD countries, the United States (US) in particular, were of the view that policies distorting investment flows could have a significant impact on trade flows, and should be subject to multilateral trade disciplines. At the start of the Uruguay Round, the US sought to negotiate rules for a long list of TRIMs, including local content, export performance, trade balancing (linking the amount of permitted imports to the amount of exports), minimum or maximum domestic sales, technology transfer and licensing, remittances, ownership limitations, and investment incentives. Many developing countries resisted such a broad agenda, arguing that investment policies in general were beyond the scope of the GATT and should remain so.

The TRIMs agreement that ultimately emerged was not very ambitious, basically prohibiting measures that are inconsistent with the GATT national treatment principle (Art. III) and the ban on the use of quantitative restrictions (Art. XI). The focus of the agreement is on policies that imply discrimination against imports by creating incentives (additional to tariffs imposed at the border) to source from domestic sources of supply. The agreement prohibits local content, trade-balancing, foreign exchange-balancing and domestic sales requirements, requires that all policies not in conformity with the agreement be notified within 90 days of entry into force of the WTO, and be eliminated within two, five or seven years, for industrialised, developing and least developed countries, respectively. While the TRIMs agreement is limited to trade policies, the second WTO agreement that affects investment policies – the GATS – goes further by including market access through establishment (FDI) and national treatment for foreign direct investors as specific commitments that signatories may decide to make on a service sector-by-sector basis (Low and Mattoo, 2000).

In 1996, a WTO ministerial meeting in Singapore led to the creation of a working group on trade and investment whose goal was to examine the relationship between trade and investment policies. This group enhanced the understanding of WTO members regarding the relationship between trade and investment, but did little to span the differences in view regarding the appropriateness of the WTO as an instrument to discipline investment policies. It was quite clear in the run-up to the 1999 WTO ministerial meeting that there was no consensus to initiate negotiations on investment.

This chapter surveys some arguments that have suggested why developing countries should support the creation of a multilateral agreement on investment. These include:

- Policies restricting entry by foreign firms are welfare-reducing because resulting rents for domestic producers are less than consumer losses. If local incumbents capturing the rents are able to block FDI liberalisation, an international agreement that grants foreign firms better market access could be beneficial not only to source countries, but also to hosts by allowing them to overcome the political opposition to adoption of welfare-improving policies.
- National investment policies may impose negative spillovers on other countries leading to an inefficient outcome for the world as a whole. Possible examples are tax competition between governments and locational distortions created by regional integration agreements (RIAs).
- Governments seeking to attract FDI may benefit from an international agreement if this serves as a mechanism through which governments can reduce investor uncertainty by making irrevocable policy commitments.
- An investment agreement could be useful as a quid pro quo for a grand bargain that addresses major concerns of developing countries such as OECD anti-dumping, agricultural protection and investment-diverting rules of origin.

We conclude that while some of these potential rationales are compelling in principle, none justify multilateral negotiations on investment policies at this time. From a developing country viewpoint, *existing agreements and international institutions* already provide substantial opportunities to pursue and commit to liberalisation of FDI where it matters most – services. The GATS includes FDI as a mode of supply, and enormous scope still exists to liberalise FDI in services through this instrument.

The chapter is organised as follows. We start with a brief discussion of the market access rationale for disciplining policies that distort FDI and summarise existing WTO rules and disciplines (Section 2). We then turn to the spillover case for international cooperation and discuss the economic rationale for financial and fiscal incentives designed to attract FDI (Section 3). Next, we turn to the issue of discrimination arising from RIAs (Section 4), followed by the case for international agreement as a strategy to gain credibility (Section 5). The grand bargain argument is the focus of Sections 6. Section 7 concludes.[1]

2. MARKET ACCESS

As noted above, the TRIMs agreement simply reaffirms that GATT rules apply to trade policies that affect investors. The agreement prohibits both mandatory

---

[1] Many of the arguments presented in this paper are presented at much greater length in Hoekman and Saggi (1999 and 2000).

measures and those 'with which compliance is necessary to obtain an advantage' (such as a tax concession or subsidy). Export performance requirements are not covered, which is somewhat inconsistent with the GATT prohibition on the use of export subsidies, as the two instruments are very similar in effect. It was agreed in the Uruguay Round that the TRIMs agreement was to be reviewed starting in the year 2000, at which time the list of prohibited measures could be expanded and the rules complemented by provisions on competition and investment policy. As the five-year review deadline coincided with the built-in negotiating mandate on topics such as services and agriculture, TRIMs were expected to be part of the negotiating agenda of the 'millennium' round, perhaps wrapped into a more general negotiating group on investment policies. Although the Seattle ministerial failed to launch a round, it was agreed that discussions would continue in the working group.

As is well known, economic theory dictates that when domestic distortions and externalities from FDI are both absent, the optimal FDI policy ought to be no policy at all – i.e. governments should allow for unfettered market transactions. For there to be a rationale for restricting FDI there must exist some other domestic policy distortions or market failures. Since multinational firms typically arise in oligopolistic industries, the existence of imperfect competition might be one motivation for policy intervention by the host economy: multinational firms wield considerable market power and will typically use it to extract rents from the host economy. Indeed, theoretical analyses of content protection and export performance requirements under conditions of imperfect competition (Richardson, 1991 and 1993; and Rodrik, 1987) illustrate that the welfare effects of such policies can be positive under certain circumstances. However, in most situations more efficient instruments than investment measures can be identified; for example, almost by definition, vigorous competition policies are better suited for encouraging competition (Bora, Pangestu and Lloyd, 2000).[2] Whatever the purported rationale of restrictive policies, the available empirical evidence suggests that local content and related policies (transfer of technology, joint ventures) are ineffective and costly to the economy (Moran, 1998).[3] Furthermore,

---

[2] In the case of other domestic policy distortions, the optimal policy is well known: remove them at the source, if necessary through appropriately designed regulatory intervention that is applied on a nondiscriminatory basis (i.e., applies equally to both foreign and domestic firms). Thus, rather than using investment policies to offset the effects of high protection, the adoption of low and uniform tariffs is referable. This point of view is implicit in the WTO, which not only aims at progressive liberalisation of trade, but also prohibits the use of most trade-related investment measures (TRIMs).

[3] Investment measures have tended to be concentrated in specific industries with automotive, chemical, and petrochemical and computer industries leading the list (Moran, 1998). Local content requirements are most important in the auto industry; export requirements are more important in the computer industry. In chemicals and petrochemicals, local content requirements and export requirements are employed extensively.

protected industries may create problems for future liberalisation as they have an incentive to lobby against a change in regime. In such a scenario, international agreement may help overcome resistance from protected industries.

In addition to investment measures that are trade-related, many countries apply licensing and approval regimes and impose related red tape costs on foreign investors. They may also prohibit entry through FDI altogether, or impose equity ownership restrictions. Such policies may reflect welfare-enhancing attempts to shift foreign profits to the domestic economy or welfare-reducing rent-seeking activities by bureaucrats and their constituents. Sometimes the effect of policies is simply to waste real resources (so-called frictional costs – see Baldwin, 1994). The TRIMs agreement does not apply to such non-trade-related policies, nor does it affect service industries. The latter are covered by the GATS, however. As mentioned, the GATS extends to FDI policies in that countries can make specific market access and national treatment commitments for this mode of supply for any or all services.

The rents for domestic industries that are associated with restrictive FDI policies will be eroded in tradable industries if a liberal trade policy stance is pursued, as foreign firms can then contest the market through exports (Hoekman and Saggi, 2000). This suggests that priority should be given to trade liberalisation and trade facilitation efforts (enhancing the efficiency of customs clearance and port services) and strengthening existing institutions through which these goals can be met. Note also that if trade barriers are low, domestic industry will not have as large an incentive to support restrictive FDI regulations (restrictions on inward FDI may be motivated in part by the existence of high trade barriers, as this provides an incentive for tariff-wall hopping FDI).

Insofar as market access is concerned, liberalisation of entry and operating restrictions is of much greater importance for non-tradables (such as many services) than it is for tradables. As in many cases local incumbents will oppose new entry by foreign firms, the desire of foreign firms for market access can be used as a tool to promote liberalisation and may provide a potential rationale for multilateral negotiations. Much can already be achieved via the GATS, however, as this agreement includes FDI as a mode of supply.

3. MARKET FAILURES AND INTERNATIONAL SPILLOVERS

Investment-related policies may rationally attempt to shift rents (profits) from source to host countries through measures that effectively tax investors. The opportunity for this is created by the fact that FDI usually occurs in imperfectly competitive markets. In this section we ask whether the reverse policy stance (i.e. the encouragement of FDI) can be desirable. Clearly, both types of policies can create international spillovers and provide a basis for international cooperation.

What follows focuses primarily on incentive policies, as strategic (rent-shifting) arguments have already been discussed (see also Hoekman and Saggi, 2000).

From an individual country's perspective, incentives to attract FDI may be justified if there exist externalities from FDI. For example, developing countries may hope that FDI will generate technological spillovers for local firms thereby making more efficient use of existing resources. Spillovers may arise by local firms adopting technologies introduced by the multinational through imitation or reverse-engineering, by workers trained by the multinational transferring information to local firms or starting their own firms; and through derived demand by multinationals for local provision of services that can also be used by local firms, thereby starting a virtuous cycle of industrial development.

There exists a large literature that tries to determine whether or not host countries enjoy 'spillovers' (positive externalities) from FDI (Caves, 1996; Markusen, 1998; and Saggi, 2000 provide surveys). The empirical support for positive spillover effects is mixed, with a number of studies using firm level data concluding that FDI has a negative effect on the performance of domestically owned firms (Aitken and Harrison, 1999; and Haddad and Harrison, 1993). The empirical evidence regarding the magnitude of labour turnover from multi-nationals to local firms is also mixed. The literature suggests that the ability of local firms to absorb the technologies introduced by multinationals may be a key determinant of whether or not labour turnover occurs as a means of technology transfer in equilibrium (Glass and Saggi, 1998).

If governments believe that there exists a solid economic case for promoting inward FDI via incentives because of positive externalities, countries may find themselves in a bidding war for attracting FDI. This can be to the detriment of the parties involved if it leads to excessive payment to the investor. The proliferation in the use of incentives to FDI suggests that this is an important possibility, and that there may be a case for international cooperation to ban or discipline the use of fiscal incentives. Clearly a key issue here is whether fiscal incentives are effective. If not, there is no argument for international cooperation. The empirical evidence on this issue is also far from clear. Many studies have concluded that incentives to inward FDI do not play an important role in altering the global distribution of FDI (see Wheeler and Mody, 1992; and Caves, 1996). Others conclude that incentives do have an effect on location decisions, especially for export-oriented FDI (see Guisinger et al., 1985; Hines, 1993; and Devereux and Griffiths, 1998).[4] When incentives do not distort the global allocation of FDI, they basically end up as transfers to multinationals and there is no good case for international cooperation on efficiency grounds. On the other hand, it is precisely when such incentives fail to attract FDI that the developing countries have the

---

[4] Fiscal incentives are found to be unimportant for FDI geared towards the domestic market. This type of FDI is more sensitive to the extent to which it will benefit from import protection.

most to gain from committing to not using them. However, the case for cooperation under these circumstances is based mainly on distributional grounds.

Even if incentives affect FDI, the efficiency case against competition for FDI is not so clear cut. Competition for FDI via incentives may actually help ensure that FDI goes to those locations where it is most highly valued. Incentive competition may act as an efficient signalling device that improves the allocation of investment across jurisdictions by ensuring that FDI moves to where it has the highest social return. Note that in such situations governments should pursue policies on a non-discriminatory basis – in particular, abiding by the national treatment principle and adopting a right of establishment would appear to be appropriate.

In practice, locational competition is generally not driven by information asymmetries. This is the case in particular for efforts by high-income countries to retain or attract FDI that would be more efficiently employed in developing countries. Labour unions and groups representing the interests of local communities may oppose plant closures and efforts by firms to transplant facilities. Similar motivations underlie the use of trade policy instruments such as anti-dumping by OECD countries. It is important therefore to distinguish between locational competition between developing countries, which may be efficient, and locational incentives used by industrialised nations. The latter are much more likely to be inefficient and focus on attracting industries that otherwise would not have come. Such incentive policies, as well as complementary policies that protect industries that cannot compete and should either exit or relocate (examples are rules of origin in regional agreements and anti-dumping) are prime candidates for international negotiations (Moran, 1998).

The foregoing suggests there are valid reasons to question the rationale for an agreement that seeks to discipline all incentives. If incentives fail to alter the global allocation of FDI, restricting their usage has mainly distributional consequences. On the other hand, if they are effective in altering location decisions, a case may exist for subsidy freedom since countries may be able to signal important information to potential investors. However, developing countries have an unambiguous incentive to push for multilateral disciplines on OECD policies that have the effect of preventing firms from relocating to developing countries.

4. SPILLOVERS ASSOCIATED WITH REGIONAL INTEGRATION

Some regional integration agreements (RIAs) have extended the reach of national treatment to investors from partner countries, in the process abolishing TRIMs. Examples include the EU, where freedom of investment is a basic principle, NAFTA, and various association agreements the EU has concluded with Central and Eastern European neighbours. Insofar as RIAs lead to discrimination between insiders and outsiders in terms of FDI policies, they impose negative externalities over and above whatever investment 'diversion' occurs because of the preferential liberalisation of trade barriers. Eliminating this discrimination can be a powerful argument in favour of multilateral rules. An important empirical question is whether such discrimination occurs and how large it is. This is very difficult to determine, as it requires careful and detailed assessments of the applicable legislation on both a horizontal and sector-by-sector basis. Some agreements – e.g., the EU and some of the agreements it in turn has negotiated with neighbouring countries – embody a right of establishment for nationals of parties. Most RIAs are limited to BIT-type disciplines, requiring national treatment (often subject to exceptions – negative lists) and disciplining the use of performance requirements. Given the role of regulation and the political sensitivity associated with foreign ownership of many service industries, one way of assessing whether RIAs have a discriminatory effect is to determine to what extent they go beyond the GATS in elimination of discrimination in service markets. Given that FDI will be a major mode of supply, the more RIAs go beyond the GATS, the greater the potential negative spillovers.

Hoekman (1999) argues that with the exception of the EU, most RIAs do not go much beyond the GATS. Most RIAs also do little to effectively constrain the ability of governments to provide incentives for FDI. The most far-reaching RIAs are those involving the EU, which seek to apply common disciplines in areas such as anti-trust, state aids, and state monopolies. Periodic disputes regarding the use of incentives by local governments to attract FDI and recurring claims of 'social dumping' illustrate that even the far-reaching EU disciplines are insufficient to constrain the ability of governments to adopt the tax and factor market policies they believe will be most conducive to stimulating investment, be it foreign or domestic.

Insofar as RIAs cause negative investment spillovers, this is most likely to arise in the area of production and trade in goods. Restrictive rules of origin and trade policies such as anti-dumping have the effect of encouraging investment in regional agreements (Moran, 1998). Such effects will be attenuated if the trade discrimination associated with RIAs is reduced by lowering external tariffs and other trade barriers. This suggests the focus of multilateral negotiation efforts should be on further trade liberalisation. This will minimise discrimination and reduce the need for restrictive rules of origin. This is likely to be a more feasible and productive strategy than attempting to strengthen WTO disciplines on regional integration (Winters, 1999) or to seek new rules on investment policies.

5. REPUTATION AND POLICY CREDIBILITY

From a national perspective, a multilateral agreement may help countries that seek FDI as a signalling device or instrument through which the perceived credibility of a set of policies intended to foster FDI can be enhanced. It is sometimes argued for example that the countries of Central and Eastern Europe sought to conclude Association Agreements with the EU in part to overcome perceptions by foreign investors that they were countries where there was a high risk of policy reversals and policy uncertainty.[5] In order to assess the relevance of the credibility argument for an investment agreement, it is necessary to identify how much of what might be embodied in such an agreement can be pursued and implemented unilaterally, and, as important, to control for the economic fundamentals.

The experience of transition economies reveals that fundamentals are crucial. Some countries with Association Agreements have attracted very little FDI (e.g., Bulgaria) in large part because privatisation was not pursued with any vigour, the political environment was uncertain, and macroeconomic policy such that inflation attained triple digits. The Czech Republic, Hungary and Poland have attracted significant FDI inflows, but it is unclear what role the investment provisions of the Association Agreements have played. A case can be made that fundamentals drove these inflows, including privatisation, re-establishment of private property rights, and geographic proximity to Europe (especially Germany).

Many countries that are looking for FDI have made use of a variety of existing credibility-enhancing institutions. One is to commit to accept arbitration of disputes under the Convention on the Settlement of Investment Disputes between States and Nationals of Other States (ICSID), by the International Chamber of Commerce (ICC), or by the UN Committee on International Trade Law (UNCITRAL),[6] depending on the preferences of the investor. Sometimes such commitments are embedded in RIAs – e.g., NAFTA. Developing countries may also negotiate bilateral investment treaties with the major home countries of FDI.

Countries that are in the market for credibility can also use existing WTO disciplines to schedule market access opening policies for services (including granting of the right of establishment), and choose to lock in low tariff regimes by binding these under GATT rules. There is still huge scope for developing countries to use the WTO as a credibility enhancing instrument – as noted

---

[5] See Markusen (1998) for a discussion of the credibility case for an investment agreement; Fernandez and Portes (1998) for an analysis of how international agreement may support credibility.

[6] An International Centre for the Settlement of Investment Disputes operates under the aegis of the World Bank to apply the Convention. The ICC has a Court of Arbitration. UNCITRAL has adopted a set of Arbitration and Conciliation Rules that can be used in the settlement of commercial disputes.

previously, the coverage of services commitments is very limited, and tariff bindings for merchandise imports are often significantly higher than applied rates. Although credibility with respect to investment-related policies can also be pursued via a multilateral investment agreement, those governments that are convinced they have a need to use external instruments to achieve such objectives could start by exploiting existing instruments much more fully.

6. ISSUE LINKAGE AND THE GRAND BARGAIN

The WTO process allows countries to define a negotiating set that allows a variety of potential tradeoffs and deals to be crafted that are superior to the status quo ante. Because countries are restricted to the equivalent of barter trade in multilateral trade negotiations, to achieve a Pareto superior (cooperative) outcome, issues must be linked. Determining when such linkage is necessary and successfully designing globally-beneficial packages is a non-trivial task, given that this occurs in the context of rent-seeking lobbying and often involves issues that are difficult to analyse (Leidy and Hoekman, 1993).

In the FDI policy context, the argument is quite simple – this is a valuable negotiating chip for developing countries as industrialised nations are the demandeurs. Indeed, insofar as governments are in a situation where domestic constraints inhibit the abolition of welfare-reducing restrictive FDI policies, using this chip comes at zero cost. Given that for most developing countries FDI exports is largely a non-issue, a good case can be made that the quid pro quo for accepting to adopt national treatment, MFN, and the right of establishment as general multilateral disciplines should be sought outside the investment area. Examples that have been mentioned include anti-dumping and restrictive rules of origin (Moran, 1998). While the argument is valid in principle, it is not clear that investment policies are a particularly valuable negotiating chip for developing countries. Other policies are likely to be more powerful in inducing offsetting concessions. Among these, further liberalisation of trade under existing agreements (GATT and GATS) figure prominently. Investment policies may prove useful at the margin, but much can already be (and will have to be) brought to the negotiating table by developing countries through utilisation of existing mechanisms and instruments. Major payoffs in terms of obtaining a quid pro quo could be expected from making significant commitments in the services area.

7. THE ARCHITECTURAL ARGUMENT

The current architecture of the WTO is quite messy: the WTO is an apex institution that oversees (embodies) three major multilateral agreements (GATT,

GATS, and TRIPs), one that incorporates FDI as a mode of supply, and another that protects investments in intellectual property. As is often emphasised, trade and investment have increasingly become complementary. It will become increasingly difficult to maintain a clear distinction between trade in goods and trade in services, as technology may give producers the choice of delivering their products in tangible form or in disembodied form. A priori, it would appear that any multilateral disciplines should apply equally to international transactions regardless of the mode of delivery.

This suggests that a case can be made that WTO members may wish to consider developing disciplines that distinguish between trade and investment, with trade in goods or services being subject to a set of common rules, and movement of factors of production being subject to another set of rules. This in effect has been the approach taken in the NAFTA, which includes a separate chapter on investment (in goods or services), which is distinct from the rules relating to cross-border trade (in goods and services). Emulating this approach would result in much greater consistency and clarity of the applicable rules and disciplines.

This is a compelling rationale for discussion of FDI-related policies in the WTO. Logic suggests that if this path is followed movement of labour should be put on the table as well. Purely from an economic viewpoint, the arguments for free movement of labour are no weaker than those for the free movement of capital. Clearly, countries that play the role of source countries in the movement of capital will play the role of host countries in the movement of labour. It is unlikely that governments will be prepared to go far down this path in the near future. The issues involved become considerably more thorny once labour mobility is introduced into the mix, and a complete revamping of the trading system will be required. In the short to medium run, efforts are better directed at arriving at a situation that would facilitate future efforts to move the WTO towards greater consistency in the rules of the game that apply to alternative modes of supply and different types of international exchange. A precondition for this is that WTO members move much closer to a free trade stance and liberalise access to their markets for goods *and* services. The GATS in particular has an important role to play in this connection as it already covers FDI in the sectors where it is most important as an instrument to contest markets – in services industries.

The fact that the GATS includes establishment as a mode of supply on which commitments can be made, significantly weakens the case for making a stand-alone investment agreement in the WTO a negotiating priority. Once substantial further progress has been made to liberalise trade in goods and services on a non-discriminatory basis, including market access through establishment in (non-tradable) service activities, it will become much clearer whether the potential benefits of seeking general rules on investment policies are large enough to justify launching a multilateral negotiation in this area. The rather limited applicability of the national treatment instrument in the GATS suggests the time is not ripe to consider launching negotiations on investment policies.

8. CONCLUDING REMARKS

Negotiating a WTO agreement on investment policies may prove useful in arriving at a grand bargain that extends to issues of particular interest to developing countries. This possibility must be considered carefully, as there may be significant scope for obtaining large returns in other areas as a quid pro quo for participating in an investment agreement. A broader agenda will be necessary in any event both for countries that confront domestic political economy constraints on the adoption of better FDI policies, and for those that seek to use FDI policies strategically. Devising a grand bargain will be difficult. Account must be taken of the potential downside – issue linkage can be a two-edged sword. Efforts to expand the agenda to investment may allow groups in society to seek cross-issue linkages in areas such as the environment or labour standards that could be detrimental to the original *raison d'être* of the WTO: to progressively liberalise international trade. Bhagwati (1998) has argued that this Pandora's box possibility provides a powerful justification for leaving general investment rules off the WTO agenda.

The failure of the OECD to reach an agreement on a Multilateral Agreement on Investment illustrates the practical difficulties that will arise.[7] The diversity in the policy environment across countries creates significant room for scepticism regarding the success of negotiations regarding an agreement on investment. If OECD countries, with their much more uniform policy environment and similar goals fail to reach an accord, how can one expect developing countries that differ more substantially from one another to agree on a common set of principles regarding investment?

In our view priority should be given to the pursuit of classic trade liberalisation to ensure markets for tradable goods are contestable through exports. This should include efforts to liberalise access to service markets on a non-discriminatory basis, an area where establishment (FDI) is often crucial. Continued non-discriminatory liberalisation of trade barriers for goods and services will also help reduce possible locational distortions for FDI resulting from RIAs and discipline the ability of countries to pursue strategic policies, as trade policy is a vital element of any such strategy. While the elimination of trade policy as an instrument to transfer profits is in theory possibly detrimental to developing countries, in practice such profit-shifting policies are very difficult to design and

---

[7] See Henderson (1999) for a comprehensive analysis of the OECD talks on investment.

implement. Any potential losses are likely to be offset many times over by the efficiency gains from trade liberalisation. Moreover, countries obtain compensation in a mercantilist sense as well, as trade liberalisation in foreign markets will be obtained as a quid pro quo.

Although we are pessimistic about the need for – and feasibility of – negotiating a multilateral agreement on investment at this time, the conclusion that new multilateral rules are not really needed urgently is a positive one. It implies that governments can achieve much of what is beneficial unilaterally – including application of the principles of national treatment and MFN, and adoption of the right of establishment in national law. It also implies governments do not have to invest resources to negotiate in (another) new area and can instead use existing institutions and mechanisms to liberalise access to markets.

REFERENCES

Aitken, B. and A.E. Harrison (1999), 'Do Domestic Firms Benefit from Direct Foreign Investment?,' *American Economic Review*, **89**, 3, 605–18.
Baldwin, R. (1994), *Towards an Integrated Europe* (London: CEPR).
Bhagwati, J. (1998), 'Powerful Reasons for the MAI to be Dropped Even From the WTO Agenda', *Financial Times* (22 October).
Caves, R.E. (1996), *Multinational Enterprise and Economic Analysis* (Cambridge: Cambridge University Press).
Devereux, M. and R. Griffiths (1998), 'Taxes and the Location of Production: Evidence from a Panel of US States,' *Journal of Public Economics*, **68**, 335–67.
Feketekuty, G. (2000), 'Assessing and Improving the Architecture of GATS,' in P. Sauve and R. Stern (eds.), *Services 2000: New Directions in Services Trade Liberalization* (Brookings Institution and Harvard University, Washington DC, ch 4).
Fernandez, R. and J. Portes (1998), 'Returns to Regionalism: An Analysis of the Nontraditional Gains from Regional Trade Agreements,' *World Bank Economic Review*, **12**, 197–220.
Glass, A.J. and K. Saggi (1998), 'Multinational Firms and Technology Transfer,' World Bank Policy Research Paper No. 2067.
Guisinger, S. and associates (1985), *Investment Incentives and Performance Requirements* (New York: Praeger).
Haddad, M. and A. Harrison (1993), 'Are There Positive Spillovers from Direct Foreign Investment?,' *Journal of Development Economics*, **42**, 51–74.
Henderson, D. (1999), *The Multilateral Agreement in Investment: A Story and Its Lessons* (Wellington: New Zealand Roundtable (www.nzbr.org.nz)).
Hines, J.R. (1993), 'Altered States: Taxes and the Location of FDI in America,' NBER Working Paper 4397.
Hoekman, B. (1999), 'Beyond National Treatment: Integrating Domestic Policies,' (World Bank, mimeo).
Hoekman, B. and K. Saggi (1999), 'Multilateral Disciplines for Investment Related Policies?,' World Bank Policy Research Paper 2138.
Hoekman, B. and K. Saggi, 2000. 'Assessing the Case for Extending WTO Disciplines on Investment-Related Policies' (World Bank and Southern Methodist University, mimeo).
Leidy, M. and B. Hoekman (1993), 'What to Expect from Regional and Multilateral Trade Negotiations: A Public Choice Perspective,' in K. Anderson and R. Blackhurst (eds.), *Regional Integration and the Global Trading System* (London: Harvester-Wheatsheaf).

Low, P. and A. Mattoo (2000), 'Is There a Better Way? Alternative Approaches to Liberalization Under the GATS,' in P. Sauve and R. Stern (eds.), *Services 2000: New Directions in Services Trade Liberalization* (Brookings Institution and Harvard University, Washington DC, ch 15).

Markusen, J. (1998), 'Multilateral Rules on Foreign Direct Investment: The Developing Countries' Stake' (mimeo).

Moran, T. (1998), *Foreign Direct Investment and Development* (Washington DC: Institute for International Economics).

Richardson, M. (1991), 'The Effects of a Content Requirement on a Foreign Duopsonist,' *Journal of International Economics*, **31**, 143–55.

Richardson, M. (1993), 'Content Protection with Foreign Capital,' *Oxford Economic Papers*, **45**, 103–17.

Rodrik, D. (1987), 'The Economics of Export-Performance Requirements,' *The Quarterly Journal of Economics*, **102**, 633–50.

UNCTAD (1997), *World Investment Report: Transnational Corporations, Market Structure, and Competition Policy* (United Nations: New York, NY).

Wheeler, D. and A. Mody (1992), 'International Investment Decisions: The Case of U.S. Firms,' *Journal of International Economics*, **33**, 57–76.

Winters, L. A. (1999), 'Regionalism and the Rest of the World' (World Bank, mimeo).

13

Trade Facilitation:
Technical Regulations and Customs
Procedures

Patrick A. Messerlin and Jamel Zarrouk

1. INTRODUCTION

T HIS chapter examines technical regulations (TRs) and customs regulations *together*, under the general headline of *trade facilitation*. Both subjects raise the same challenge: how to minimise the unnecessary burden – for trading partners and domestic consumers – of the application and enforcement of national laws and regulations. Such national measures reflect each WTO Member's right to regulate its own economy as it wishes. In both areas symmetrical demands are triggered from industrial and developing countries, suggesting beneficial trade-offs in future WTO negotiations.

Industrial countries perceive that customs procedures in developing countries have not adjusted enough to the rapidly growing volume of trade of the last decade. Their complaints are echoed by service providers, such as express mail couriers which handle a substantial proportion of all customs entries (more than 30 per cent in their largest markets). The ability of such firms to provide their services depends heavily on efficient customs procedures (e.g., a guaranteed delivery time for parcels). Conversely, developing countries are increasingly concerned by the imposition of ever expanding TRs by industrial countries, arguing that TRs are beyond their technical competence or do not take into account special development needs and technological problems (UNCTAD, 1999). Industrial countries also complain about the adoption by some developing countries of TRs that seem to be substitutes for quantitative restrictions and similar instruments, while developing countries complain about the 'spaghetti bowl' of rules of origin included in the customs procedures of the industrial countries (in particular, those which are hubs of regional agreements).

These complaints have become noisier because many tariffs and non-tariff barriers (such as quantitative restrictions or voluntary export restrictions) have been reduced or eliminated. But other factors also explain the fact that trade facilitation is rising on the agenda of trade negotiations. First, the growth of intra-firm trade (where the same firm is at both ends of the trade flows concerned) makes large firms less willing to accept unexpected or duplicative constraints on their cost-minimised internal production process. Second, small and medium enterprises are playing an increasing role in world trade: TRs and customs procedures are for them new problems – in contrast with large firms having an experience in these issues – fuelling the feeling of unfair competition. This factor plays a strong role in developing countries (large firms in these countries are generally small firms by world standards), as documented in detail by a recent study (ITC-UNCTAD-WTO, 1997). Last, but not least, TRs impinge on sensitive issues such as health, safety and the environment, while inefficient customs regimes can have major detrimental repercussions for traders. The prominence of both aspects of trade facilitation is greatly magnified by small and well-organised interest groups, including non-governmental organisations (NGOs) with strong views on the 'best' TRs, are skilled in getting attention in the media, and are able to convey their messages quickly worldwide.

This chapter asks what can be done at the multilateral level during the coming decade in this vast trade facilitation field. It is organised as follows. Section 2 tries to provide some quantitative estimates of the importance of trade facilitation issues. Section 3 looks at the possibility for multilateral actions for addressing the issues raised by the *design* of trade facilitation-related regulations. Section 4 does the same, but at the level of the *enforcement* of trade facilitation-related regulations. Section 5 concludes.

Two general conclusions emerge from the chapter. First, *designing* similar TRs is likely to be a costly approach at the multilateral level, and a source of distortions when done at the regional level. By contrast, multilateral initiatives for *enforcing* TRs offer much better perspectives if trade facilitation activities are conceived as 'services' to be included in the WTO negotiations on services liberalisation (with accompanying adequate domestic regulatory reforms). Second, *private* initiatives can be very useful at both levels (design and enforcement) because they are much more flexible and more responsive to consumers' demand than public actions, and because the associated risks of private collusive behaviour (which could lead to trade distortions) can be handled by competition policy.

2. THE IMPORTANCE OF TRADE FACILITATION-RELATED ISSUES

TRs comprise mandatory 'norms' and voluntary 'standards.' They are introduced for a wide range of reasons (including at times simply to give the impression of public action). They can be applicable to products, production or producers (licensing requirements for service suppliers), or to consumption (e.g., bans of certain products, such as in the beef hormone case). The scope and types of prevailing TRs reflect a society's attitudes toward the level of acceptable risks, its environmental factors (endowments), and its knowledge and ability to manage risk.

The last 50 years have witnessed a considerable increase in TRs in almost all countries, as best illustrated by the EC. The main argument for creating European TRs during the 1970s was the great expansion of new national TRs adopted by Member states (in 1992, EC Member states were enforcing more than 80,000 norms, compared to less than 2,000 European norms (WTO, 1993, p. 111)). Today, EC TRs represent the largest body of EC regulations: the number of Directives (laws in EC parlance) devoted to TRs amount to more than a third of all the Directives adopted since 1958.[1] The same boom can be observed for customs procedures, and is explained by a variety of reasons ranging from the need to create new tariff codes for products subject to anti-dumping duties to ever expanding and more detailed rules of origin. As is documented by Hoekman (1998), this evolution is common to most WTO Members, and has led to a multiplication of duplicative requirements imposed at customs borders, rapidly becoming more important barriers to international trade.

a. The Extent of Technical Regulations

Are trade facilitation-related costs relatively uniformly spread over all the trading partners of a country, or do they tend to hurt certain countries more than others? Differentiated effects can flow from various sources. First, certain products are more subject to TRs than others. Second, bilateral or regional agreements on common TRs could result in discrimination and trade distortions between members of the agreement: in this respect, common TRs are potentially similar to endogenous tariff formation in the context of a free trade zone, hence favouring the dominant industries and firms of the zone (Olarreaga and Soloaga, 1998). Third, bilateral or regional agreements to establish common TRs could result in discrimination and trade distortions between members and non-members: in this respect, common TRs are potentially equivalent to a common external tariff leading to trade-creation and trade-distortion effects between a customs union and the rest of the world).

---

[1] The two next largest packages of Directives cover agriculture and environment (another third of all Directives) with a substantial proportion of them being TR-related.

It is thus important to have a sense of the magnitude of all these possible differentiated effects. A relatively detailed analysis of the EC experience in the manufacturing sector suggests two main conclusions (Messerlin, 1998). First, sectors with a high index of failure in regard to establishment of EC TRs policy (this index is based on an industry survey) represent one-third of intra-EC trade and of EC imports from the world, suggesting that introducing common TR is slow and difficult (a point worth recalling in the next section). Second, sectors dominated by the process of adopting common TRs represent one-third of EC value added and of intra-EC trade, but only one-fourth of EC imports from the rest of the world – with substantial differences between the various EC trading partners (these sectors represent one-fourth of EC imports from the US, Japan, and Central European countries, but only one-sixth of EC imports from the emerging economies (Hong Kong, Korea, Indonesia, Malaysia, Singapore, Taiwan and Thailand) and almost one-third of EC imports from ACP countries). These findings are consistent with TR-related discriminatory effects on extra-EC trade, all the more because the sectors involved are subject to high rates of EC global protection (Messerlin, 1999).

b. Customs Procedures and Trade Costs

Excessive control of and inefficiencies in customs procedures, combined with a monopoly of service providers in key entry points in importing countries, are prevalent in many parts of the developing world. Valuation procedures are a major source of uncertainty for importers (customs generally expect under-invoicing). In some Middle East and North African countries, customs officers question every invoice in order to charge penalties or collect 'rewards.' Resulting costs can exceed tariffs in many cases. Documentary red tape in customs procedures can increase the cost of imports substantially – according to one estimate by some 7–10 per cent of the value of world trade (Staples, 1998). Anecdotal evidence of administrative customs inefficiencies and its impact in several developing countries is abundant.

Customs-related barriers to trade facilitation are a major problem facing transport operators when crossing frontiers. The International Road Transport Union has reported that the most restrictive cross-border transportation policies are found in some parts of Europe and the Middle East and North Africa (WTO, 1998). The cost of the associated delays affecting international trade is estimated to be about six per cent of total transport time in some countries of Central and Eastern Europe. Complaints from the transport profession also include excessive charges that impair the freedom of transit required by Article V GATT. For instance, monopoly port service providers and inefficient regulation of port operations gives rise to implicit tariffs of 5–15 per cent on exports in Latin America (Guasch and Spiller, 1999). The cost per ton of handling a container in the port of Alexandria (in Egypt) is reported to be a multiple of that in other Mediterranean countries. The lack of competition in trade-related services (such as insurance) translates into higher insurance premia for trade coverage (Hoekman, 1995).

c. Trade Facilitation and WTO Dispute Settlement Cases

Both components of the trade facilitation agenda discussed in this chapter (TRs and customs procedures) have emerged as a recurrent theme in WTO dispute settlement cases. Customs-related disputes have included customs classification, duty collection, GSP coverage, quota management and import measures. Although only a handful of TR cases have been brought (tuna-dolphin, shrimp-turtles, beef hormones, and asbestos), the provisions of the Uruguay Round Technical Barriers to Trade Agreement (hereafter TBT) have been invoked in many other complaints. All these cases have involved industrial and developing countries, both as complainants and defendants.

So far, the disputes have had a very different fate, depending on whether customs procedures or TR are at stake. Cases on customs procedures have been dealt with at the technical level without too many fights, and losing parties have complied with recommendations (or, at least, issued an official statement to comply). In sharp contrast, cases involving TRs have generated heated debates, and compliance with panel rulings seems to be far from automatic (in particular since the EC decision not to implement the WTO ruling on beef hormones). The main lesson to be drawn from these cases is that the 'science-based' approach used by the WTO (and by each WTO Member state) does not provide the robust guidelines necessary for a satisfactory handling of multilateral trade disputes. This reliance on science leads to two typical situations. Either the scientific community can assess risks and largely agrees, but defending governments dismiss scientific evidence because they are captured by vested interests (or are simply unable or unwilling to act).[2] Or the scientific community is unable to assess risks – a situation which is not so rare, particularly for technologies lacking the data necessary for risk assessment because evidence has to be found *ex post* (asbestos) or because relatively new technologies are involved (genetically modified organisms or GMOs). The problem of the science-based WTO approach flows simply from the fact that, almost by definition, trade conflicts are most

---

[2] This is best illustrated by the beef hormone case. In 1988, the EC banned the use of six hormones for cattle growth-promoting purposes, after years of strong intra-EC conflicts. Few experts (including in Europe) believe that there is a serious health risk related to beef hormones: in fact, three of the six hormones are authorised in the EC for therapeutic uses. Moreover, there are constant rumours reporting a sizeable illegal (that is, growth-promoting) use of all these hormones in the EC – suggesting that the ban is motivated by the depressed situation of the beef market and the inability to reform the CAP (hormones can increase beef production by 20 per cent).

likely to arise in the two above-mentioned situations – the first one being highly correlated with traditional protectionist behaviour, the second one with the emergence of a more efficient production pattern.

Far from being specific to the WTO, these problems mirror those faced by WTO members at the national level. In North America, an additive to gasoline for cars (methylcyclopentadienyl manganese tricarbonyl, or MMT) has been banned on health grounds by the US EPA, but not by Health Canada, fuelling one of the most bitter disputes in Canada–US trade, and playing an important role in the OECD-based negotiations on a Multilateral Agreement on Investment. In the EC, Finland (which produces cadmium-free phosphates) believes that cadmium in phosphate is damaging for health in the long run, whereas Spain and Italy (which import cheap phosphates with a relatively high cadmium content from Morocco) do not.

Such examples abound. If anything, they show the difficulties (to say the least) that arise in providing a robust definition of the 'precautionary principle.' The resulting chaotic situation is illustrated by the fact that many Europeans (Americans) find acceptable (unacceptable) the EC ban on imports of beef hormones, but unacceptable (acceptable) US restrictions on EC exports of non-pasteurised cheeses (despite risks of salmonella). It also leads to chaotic situations within regional trade zones, such as in the EC: since the 'mad cow' disease, France (and Germany) bans beef imports from Britain, whereas imports of tobacco (which kill 60,000 French citizens every year) are left free.

3. MULTILATERAL RESPONSES TO TRADE FACILITATION: A VERY LIMITED ROLE FOR THE WTO

Eliminating differences between TRs by *designing* common TRs at the multilateral level seems *a priori* the best way to eliminate TR-related conflicts in the WTO. The same could be said for customs regulations. However, what follows suggests that it would be a costly approach. *Private* initiatives to design global TRs are more preferable.

The distinction between mandatory norms and voluntary standards is essential in the WTO context. WTO Members differ substantially in terms of the proportion of the two sources of TRs: norms remain dominant in many former centrally-planned economies and developing countries, whereas standards are a dominant force in industrial countries (except for health- and environment-related issues) because firms are regarded as the only economic operators knowledgeable enough to master adequately the problems raised by technical progress. As a result, firms in industrial countries are left free to develop and monitor their own appropriate standards in which they invest their own credibility (loose standards would damage the firm's reputation and profits). Of course, firms can act collectively (*collective* action does not necessarily mean *government* action).

The norm-based and standard-based approaches also have quite different potential impacts on trade. It seems reasonable to assume that the deeper the involvement of public authorities is, the more likely the *impact* of TRs is a protectionist and discriminatory one, leading to trade conflicts. This hypothesis does not mean that industry-based standards have no protectionist or discriminatory *content* (they do, maybe even more than mandatory standards designed by public authorities). However, firms are generally unable to *enforce* trade barriers in the long run without the help of public authorities.

a. Harmonisation

Designing common TRs could be done by *harmonising* WTO Members' TRs (that is, by substituting multilateral TRs for national TRs) or by promoting the *mutual recognition* of Members' TRs by other Members (possibly around a minimal core of common regulations). Designing common TRs is a task which could be conceived for both norms and standards (firms from different countries might wish to design a common standard), but of course, it raises more issues in case of mandatory norms. Indeed, this is suggested by a direct interpretation of Articles 2:4 (harmonisation) and 2:7 (mutual recognition) of the TBT Agreement.

During its first 28 years (1958–1985), the Community used the *harmonisation* approach to TRs by adopting European norms proposed by the Commission and negotiated by the Member states in the Council of Ministers. This process proved to be extremely slow and difficult. EC efforts to break this deadlock by reducing the scope of harmonisation (making harmonisation optional, partial, minimal, alternative, or piecemeal) led to the adoption of a much larger number of TRs, but at a high cost: the product coverage of each EC TR was very narrow, with most of these TRs being drafted in an extremely detailed manner. As a result, frequent and substantial redrafting has been (still is) required, leading to recurrent and difficult conflicts.[3]

The EC experience suggests that it would be unproductive for the WTO to play a role in the design of multilateral norms (mandatory TRs). In contrast, the multilateral harmonisation of standards (voluntary TRs) seems much easier, but must flow from collective efforts by firms with enough technical competence and prestige to generate multilateral standards in their sector. Numerous examples of such efforts exist. For instance, in the 19th century, international railway unions in Europe promoted the establishment of networks by adopting the same rail

---

[3] For instance, the EC Directive on 'braking devices on certain categories of motor vehicles and of their trailers' has been revised eight times. The last version is 146 pages long.

gauge, standardising rolling equipment, driving on the left, adjusting signals, brakes and timetables to each other, etc. Interestingly, these inter-firm agreements had spillovers on related services, such as the mutual repair and cleaning of freight cars or the adoption of a single document for all trans-European shipments, and they even culminated in trade liberalisation, e.g., abolition of transit duties on goods shipped by rail (Hoekman, 1998). Today, such cases of cooperation are likely to be more frequent because of the emergence of global firms that are very sensitive to the high costs associated with reputation losses in the case of failure or accident.

Between norms and standards, there is room for (voluntary) standards generated by 'recognised' bodies. More than 30 intergovernmental organisations were created between the late 19th and early 20th centuries, from mail (1863) to aerial navigation (1910), and a few others have been added since the Second World War (for labour markets or banking supervision rules). A few regulatory bodies from one country have also gained a worldwide influence, as best illustrated by the US Federal Aviation Authority on aircraft safety.

In sum, firms may achieve multilateral cooperation much more easily than governments. A firm-based approach raises the possibility of firms generating market dominance (and its potential abuse) through common TRs, as illustrated by the inter-war efforts to cartelise national European steel industries by using:

> complex systems for documentation and classifying raw materials and finished goods to favour their own producers, ports, cities or transfer points (Murphy, 1994, p. 109).

However, using potential collusion as an argument for dismissing the gains from private efforts to design common TRs, and for substituting public efforts for private initiatives, is not a good argument: a better policy is a mix of allowing the emergence of standards and using competition policy for deterring collusion. In fact, the use of competition policy could be promoted by the WTO legal framework if it is explicitly included in the Code of Good Practice on the Preparation, Adoption and Application of Standards (Annex 3 of the TBT Agreement).

Nascent conflicts about GMOs illustrate the fact that public intervention tends to make issues more conflictual. Producers of GMO anxious to recoup huge R&D outlays lobby their governments for 'market access' in the rest of the world, whereas farmers in the importing countries claim to be safeguarding consumers' interests (but in fact are concerned about an increase in quasi-vertical integration links between users and GMO producers). In contrast, certain US and EC firms have recently started to build a reputation for the absence of GMO inputs – shifting the issue from an international dispute case to one centring on individual decisions taken by well (or better) informed consumers *within* each country.

b. Mutual Recognition

The failure of the harmonisation approach led the EC to create the notion of 'mutual recognition' (hereafter, MR) for *designing* EC TRs: harmonisation is limited to the minimum core of technical aspects ('essential requirements'), and each trading partner *recognises* the validity of all the other aspects of the relevant TR of its partners.

The MR approach looks flexible enough to be an interesting solution for the WTO. However, it has required a legal infrastructure that does not exist at the WTO: rulings from the European Court of Justice, and an elaborate system of safeguards that are difficult to introduce in the legally loose WTO framework. These legal difficulties should not hide a more profound problem: the efficacy of the MR approach. At a first glance, the EC MR approach seems successful: it covers more products (e.g., one EC Directive covers 55,000 types of machines), and hence appears more efficient in establishing wide coverage than the Directives based on harmonisation. But in fact, the average index of success of the EC MR approach is not very much different from that of the harmonisation-based approach. This is because MR has three limits, all of them suggesting that only a very limited use of MR can be achieved at the multilateral level. First, the process of establishing MR is awfully complex: essential requirements developed by Member states are often too vague to be useful, leading to unclear mandates for the technical work to be done by technical bodies. Second, creating *operational* standardisation bodies has proven to be much more difficult than expected. Third, *designing* a mutually recognised TR is only one aspect of a complete TR regime: it leaves unaddressed (and indeed exacerbates) key problems at the *enforcement* level (see Section 4).

These difficulties may be more easily overcome at the regional level than at the multilateral level. Indeed, there are many regional experiences – from the Trans-Tasman Mutual Recognition Arrangement (TTMRA) which covers all goods and services (except medical practitioners) and which reduces to nothing the essential requirements (goods legally sold in one country can be sold in the other, and service providers registered in one country can practise in the other) to the much more limited NAFTA approach (Hoekman, 1998; and Beviglia Zampetti, 1999). However, all these regional MR procedures create risks of discrimination against non-members of the regional agreements. As a result, the key issue raised by regional agreements from a multilateral perspective is whether foreign products imported in one Member state can be exported to other Member states without further formalities. This condition may be respected in the case of a customs union (because it is required by the notion of a 'single market,' as in the EC) but not necessarily in the case of free trade areas. An essential role for the WTO is to ensure that such discrimination is minimal by ensuring that the principles of open access and conditional MFN are applied to third parties seeking to join the regional agreement (Messerlin, 1996; and Hoekman, 1998). In particular, any country meeting the 'essential requirements' should be able to participate in a regional agreement on TRs.

The WTO may have an additional role: imposing or enhancing notification requirements for norms. The Uruguay Round introduced three provisions on notification of TRs: (i) the creation of an 'enquiry point' in each WTO Member (TBT Agreement, Article 10), (ii) the creation of a WTO standards information system (Ministerial Decision on Proposed Understanding on WTO-ISO Standards Information System) and (iii) regular review of the notification requirement by WTO Members (Ministerial Decision on Review of the ISO/IEC Information Centre Publication). However, these WTO measures are far from attaining the major reasons for the (relative) success of the EC notification process: in particular, there is no institution equivalent to the Commission which could discuss proposed TRs in the same room with Members' delegates. As a result, it is necessary to improve the current WTO notification procedure by opening it to *active* participation by firms, possibly through institutions or fora such as the International Chamber of Commerce, where firms' rights could be exercised.[4]

c. Simplification and Harmonisation of Customs Procedures

Unilateral reforms of customs administrations and procedures have been initiated by many developing countries. They deal with national customs procedures and regulatory requirements imposed by other agencies on cross-border trade, and aim at ensuring both more efficient revenue collection and trade facilitation by following 'best practice' guidelines. Some developing WTO members have stepped up efforts to improve inspection and clearance activities in anticipation of the full implementation of WTO Agreements that have a direct relation to trade facilitation. But many countries need longer transition periods with regard to the implementation of some parts of the agreements. Many countries have asked for an extended period of three years to implement the Agreement on Customs Valuation, and a draft decision to this effect was included in the Ministerial Declaration that was under discussion at the failed Seattle meeting.

Multilateral initiatives seem useful for generating guidelines based on best practices, and for accelerating domestic reforms. Following the many Uruguay Agreements that have implications for customs procedures – Customs Valuation, Import Licensing Procedures, Preshipment Inspection, Rules of Origin, TBT, and Sanitary and Phytosanitary Measures – the 1996 Singapore Ministerial added trade facilitation to the WTO agenda. Among the major

---

[4] TBT notifications are derestricted documents, available from the WTO web-site. In other words, 'passive' transparency does exist.

issues related to customs procedures that have been listed are excessive documentation requirements, lack of automation and information technology, lack of transparency in regulatory requirements, non-use of risk assessment techniques and audit-based controls, and absence of cooperation among customs and other government agencies.

Guidance on good customs procedures can be obtained from the WCO's International Convention on the Simplification and Harmonisation of Customs Procedures, known as the Kyoto Convention. This comprises a set of principles and 31 Annexes that lays out standards and best practices for customs procedures and related arrangements. The Kyoto Convention has not been a very successful multilateral instrument since it was drawn up in 1973, because of its non-binding nature and the fact that some of its Annexes have become outdated, no longer reflecting modern techniques, e.g., in the areas of risk assessment and audit-based systems of control and automated systems. Revisions to update the provisions of the Kyoto Convention to set 'international standards and facilitative customs procedures in the 21st century' were completed in 1999 (WCO, 1999). Implementing and enforcing the revised Kyoto Convention will require substantial effort, as well as money (Finger and Schuler, 2000). As discussed below, a key issue will be whether the revised Kyoto Convention will be binding on signatories.

4. ENFORCING TRADE FACILITATION REGULATIONS: A KEY ROLE FOR THE WTO?

Trade facilitation raises issues not only at the level of *designing* multilateral TRs and customs practices, but also at the level of *enforcing* existing (national or multilateral) norms. Enforcement of TRs or customs regulations can be split in two major groups of activities: (i) monitoring the application of TRs and standards for customs administration, including conformity assessment procedures (CAPs) such as testing, certification, and marking; and (ii) market surveillance which aims at ensuring that a product or service available on the domestic market conforms to the country's TRs and customs requirements.

Designing common TRs will not automatically solve enforcement problems. Common TRs can generate costs if traded products or services are subject to CAPs in *both* the exporting and importing countries, or if they are subject to severe constraints on the choice of CAP entities (these constraints are equivalent to quantitative restrictions if too few CAP bodies are available, or to higher transport or transaction costs if enough CAP units are available). Similarly, excessive or redundant customs procedures can create costs by requiring firms to spend wasted resources. In sum, efforts to *design* common TRs (be it harmonisation or mutual recognition) can lead to a waste of resources if serious problems exist at the *enforcement* level. The optimal balance between design and enforcement is one of the most important issues arising in the context of trade facilitation.

a. Conformity Assessment Procedures (CAPs) for TRs

The huge increase in CAP activities in many countries suggests they be considered a fully-fledged services industry. CAPs are performed by specialised units of all kinds (laboratories, public agencies, private firms). In the EC, enforcing the 80,000 existing TRs involves some 10,000 independent CAP units employing 200,000 workers, with a turnover of ECU 10 to 11 billion (these estimates date from the mid-1990s).

Analysing CAP units as service providers has many advantages. It allows inclusion of CAP units in the general framework for service industries provided by the GATS. This would subject them to the concept of progressive liberalisation and help apply the concept of *domestic* regulatory reform to the sector. This is important as CAPs can be used to achieve protectionist objectives. They cover a wide range of procedures – from confidence in private behaviour (manufacturers have strong interests to safeguard their reputation which is an essential part of the firm's capital) to reliance on *ad hoc* public agencies. As suggested in the Introduction, the greater the reliance on public intervention, the easier protectionist action may be to pursue. In most WTO Members, CAPs traditionally rely mostly on state-related agencies.

The necessary mix of liberalisation and domestic regulatory reforms is well illustrated by the EC MR approach. In 1993, an EC Decision defined a conceptual framework involving 14 'modules' describing the CAP tasks that were to be implemented, the responsible operators (manufacturers or CAP units) and the allocation of their responsibilities. Each EC Directive determining the TR for a given product also identifies which of the 14 CAP modules are effectively available to the manufacturers and to the CAP units. The Directive may require that Member states 'accredit' CAP units that are competent to carry out the CAP activities in question. Currently, there are 600 accredited CAP units (compared to a total of 10,000 CAP units in the EC). These have a pivotal role: the technically correct and economically sound implementation of the whole EC MR approach depends on the competence of this relatively small number of organisations. However, in a recent survey, the Commission found that the 'accreditation' of CAP units by Member states is associated with such a wide range of rules, methods and procedures (or rather, such an absence of rules, methods and procedures) that it represents a threat to the credibility of the whole EC MR regime. This conclusion has induced the Commission to table several proposals for 'harmonising' accreditation procedures (in particular, related to ethical behaviour, such as the independence and qualification of the CAP unit staff, the confidentiality and traceability of the work done by the CAP unit, etc.).

These proposals represent domestic regulatory reforms that are required by intra-EC liberalisation in TR matters.[5]

The envisaged domestic regulatory reforms in the EC imply more public intervention, leading ultimately to a European (regional) system of CAPs – echoing Article 9 of the Uruguay TBT Agreement. However, one may wonder whether this system is an optimal solution: it eliminates the gains from competition in the 'easy' (non-conflictual) cases, without being a workable solution in the 'difficult' cases involving powerful lobbies (such as the current intra-EC conflict on 'mad' cow disease). A better alternative could be to promote more competition between CAP units by allowing entry of foreign CAP units in domestic markets – echoing Article 6:4 of the Uruguay TBT Agreement. Taking the EC case as an example, a CAP unit located in a Member state could decide to provide the 'best' CAP services for only a limited range of goods (those for which the agency believes it has the best expertise, that is, 'comparative advantage') for the whole EC.[6] If the 'specialised' CAP unit has rightly assessed its abilities, it will attract manufacturers from the whole EC (not only those of its Member state of origin, as today).

Looking at enforcement of TRs as a service industry, to be subject to domestic regulatory reforms combined with liberalisation, makes the CAP industry a good candidate for inclusion in the coming WTO negotiations on services liberalisation. It should also induce the negotiators to develop further the various Articles of the Uruguay TBT Agreement (such as Article 6:4) which are competition-oriented.

An alternative to WTO negotiations is *unilateral* liberalisation. The scope for this is illustrated by the International Conformity Certification Programme (ICCP) established by the Saudi Arabian Standards Organisation (SASO), which is the primary agency responsible for CAPs in Saudi Arabia. The ICCP is a pilot conformity assessment procedure that relies on the private sector to inspect shipments for compliance verification in the exporting countries. The ICCP combines conformity assessment, preshipment inspection and certification of shipments of selected categories of products prior to shipment to Saudi Arabia (the Programme currently applies to 76 product categories covering food, automobiles, electronic and chemical products). The key element of the SASO Programme is that each shipment must provide evidence of conformity to SASO norms (or their approved equivalents) before the certificate of conformity

---

[5] Problems raised by CAPs outside the scope of the MR approach are similar. But they are even more difficult because of the wider range of CAP activities (not limited to the 14 basic modules), the larger number of operating CAP units (10,000 units), and a wider scope of CAP units (which range from the large organisations, such as SGS or Veritas, to small in-house private units, to large government laboratories).

[6] *En passant*, such a reform is much more consistent with the once popular EC view of subsidiarity according to which the MR approach was a way to promote competition between rules and between regulators as a better alternative to increasing public intervention (see Rollo and Winters, 2000).

(required for every consignment) can be issued, and ensures both exporters and importers of a streamlined customs process which allows goods to clear faster and to face a minimum rejection risk at the port of entry (SASO, 1998).

So far, the SASO Programme has not been a complete success: it is considered a costly process by major exporters to Saudi Arabia, with complaints about high fees for obtaining certificates of conformity, and high storage fees (as each consignment has to be isolated in storage during the testing stage). But the interesting aspect of the SASO Programme is that test data can be produced by nationally or internationally accredited laboratories approved by SASO, or by the manufacturer's declaration of conformity. At the conclusion of the SASO-approved laboratory testing, a Conformity Test and Evaluation Report is issued and submitted to the Regional Licensing Centre for verification of Conformity to SASO Programme Requirements. The SASO Programme closely follows ISO/IEC Guide 28 (General Rules for a Model Third Party Certification System for Products). SASO has contracted an international firm to carry out these activities. This firm is in turn assisted by a network of accredited testing laboratories and inspection bodies around the world. The SASO experience shows that compliance verification of national standards might be better and more cost-effectively served through mutual recognition agreements (MRAs) that improve the certification time and reduce the induced cost for exporters. In sharp contrast with the SASO Programme, most of the existing MRAs relating to CAPs signed by WTO Members do not generate a worldwide web of CAP units. They aim more at eliminating excess costs from duplicate CAPs or from artificial constraints on CAPs than at reducing costs by improving the competitive conditions on the market for CAP activities.

What are possible implications for the WTO? It could work in two directions. First, the WTO should ensure that MRAs for CAPs do not distort trade by favouring MRA signatories to the detriment of non-signatories. This goal is similar to the objective mentioned above at the level of *designing* common TR and, as said in Section 2, it could be achieved by establishing clear 'essential requirements,' the fulfilment of which would be an automatic passport to be a signatory of the MRA in question. If this condition is met, there should be few concerns about the burgeoning of bilateral and regional MRAs (in fact, the European Accreditation of Certification Bodies in 1990 and the European Cooperation for Accreditation of Laboratories in 1994 were preceded by a series of bilateral MRAs signed by France, the Netherlands and Sweden in the early 1980s).

Second, the WTO should be the best place to discuss CAP issues within the global framework of service liberalisation, ultimately giving rise to exchanges of concessions between WTO members on market access for CAP units.[7] At the

---

[7] The proposal of an 'APEC-wide Recognition of Product Certification,' based on an 'APEC Laboratory Recognition Centre,' is a regional variant of such an approach (Wilson, 1995).

beginning, only industrial countries may be interested in such liberalisation, given that many developing countries reject test data or product certifications issued by foreign laboratories and firms (allegedly not competent to serve domestic safety standards). However, increasing competition between CAP units from industrial countries will decrease CAP-related costs and enlarge the choice of developing countries of foreign laboratories and firms that they could accredit – potentially eroding developing countries' opposition to a progressive liberalisation of the CAP sector.

b. Enforcement of Norms for Customs Procedures

The 1973 Kyoto Convention was not a mandatory agreement, and its provisions were not enforceable. Pressures have been exerted by some parts of the trading community to embody the revised Convention into the WTO. In principle, the WCO – which cooperates with member customs administrations around the world – is the appropriate institution to oversee and enforce the Kyoto Convention. However, enforcing its procedures requires a 'dispute settlement' mechanism – something the WCO lacks. As a result, it has been suggested that the WTO extend its 'dispute settlement' mechanism to enforce the Kyoto Convention. This has met resistance: some WTO members have argued that the WTO should not be used to enforce an instrument developed by another organisation. A counter-argument is that the WTO has a mandate to achieve greater coherence in global economic policy by cooperating with other international organisations.[8] A way to get the benefits from greater WTO-WCO cooperation and to appease the fears associated with the use of the WTO as an enforcer would be to negotiate a 'restricted' list of international organisations with which the WTO could have deeper and more institutional relations. The list could start with only one item in the coming Round – the WCO – but it could be subject to review in every Round.

5. CONCLUSION

The chapter has addressed trade facilitation issues broadly defined to include both technical regulations (TRs) and customs procedures. Both issues constitute an increasing source of trade conflicts that can be particularly acrimonious and damaging for the world trade system when they concern health and environment issues. But, they also constitute opportunities for symmetrical concessions in the

---

[8] See WTO (1998) for a synopsis of views. WTO members have already given the WCO the responsibility for developing the rules of origin for non-preferential trade, in addition to the responsibility for promoting the WTO Agreement on Customs Valuations.

context of WTO negotiations on liberalisation. The chapter suggests two conclusions.

Although at a first glance, designing common public norms may seem the best way to eliminate TR-related trade conflicts, the EC experience suggests it is likely to be very costly in terms of time and effort in a multilateral framework. This conclusion is reinforced by the fact that 'scientific' evidence has proven to provide poor support for the WTO in case of dispute settlements. In contrast, private initiatives to design standards have been numerous and often successful. It appears that this approach (possibly monitored by competition policy) should be encouraged.

Multilateral actions for enforcing existing TRs (be they national norms and standards, or multilateral standards) can be a source of large gains. The WTO should ensure that bilateral or regional MRAs on standards do not distort trade by favouring the MRA signatories to the detriment of non-signatories. This goal could be achieved by establishing clear essential requirements, the fulfilment of which would be an automatic passport to become a signatory of the MRA in question. Moreover, enforcement issues related to trade facilitation should be included in the global framework of service liberalisation: increased competition between the agencies, firms and institutions in charge of conformity assessment would be beneficial. Such an increased competition would flow from domestic regulatory reforms that accompany trade liberalisation – a process that is driving the WTO negotiations on services.

REFERENCES

Beviglia Zampetti, A. (1999), 'Market Access through Mutual Recognition: The Promise and Limits of GATS Article VII' (Washington, DC: World Services Congress).

Finger, J.M. and P. Schuler (2000), 'Implementation of Uruguay Round Commitments: The Development Challenge', this issue.

Guasch, J.L. and P. Spiller (1999), 'Managing the Regulatory Process: Design, Concepts, Issues, and the Latin America and the Caribbean Story' (Washington, DC: The World Bank Institute).

Hoekman, B. (1995), 'The WTO, the EU and the Arab World: Trade Policy Priorities and Pitfalls', Paper No. 1226 (London: Centre for Economic Policy Research).

Hoekman, B. (1998), 'Beyond National Treatment: Integrating Domestic Policies' (Washington, DC: World Bank).

International Trade Centre UNCTAD/WTO (1997), Principal Bottlenecks to International Business Development and Related Technical Cooperation Needs of Least Developed Countries: A Business-Sector Perspective (Geneva: UNCTAD/WTO).

Messerlin, P.A. (1996), 'A Transatlantic Free Trade Agenda on Non-tariff Barriers', in Bruce Stokes (ed.), Open for Business: Creating a Transatlantic Marketplace (New York: Council on Foreign Relations).

Messerlin, P.A. (1998), Technical Public Regulations and Industry Standards: The EC Regime (Washington, DC: The World Bank).

Messerlin, P.A. (1999), Measuring the Costs of Protection in Europe (Washington, DC: Institute for International Economics, forthcoming).

Murphy, C. (1994), *International Organization and Industrial Change: Global Governance Since 1850* (New York: Oxford University Press).

Olarreaga, M. and I. Soloaga (1998), *Endogenous Tariff Formation: The Case of Mercosur* (London: Centre for Economic Policy Research).

Rollo, J. and L.A. Winters (2000), 'Subsidiarity and Governance Challenges for the WTO', this issue.

Saudi Arabian Standards Organisation (SASO) (1998), 'Conformity Certification Program: ICCP' SASO Website (http://www.saso.org/SERVICES/iccp.htm).

Staples, B.R. (1998), 'Trade Facilitation' (Washington, DC: World Bank, www.worldbank.org/trade).

United Nations Conference on Trade and Development (UNCTAD) (1999), 'Preparing for Future Multilateral Trade Negotiations', UNCTAD/ITCD/TSB/6 (Geneva).

Wilson, J. (1995), *Standards and APEC: An Action Agenda* (Washington, DC: Institute for International Economics).

World Customs Organisation (1999), 'International Convention on the Simplification and Harmonization of Customs Procedures (as Amended)' (Brussels: WCO).

World Trade Organisation (1993), *Trade Policy Review – European Communities* (Geneva: WTO).

World Trade Organisation (1998), 'WTO Trade Facilitation Symposium, 9–10 March, Report by the Secretariat', Document G/C/W/115 (28 May, Geneva: WTO).

14

Competition Policy and Intellectual Property Rights in Developing Countries

Keith E. Maskus and Mohamed Lahouel

1. INTRODUCTION

C OMPETITION policy is a broad term, covering all aspects of government actions that affect the conditions under which firms compete in a particular market. The term competition law refers to legislation, judicial decisions, and regulations specifically aimed at avoiding the concentration and abuse of market power. However, many regulations stipulate exemptions from competition disciplines for purposes of achieving various social goals. Competition policy is therefore complex in its intentions and effects.

Competition law has emerged as an issue for the WTO largely because exporting firms in the high-income developed economies argue that anti-competitive practices of competitors in foreign markets hinder their ability to penetrate those markets. Such practices may be largely private in nature and could be facilitated by the absence or weak enforcement of local competition laws. These issues have prompted a number of proposals for negotiating a limited agreement on multilateral principles and disciplines in competition law within the World Trade Organisation (WTO).[1] However, the debate is contentious and no consensus has emerged on whether and how to address competition law and regulations within the WTO.[2]

We argue in this chapter that developing countries would gain if a WTO agreement were reached that recognised the principle that competition law should promote open competition, emphasised international cooperation in competition

---

[1] See Brittan (1997), Scherer (1994), Graham and Richardson (1997a) and Fox (1997).
[2] See Lloyd (1998), Neven and Roller (1999) and Hoekman (1997).

enforcement, and disciplined the most anti-competitive forms of public and private restraints against market contestability. Developing countries have a great interest in implementing active domestic competition policies, encompassing both appropriate, pro-competitive regulations in the narrow sense and market liberalisation in the broader sense. An important reason is that existing WTO Agreements, especially the Agreement on Trade-Related Intellectual Property Rights (TRIPs), invite a full consideration of policies for competition maintenance in countries where such policies are weakly developed.

In the next section we discuss aspects of competition policy in developing countries. Some illustrations are provided from competition problems in Tunisia. We then turn specifically to linkages between intellectual property rights (IPRs) and competition rules, and consider the form in which a limited agreement on competition approaches would be potentially beneficial for developing countries. A welfare-enhancing accord would focus on basic principles, cooperation in procedures, and disciplines against clearly anti-competitive measures.

2. COMPETITION POLICY IN DEVELOPING COUNTRIES

While competition law remains nascent in most developing countries, it is misleading to claim that such countries do not have competition policies in the broader sense. For example, weak patent protection may be construed as a channel for promoting technical change through imitation and diffusion. Industrial policies that aim to achieve scale economies and industrialisation through the protection of state-owned monopolies or private enterprises explicitly limit competition. Subsidies, state aids, and procurement preferences further limit accessibility of important markets.

Interventionist competition policy of this nature is inherently anti-competitive and counterproductive. Trade barriers choke off imports of technologically sophisticated capital goods and material inputs. Protected and subsidised enterprises have limited incentives to innovate or adapt new technologies. Small and segmented markets limit the attainment of meaningful scale economies. Monopolies in important service markets tend to be unresponsive to changing consumer needs. Weak IPRs promote significant imitative activities but restrain the development of innovative local enterprises and discourage the acquisition of high-quality foreign technologies. Tolerance of cartels and monopolies limits competitive entry by both foreign competitors and new domestic firms.

In many developing countries the public sector is at least as responsible as the private sector for anti-competitive conduct. In Tunisia, for example, investment licensing that restricted entry was the rule rather than the exception until the late 1980s. Even though significant trade liberalisation has occurred, trade and industrial policies still hinder competition on the domestic market. Imports of several products remain monopolised by state trading boards or public enterprises. A state-owned telecommunications enterprise holds the monopoly of both fixed and cellular telephone services. Licences for internet services have been restricted to two providers. In public procurement, domestic firms in Tunisia are granted a preferential margin of 20 per cent, but this treatment will be phased out by the year 2003 under the terms of the Euro-Med Agreement.

Increasingly, developing countries recognise that promoting effective competition on their markets promises substantial net benefits over the long term. This may be seen from the fact that over 40 developing countries unilaterally strengthened their IPRs regimes in the 1990s and that, as of 1997, 58 developing countries or economies in transition had adopted or were in the process of adopting competition legislation.[3] These policy changes are consistent with extensive and ongoing liberalisation of trade and investment barriers and with privatisation of public enterprises. Competition law is an important complementary support to general market liberalisation.

a. Objectives of Competition Law

Competition law aims primarily at protecting the processes underlying efficient functioning of markets. Markets are inherently dynamic and experience the birth of new firms and products, the death of inefficient firms and outmoded products, and the natural expansion, contraction, and reorganisation of enterprises. Competition may come from domestic producers, subsidiaries of foreign enterprises, and trade flows. Thus, an effective competition regime ensures that entry is not artificially blocked, that exit from production is orderly, and that efficient combinations of enterprises and activities are permitted. Free exit is a critical feature and effective bankruptcy laws are an important element of competition regulation. Competition law further recognises that firms compete in both static and dynamic terms, requiring that some balance must be struck between ensuring competitive access and encouraging innovation.

Put simply, the fundamental purpose of competition law is to ensure that markets are effectively contestable, meaning that incumbent firms are not able to sustain anti-competitive practices for extended periods of time. Such practices include merging with competitors to attain monopoly, refusing to supply goods or to license technologies on market terms in order to prevent competition, and agreeing with other firms to establish collusive restraints on trade. In this context, competition law aims at preventing or disciplining such abuses by establishing conditions or guidelines under which they would be examined for legality.

---

[3] See Maskus (2000) and Hoekman (1997).

This task is complex. For example, published guidelines differ considerably across the United States, the European Union, and Japan in which practices are viewed as potentially anti-competitive, which practices should be banned outright, and what circumstances should be investigated by authorities for anti-competitive effects. Indeed, the underlying analytical issues are typically so complicated that there can be no 'ideal' definition or application of competition law.

Competitive processes in markets may suffer even more broadly because of public restraints on entry, such as import quotas, widespread procurement preferences, government-sanctioned monopolies, targeted subsidies, and reserved positions for service providers and distributors. In such cases, competition law can take on the useful role of competition advocacy, whereby anti-trust authorities question the need for such restrictions and publicise their costs. Competition advocacy is rare in developing countries. For example, Tunisia is one of the few countries in the Middle East-North Africa region with a competition law. However, the Competition Council has insufficient resources to be a competition advocate and has been almost completely inactive. One reason is that it has only a limited mandate to take initiatives. Indeed, it does not have the authority to initiate *ex officio* investigations; instead it can only respond to requests for investigations by the Ministry of Commerce.

Competition law could have goals in addition to its fundamental one of supporting market processes.[4] Many countries establish exceptions for small enterprises, set-asides for minority entrepreneurs, and guarantees in order to promote servicing of rural regions. While such exemptions may spring from valid social objectives, the need to pursue them must be balanced against the gains from open competition.

Some observers in developing countries argue that competition law conflicts with the fundamental goal of industrialisation, because open competition favours efficient and established foreign enterprises over inefficient domestic firms. However, the goal of competition maintenance is not to favour any particular interests but rather to support the development of markets. This emphasis should bear long-run payoffs in terms of efficient restructuring of enterprises and raising incentives for product development as entry barriers are reduced.

b. Competition Issues of Particular Concern to Developing Economies

Competition law and enforcement are potentially important in supporting contestable internal markets in developing countries. Many of the most significant restrictions on competition come from public supports, state monopolies, exclusive rights, commercial policies, and restrictions on FDI and rights of establishment for

---

[4] See Graham and Richardson (1997a and 1997b).[5] We can only provide a brief overview here.

service providers. The most effective *competition policy* would be continued liberalisation of these restrictions, buttressed by safeguards against higher private entry barriers being substituted for lower public entry barriers.

Regarding the preparation and implementation of *competition law*, a number of difficult issues arise.[5] It may be impossible to identify particular behaviour as anti-competitive or monopolistic. For example, setting predatory prices to drive competitors out of an industry should be disciplined, in principle. However, evidence indicates that predatory behaviour in open, competitive markets rarely occurs in practice. In contrast, numerous regulations aimed at protecting domestic competitors from efficient entrants, in the guise of avoiding predation, have injured competitive processes. The most prominent example of this problem is the anti-competitive application of anti-dumping laws in developed countries.

It may be easier to identify horizontal cartels among competitors as an attempt to monopolise a market. Virtually all developed competition regimes take a harsh view of such cartels to the extent they operate in the domestic market. Note that cartels may be both informal and formal, so that competition authorities need to be armed with investigative powers. However, as Graham and Richardson (1997a) emphasise, not all cartels among competitors are inefficient. For example, rationalisation cartels may win temporary exceptions from anti-trust enforcement in order to permit orderly exit of firms from markets. At the same time, such cartels may inefficiently delay effective resource reallocation. The best policy would be to assist firms to exit markets through transparently provided subsidies and adequate bankruptcy laws.

It is often unclear whether mergers, joint ventures, and other combinations should be deemed anti-competitive or pro-competitive. An important factor is determination of the 'relevant market' within which firms compete. Even if domestic production were to become concentrated any resulting price increases could be outweighed by gains in scale efficiency. Similar comments apply to joint ventures, which may bring cost-reducing technological advantages to the economy but result in additional concentration. Thus, examination of mergers requires legal and economic expertise.

In this context, it is evident that trade and investment liberalisation form important complements to competition maintenance, for the former processes provide competitive discipline against merger-induced restraints. Mergers and privatisation of monopolies in small and relatively closed markets embody considerably higher risks of concentration. Open trade in goods is not a complete solution, however, for many services are non-traded and potentially subject to competitive abuse. The classic example is a telecommunications monopoly, which might refuse access to its network to foreign suppliers of equipment and

---

See the papers in Graham and Richardson (1997b).

telephone service. Similarly, monopolised port services can act as a significant drag on export development.

Whereas horizontal restraints among competitors may be generally anti-competitive, vertical restraints within enterprises may enhance competition, depending on circumstances. For example, manufacturers may award exclusive territories to distributors in order to induce them to invest in marketing products and building distribution facilities. These investments can increase the supply of goods and services on a market and raise investments in product quality. This is especially the case in markets where interbrand competition is sufficiently vigorous that competition is not harmed by private restraints on intrabrand competition.

It is possible that vertical agreements could have the effect of closing distribution markets to potential domestic and foreign competitors. Indeed, this was the crux of the American claim in the WTO against Japan in the Fuji-Kodak case. In this context, three issues of particular concern for developing countries emerge. First, if there is limited interbrand competition among manufacturers, vertical arrangements can support monopolistic collusion. Second, industrial firms in developing countries tend to be small or medium-sized and cannot readily establish their own distribution channels, raising some concerns about forestalled entry on the part of domestic firms.[6] Third, vertical arrangements may become anti-competitive to the extent they are supported by government controls on distribution. For example, many developing countries have laws dictating exclusive national dealerships for trademarked foreign goods. Such mandates permit only one dealer in the country, thereby completely foreclosing intrabrand competition. They also invite rent seeking, support monopolistic practices and likely result in smaller quantities and inferior services. Elimination of such restrictions should be high on any government's competition agenda.

Even in developing countries where competition law prohibits exclusive arrangements, enforcement is difficult. The Tunisian law differs in this regard from that of many other countries in that it prohibits such arrangements in principle unless they were authorised by competition authorities. In practice the law has proven difficult to enforce and exclusive arrangements are the general rule.

Thus, developing countries have much to gain from improving competitive processes in their markets. In greatest measure, such gains would come from additional market liberalisation and deregulation of government supports that block market contestability. Establishing an institution for competition advocacy is particularly important. There is also scope for developing procedures for

---

[6] Note further that such firms are unlikely to invest in the substantial fixed costs of building distribution channels in developed countries. Thus, exclusive arrangements in those nations may prevent developing-country exporters from entering their markets.

competition maintenance if private market power becomes more concentrated. However, appropriate application of such procedures is complex, requires considerable expertise, and must be transparent. Establishing an interventionist competition regime that serves mainly to protect entrenched firms from new entrants would be counterproductive.

3. THE INTERFACE BETWEEN COMPETITION POLICY AND INTELLECTUAL PROPERTY RIGHTS

Intellectual property rights and competition regulation are intimately related.[7] The former provide exclusive rights within a designated market to produce and sell a product, service or technology that results from some form of intellectual creation and that meets specific requirements. These inventions and creations are protected by patents, copyrights, trademarks, trade secrets, or *sui generis* forms of protection. Thus, IPRs designate boundaries, within which competitors may exercise their rights. They exist to solve the fundamental appropriability problem arising from investment in information, which is a non-rival and often non-excludable public good.

In principle, IPRs create market power by limiting static competition in order to promote investments in dynamic competition. In competitive product and innovation markets the awarding of IPRs rarely results in sufficient market power to generate significant monopoly behaviour. However, in some circumstances a portfolio of patents could generate considerable market power through patent-pooling agreements among horizontal competitors. In countries without a strong tradition of competition and innovation, strengthening IPRs could markedly raise market power and invite its exercise.[8]

For its part, competition regulation aims at curbing attempts to extend exploitation of an intellectual asset beyond the boundaries provided by IPRs. Thus, there is an inherent tension between competition laws and IPRs, particularly if competition laws emphasise static market access and IPRs emphasise incentives for dynamic competition. Structured properly, however, the two regulatory systems complement each other in striking an appropriate balance between needs for innovation, technology transfer, and information dissemination.

In this context, an important reason for developing countries to consider implementation and reform of competition regulations is that the TRIPs

---

[7] We provide here an analytical overview. For an excellent discussion of the economics and law of this interrelationship, see Gallini and Trebilcock (1998). See also Maskus (2000).
[8] Smith (1999) provides indirect evidence of this possibility through an examination of trade data. See also Maskus (2000) and UNCTAD (1996).

Agreement envisions a clear link between strengthened protection of IPRs and the need to control anti-competitive uses of IPRs. Countries must adopt minimum standards of protection for IPRs that are, in many dimensions, markedly stronger than those prevalent in many developing economies. Chief among these are the provision of pharmaceutical product patents, reversal of burden of proof in process patent cases, limitations on the issuance of compulsory licences, designation of a protection system for plant varieties, recognition of copyrights for computer programs, protection of well-known trademarks, security of trade secrets and confidential information from unfair revelation by competitors and governments, and a comprehensive system of enforcement.[9]

In response to concerns that such protection would invite unwarranted exploitation of market power, Article 40 of TRIPs provides considerable discretion to WTO member states in specifying licensing practices or conditions that may constitute an abuse of intellectual property rights. The Article goes on to specify three examples of potentially abusive licensing practices (exclusive grantback conditions, conditions preventing challenges to validity, and coercive package licensing) but this list is not exhaustive. Read broadly, the Article could cover any potential abuse of IPRs, including monopoly pricing, refusals to license, effectuating horizontal cartels through patent pooling, and exclusive vertical arrangements that forestall competition.

a. IPRs Standards as Competition Regulation

In an important sense IPRs and competition laws overlap in that the scope of exclusive rights granted by the former determines the degree of potential market power. An immediate opportunity arises for many developing countries to define and implement minimum standards for IPRs, consistent with TRIPs requirements, that are dynamically pro-competitive.[10] Economic development is a dynamic process and IPRs may be used fruitfully to help convert 'free riders' into 'fair followers' in Reichman's (1993) apt phrase.

A brief review of how certain standards may be selected is useful. Consider patents first, which must apply for a minimum 20-year term under TRIPs. However, countries may exclude inventions from patent eligibility for purposes of maintaining public order, national defence, and environmental protection. They may exclude therapeutic, surgical, and diagnostic techniques and patents need not be extended to discoveries of nature, scientific principles, and mathematical formulas and algorithms. Patents need not pertain to higher life forms, nor must plant varieties be patented if they are protected by another system. Finally, TRIPs does not require that computer programs be awarded

---

[9] See UNCTAD (1996), Maskus (2000), Watal (2000) and Primo Braga (1996).
[10] See UNCTAD (1996) and Maskus (2000) for further analysis.

patent protection. Countries also have flexibility in defining the conditions for protection. Patents might recognise only narrow claims in order to promote the ability of competitors to invent around them.

Article 30 of TRIPs provides that member states may issue compulsory licences of patented inventions under certain circumstances. In practice, this allows countries to permit limited use for private and non-commercial purposes, for research and experimental or teaching purposes, for obtaining approval of generic drugs, and for preparation of individual medicines by pharmacies. The research and teaching exceptions are particularly important for promoting learning and dynamic competition. The TRIPs agreement places new limits on the use of compulsory licences but provides much leeway for specifying conditions under which they may be used (Watal, 2000). For example, the new Argentine patent law anticipates the use of compulsory licences, permitting domestic pharmaceutical firms to retain relatively flexible access to foreign-owned patented drugs and chemical processes.

Regarding trade secrets, Article 39 requires laws or judicial mechanisms aimed at preventing unfair acquisition of confidential information. Left undefined are the acts that are deemed unfair, leaving some flexibility to member states. States must protect against commercial bribery and industrial espionage. Reverse engineering is generally considered to be an honest form of competition that promotes dynamic efficiency and learning. Indeed, a regime of trade secrets with liberal treatment of reverse engineering poses one of the greatest potential dynamic benefits for developing economies in the area of IPRs.

Trademark protection can be valuable in developing nations, for it provides incentives to develop local crafts, clothing, and foods, among other goods and services.[11] There is little effective market power associated with all but well-known international marks. To the extent that trademark owners impose unreasonable or anti-competitive commercial conditions on licensees, recourse may be made to competition policies.

In copyrights, countries may adopt a fair-use doctrine permitting the unauthorised use of copies for purposes of achieving social objectives. It is acceptable to allow limited copying for educational and research purposes and many countries permit a single 'private-use' exception. Wholesale copying of computer software must be prohibited but TRIPs allows for reverse engineering by honest means. In this context, programs that deliver essentially similar functional performance as original software are legitimate forms of competition.

b. Regulation of IPRs through Competition Policy

A broader issue is the use of competition rules to discipline anti-competitive practices in the post-grant use of IPRs. Claims that a rights holder has engaged in

---

[11] Maskus (1999) provides evidence on this point in Lebanon.

anti-competitive activity are often complex and require significant judicial and legal expertise in their interpretation. In countries with developed competition law, three general issues dominate discussion over the interrelationships between competition regulation and IPRs.

First, concern over monopoly pricing reflects fear of one potential abuse. However, in developed countries prices are rarely the focus of competition policy *per se* and more often the subject of price regulation for purposes of maintaining public health and nutrition. Firms set prices in recognition of market substitutes that are rarely absent (both in a static and dynamic context), suggesting that policy concern over monopoly pricing is misplaced.

However, this optimistic view may not be shared by developing countries, both because the number of available substitutes may be more limited and because most innovations protected by IPRs are owned by foreign interests. In that context, price monitoring may take on additional scope in developing countries.

Second, most abuses of IPRs relate to business strategies, including selling practices and licensing restrictions. There are few concrete guidelines in the area because of the complicated nature of markets for information and technology. Vertical licensing agreements, for example, may serve the purpose of ensuring downstream product quality on the part of local vendors, which aids competition. However, tie-in sales of unrelated products to technology purchasers could be injurious to competition.

Several potential competitive problems are raised by the exploitation of IPRs. One is potential cartelisation of horizontal competitors through licensing agreements that fix prices, limit output, or divide markets. Competition authorities in developed countries have found it difficult to set rules covering such licensing agreements. Instead, the focus has been on whether agreements present the potential for cartelisation of a significant share of the market. Thus, authorities apply a 'rule of reason' approach in such cases. Concerns also arise over agreements among licensors and licensees that require resale price maintenance of distributors' prices. Such agreements may be disguised price-fixing arrangements. It is evident that such risks are greater, the more regulated is entry into distribution contracts, a common problem in many developing countries.

A second difficulty relates to exclusionary effects of licence agreements. Such agreements could exclude other firms from competing in particular markets. This could happen through required tie-in sales and mandates that licensees may only use the licensor's present and future technologies. Further, licensors may seek to hinder the development of competing technologies through exclusive grant-back provisions. Again, competition policy must attempt to assess the potential anti-competitive impacts of such arrangements. These impacts depend critically on the structure of the markets in which agreements operate, the share of markets covered, and the difficulty of entry of licensors and licensees.

A third class of problems relates to attempts to acquire market power beyond a firm's own protected technology or product by purchasing exclusive rights to competing technologies and products. Such efforts effectively are horizontal mergers, which may be analysed in terms of their impact on current and future market concentration.

Thus, there are complex relationships between IPRs and their potential abuse. Competition authorities must develop the capability to distinguish various forms of behaviour and potential impacts on static and dynamic competition. Further, in those developing economies in which entry is made difficult by protected monopolies, exclusive-distributor laws, restrictions on trade and investment, and weak bankruptcy laws, the anti-competitive exploitation of IPRs could be particularly problematic. The remedy is not to delay implementation of IPRs but to develop procedures for ensuring effective competition and engaging in wider liberalisation and market reform.

c. Treatment of Parallel Imports

Parallel imports are goods brought into a country without the authorisation of the patent, trademark, or copyright holder after those goods were placed legitimately into circulation elsewhere. Policies regulating parallel imports stem from specification of the territorial exhaustion of IPRs. Under national exhaustion, rights end upon first sale within a nation but IPRs owners may prevent parallel trade with other countries. Under international exhaustion, rights are exhausted upon first sale anywhere and parallel imports are permitted. A third option is regional exhaustion, by which rights are completed within a group of countries, thereby allowing parallel trade among them, but are not exhausted.

Despite efforts by US negotiators in the Uruguay Round to incorporate a global standard of national exhaustion into TRIPs, it was impossible to reach such an agreement. Rather, Article 6 simply preserves the territorial prerogative to regulate parallel trade, subject to national treatment and MFN obligations.[12] Considerable debate persists over the question of whether to amend TRIPs to achieve a global approach. Some analysts advocate a global ban on parallel trade as a natural extension of the rights of intellectual property owners to control international distribution.[13] Others prefer a consistent rule of international exhaustion, placing no restrictions on parallel imports, in order further to integrate markets (Abbott, 1998).

Exhaustion policies vary widely, even among developed economies. The European Union adopts exhaustion in all fields of intellectual property within the Community but bars parallel imports coming from outside its territory.

---

[12] See Abbott (1998), Cottier (1998) and Bronckers (1998).
[13] See Barfield and Groombridge (1998).

American policy on parallel imports is mixed. The United States maintains a 'common-control exception' in the case of trademarked goods, permitting some parallel imports. Owners of US patents and copyrights are protected against parallel imports. Japan permits parallel imports in patented and trademarked goods unless they are explicitly barred by contract provisions. Japan is more open to parallel imports than is the United States. New Zealand and Australia have recently removed restrictions against parallel imports of copyrighted music and videos.

Few developing countries restrict parallel trade in any field of protection, although 'sole agency' laws (exclusive distribution arrangements) can have the effect of greatly restraining the ability of traders to engage in such activities. The absence of regulations in this area partly reflects the general absence of competition policies. However, parallel imports may be seen as a useful policing device against price collusion emanating from exclusive territorial restraints. Further, parallel exports may be viewed as a channel for penetrating foreign markets. Indeed, many countries consider potential global restrictions on parallel trade as back-door attempts by industrial countries to close their markets through implicit non-tariff barriers.

As this wide disparity in policies and attitudes toward parallel imports accurately suggests, there is no obvious answer to the question of whether they are beneficial or harmful in welfare terms. Arguments favouring parallel trade begin with the view that restrictions on parallel imports amount to non-tariff barriers to goods that have legitimately escaped the control of IPRs owners. A second argument is that parallel imports can discipline abusive price discrimination and collusive behaviour based on private territorial restraints. The final argument is that government enforcement of territorial rights invites rent-seeking on behalf of firms that claim to need relief from free-riding competitors but are actually interested in setting collusive prices.

Many arguments are made in favour of banning parallel imports. First, international price discrimination need not be harmful and under certain circumstances can raise economic welfare. Countries with small markets and elastic demand, typically developing economies, could face low prices under price discrimination. In the presence of parallel trade, foreign rights holders may choose not to supply such countries because local demand is insufficient under uniform pricing.[14] In this view, international exhaustion would lower welfare of developing economies through higher prices and lower product availability. However, this notion may be inaccurate because restrictions against parallel imports limit intra-brand competition, a significant problem in small developing countries. Indeed, most developing countries express opposition to restricting parallel trade, in part over concerns that domestic prices could actually be higher

---

[14] See Malueg and Schwarz (1994).

for imported goods under price discrimination. This problem is expressed most often in the context of pharmaceuticals trade.

A second argument is that parallel traders free ride on the investment, marketing and service costs of authorised distributors. Indeed, this is the primary motivation for permitting privately contracted exclusive territories in the first place. Such restrictions may be pro-competitive by overcoming the dynamic problem that markets may be underserved. Moreover, exclusive territorial representation lowers the rights-holder's costs of monitoring and controlling product and service quality. In this sense restrictions against parallel imports may be viewed as welfare improving.

An important issue is that international price differences may be the result of national price regulations established for purposes of achieving social objectives. The most prominent example is pharmaceuticals. Virtually all nations regulate prices in order to limit consumer costs or health procurement budgets. Such regulations differ widely across countries and account for significant price variations (Danzon, 1997). In this context, it may be appropriate to bar parallel exports from regulated markets on the theory that such regulations amount to a sector-specific export subsidy.

The question of whether regulating parallel imports is beneficial or harmful is ultimately an empirical question and depends on circumstances. Unambiguously, restrictions on parallel trade raise profitability of intellectual property developers, which are overwhelmingly located in developed countries. The possibility that price discrimination could result in lower prices in developing countries must seem a leap of faith to those unschooled in industrial organisation theory. Moreover, even in relatively low-income economies with large markets there may well be lower-priced sources of goods in regional trade. Given this situation, it is impossible to place confidence in either the prescription for banning parallel imports or mandating that there be a free global regime in parallel trade. The best advice seems simply to permit the *status quo ante* to continue, with each country or region selecting its own policy.

4. MULTILATERAL AGREEMENT ON COMPETITION POLICY?

With this background, consider the justifications that may be put forward for reaching an agreement on competition issues in the WTO. First, many public and private restraints on competition have cross-border anti-competitive effects and distort trade. Second, mergers that take place across borders involve multiple reviews of potential impacts on competition, while even mergers among firms domiciled within a single country may have effects on competition abroad. Third, anti-dumping laws have the effect of limiting the contestability of markets in which they are used. Fourth, the need to implement stronger IPRs raises important concerns about anti-competitive cross-border behaviour. Finally, countries may engage in opportunistic or strategic use of competition policy in order to extract rents from foreign firms or consumers. Thus, there may be a policy coordination failure in competition regulation that could be eased by multilateral agreement.

For reasons discussed earlier, it is neither possible nor desirable to subject all domestic public and private competitive restraints and exceptions from competition law to specific WTO disciplines. Cases in which such restraints operate to nullify or impair the benefits anticipated by trading partners from other trade liberalisation may be subject to non-violation complaints, a route that exists already in the WTO but is rarely undertaken. In most cases, an agreement to engage in bilateral consultation, information sharing and enforcement under the rule of positive comity may be most effective.[15]

Even if it were not comprehensive, a multilateral approach embodying a minimum set of principles would be in the interest of developing countries. In present circumstances, developing countries have little leverage to prevent or sanction anti-competitive practices by enterprises that spill over borders. At a basic level, a multilateral commitment to banning cartels and horizontal agreements would be beneficial, whether the markets targeted are domestic or foreign.

One of the greatest threats to global competition is the international proliferation of anti-dumping actions. While use of these laws remains largely the practice of developed countries, their adoption and use is rising sharply in developing countries as well. In order to avoid restricting genuine competition on their markets, it would be advisable to revise anti-dumping actions to meet relevant competition principles and to place them under the jurisdiction of national competition authorities.[16] Reaching a WTO agreement on such reform would be difficult in light of the strong political interests in favour of anti-dumping (Hoekman and Holmes, 1999). Yet it might be feasible by trading greater access to developing-country markets, engineered through a commitment to competition enforcement, for partial disarmament in anti-dumping in OECD countries.

The close linkages between IPRs and competition regulation raise further avenues for an agreement on competition policy. Indeed, if TRIPs were to be revisited in the next round of negotiations, its broad limitations on IPRs exploitation in the name of competition could come up for review. Developing countries should consider carefully the extent to which they wish to retain and justify these limitations. In turn, multilateral cooperation to identify anti-

---

[15] Indeed, this approach is anticipated by TRIPS, in which members that feel aggrieved by competition actions against firms domiciled in their jurisdiction regarding their alleged abuse of IPRs are to be accorded sympathetic consultation.

[16] See Messerlin (1996) and Scherer (1994).

competitive licensing practices that would attract competition enforcement could be beneficial. Finally, it seems advisable to maintain national discretion over the regulation of parallel imports.

Our view about the form of a desirable WTO agreement supplements that in Fox (1997). In her model, contracting nations would negotiate shared competition principles for the trading system, including a rule outlawing cartels and an agreement to make markets accessible. Enforcement would involve national treatment by considering harm to foreign interests with the same gravity as harm to domestic competition. Members would make their anti-dumping enforcement more consistent with competition principles. Nations would agree on principles under which to recognise that some market arrangements potentially enhance efficiency. Members that have experienced damages from actions of another member could petition for enforcement there and, failing satisfactory resolution, have access to dispute resolution within the WTO. A strong emphasis would be placed on cooperation and transparency.[17]

5. CONCLUDING REMARKS

In this chapter we have provided an overview of the advantages of an active competition policy, broadly construed, for developing countries. As they adopt and implement competition laws, it is important to recognise the synergies between them and intellectual property rights, market openness, and deregulation. Competition policy must be confronted in any event because of the need to implement new standards of protection for IPRs. To an important degree, the scope of such rights determines how they may be used and constitutes itself a form of competition regulation. However, there is some tension between IPRs and competition regulation, which needs to be addressed in a dynamically pro-competitive framework.

The next round of trade negotiations should incorporate competition regulation, with a view toward enhancing global market accessibility. Developing countries could achieve gains from such an agreement if it is structured in a way that assists the establishment of competition on their markets and disciplines the most anti-competitive measures undertaken by developed countries, including anti-dumping. While it may be unrealistic to anticipate more than an agreement on basic transparency and cooperation, a broader vision could succeed in bringing competition principles more fully into the global trading system.

---

[17] See Graham and Richardson (1997a) for a more limited proposal and Hoekman and Holmes (1999) for a sceptical dissent.

REFERENCES

Abbott, F. (1998), 'First Report (Final) to the Committee on International Trade Law of the International Law Association on the Subject of Parallel Importation', *Journal of International Economic Law*, **XX**, 607–36.

Barfield, C.E. and M.A. Groombridge (1998), 'The Economic Case for Copyright Owner Control over Parallel Imports', *The Journal of World Intellectual Property*, **1**, 903–39.

Brittan, Sir L. (1997), 'Competition Policy and the Trading System: Towards International Rules in the WTO', Paper presented to the Institute for International Economics (Washington, DC, 20 November).

Bronckers, M.C.E.J. (1998), 'The Exhaustion of Patent Rights Under World Trade Organization Law', *Journal of World Trade*, **32**.

Cottier, T. (1998), 'The WTO System and Exhaustion of Rights', Paper presented at Conference on the Exhaustion of Intellectual Property Rights and Parallel Importation in World Trade, Committee on International Trade Law (Geneva, 7 November).

Danzon, P.M. (1997), *Pharmaceutical Price Regulation* (Washington, DC: American Enterprise Institute Press).

Fox, E.M. (1997), 'Competition Law and the Agenda for the WTO: Forging the Links of Competition and Trade', *Pacific Rim Law and Policy Journal*, **4**, 1–36.

Gallini, N.T. and M. Trebilcock (1998), 'Intellectual Property Rights and Competition Policy: A Framework for Analysis of Economic and Legal Issues', in R. Anderson and N.T. Gallini (eds.), *Competition Policy and Intellectual Property Rights in the Knowledge-Based Economy* (Calgary: University of Calgary Press).

Graham, E.M. and J.D. Richardson (1997a), *Competition Policies for the Global Economy* (Washington, DC: Institute for International Economics).

Graham, E.M. and J.D. Richardson (eds.) (1997b), *Global Competition Policy* (Washington, DC: Institute for International Economics).

Hoekman, B. (1997), 'Competition Policy and the Global Trading System', *The World Economy*, **20**, 383–406.

Hoekman, B. and P. Holmes (1999), 'Competition Policy, Developing Countries, and the WTO', *The World Economy*, **22**, 875–93.

Lloyd, P.G. (1998), 'Multilateral Rules for International Competition Law?' *The World Economy*, **21**, 1029–49.

Malueg, D.A. and M. Schwartz (1994), 'Parallel Imports, Demand Dispersion, and International Price Discrimination', *Journal of International Economics*, **37**, 167–96.

Maskus, K.E. (1999), 'Intellectual Property Rights in Lebanon', in B. Hoekman and J. Zarrouk (eds.), *Catching Up With the Competition: Trade Opportunities and Challenges for Arab Countries* (Ann Arbor: University of Michigan Press, forthcoming).

Maskus, K.E. (2000), *The Protection of Intellectual Property Rights in the Global Economy: Analysis, Evidence, and Policy* (Washington, DC: Institute for International Economics, forthcoming).

Messerlin, P.A. (1996), 'Competition Policy and Antidumping Reform: An Exercise in Transition', in J.J. Schott (ed.), *The World Trading System: Challenges Ahead* (Washington, DC: Institute for International Economics).

Neven, D. and L.-H. Roller (1999), 'International Antitrust', Paper presented to the NBER-CEPR International Seminar on International Trade (June).

Primo Braga, C.A. (1996), 'Trade-Related Intellectual Property Issues: The Uruguay Round Agreement and Its Economic Implications', in W. Martin and L.A. Winters (eds.), *The Uruguay Round and the Developing Countries* (Cambridge: Cambridge University Press).

Reichman, J.H. (1993), 'From Free-Riders to Fair Followers: Global Competition Under the TRIPs Agreement', *New York University Journal of International Law and Politics*, **29**, 11–93.

Scherer, F.M. (1994), *Competition Policies for an Integrated World Economy* (Washington, DC: Brookings Institution).

Smith, P.J. (1999), 'Are Weak Patent Rights a Barrier to U.S. Exports?' *Journal of International*

Economics, **48**, 151–77.
United Nations Conference on Trade and Development (1996), *The TRIPS Agreement and Developing Countries* (Geneva: UNCTAD).
Watal, J. (2000), *Intellectual Property Rights and Developing Countries in the World Trade Organization: The Way Forward* (Delhi: Oxford University Press, forthcoming).

15

Market Access Advances and Retreats: The Uruguay Round and Beyond

J. Michael Finger and Ludger Schuknecht

!. INTRODUCTION

𝕿 HE Uruguay Round has been justly celebrated for the innovations it represents: coverage extended to services, intellectual property, trade-related investment issues, much greater attention to the rules of trade-policy making and administration, a new and unified organisation to administer the agreements. At the same time, the Uruguay Round dealt significantly with the more or less traditional subject of the GATT – market access: tariff cuts as broad in scope as those of any previous round were agreed, policies that affect trade in agricultural products were taken up for the first time, agreement was reached to eliminate restrictions on trade in textiles and clothing under the Multi-Fibre Arrangement.[1] This chapter deals only with market access. In it we present a tally of:

- implementation of market access commitments, i.e., of the agreed removal or reduction of import restrictions, and
- use of various 'safeguard' and other measures that the agreement provides that allow a member government to introduce new trade restrictions.

Our report has no thesis to advance. It is not an essay, but is a tabulation of the amount of liberalisation that has resulted from the Uruguay Round Agreements, and of slippage from that liberalisation. Our objective is not to count up to see which part is larger, the agreed liberalisation versus the allowed 'backsliding.' No doubt, the liberalisation has been larger, by several orders of magnitude.

---

[1] We do not review in this chapter these 'rules' areas of the Uruguay Round agreements; they are taken up in the chapter by Finger and Schuler in this volume.

Nevertheless, it is important to keep a close watch on the use of allowed backsliding.

Our major findings are the following:

1.   Much was achieved. Tariff cuts compare well to the coverage and depth of cuts achieved at the Tokyo and Kennedy Rounds. Agricultural protection was dealt with substantively for the first time, VERs outside of MFA have been phased out. The agreement to remove MFA-based quantitative restrictions on imports of textiles and clothing is of itself a major accomplishment.

2.   There has been minimal backsliding, minimal use of the special or general provisions for imposing new restrictions that the various WTO agreements provide. Anti-dumping is the one exception.

3.   Tariff cuts by developing countries were as broad and at the same time, deeper, than those conceded by the developed economies.

4.   The major part of what developing economies *gave* is due now, the major part of what they *receive* will not be delivered until 2005, or is yet to be negotiated. What they gave (apart from the exchange of tariff cuts) was mainly acceptance of 'codes' on major areas of domestic as well as import regulation/institutions (e.g., intellectual property, technical and sanitary standards, customs valuation, import licensing procedures). What they got in return from the developed economies is MFA elimination – not due until 2005 – trade liberalisation and reduction of domestic support on agricultural products – yet to be negotiated. Details are provided below.

2. TARIFF NEGOTIATIONS

At the Uruguay Round, some 130 countries or customs areas made tariff concessions. Within the mechanics of the GATT/WTO, a member makes a concession by submitting to the organisation a schedule of commitments, of bound rates. In doing so, the member accepts a legal obligation not to impose a duty on any listed product at a rate higher than the specified bound rate. Its schedule of bound rates defines a member's legal obligations on tariff rates – there was no legal commitment to cut tariffs by a specified amount and thus no 'official' measure of the tariff reductions exchanged at the Round.

As the negotiations matured, a frequently mentioned 'target' was that developed members should reduce their tariffs by one-third, developing members should reduce theirs by one-quarter. The discussion surrounding these targets was not precise, e.g., as to whether the base should be all merchandise imports or only industrial goods, all tariff lines vs. all dutiable tariff lines, or even if the

TABLE 1
Uruguay Round Tariff Concessions Given and Received

	Bindings (percentage of 1989 imports)		Tariff Reductions	
	Pre-UR	Post-UR	% of Imports	Depth of Cut $(dT/(1+T))$
Tariff Concessions Given – All merchandise				
Developed Economies	80	89	30	1.0
Developing Economies	30	81	29	2.3
All	73	87	30	1.2
Tariff Concessions Received – All merchandise				
Developed Economies	77	91	36	1.4
Developing Economies	64	78	28	1.0
All	73	87	33	1.3
Tariff Concessions Given – Industrial goods				
Developed Economies	85	92	32	1.0
Developing Economies	32	84	33	2.7
All	77	91	32	1.3
Tariff Concessions Received – Industrial goods				
Developed Economies	79	93	37	1.5
Developing Economies	72	86	36	1.2
All	77	91	37	1.4

appropriate formula was dT/T or $dT/(1+T)$. Members also engaged in a related discussion of how bindings of unilateral liberalisations would be treated, all of this complicated by an imprecision as to what date should be used to determine the 'before' tariff rates.

In Table 1 along with Figures 1 and 2, we summarise our measures of the increase of bindings and the tariff reductions that will result from Uruguay Round commitments. [2]

a. Increases of Bindings

Expansions of bindings are simple to conceptualise – the amount of some base year's imports that would be covered by the new bindings versus the old. Increased bindings by developing economies are evident from Figure 1. Developing economies sometimes bound tariffs at levels above currently applied rates and some members' tariff concessions consisted of binding tariffs at rates to which they

[2] Though we use here the labels 'developed' and 'developing,' the classification of countries used in these calculations is the World Bank's sorting of countries as either high-income economies (HIES) or low and middle income economies (LMIEs), that includes transition economies. Footnote 3 provides details of country coverage of the two categories.

FIGURE 1
Coverage of GATT Tariff Bindings, Pre- and Post-Uruguay Round
(Industrial Goods)

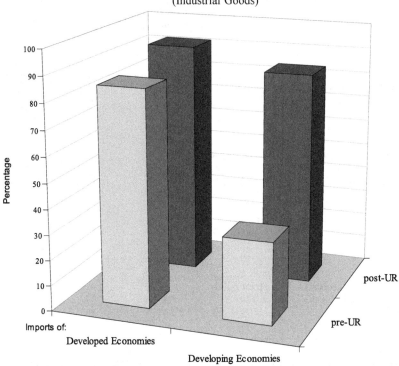

had previously been reduced unilaterally. More information will be provided below both on ceiling bindings and on bindings of unilateral concessions.

b. Tariff Reductions

We find that Uruguay Round commitments by the developing economies to reduce their tariffs compare well with the commitments of the developed economies.

- Developing economies' tariff cuts cover approximately the same percentage of imports.
- Developing economies' tariff cuts are actually deeper.

(i) Depth of cut[3]

Our calculations of depth of tariff cut depart in two ways from the way that the GATT tariff cuts are traditionally measured. First, GATT tariff cuts are usually

---

[3] The results reported in this section come in large part from Finger, Ingco and Reincke (1996). That source provides more extensive information on tariff concessions given and received by major

FIGURE 2
Depth of Tariff Cuts Agreed at the Uruguay Round
(Industrial Goods)

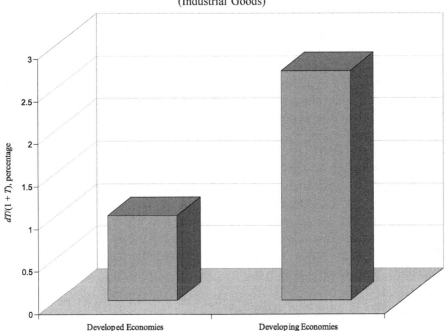

measured only over the import categories on which cuts are made; e.g., 'a 30 per cent cut on 40 per cent of imports' does not mean that the tariff, on average, is now 30 per cent lower. It means that the tariff is, on average, 0.4 × 30 per cent, or 12 per cent lower. We include 'zero cuts' in our average.[4]

Second, it is obvious that a 50 per cent reduction of a 2 per cent tariff rate does not improve market access the same as cutting a 40 per cent rate in half. Taking

Uruguay Round participants. It also provides a detailed discussion of which dates were taken as the 'before' and the 'after' Uruguay Round tariff rates. Conceptualisation of 'before' and 'after' followed practice developed by the GATT/WTO Secretariat, the dominant concern being to isolate tariff cuts that took place as a result of Uruguay Round commitments, not to count politically unilateral tariff cuts that took place while the round was under way. The basic data source for Finger, Ingco and Reincke (1996) is the GATT/WTO Integrated Data Base (IDB) that provides electronic data on the Uruguay Round schedules of commitments plus corresponding trade data for 40 major participants in the Uruguay Round negotiations (counting the then 12 members of the European Union as one participant). The IDB covers 98 per cent of merchandise (excluding petroleum) imports of the GATT contracting parties at the time of the round. Using the World Bank convention of dividing economies into high income vs. low and middle income, the IDB covers 14 high-income economies plus 26 'transition' and 'developing' economies. With the exception of Hong Kong, all of the countries classified as high income are OECD members. Mexico and Korea, though OECD members, are classified as developing countries.

[4] That we are focusing on market access may seem an obvious point, but experience with previous drafts indicates that readers will view our information from different perspectives. Some, for example,

this into account, we have calculated tariff changes from the formula:

$$dT/(1+T)$$

where T is the *ad valorem* tariff rate, or *ad valorem* equivalent. From the perspective of an exporter, $dT/(1+T)$ measures the percentage by which she can reduce her delivered price in the importing country while keeping the net price she collects (after the tariff) the same. This comes to less than 1 per cent if a 2 per cent rate is cut in half, to more than 14 per cent if a 40 per cent rate is cut in half. We consider, thus, the formula $dT/(1+T)$ to provide the more appropriate measure of market access improvement.

Because of the tariff cuts, exporters on average will be able to reduce an additional 1 per cent of what buyers pay in developed economies, 2.3 per cent more of what buyers pay in developing economies. These figures are less exciting than reports of 'tariffs being cut world-wide by an average of 40 per cent,' that were in newspapers the day after the agreement was completed.[5]

Generally, the tariff cuts were made in five annual stages, the last on 1 January 1999. There were some exceptions in each direction, toward quicker implementation and toward slower.

(ii) *Bindings of unilateral reductions*

Table 2 reports for selected countries the percentage of recent tariff reductions that have been bound at the Uruguay Round.[6] The countries in Table 2 are not the only countries that implemented unilateral liberalisations, they are the countries for which we could find data to measure the unilateral tariff liberalisation, as well as the reduction agreed at the Uruguay Round.

Overall, our figures show that the countries in the group have bound somewhat less than half of the unilateral concessions that they have implemented since 1986. Measured by the $dT/(1+T)$ formula, that comes to a bound cut of 8 to 12

---

have commented that in calculating the percentage of imports subject to tariff cuts, we should have excluded already duty-free imports from the denominator – that a country with 80 per cent duty free imports at the beginning *could not have done more* than make cuts of 20 per cent. Our figures compare the percentage of countries' imports affected by Uruguay Round concessions, on who did what. They do not compare who was more generous, who might have done what, or who tried harder.

[5] The quote in this sentence is from the *Financial Times*, 16 December, 1993, p. 1.

[6] These results are taken from Finger and Winters (1998). The data that were used and the formulas for calculating total, bound and reciprocal reductions are explained there. Intuitively, suppose an applied tariff rate, initially 50 per cent, is reduced in a unilateral liberalisation to 20 per cent. Suppose the country also agrees to bind the rate on that tariff line at 30 per cent. The Total reduction is (50–20) or 30 percentage points; the Bound Reduction is (50–30) or 20 percentage points. The Reciprocal Reduction, the reduction conditioned on the Uruguay Round, is what the Uruguay Round adds to the Total Reduction. In this example, the bound rate is above the unilaterally assigned applied rate, so the Reciprocal Reduction is zero. Had the Uruguay Round bound rate been 10 per cent, the Total Reduction would be (50–10), the Bound reduction would be (50–10) and the Reciprocal Reduction would be (20–10).

TABLE 2
Uruguay Round Total, Bound and Reciprocal Reductions of Selected Developing Countries

Country	Total Reduction	Bound Reduction	Reciprocal Reduction	Percentage of Total Reduction Bound
Argentina	16	9	0.001	57
Brazil	25	12	0.007	47
Chile	19	8	0.000	39
Mexico	27	8	0.004	30
Peru	20	9	0.03	46
Uruguay	6	3	0.009	41
Venezuela	19	2	0.200	12
India	27	22	4.800	82
Average, weighted by import value				39

per cent for a number of Latin American countries and a 22 per cent cut for India. Again, such figures compare favourably with the tariff cuts agreed and bound by the developed economies at the Uruguay Round.

c. Remaining Tariffs

Table 3 presents post Uruguay Round averages of bound and of applied rates. Even though the developing economies agreed to larger cuts at the Uruguay Round, and a number of them also implemented unilateral reductions, their tariffs are still on average considerably higher than those of the developed economies.

Figure 3 provides the same information graphically. Generally, remaining patterns of tariff protection have the following characteristics.

1. Tariffs are disproportionally imposed *against* the exports of developing economies.
2. Tariffs are disproportionally imposed *by* the developing economies.
3. Biases against developing country exports are in *developing* economies' tariffs as much as in the *developed* economies' tariffs.

TABLE 3
Post-Uruguay Round Tariff Rates, All Merchandise

	Bound Rate, Average Ad Valorem	post-UR Bound Rate Rate Above Applied Rate[a]	Applied Rate, Average Ad Valorem
Developed Economies	3.5	19	2.6
Developing Economies	25.2	37	13.3
All	6.5	22	4.3

Note:
[a]Percentage of 1989 imports.

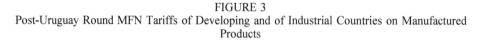

FIGURE 3
Post-Uruguay Round MFN Tariffs of Developing and of Industrial Countries on Manufactured
Products

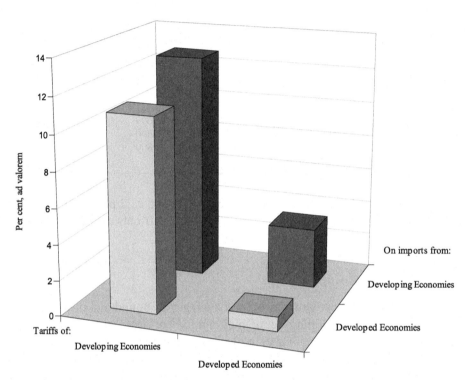

Beneath the low average tariffs of the developed economies there remain some significant tariff peaks, i.e., rates which are more than three times the national average. In several developed economies more than 10 per cent of tariff lines bear rates more than three times as high as the national average (Laird, 1999). The sectors with such peaks tend to be those of greater export interest to developing economies: footwear, leather and leather goods, food products, agriculture and textiles/clothing (UNCTAD/WTO, 1998) (a separate discussion of these latter product categories follows below). Both developing and developed economies display this tendency to impose higher import duties on goods of particular export interest to developing economies. That is why we see the pattern that Figure 3 reports.

d. Tariff Reductions since the Uruguay Round

WTO members at several negotiations since the Uruguay Round have agreed to significant further tariff reductions (Table 4). The largest of these reductions came together in the Ministerial Declaration on Trade in Information Technology Products which by the fall of 1997 had accumulated 43 signatories who thereby

TABLE 4
Post-Uruguay Round Tariff Concessions

Products	Countries	Concessions	Trade covered
Pharmaceutical Products	Canada, EC, Japan, Macau, Switzerland/ Liechtenstein, USA	Duty free treatment for 465 pharmaceutical products from 4/97 and for another 639 products from 7/99. At the Uruguay Round, these Members agreed to duty free treatment of some 6000 products.	–
Information Technology Products	43 WTO Members and acceding Members	Stepwise elimination of tariffs on information technology products until January 2000, selected countries until 2005 (see ITA for product coverage)	Covers about 10% of world – 93 per cent of world trade in IT products of US$ 500 billion in 1997
Distilled Spirits	USA, EC	Tariff reductions for distilled spirits in 1997; most tariffs will be reduced to zero by 2000	–

Source: Rectifications and Modifications of Uruguay Round Schedules.

committed to a stepwise tariff elimination on an MFN basis – on information technology products.[7]

This liberalisation is impressive in both scope and depth. The Information Technology Agreement covers some big items like semiconductors, computers, scientific instruments and software – in 1997, more than 10 per cent of world merchandise trade. Uruguay Round tariff cuts, we noted above, covered about 30 per cent of world merchandise trade. The tariffs in question are more or less in line with the averages in most of the countries involved, hence the depth of cut will be in the same range as the depth of the Uruguay Round cuts.

Another post Uruguay Round liberalisation involved Canada, the European Union, Japan, Macau, Switzerland-Liechtenstein, and the US who agreed to eliminate tariffs by April 1997 on 465 pharmaceutical products, and on another 639 products by July 1999. These negotiated tariff eliminations followed an understanding during the Uruguay Round to hold such negotiating meetings at least every three years. These eliminations come in addition to 6,000 duty-free

---

[7] For most of the signatories, tariffs were eliminated by January 2000, for a few, by January 2005.

products already covered under the pharmaceutical initiative in the Uruguay Round.

The third instance, the EU and the US agreed in 1997 to reduce tariffs on distilled spirits, with the objective of eliminating tariffs on most of these products by 2000.

e. Policing the Tariff Cuts

WTO Members created no specific mechanism to monitor the implementation of tariff commitments. 'Monitoring' will be done by traders – if a trader is asked to pay a duty above the importing country's bound rate, the trader's government can take the situation to the WTO dispute settlement process. As of March 1999, only one such situation has been brought to WTO dispute settlement, and the case is now under consultation.

The Integrated Data Base[8] itself is an important instrument for monitoring implementation of tariff commitments and increasing the transparency of tariff protection. The IDB was first pulled together to aid negotiators during the Uruguay Round. Since July 1997, members are required[9] to notify annually bound and applied tariff rates plus annual import statistics at the tariff line level. As of January 1999, 52 countries had made submissions to the IDB and a further seven had requested technical assistance to do so. Submissions, however, were not always complete, bound rates have been included in only 33 of the 52 submissions.[10]

3. QUANTITATIVE RESTRICTIONS

The Uruguay Round re-emphasised GATT's concern to discipline the use of quantitative restrictions and similar instruments, and made considerable progress toward that end. Rules that allow such restrictions[11] have been tightened, and

---

[8] The IDB is an electronic database. All Members have submitted (at least) paper copies of their schedules of commitments.

[9] General Council decision of 16 July, 1997 (WT/L/225).

[10] Adapting data to recent changes and the technical challenge of producing submissions for 8 or 10 thousand tariff lines are the major reasons for delays.

[11] The Agreements on Safeguards, on Agriculture and on Textiles and Clothing allow quantitative restrictions in certain circumstances. GATT 1994 under Article XI:2 allows quantitative export restrictions to deal with domestic shortages, also quantitative import restrictions for the application of standards and regulations, etc. Article XVII allows quantitative restrictions for the allocation of import licences through state trading companies, Article XVIIIB for balance of payment reasons. Quantitative restrictions might also be justified under the general and security exceptions of Articles XX and XXI. For agricultural products, Article 4:2 of the Agriculture Agreement supercedes Article XI:2c of GATT 1994.

those outside the new rules must be phased out. Grey-area measures such as voluntary export restraints are now illegal and existing measures must be phased out. In this section we will review notifications to the WTO of legal quantitative restrictions, and of those made illegal by the Uruguay Round Agreements and scheduled for elimination. In later sections we will review restrictions that have been imposed under various of the safeguard provisions in the Uruguay Round Agreements – some of which provisions allow for quantitative restrictions.

a. GATT-Legal Measures

Several GATT provisions that allow quantitative restrictions do not include notification requirements. Principal among these are Articles XX, General Exceptions, and XXI, Security Exceptions. Article XX covers, *inter alia*, restrictions to protect public morals (e.g., prohibition of importation of pornography) to apply technical or sanitary standards, to preserve human, animal and plant life, restrictions against imports produced by prison labour.

Some countries notify such restrictions, others do not. Table 5 provides indicative information about the mix of legal quantitative restrictions that Members apply, but it does not provide reliable information about which Members apply legal quantitative restrictions.[12] Virtually all countries have controls on some imports, e.g., of arms. The WTO Agreements do not require that Members report these restrictions and Table 5 indicates that few Members have chosen to report them.

In Table 5 we see that 49 times out of 57 (86 per cent) Article XX or XXI was the justification cited for a quantitative restriction. The most frequently cited paragraph of Article XX is the one allowing restrictions to protect human, animal or plant life or health. Outside of Articles XX and XXI, Article XVIII.B, allowing developing countries to use quantitative restrictions to defend the balance of payments, is the most frequently cited Article.[13]

Though Articles XII and XVIII.B still provide for trade restrictions to defend the balance-of-payments, the Uruguay Round Understanding on Balance-of-Payments Provisions limited the scope for use of such. Even before that agreement, developing economies had been under considerable pressure to remove such restrictions, and use of the provision has declined. Only India, Nigeria, Tunisia, Bangladesh and Pakistan maintain restrictions under XVIII.B, and schedules for phasing out balance-of-payment based non-tariff-measures have already been agreed with Tunisia and Pakistan. India's restrictions justified under XVIII.B are subject to a dispute settlement proceeding, and India has re-

---

[12] GATT articles that allow restrictions have proven to be fungible in that almost any restriction can be at least arguably justified under several GATT provisions (Finger, 1996). There will thus be a vague margin between restrictions that the GATT allows in principle and those it allows in fact.
[13] Notification of measures justified under Article XVIII.B is required.

TABLE 5

Indicative List of Notifications of GATT-Consistent* Quantitative Restrictions and Justifications, by Member

Member	GATT Articles or Paragraphs Cited		Product Categories	Type of QR(***)	Year of Last Notification
	Which Ones (**)	Number: Articles XX, XXI/ Total			
Argentina	XX(b)	1/1	Vehicles	Q	1997
Australia	XX(b)	1/1	Chemicals (Ozone depleting substances)	P	1996
Chile			Used Vehicles	P	1996
Cyprus	XX(b),(d), XXI(a),(b)	4/4	Various Industrial Products	L	1996
Fiji	XX, XXI	2/2	Drugs, Arms etc. (anything seditious)	P	1997
Hong Kong	XX(b)	1/1	Agricultural Chemicals (s.a)	Q,P	1996–1998
Hungary			Food, Textiles, Wood, Jewellery, Motor Vehicles	Q,L	1996
India	XVII, XVIII:B, XX(b),(c), (d), XXI(b)	4/6	Food, Chemicals, Machinery, Wood, Minerals, Metals, etc.	L,P,O	1996–1997
Jamaica	XX, XXI	2/2	Vehicles, Arms, Chemicals	L	1998
Japan	XI:2(c), XX (b),(g), XXI(b)(I)	4/5	Food, Mineral Products, Chemicals, Machinery, Arms	Q, O	1998
Korea	XVII, XVIII:B	0/2	Food, Mineral Products, Textiles	L	1997
Macau	XI:2(b), XX (b)	1/2	Agricultural Products, Chemicals, Arms, Machinery	L, P	1996
Malta			Food, Chemicals, Minerals, Wood, Metals, Vehicles, etc.	L	1996
Morocco	XX(b),(f),(g), (j), XXI	5/5	Various	L	1997
New Zealand	XX(b),(g),(j)	3/3	Chemicals (Ozone depleting substances)	P	1966
Pakistan	XX	1/1	Food, Chemicals, Arms	P	1997
Peru	XX(b),(g)	2/2	Used Textiles and Vehicles	P	1996–1997
Philippines	XVIII:B	0/1	Agricultural Products, Oil, Arms. Vehicles, Rubber Products, etc.	L,P	1996
South Africa	XX(a),(b),(c), XXI:b(ii)	4/4	Agricultural Products, Oil, Arms, Chemicals, Rubber, Metals, etc.	L	1996
Turkey	XI:2(a), XX(a),(b),(c),(d),(f), (g),(h); XXI:(b)(i), (b)(ii)	9/10	Animals, Food, Chemicals, Textiles, Arms	Q,P	1996–1998
Venezuela	XX(b),(g),(I)	3/3	Minerals, Chemicals, Rubber, Textiles, Used Vehicles	L,P	1996
Zambia	XX(g), XXI	2/2	Ivory, Wood, Metals	P,L,O	1996
Totals		49/57			

Note:
Countries which notified that they do not maintain quantitative restrictions and year of notifications: Bahrain (1997), Bolivia (1997), Brunei Darussalam (1996), Costa Rica (1998), Dominican Republic (1996), Gambia (1997), Haiti (1998), Honduras (1997), Iceland (1996), Liechtenstein (1997), Mongolia (1998), Paraguay (1998), Singapore (1996), Switzerland (1997), Trinidad/Tobago (1996-1998), Uganda (1996), United Arab Emirates (1997), Uruguay (1996).

Source: Notifications submitted by Member Countries to the Market Access Committee.
(*) Only GATT Articles.
(**) Four countries in addition to the three listed here maintained at the end of 1998 quantitative restrictions under the balance of payment provision (Article XVIII.B). They are Bangladesh, Nigeria (no conclusion of last consultation), Pakistan and Tunisia.
(***) P=Prohibition, Q=Quota, L=Licensing, O=Other.
P includes: Prohibition (P), Prohibition except under defined conditions (CP).
Q includes: Global quota (GQ), Global quota allocated by country (GQC), Bilateral quota (BQ).
L includes: Automatic licensing (AL), Non-automatic licensing (NAL).
O includes: QR made effective through state trading (STR), Mixing regulation (MXR), Minimum Price (MPR), Voluntary Export Restraint (VER).

notified some of the measures under other GATT articles Nigeria's BOP-based quantitative restrictions have also been questioned.

b. Measures Notified for Post-Uruguay Round Elimination

The Uruguay Round Safeguards Agreement imposes time limits on all new safeguard measures. In concert it requires the phase-out of all existing safeguard measures now legal under GATT Article XIX. It also requires the elimination of all VERs and other restraints that would not be allowed under the Uruguay Round safeguard rules.[14] Table 6 lists all such measures notified by WTO Members. Only eight of the measures notified are measures taken under Article XIX that now come under sunset provisions. The brevity of this list, say, in comparison with the number of anti-dumping measures in place (below) reflects how infrequently Article XIX measures have been used to deal with troublesome imports. The other 18 measures listed are notified as inconsistent with the new Safeguard Agreement and subject to phase-out. Most of the measures (of both types) have been eliminated already, the remaining three are scheduled for elimination at the end of 1999.

The information in Table 6 demonstrates that VERs have disappeared. To confirm that finding we looked for other information on VERs. A GATT tabulation (GATT, 1992) identifying 79 such restraints outside agriculture and textiles/clothing that were in place as of 1992. Korea (46) and Japan (23) were most frequently involved on the exporters' side. On the importers' side, the European Union and the US accounted for 33 and 17 VERs each. Notifications since the Uruguay Round indicate that these arrangements are gone or will be gone on the deadline specified

---

[14] Of course, the fungibility of GATT/WTO rules (footnote 12) means that a country wishing to maintain a grey area measure had several options for defending its legality.

TABLE 6

Pre-existing Measures Notified by Members as Subject to Elimination Under Rules Adopted at the Uruguay Round (grey area measures and measures legal under Article XIX now subject to sunset provisions)

Importing Member	Restrained Exporters (if available)	Product	Instrument	Elimination Date	Sfg. Agm. Article[a]
Cyprus	All countries	Most imports	QRs, Prohibitions, discretionary licensing	31.12.98	11
EC		**Dried Grapes**	**Minimum Import Price**	**31.12.99**	**10**
EC		**Preserved Cherries**	**Minimum Import Price**	**31.12.99**	**10**
EC	Non-EC Countries	Live Bovine Animals	QR (Import Licence)	01.07.95	11
EC	Non-EC Countries	Swine and Meat of Swine	QR (Import Licence)	01.07.95	11
EC	Non-EC Countries	Rabbit Meat	QR (Authorisation)	01.07.95	11
EC	All countries	Potatoes	QR (Certificates)	01.11.98	11
EC	Non-EC Countries, except those with a preferential agreement with the EC	Preserved Sardines	QR (Global Quota)	31.12.96	11
EC	Non-EC Countries, except those with a preferential agreement with the EC	Preserved Tuna	QR (Global Quota)	31.12.96	11
EC	Non-EC Countries	Lignite	QR	31.12.96	11
EC	Non-EC Countries	Coal	QR (Authorization)	31.12.97	11
EC	**Japan**	**Motor Vehicles**	**VER**	**31.12.99**	**11**
EC	Korea	Microwave Ovens	VER	02.06.97	11
EC	Korea	Colour Picture Tubes	VER	02.06.97	11
EC	Thailand	Manioc	VER	30.06.95	11
Japan	Korea	Chestnuts, shelled	VER	31.12.98	11

Korea	People's Rep. Of China	Hot Bean Paste	QR (Import Licence)	31.12.99	10
Nigeria	All countries	Wheat Flour	Import Prohibition	No date provided	10
Nigeria	All countries	Sorghum	Import Prohibition	No date provided	10
Nigeria	All countries	Millet	Import Prohibition	No date provided	10
Nigeria	All countries	Gypsum	Import Prohibition	No date provided	10
Nigeria	All countries	Kaolin	Import Prohibition	No date provided	10
South Africa	All countries	Oil and Oil Products, Petroleum, Chemicals, Rubber, Plastic	QR (Import licenses)	31.12.98, 31.1 2.96, 31.07. 96, 28.02.97	11
UK, Germany	Korea	Stainless Steel Flat-ware	VER	31.12.98	11
All countries	Slovenia	Wood in various forms, Metal Waste and Scrap	Special Export Tax, rates 10 to 25%	01.01.97 and 01.01.98	11
All WTO Members	Korea	Oysters in airtight containers	VER	31.12.98	11

Source: Notifications submitted by Member Countries to the WTO Committee on Safeguards
[a] Article 10, GATT XIX measures; Article 11, VERs and other measures inconsistent with the Safeguards Agr.

in the agreement. Among exporters, Japan submitted no report of continuing VERs,[15] Korea's report indicates that all VERs with the US and the European Union have been eliminated. Thailand's notification indicates the same for the Thai VER on manioc to the European Union. Though the WTO does not require such notification, 18 Members have notified the WTO that they maintain no quantitative restrictions. They are listed in the note to Table 5.

WTO Trade Policy Reviews further support the conclusion that VERs have disappeared. The most recent TPR for Japan reports that all VERs in which Japan participated have been eliminated except the Japan-EU VER on cars – and that one will be gone by end 1999 (WTO, 1998). The 1996 Trade Policy Review for the US reports that the VERs agreed with other countries had been removed (WTO, 1997). The accuracy of that finding is confirmed by the fact that it was not contested in discussion of the Trade Policy Reviews.

Despite this 'elimination' of VERs, there are still WTO-legal ways for trade disputes to be resolved by exporters agreeing to restrain shipments. The anti-dumping and subsidies, countervailing measures agreements allow such 'under-takings.' Following the filing in 1998 of anti-dumping and countervailing duty cases by the US steel industry, the US reached agreement to a VER with non-WTO member Russia. As of March 1999 when this study was written, Brazil had proposed to curb exports voluntarily if a US anti-dumping case is suspended, and much pressure is being put on Japan to reduce exports to the US.

c. Overall Progress on NTBs

Tables 7 and 8 provide a view of recent reductions in the application of NTBs. The tabulations summarised in the tables cover export restraints, non-automatic licensing, variable charges and quantitative restrictions and price-quantity measures, but exclude anti-dumping and countervailing duties.

Among OECD countries, the principal finding is that the share of tariff lines affected by such measures declined significantly, or remained at a very low level (Australia and New Zealand) in all countries covered. In those two, the index remained constant. The decline in the NTB index for Norway is mainly due to the tariffication of a large number of agricultural tariff lines, the elimination of VERs is a key reason for the decline in NTBs in the US and the EU.

Information on developing economies' use of NTBs extracted from WTO Trade Policy Reviews suggests a significant reduction in use of NTBs.[16]

---

[15] The EU notified the VER on Japanese exports of cars that the EU has notified under the phasing out provision of the Safeguard Agreement.

[16] The OECD and the WTO-Trade Policy Reform tabulations are based on data at different levels of aggregation, hence we cannot compare the incidences of NTBs for developed economies (from the OECD tabulation) with those for developing economies (from the WTO-Trade Policy Reform tabulation).

TABLE 7
Core Non-tariff Measures* in Selected OECD Countries
(Share of tariff lines with at least one NTB, in percentage)

Country	1993	1996
Australia	0.3	0.3
Canada	1.4	1.2
EU	9.4	4.2
Iceland	2.8	0.7
Japan	3.8	2.6
Mexico	2.0	1.0
New Zealand	0.0	0.0
Norway	24.0	3.8
Switzerland	3.5	0.2
Turkey	0.1	0.2
US	10.3	2.9

Note:
* Core Non-tariff Measures include: export restraints, non-automatic licensing, other quantitative restrictions, variable charges and other price control measures. The figures do not cover anti-dumping, countervailing duties and voluntary export/price restraints.

Source: OECD (1997).

TABLE 8
Core Non-tariff Measures in Selected Developing Economies

Economy	Relative Incidence of NTBs 1995–98[b]
Hong Kong	0
Singapore	1
Argentina	2
Chile	6
South Africa	9
Colombia	11
Mexico	14
Morocco	14
Thailand	19
Malaysia	21
Korea	27
Indonesia	33
Brazil	48
India	100

Notes:
[a] Core Non-tariff Measures include: export restraints, non-automatic licensing, other quantitative restrictions, variable charges, and other price control measures. The figures do not include coverage of anti-dumping, countervailing duties and voluntary export/price restraints.
[b] Relative NTB incidence where NTB incidence is measured by the share of 85 broad data categories with at least one NTB.

Source: WTO Trade Policy Reviews to April 1999.

Colombia, Indonesia, Korea, Malaysia, Mexico, Morocco, South Africa and Thailand now take much less recourse to such trade restrictions. Among the developed economies listed in Table 8 (which is based on TPRs) only one, Brazil, had a higher NTB index value in 1995–98 than 1989–94, and for Brazil the increase was small, less than two percentage points

WTO Trade Policy Reviews explicitly acknowledge the implementation of the Uruguay Round Agreements in bringing down NTBs in Mexico and Thailand by about 50 per cent. In Colombia and Korea, the elimination of quantitative restrictions under the balance of payments provision has resulted in a major reduction of NTBs. The decline in the use of the balance of payments provision has been an important achievement in the post-UR period, although it was not explicitly part of the Uruguay Round package.[17]

4. TEXTILES AND CLOTHING

Since the 1930s, developed economies have used negotiated or 'voluntary' export restraints to limit their imports of textiles and clothing.[18] Finally, in the Uruguay Round Agreements, the international community decided to put an end to this practice. The major provisions for eliminating quotas and VERs on textiles and clothing are as follows:

- all textiles and clothing products will be 'integrated into GATT 1994' in four stages (1/1/1995, 1/1/1998, 1/1/2002, 1/1/2005), encompassing 16 per cent, 17 per cent, 18 per cent and 49 per cent (by 1990 volume) of imports of all specified textiles and clothing products;
- import growth rates for all products not so integrated (i.e., that remain under restraint) will be increased in each of the three intervals between stages by 16 per cent, 25 per cent and 27 per cent, respectively;[19]
- each of the four groups into which the spectrum of textile products has been divided (tops and yarns, fabrics, made up textile products, clothing) must be included in each of the integration.

The percentages listed in the first bullet above apply to 'the total volume of the Member's 1990 imports of the products in the Annex.'[20] The annex runs to more than 30 pages of six-digit HS products and includes all textile and clothing

---

[17] Trade Policy Reviews for the other developing countries in Table 8 did not look into the reasons for the decline of NTBs.

[18] Finger and Harrison (1996) provide a history of MFA-related restrictions on developed economies' imports of textiles and clothing, beginning with VERs by Japan in the 1930s.

[19] The percentages apply to growth rates, not to growth; e.g., if the agreed quota growth rate is 3 per cent, in the first interval this rate must increase to (1.16)x3, equals 3.48.

[20] Agreement on Textiles and Clothing, Article 2, paragraph 6.

products that were subject to MFA or MFA-type restraints in at least one importing country.[21] Any one Member is unlikely to have restraints on all of the products on the list, and hence in the early stages will have the opportunity to 'integrate' products on which it has no restrictions. As a matter of semantics then, the operative phrase in the agreement, *to integrate into GATT 1994* is better described as 'certifying that a product is clean of restrictions'[22] than as 'removing MFA restrictions.'

- A transitional safeguard measure may be applied by a Member[23] to any product in the Annex, except for products already integrated into the GATT, i.e., liberalised as per the first bullet above.

Constraints for using the transitional safeguard mechanism are tighter than those for, say, the safeguards agreement – e.g., a transitional safeguard cannot extend beyond three years. Transitional safeguards may, however, be applied against specific exporters.

a. Implementation – Concentrated on Relatively Unrestricted Products

The developed economies' policies toward these imports are among their most restrictive. Hufbauer and Elliott estimate, for example, that almost 9/10 of the cost to the US economy of US import restrictions are accounted for by restrictions on imports of textiles and clothing. At the same time, textiles and clothing account for more than 20 per cent of developing economies' industrial exports, hence there is much to gain all around from liberalisation.

Implementation has proceeded through the first two stages; thus, each importing country has integrated into GATT 1994 products accounting for at least 33 per cent of its imports. There have been, however, loud complaints that minimal liberalisation has resulted from this implementation. The most often voiced complaints are that each importing Member has weighted its liberalisation toward products:

- that were not under restraint in that country,
- with little value added or on which developed economies do not have comparative advantage, e.g., yarns and fabrics rather than clothing,
- with high tariffs,
- and that they have overused transitional safeguards or have applied antidumping and other WTO-legal restrictions disproportionally against textiles and clothing.

---

[21] WTO Secretariat (1999, p. 66).

[22] Those that would be illegal under GATT 1994.

[23] This includes Members who did not have in place restrictions under the MFA, but who notified the Textiles Monitoring Board that they retained the right to use the transitional safeguards provision. Sixty-four Members so notified. Nine Members notified that they did not wish to retain the right to use transitional safeguards (WTO G/L/179, p. 14).

TABLE 9

Numbers of MFA Quota Limits Notified and Eliminated in Stages 1 and 2
(Stage 1 plus stage 2 requires integration of 33 per cent, by import volume)

Member	Notified, Number	Eliminated Number	Eliminated Percentage
United States	650	8	1
European Union	199	14	7
Canada	205	28	14
Norway	54	46	85

Source: WTO Doc. G/L/179, p. 29. Norway G/C/M/23, p. 23.

TABLE 10

Clothing as a Percentage by Volume of
Products Integrated in Stages 1 and 2

Member	Percentage
United States	12.4
European Union	7.2
Canada	7.9
Norway	10.6

Source: WTO Doc. G/L/179, p. 29.

We will review below available evidence on each of these.

The tabulation in Table 9 – taken from information notified to the Textiles Monitoring Board – does indicate that importers have selected items that were not under restriction. Norway, of the countries in the table, is the exception. Norway has decided to liberalise more rapidly than the agreement requires.[24]

For the US and Canada (combined) textile imports and clothing imports are about equal, for Western European countries (combined) clothing imports are considerably larger than textile imports.[25] Even so, clothing has made up a small part of the products the countries listed in Table 10 which have been integrated into GATT 1994 – among the best of them, hardly more than 10 per cent.

b. Tariff Cuts and Remaining Tariffs

Tariffs on textiles and clothing remain high relative to those on industrial products generally (Table 11). Table 11 also reports that the Uruguay Round tariff cuts on textiles and clothing were relatively *large*. Not only were the cuts (measured by $dT/(1 + T)$) deeper on textiles and clothing, they were applied to a larger fraction of imports.

---

[24] WTO document G/C/M/23, p. 23.
[25] WTO, Annual Report (1997, Tables IV.53 and IV.60).

TABLE 11
Post Uruguay Round Applied Tariff Rates and Uruguay Round Tariff Cuts on Textiles and Clothing
and on All Industrial Goods

	Post-UR Applied Rate		UR cut[a] $dT/(1+T)*100$		Percentage of Imports Subject to Cut	
	Textiles and Clothing	Industrial Goods	Textiles and Clothing	Industrial Goods	Textiles and Clothing	Industrial Goods
Selected Developed Economies						
Australia	22.6	9.7	9.0	3.8	54.1	46.2
Canada	14.2	2.6	3.7	1.1	64.8	22.5
European Union	8.7	2.9	1.4	1.3	70.5	43.3
Japan	7.2	1.4	1.9	1.1	83.5	42.1
United States	14.8	3.1	1.7	1.2	86.0	42.5
Selected Developing Economies						
Brazil	15.5	11.8	0.0	0.0	0.0	0.1
Colombia	15.9	10.4	0.0	0.0	0.0	0.6
Czech & Slovak Customs Union	6.6	3.7	1.7	0.9	72.8	72.8
India	42.4	29.0	7.4	6.8	41.1	41.1
Korea	13.0	7.6	5.1	6.2	71.1	71.1
Thailand	28.9	26.8	19.6	5.4	41.4	41.4
Turkey	44.2	24.2	10.5	2.6	41.7	41.7
Zimbabwe	17.6	4.5	1.3	0.1	2	2
All developed economies in the IDB	8.4	2.5	1.4	1.0	53.0	32.3
All developing economies in the IDB	21.2	13.3	4.1	2.7	48.6	33.4
All economies in the IDB	9.8	4.2	1.6	1.3	52.6	32.4

Note:
[a] Averaged over all textiles and clothing tariff lines, including those with zero cuts.

c. Transitional Safeguards

Table 12 lists all transitional safeguard measures implemented from implementation of the Uruguay Round Agreements through 19 March, 1999. Soon after the agreement went into force, the United States applied a number of transitional safeguards, all but one of which had been lifted by March 1999. The US has not imposed a transitional safeguard since March 1996. Brazil's actions, all imposed in January 1996, are mostly still in place. The only other country to apply a transitional safeguard measure was Colombia, but the two measures applied by Colombia in 1998 have both been rescinded.

TABLE 12
Transitional Safeguards in Textiles and Clothing since 1/95

Member Requesting Consultations	Member Subject to Request for Consultation	Product	Measure Introduced On	Type of Safeguard Measure Introduced	Review by the TMB	Follow-up of the TMB Review	Measure Still in Force (on 19.03.1999)
United States	El Salvador	Cotton and man-made fibre pyjamas and other nightwear	27.03.95	Agreed restraint	United States rescinded	United States rescinded	No
United States	Honduras	Cotton and man-made fibre pyjamas and other nightwear	27.03.95	Unilateral restraint	Yes	United States rescinded	No
United States	Jamaica	Cotton and man-made fibre pyjamas and other nightwear	27.03.95	Agreed restraint	United States rescinded	United States rescinded	No
United States	Costa Rica	Cotton and man-made fibre underwear	27.03.95	Unilateral restraint	Yes	Dispute settlement panel	No
United States	Dominican Republic	Cotton and man-made fibre underwear	27.03.95	Agreed restraint	Yes		No
United States	El Salvador	Cotton and man-made fibre underwear	27.03.95	Agreed restraint	Yes		No
United States	Honduras	Cotton and man-made fibre underwear	27.03.95	Unilateral restraint	Yes	Subsequent agreed restraint, reviewed	No
United States	Turkey	Cotton and man-made fibre underwear	28.03.95	Unilateral restraint	Agreed restraint during Review	Agreed restraint reviewed	No

United States	Colombia	Cotton and man-made fibre underwear	29.03.95	Agreed restraint	Yes	No
United States	Thailand	Cotton and man-made fibre underwear	29.03.95	Unilateral restraint	United States rescinded during review	No
United States	India	Woven wool shirts and blouses	18.04.95	Unilateral restraint	Yes — Dispute settlement panel	No
United States	India	Women's and girl's wool coats	18.04.95	Unilateral restraint	Yes Dispute settlement panel requested, US rescinded. India requested termination of further action in pursuance of decision to establish a panel	No
United States	India	Men's and boys' wool coats other than suit-type	18.04.95	Unilateral restraint	Yes — United States rescinded	No
United States	Honduras	Women's and girls' wool coats	24.04.95	Unilateral restraint	Agreed restraint during review	No
United States	Philippines	Man-made fibre luggage	24.04.95	Unilateral restraint	Rescinded before review	No
United States	Brazil	Men's and boys' wool coats other than suit-type	26.04.95	None		No
United States	Hong Kong	Woven wool shirts and blouses	27.04.95	Unilateral restraint	Yes — United States rescinded	No
United States	Sri Lanka	Man-made fibre luggage	27.04.95	Agreed restraint	United States rescinded	No

TABLE 12 (Continued)

Member Requesting Consultations	Member Subject to Request for Consultation	Product	Measure Introduced On	Type of Safeguard Measure Introduced	Review by the TMB	Follow-up of the TMB Review	Measure Still in Force (on 19.03.1999)
United States	Thailand	Man-made fibre luggage	28.04.95	Unilateral restraint	Rescinded before review		No
United States	Thailand	Artificial staple yarn	28.04.95	Unilateral restraint	Agreed restraint reviewed		No
United States	Guatemala	Cotton and man-made fibre skirts	31.05.95	Agreed restraint	Agreed restraint reviewed		No
United States	Colombia	Women's and girls' wool suits	31.05.95	Agreed restraint	Agreed restraint reviewed		No
United States	Philippines	Women's and girls' wool suits	31.05.95	Unilateral restraint	Rescinded before review		No
United States	Costa Rica	Cotton and man-made fibre pyjamas and other nightwear	29.06.95	Unilateral restraint	Rescinded before review		No
United States	El Salvador	Cotton and man-made fibre skirts	29.03.96	Unilateral restraint	Agreed restraint before review		Yes
United States	Pakistan	Yarn for sale, 85% or more by weight cotton ring spun	Not introduced				No
Brazil	Hong Kong	Woven artificial filament fabric	01.06.96	Unilateral restraint	Yes	Brazil rescinded	No

Brazil	Hong Kong	M&B shirts, knitted or crocheted, of other textile material	01.06.96	Unilateral restraint	Yes	Brazil rescinded	No
Brazil	Korea	Woven fabric containing 85% or more by weight artificial staple	01.06.96	Unilateral restraint	Agreed restraint before deferred review		Yes
Brazil	Korea	Woven artificial filament fabric	01.06.96	Unilateral restraint	Agreed restraint before deferred review		Yes
Brazil	Korea	Polyester filament fabric	01.06.96	Unilateral restraint	Agreed restraint before deferred review		Yes
Brazil	Korea	Other synthetic filament fabric	01.06.96	Unilateral restraint	Agreed restraint before deferred review		Yes
Brazil	Korea	Sheeting of staple filament fibre combinations	01.06.96	Unilateral restraint	Agreed restraint before deferred review		Yes
Colombia	Brazil	Denim	17.07.98	Unilateral restraint	Yes	Colombia rescinded	No
Colombia	India	Denim	17.07.98	Unilateral restraint	Yes	Colombia rescinded	No

Source: Reports of the Textiles Monitoring Body of the WTO.

d. Anti-dumping

Table 20 reports recent anti-dumping initiations by sector. From these dates it appears that the EU has initiated a significant number of cases against textile and clothing imports. These cases however were not on products that the EU liberalised in the first two rounds of phasing textile and clothing tariff lines into the GATT 1994.

5. AGRICULTURE

The agriculture negotiations focused on three categories of policy: import restrictions, domestic support programmes, and export subsidy programmes. We will pay attention principally to import restrictions.

a. The Intent of the Negotiators

On import restrictions, the major objective of the agreement is to establish a 'tariffs only' regime – to eliminate all forms of import restriction other than bound tariff rates. To do so, all members were required to 'tariffy' their non-tariff import restrictions. This conversion was based on the price gap methodology, with the methodological details being set out in technical guidelines on how to measure the gap between the domestic price (the price inside the protection wall) and the world price.[26] The base period for the conversion, members agreed, would be 1986–1988, a period when many agricultural prices had been unusually low. Because agricultural policies try to maintain a relatively stable – and high – domestic price, the price gap calculated from this base period coupled, in some cases, with other adjustments allowed by the technical guidelines, frequently resulted in high tariff rates. Developing countries had the option to submit ceiling rates on previously unbound tariff items, with the additional proviso to remove all agriculture-specific non-tariff measures. Each member's legal obligation is defined by its schedule of tariff rates annexed to the GATT 1994.[27]

---

[26] Following their use to establish the draft schedules of concessions and commitments, the technical guidelines were re-issued as Uruguay Round document MTM.GNG/MA/W/24, Modalities for the Establishment of Specific Binding Commitments Under The Reform Program, 20 December, 1993.

[27] The reader should be careful to recognise the difference between the negotiating process through which legal commitments are agreed and the legal commitments themselves. The conversion guidelines were part of the negotiating process. They likely influenced what tariff rates one Member was willing to accept from another, but once a Member's schedule of rates was accepted and annexed to GATT 1994, the conversions guidelines became irrelevant. No Member can be taken to the dispute settlement mechanism on its bound rates being higher than those calculated with the formulas of the conversion guidelines.

According to the WTO Secretariat, 40 countries participated in the tariffication process which covered (in aggregate) about 22 per cent of their tariff lines.[28] Finger-Ingco-Reincke (1996) calculations over the IDB show that tariffication covered, by value, just over one-third of tariffying countries' agriculture imports.

The modalities document also gave targets for tariff reductions. A developed country member was to reduce its duties, including those resulting from tariffication, across all agricultural tariff lines by a simple average of 36 per cent over six years, with a minimum reduction of 15 per cent on individual products. A developing country member was to reduce its duties by 24 per cent over ten years, and least developed countries were not required to make reductions.[29]

(i) Tariff quota commitments

As part of the tariffication package, WTO Members agreed to maintain, for tariffied products, 'current' import access opportunities at levels corresponding to those existing during the 1986–88 base period at terms not less favourable than in that period. Where such current access had been less than five per cent of domestic consumption of the product in question in the base period, the agreement required an (additional) minimum access opportunity on a most-favoured nation basis[30] at a low tariff rate. This was to ensure that in 1995, current and minimum access opportunities combined represented at least 3 per cent of base-period consumption and are progressively expanded to reach 5 per cent of that consumption in the year 2000 (developed countries) or 2004 (developing countries), respectively.[31]

b. Estimating How the Agreement has Changed Market Access

Implementing the tariff part of the agreement involves the following steps:

- As explained above, convert to tariffs-only, i.e., determine new tariff rates for all tariff lines with NTBs, eliminate the NTBs. (Many of the new rates are specific rates, not *ad valorem* rates.)
- Bind all tariff lines – those on which NTBs have been converted to tariffs and those on which there were tariffs only, i.e., no NTBs.
- Reduce the bound rates.

---

[28] WTO Secretariat (1999, p. 136).

[29] Again the schedules of commitments, not the formula, define legal obligations.

[30] Importers can, however, count special arrangements as part of their minimum access commitments and can allocate their minimum access to exporters that have special arrangements. Thus sugar, beef, etc., imports of the US and the European Union will be allocated as before (Hathaway and Ingco, 1996, p. 48).

[31] Again, legal commitments are defined by the schedules, which specify at which quantities the higher tariff rate will go into effect.

Legal commitments are those specified in the schedules of rates attached by Members, possibly higher – even including staged reductions – than the tariff equivalent of initial measures. The Finger-Ingco-Reincke calculations that we report here are based on work by Ingco (1995) that used 1986–1988 as the base period for calculating (a) the *ad valorem* equivalents of overall protection applied in that period, and (b) the *ad valorem* equivalents of the tariffied bound rates.

Ingco found that many of the new bound rates were above the rates actually applied in the base period, and that some of the post-Uruguay Round bound rates – the rates that incorporate all of the scheduled reductions – are above the tariff equivalents of all protection applied before the Uruguay Round. While the focus of the Finger-Ingco-Reincke calculations we report here is on isolating the instances in which the Uruguay Round schedules do imply a reduction of protection, we will pay attention to her evidence on this 'dirty tariffication.'

Suppose for example, that the *ad valorem* equivalent rates for a particular *tariffied line*, as of the base period, were as follows:

Base period applied protection	20%
including the tariff equivalent of NTBs)	
Immediate post UR bound rate	30%
Final post-UR bound rate that	
incorporates the scheduled reductions	18%

In this instance, the Finger-Ingco-Reincke calculations would take as the 'before-UR' rate the 20 per cent applied rate, not the 30 per cent bound rate. Only if the final-UR bound rate is below the 'before-UR' applied rate does the country's Uruguay Round commitment imply a tariff reduction. Thus the 'after-UR' rate in the Finger-Ingco-Reincke calculations is the lower of the 'before-UR' rate or the post-UR bound rate.

The guideline of a 36 per cent reduction is met in this example – the reduction of the *bound* rate from 30 per cent to 18 per cent is more than a 36 per cent reduction. The Finger-Ingco-Reincke calculations, however, look at how the Uruguay Round has reduced applied protection, and would include only the reduction from the previously applied rate, i.e., from 20 per cent, to 18 per cent. If the final-UR bound rate were at or above the base period applied rate – in this example, at or above 20 per cent, the Finger-Ingco-Reincke calculations would attribute zero reduction to the Uruguay Round.[32]

---

[32] The 'after' rate is always the lower of the applied and the post-UR bound rate; hence, the Uruguay Round reduction is never negative.

TABLE 13
Agricultural Products: Uruguay Round Tariff Bindings

	Per cent of Imports GATT-bound		Post-UR Bindings that Reduce Protection[a]
	Pre-UR	Post-UR	
Tariffied Products			
All Economies that Tariffied	66	100	14
Untariffied Products			
Developed Economies	71	100	35
Developing Economies	37	100	17
Tariffied and Untariffied Products			
Developed Economies	72	100	26
Developing Economies	37	100	17

Notes:
[a] Tariffied products: percentage (by value) of imports with final-UR bound rates (rates that include reductions) below the tariff equivalent of base period protection. Untariffied products: percentage of imports with final-UR bound rates below base period applied rates.

Source: Finger-Ingco-Reincke (1996, Tables G2).

c. Results: Tariff Bindings and Reductions

Judging from the sample of countries in the IDB, Table 13 reports that both developed and developing economies have now bound virtually 100 per cent of their agricultural tariff lines, overall an expansion of coverage of about two-thirds for the developing economies, one-quarter for the developed economies. Uruguay Round adjustments imply reductions of tariff rates on about one-quarter of developed economies' imports, on about one-fifth of developing economies' imports. The developing economies were expected to make smaller cuts, but our results show a larger depth of cut for developing economies.[33]

The figures for scope and depth of cut by the developing economies in the IDB, are probably not representative of developing economies in general. The IDB covers all of the developed economy members of the WTO, but it covers none of the least developed countries, who were not expected to make reductions of their agricultural tariffs. The developing economies in the IDB tend to be those that have implemented significant trade reforms.

Figure 4 converts the extent and depth of tariff cuts by the developing economies into multiples of performance by the developed economies. We see there the same pattern we found for tariffs overall. Developing economies' tariffs are still considerably above those of developed economies; the extent (import coverage) of developing economies' Uruguay Round tariff reductions was

---

[33] Developing economies' tariff rates tend to be higher (Table 14), we measure the depth of tariff cut by $dT/(1+T)$ which for a given dT/T is larger as T is larger. Negotiating guidelines were not precise, but in GATT/WTO affairs, dT/T is usually the implicit measure for depth of cut.

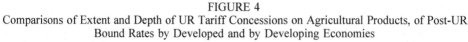

FIGURE 4
Comparisons of Extent and Depth of UR Tariff Concessions on Agricultural Products, of Post-UR
Bound Rates by Developed and by Developing Economies

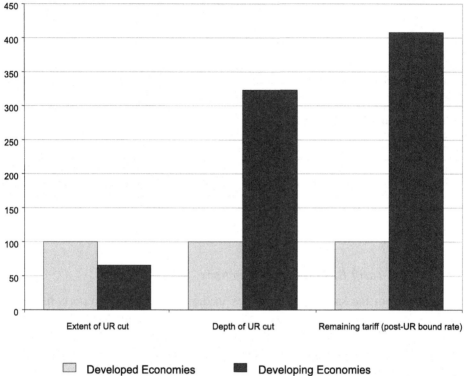

smaller. But the depth of cut when we measure by how it will affect trading partners' market access was considerably more by the developing economies – at least for those who are in the IDB.

(i) Tariff quota commitments

The above figures do not take into account how the minimum access commitments (implemented through tariff quotas) have affected the scope of liberalisation. This impact depends, of course, on which of a country's tariffied products have imports below five per cent of base period domestic consumption, and by how much.[34] At the maximum (i.e., if imports of all tariffied products were below the minimum) minimum access opportunities would affect the 22 per cent of tariff lines, or approximately one-third of imports, by value, that were tariffied. Hathaway and Ingco (1996, p. 49) estimate that Japan and Korea's minimum access commitments on rice will result in nearly a million tons per year

---

[34] The commitments apply to opportunities, as defined by the volume at which the higher tariff quota rate applies. They are not minimum import commitments.

TABLE 14
Average Uruguay Round Tariff Cuts on Agricultural Products, Average Post-Uruguay Round
Applied and Bound Tariff Levels

	UR Reduction[a]	Post-UR Applied rate[b]	Post-UR bound Rate[b]
Tariffied Lines			
All Economies that Tariffied	4.4	25	32
Not Tariffied Lines			
Developed Economies	1.6	5	7
Developing Economies	0.9	19	66
Tariffied and Not Tariffied			
Developed Economies	1.5	14	15
Developing Economies	4.7	18	60

Notes:
[a] Change measured as $dT/(1+T)$, expressed as a percentage. Tariffied products: change from the tariff equivalent of base period protection to final-UR bound rate. Untariffied products: change from base period applied rate to the lower of base period applied rate and final-UR bound rate.
[b] *Ad valorem* equivalent based on 1986–1988 prices.

Source: Finger-Ingco-Reincke (1996, Tables G2).

of new imports, an expansion of world trade in rice of 7.5 per cent over its 1992 level. Otherwise, they conclude that 'the minimum access commitments will provide relatively little additional access and even less additional trade,' no more that 0.5 per cent for wheat and sugar (pp. 48–9).

d. Tariffication Above Existing Levels of Protection

On agriculture products as on manufactures, developing economies committed to ceiling bindings above their applied rates. Averaged over the developing economies in the IDB, the average applied rate in the base period was 18 per cent, their bound rates average almost 60 per cent.

Countries that converted NTBs to tariffs have in some cases posted rates higher than the base year tariff equivalent of those NTBs. Japan, for example, has announced that beginning in April 1999 its tariff on rice will be $3.05 per kilo. *International Trade Reporter* (1998) estimates that this rate is equivalent to 1,000 per cent, *ad valorem*. This rate applies, of course, only to imports in excess of Japan's minimum access commitment. Hathaway and Ingco calculate that Japan's actual base period protection on rice had a tariff equivalent of about 650 per cent.[35] Ingco identifies other instances in which a developed economy's post-UR bound rate is above the tariff equivalent of its base year protection.

---

[35] The specific duty is above the domestic cost of production, hence only the minimum access commitment will affect the amount of rice Japan imports.

e. Special Safeguards

The provision on special safeguards applies only to products that were subject to tariffication. They allow additional duties to be applied in case of a precisely defined surge of import quantity, or cases of imports at prices below a precisely defined reference level. A member can apply a special safeguard to a product for the remainder of the relevant year, on a shipment by shipment basis, only if the member noted in its schedule of commitments that it claimed the right to (eventually) do so. Thirty-eight members have reserved that right, on varying numbers of products. For all relevant Members combined, these reservations imply a potential for imposing special safeguards on almost 6,100 tariff items. During the period January 1998 through September 1998, volume-based actions were taken by five Members affecting a total of 128 tariff items and price-based actions were also taken by five Members affecting a total of 72 tariff items.

6. ANTI-DUMPING

The Uruguay Round Anti-dumping Agreement (formally, Agreement on Implementation of Article VI of the GATT 1994) adds considerable detail, e.g.:

- specificity has been added on the required evidence and methodology for determining dumping and injury,
- rules regarding support from domestic industry of the anti-dumping claim are now spelled out,
- procedural rules for hearing both sides and the time frame of investigations have been tightened,
- a '*de minimis*' clause (specifying that the dumping margin has to be at least two per cent) have been added,
- notification requirements are explicit,
- a sunset clause and requirement for review have been added.

a. Developing Economies Become Major Users

The use of anti-dumping has spread significantly from the five original industrial country users (Australia, Canada, the EU, New Zealand and the US). In a first wave, a number of advanced developing countries including Mexico, Brazil and Argentina starting using anti-dumping in the late 1980s. More recently, many smaller and poorer developing countries have sporadically taken recourse to anti-dumping, so that the total number of countries which have used this means of trade protection now exceeds 30. The use of anti-dumping per dollar of imports is notably higher among developing economies than among developed economies.

Among the traditional users of anti-dumping, the number of initiations has declined since the Uruguay Round Agreements have been in effect, i.e., since 1 January, 1995. The filing of a number of anti-dumping cases by the US steel industry at the time of this writing (March 1999) may, however, reverse the decline in the United States. Among new users, for which data are available – Argentina, Mexico, Korea and Turkey report an increase in the number of tariff lines the trade covered by anti-dumping measures. Among the developing economies for which data are available, only Brazil applies anti-dumping measures to a declining share of tariff lines (Michalopoulos, 1999). Table 15 along with Figures 5 and 6 illustrates the development of anti-dumping investigations over the 1991–98 period.

Table 16 contains the countries most frequently affected by anti-dumping cases between 1992-94 and 1995-97. China has been targeted most frequently during both periods. The United States, one of the most frequent users of anti-dumping, is also one of the most targeted countries, second after China and targeted more than twice as often as Japan. After China and the US, Korea and Brazil were the main targets during the early 1990s; while Korea, Germany and Taiwan attracted the most investigations in the latter period. Industrial countries mostly target other high income and transition countries, with less than one quarter of the investigations involving developing countries (and about half of

FIGURE 5
Anti-dumping – Total Number of Initiated Investigations, All WTO Members

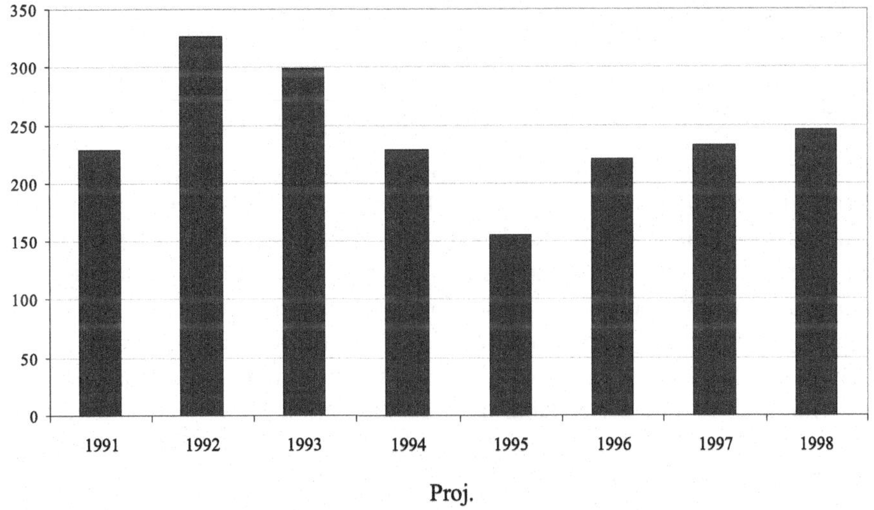

Proj.

Source: WTO Rules Division; Anti-dumping Measures database.

FIGURE 6

Numbers of Anti-dumping Initiations by Developed and by Developing Economies

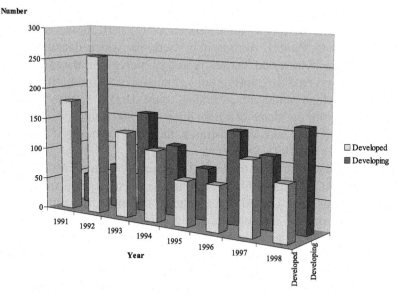

those, China). Developing countries by contrast initiate an almost equal share of investigations against either of the three country groups (Miranda, Torres and Ruiz, 1998). As to sectoral distribution, we find that producers of base metals, chemicals, machinery, electrical equipment, plastics and textiles frequently seek anti-dumping protection.

b. Undertakings, Magnitude of Anti-dumping Measures

The share of initiated investigations (Table 17) that lead to a restrictive outcome (provisional measures and affirmative findings) tend to be similar among all the countries in the table – except Australia, where the proportion of cases there that lead to restrictive outcomes, particularly restrictive final outcomes, is notably below the figure for any other country.

Another important dimension of such protection is the use of price undertakings (exporters agreeing to maintain minimum export prices) versus tariffs. For lack of time-series data, we did a tabulation for seven of the main anti-dumping users for 1997. In this year, only Korea and the EU report a significant share of final measures being price undertakings (Table 18). In Korea this share exceeds 50 per cent, and in the EU 20 per cent. In the other five countries for which data was readily available, 98–100 per cent of final measures consisted of duties.

TABLE 15
Anti-dumping Initiations by Economy Taking Action

Economy	Number of Anti-dumping Initiations		Index of Anti-dumping Initiations 1995–98 Per Dollar of imports, USA=100[a]
	1991–94	1995–98	
Developed Economies			
Australia	213	77	1096
Canada	84	39	199
EU	135	122	210
US	226	94	100
All developed economies	678	353	74
Developing Economies			
Argentina	59	72	2627
Brazil	59	54	871
India	15	78	1875
Korea	14	34	204
Mexico	127	31	275
South Africa	16	72[b]	2324
All developing economies	394	509	313

Notes:
[a] Based on numbers of anti-dumping initiations 1995–98 and values of merchandise imports for 1996.
[b] 1995–97 figure.

Source: WTO Secretariat, Rules Division; Anti-dumping Measures Database.

TABLE 16
Anti-dumping Initiations by Exporting Economy

Economy	Number of Anti-dumping Initiations		Index of Anti-dumping Initiations per Dollar of Exports, USA=100
	1992-94	1995-97	
Developed Economies			
France	26	8	34
Germany	35	30	70
Italy	16	16	77
Japan	32	23	67
UK	20	16	74
US	70	48	100
Developing Economies			
Brazil	50	23	585
China	115	94	751
India	24	21	779
Korea	50	40	385
Taiwan	31	30	323
Thailand	26	21	451

While the trade coverage of anti-dumping is small, the level of tariffs applied on average is quite high and has in some instances reached several hundred per cent. The last column of Table 18 provides average duties imposed as part of final measures in the same seven users in 1997. Colombia applies the highest average tariff of 60 per cent and Korea the lowest of 28 per cent. Four of the other countries apply average rates of 30 to 40 per cent. This is very high compared to 'normal' average tariffs of about 4 per cent on industrial products in developed economies, 8 per cent to 12 per cent in developing economies. The EU's 40 per cent for 1997 are also much higher than the 23 per cent applied for the 1980–87 period (Messerlin, 1989).

Because of the sunset clause in the Uruguay Round Agreement, reviews of measures already in place make up an increasing share of investigations. In the EU, 79 out of 190 investigations have been reviews in the 1995–1998 period, in the US 116 reviews of measures in place when the Uruguay Round agreements came into effect were conducted in 1998.

c. WTO Disputes Over Anti-dumping Cases

A variety of disputes regarding procedures, standards for initiating and conducting investigations, as well as substantive elements necessary for imposing duties are emerging. The recent dispute between Guatemala and Mexico on Portland cement has illustrated that the procedural and technical requirements to conduct an anti-dumping investigation consistent with WTO rules are quite stringent. Many developing countries are likely to find it difficult to meet these requirements and may find themselves increasingly challenged, especially by the high-income countries. Developing economies have not been reluctant to challenge anti-dumping actions by the developed economies: Korea's case against the US on D-Ram and India's dispute with the EU on unbleached cotton fibres are examples.

The real test of the use or abuse of anti-dumping, however, may still be lying ahead. In recent years, the world economic climate has been quite favourable, and previous studies have shown that the use of anti-dumping is strongly correlated with the business cycles (see, e.g., Leidy, 1996). The slowdown in economic growth since the outbreak of the Asian crisis could, with a lag, lead to a rebound in anti-dumping measures and more retreats in market access commitments. The sabre-rattling in the US and the considerable increase in cases by several countries in 1998 are, we hope, a transitory phenomenon.

d. Anti-dumping as Affected by the Asian Crisis

One could hypothesise that the Asian crisis would change the pattern of user and target countries for anti-dumping. As to the Asian countries affected, each

TABLE 17
Share of Completed Investigations Resulting in Provisional and Definitive Measures, 1987–1997

	Number of Completed Investigations	Proportion Provisional Measures	Proportion Affirmative Outcome
United States	423	83	64
Canada	186	83	63
EC	308	55	60
Korea	43	58	58
New Zealand	54	39	57
Mexico	182	63	53
Argentina	94	48	51
Brazil	75	41	43
South Africa	62	48	42
Australia	408	53	29

Source: WTO Secretariat, Rules Division; Anti-dumping Measures Database.

experienced a marked currency devaluation, which is likely to reduce import competition and hence pressures for protection. Consistent with this, we found that the five Asian countries affected by crisis initiated fewer new cases but became the target of investigations more often in 1998 as compared to 1997. Korea and Malaysia which had used anti-dumping to a moderate extent in 1996/97 almost stopped initiating new investigations in 1998. Indonesia continued using anti-dumping to some degree while Thailand and the Philippines had never been very active users.

As to anti-dumping initiations against the Asian crisis countries, there is no uniform development although some increase has probably taken place. The US

TABLE 18
Anti-dumping Duties vs. Price Undertakings, 1997

	Share of Affirmative Decisions Ending in Duty (in %)	Share of Affirmative Decisions Ending in Price Undertakings (in %)	Average duty in 1997[a]
Canada	98.0	2.0	34.1
Colombia	100.0	0.0	60.3
EC	79.5	20.5	40.4
Korea	46.7	53.3	27.9
Mexico	100.0	0.0	53.7
South Africa	100.0	0.0	34.1
US	99.4	0.6	30.5

Note:
[a] In per cent; average all final measures per country in 1997; when a decision ended in a range of duties, the mean value was taken.

Source: WTO Rules Division; Anti-dumping Measures Database.

and South Africa increased the number of anti-dumping investigations against South East Asia from two to six and from two to nine respectively. The European Union, on the other hand, initiated only four new cases in 1998 (all of them against Korea) after ten cases in 1997. Brazil and Mexico neither used anti-dumping in 1997 nor in 1998 against these countries (Table 19).

e. Anti-dumping Cases in Sectors with Notable Liberalisation

It could be hypothesised that sectors with disproportionately large liberalisation would also report a stronger increase in anti-dumping cases since the end of the Uruguay Round. However, there is little evidence of this for four of the main user countries. In India use of anti-dumping has jumped since the end of the Uruguay Round, but it is not obvious that there is a correlation between new anti-dumping cases and sectoral liberalisation. Disproportionate liberalisation in wood products (EU, Australia) and in textiles/clothing/footwear (EU) may be responsible for an increase in anti-dumping claims in these two sectors (Table 20).

f. Subsidies, Countervailing Duties

Like the anti-dumping rules, the GATT rules on subsidies and countervailing duties were superseded by a comprehensive Uruguay Round Agreement. The Subsidy Agreement distinguishes three types of subsidies. Subsidies contingent upon export performance or on the use of domestic over imported inputs are prohibited. They can lead to both countervailing duties and a dispute settlement case. Subsidies not specific to an enterprise or industry are considered 'non-actionable.' They cannot be subject to countervailing duties or dispute settlement challenges although they can be brought to the Committee on Subsidies and Countervailing Measures if they result in serious adverse effects in another country. All other subsidies are 'actionable', i.e., they may be subject to multilateral dispute settlement challenge or to countervailing action if they adversely effect another WTO Member.

Industrial countries had to phase out prohibited subsidies by 1998. Least developed countries have until 2003 to eliminate subsidies contingent on the use of domestic inputs, but are not required to eliminate export subsidies. Other developing countries must eliminate subsidies contingent on the use of domestic inputs by 2000, export subsidies by 2003. Special Provisions for transition economies are more complex, involving a requirement that prohibited subsidies be phased out by 2002, but at the same time providing some lee way to apply programmes and measures necessary for transformation from a centrally-planned to a market, free-enterprise economy.

Like in anti-dumping, the subsidy agreement added considerable specificity on procedures and criteria for a countervailing duty investigation. The agreement

TABLE 19

Anti-dumping Initiations Against South-East Asian Countries in 1997 and 1998

	Korea		Indonesia		Thailand		Philippines		Malaysia		Total	
	1997	1998	1997	1998	1997	1998	1997	1998	1997	1998	1997	1998
EU	4	4	1	0	2	0	0	0	3	0	10	4
US	2	4	0	2	0	0	0	0	0	0	2	6
Brazil	0	0	0	0	0	0	0	0	0	0	0	0
India	1	3	0	0	0	0	0	0	1	0	2	3
Mexico	0	0	0	0	0	0	0	0	0	0	0	0
South Africa	2	5	1	1	0	0	0	0	1	3	4	9

Source: WTO Secretariat, Rules Division; Anti-dumping Measures Database.

TABLE 20
Anti-dumping Claims by Sectors with Above Average Liberalisation, Selected Countries

	1992	1993	1994	1995	1996	1997	1998
United States							
Metals	68	15	33	4	8	11	13
Chemicals	9	12	7	0	6	0	0
Other Manufacturing	0	2	2	0	0	0	0
Textiles/Clothing	0	0	0	0	0	0	0
European Union							
Wood	1	0	0	1	0	7	0
Metals	9	5	10	7	11	3	15
Chemicals	13	5	6	3	0	6	0
Machinery	13	7	4	10	0	14	0
Other Manufacturing	0	0	0	0	0	0	0
Textiles/Cloth/Footwear	1	1	17	6	10	8	6
India							
Wood	0	0	0	3	0	0	...
Text/Clothing	0	0	0	3	0	9	...
Metals	0	0	3	0	3	3	...
Chemicals	1	5	2	1	4	8	...
Machinery	0	0	0	8	0	6	...
Australia							
Wood	0	8	0	0	0	14	1
Metals	2	3	2	0	0	2	0
Machinery	2	4	0	1	1	1	0

also requires that countries notify their specific subsidies (as defined under the Subsidy Agreement) on an annual basis, and countervailing duty activities on a semi-annual basis.

g. Use of Countervailing Duties

There are two notable developments in the use of countervailing duties:

- Overall use has declined considerably since the end of the Uruguay Round, with much of this decline due to the absence of steel cases,
- The EU has become a user of countervailing measures since 1996 after hardly having used this instrument before.

The 1992 to 1994 period saw 137 cases, with the US, Australia, Brazil and Mexico being the principal users (Table 21). The European Community and its individual members, Brazil and South Africa were the main targets of countervailing duty cases for that period. Since the Uruguay Round agreements have come into force, the number of initiations has declined drastically. The

TABLE 21

Numbers of Initiations of Countervailing Duty Investigations, by Initiating Member

Country	Number of Initiations by Country	
	1992–94	1995–97
Argentina	4	3
Australia	19	1
Brazil	23	0
Canada	2	3
Chile	8	0
EU	0	5
Mexico	16	1
New Zealand	0	6
USA	60	10
Other	5	4
Total	137	33

Source: WTO Secretariat, Rules Division; Countervailing Measures Database.

1995–1997 period witnessed only 33 cases, one quarter of the cases during the preceding 3 years. Apart from the US, the EU and New Zealand have become the main users of this provision, with EU countries and South Africa remaining the main targets (Table 22). Although 1998 data are incomplete at the time of this writing, there are indications that the number of cases will be near the annual rates of 1992–95; considerably higher than the low rates in 1995–97.

Data on the trade coverage of countervailing cases is very limited. The US reports that cases initiated over the past ten years (1988–1997) affected only 0.7 per cent of total US imports. This is a decline by 50 per cent compared to the 1984–94 period, when 1.4 per cent of imports were affected (US ITC, 1998). We mentioned above that the EU does not report trade coverage of countervailing cases separately

TABLE 22

Numbers of Initiations of Countervailing Duty Investigations, by Affected (Exporter) Member

Country	Number of Initiations against Country	
	1992–94	1995–97
Brazil	13	1
Canada	4	2
EC	12	5
Germany	6	1
India	4	4
Italy	6	6
South Africa	10	3
US	7	1
Venezuela	5	1
Other	70	9
Total	137	33

Source: WTO Secretariat, Rules Division; Countervailing Measures Database.

from anti-dumping. However, given that the first EU countervailing case of the 1990s was brought about in 1996 and only nine cases were reported for 1996/98, trade coverage should be very small. The four cases from 1998, for example, affected trade of US$ 140 million.

Data on the share of decisions leading to duties versus undertakings and on the average tariff rates are also scarce, but available data for two countries suggest that countervailing duties are much lower than anti-dumping duties. New Zealand reports two decisions leading to duties and price undertakings, each with an average duty of 7.5 per cent. The US notified over 80 per cent of decisions leading to duties, and average tariffs only average 4.2 per cent.

There were a number of conflicts over the application of the Subsidy Agreement and the use of countervailing duties during the 1995–98 period. With respect to multilateral challenges to subsidies applied by Members, the only adopted dispute settlement panel report (by March 1999) in this area on Indonesia's national car programme was decided in favour of the plaintiff, the EU. However, a number of other subsidies panels are ongoing as of this writing, mostly dealing with subsidies that the plaintiff interprets to be in the prohibited category. There are also in process a number of cases on the application of countervailing measures.

Notifications regarding subsidies and countervailing duties seem to be provided relatively regularly. However, developing countries report subsidy data much less frequently, and all subsidy notifications are frequently late and incomplete.

There are no firm plans for new negotiations in this area, but some challenges remain. Given the upcoming deadlines to bring Members' subsidy schemes in line with WTO rules, there is considerable concern about developing and transition countries' ability to meet these deadlines.

7. SAFEGUARDS

The Agreement on Safeguards specifies the rules for the application of Article XIX emergency action measures. Under the agreement, action can be taken against imports only a determination of 'serious' injury caused or threatened to be caused by imports.[36] Either quantitative restrictions or duty increases beyond bound rates are allowed, but measures are time bound and must be progressively reduced. The need to make compensation and the right of exporters to retaliate can be avoided by keeping the restrictive measure within certain parameters.[37]

---

[36] There seems to be a legal consensus that 'serious injury' is a somewhat higher level of injury than 'material injury' as specified under anti-dumping and countervailing duty rules. The difference is, however, difficult to isolate in an accounting or economic sense.

[37] The conditions are provided in the WTO homepage under www.wto.org/WTO/goods/safeguar.htm.

This restriction on compensation-retaliation was intended to make the use of safeguards measures more attractive, and aims at preventing the re-emergence of voluntary export restraints or orderly marketing arrangements. The agreement also requires that existing safeguard measures be notified and phased out according to a schedule similar to the sunset provision that applies to new measures.

There has been a minor increase in cases since the Uruguay Round agreement came into effect, but safeguards remain an infrequently used trade remedy – only 19 safeguard investigations were initiated from 1995–97 as compared with 33 countervailing duty investigations and over 600 anti-dumping initiations[38] (Table 23).

Total imports affected by investigations amounted to about 2 billion US$ between 1995 and 1998, or about one quarter of 1 per cent of annual imports of the countries initiating investigations.[39] Two of the eight cases which have been decided affirmatively resulted in a quantitative restriction, the other six in tariffs. Import quotas were allocated in both cases on the basis of previous relative import shares. Four cases were terminated or ended in a negative decision, and four decisions were outstanding at the time of this writing.

Our findings on safeguards confirm earlier findings that market access retreats through existing provisions have so far been limited. At the same time, the new UR Agreements have been successful in curtailing protection outside the multilateral framework. Between 1995 and spring 1999, there have been no complaints that the prohibition of grey area measures under Article 11 of the SGA has been violated. Anticipation that degressive and time-bound safeguard measures would replace anti-dumping as an instrument for dealing with specific import problems has not been realised.

8. SERVICES

Since the Uruguay Round, the multilateral trading system includes disciplines and liberalisation commitments covering trade in services. Although experts who have reviewed the outcome of the negotiations have concluded that the first round of services negotiations did not result in far-reaching trade liberalisation, they also point out that the importance of bringing services under the multilateral umbrella of the WTO should not be under-estimated (Snape, 1998; and Hoekman, 1996). In most countries, at least half of GDP is generated in the services sectors and the share is increasing. At the same time less than one-quarter of world trade,

---

[38] Finger (1998) demonstrates that the various trade remedies the GATT/WTO permits are quite fungible.
[39] The five cases by the US covered in total about 0.15 per cent of US annual imports, the two cases by Argentina covered 1 per cent of Argentine imports.

TABLE 23

Safeguard Investigations Initiations, 1991–1998

Country	1991	1992	1993	1994	Total 1991–94	1995	1996	1997	1998	Total 1995–98
Argentina					0			1	1	2
Australia					0				1	1
Austria	1		1		2					0
Brazil					0		1			1
Canada	1		1		1					0
Czech and Slovak	1				1					0
EEC	3		1		4					0
Egypt					0				1	1
Hungary		3			3					0
India					0			1	5	6
Korea					0	1	2			3
USA					0	1	2	1	1	5
All countries	5	3	3	0	11	2	5	3	9	19

TABLE 24
Safeguard Measures, Since 1/95

Notifying Member	Type of Product Concerned	Import Value, Year Prior to Investigation (Million US$)[1]	Share of Total Merchandise Imports (%)	Initiation of Investigation (Year)	Outcome of Injury Investigation	Type of Measure	Type of Measure and Quantification[2]
Argentina	Footwear	116.6	0.49	1997	Affirmative	Tariff	4.96 $ per pair (average), 4.04 $ per pair (average)
Australia	Toys	155.1	0.51	1998	Ongoing		
	Swinemeat	27.6	0.04	1998	Affirmative		
Brazil	Toys	133.1	0.25	1996	Affirmative	Tariff	43%,29%,15% plus 20% regular tariff
Egypt	Safety matches	1.7	0.01	1998	Affirmative	Tariff	34%,22%,11% plus 30% regular tariff
India	Acetylene black			1997	Affirmative	Tariff	18% up to Re 12,950/metric tonne, 5% up to Re 8,830/metric tonne /3
	Carbon black	24.5	0.07	1998	Affirmative	Tariff	10%
	Slabstock polyol	13.1	0.04	1998	Ongoing		
	Propylene glycol	3.4	0.01	1998	Ongoing		
	Hardboard	0.2	0.00	1998	Negative		None
	Styrene butadiene rubber			1998	Terminated on 01.05.98		None
Korea	Soybean oil			1995	Affirmative	Import	None
	Dairy products	69.4	0.05	1996	Affirmative	Quota	rising from 55.6 to 65.2 % of pre-investigation imports
USA	Bicycles and parts	38.9	0.03	1996	Affirmative		None
	Tomatoes	191.9	0.03	1995	Negative		None
	Brooms	12.1	0.00	1996	Affirmative	Tariff	33%,32.5%,32.1% from 32% current bound rate
	Tomatoes and peppers	843.1	0.10	1996	Negative	None	
	Wheat gluten	90.5	0.01	1997	Affirmative	QR	
	Lamb meat	123.5	0.01	1998	Ongoing		...
		Total 1,844.7	Average across countries 0.24				

Notes
[1] The year closest to the initiation of the investigation was chosen, in most cases this was the year prior to it.
[2] More than one figure for one measure describes the steps of progressive liberalization.
[3] A duty charged up to a maximum of value (Re) per quantity (metric tonnes).
Source: Notifications submitted by Member Countries to the WTO Committee on Safeguards.

as reported in countries' balance of payments, is in services; 60 per cent of which falls under tourism and transport. Low, Mattoo and Schuknecht (1999) show that trade-openness in most services sectors is still much lower than in merchandise trade, and further technical progress and market opening could hence create enormous new trading opportunities.

a. The Agreement

The rights and obligations of WTO Members regarding services trade are specified in the General Agreement on Trade in Services (GATS). Many GATS obligations parallel those of the GATT, although there are important structural differences between the two agreements. National treatment, for example, is an unconditional obligation under GATT but negotiable under the GATS. It applies only to sectors that a country itself specifies in its schedule of commitments and can be made subject to limitations even in these cases. Moreover, the GATS permits exempting measures from the most-favoured-nation treatment for limited periods.[40] The GATS, like the GATT, provides for the withdrawal of commitments for Balance-of-Payment reasons (Article XII), and under general exceptions (Article XIV). It contains a broad carve-out for prudential reasons in financial services (Annex on Financial Services) and establishes a framework for modifications of schedules (Article XXI). In some areas, negotiations on the need for and possible content of specific rules are still ongoing (see also Croome, 1996 and 1998).

Like the tariff agreements under the GATT, the GATS provides no special monitoring system for Members' compliance to their commitments. The small number of complaints and conflicts brought to the Services Committee and the Dispute Settlement Body suggest that compliance is so far not a big problem. Early dispute settlement cases have however helped to establish important principles. The banana case against the European Union, for example, established that GATS commitments must not be impaired indirectly – in the bananas case, through the application of trade measures on goods that would otherwise be allowed.

b. Liberalisation

The GATS schedules of commitments are structured along three dimensions: (i) sector,[41] (ii) type of commitment (essentially market access and national

---

[40] Slightly more than half of the WTO membership has used this possibility and annexed MFN exemptions to their schedules.

[41] Members in making commitments for specified sectors usually followed from a nomenclature prepared to facilitate negotiations. That nomenclature divides services activities into some 160 sectors.

treatment), and (iii) mode of supply. Unlike the GATT, the GATS covers not only cross-border trade (mode 1) but also consumption abroad (mode 2), foreign commercial presence (mode 3), and the movement of natural persons (mode 4).[42] GATS commitments are based on a positive list, i.e., apply only to sectors explicitly listed in schedules. A country that makes a commitment for a sector for a type of commitment say, national treatment, may, however, put limitations on that commitment. Country schedules vary from one page covering one subsector to more than 100 pages covering most services sectors. Malaysia, for example, has made commitments in the largest number of sectors (over 130), and another 30 countries have made commitments in over 100 sub-sectors. Almost all WTO Members have made commitments in tourism, but only 10 regarding rail services.

Tables 25 and 26 present a tally of Members' commitments under the most frequently used modes of delivery, mode 1 (cross-border) and mode 3 (commercial presence).[43] The tables list the numbers of countries that have made national treatment and market access commitments in the most important service sectors. The information in Tables 25 and 26 is summarised in Tables 27 and 28.[44] We see in Table 27 that across all of the sectors, developing economies agreed to allow unlimited cross-border market access to foreign sellers in only 8 per cent of the country-sector possibilities. Developed economies were even less forthcoming, granting full cross-border access in only 7 per cent of the country-sector possibilities. There are even fewer unrestricted commitments to allow foreign sales through a foreign commercial presence. Overall, there were slightly more commitments to allow unqualified national treatment to foreign sellers.

While Table 27 asks how many countries granted *unrestrained* access to foreign sellers, Table 28 asks how many countries granted *at least some* access, e.g., allowed foreign commercial presence but limited the size of the foreign establishment, allowed cross-border access to some forms of banking deposits but

---

[42] Examples: tourist travel abroad (mode 2), buying an insurance policy from a foreign-owned but domestically established branch office (mode 3), and the temporary contract for a business consultant abroad (mode 4). Trade statistics comparing trade across modes are limited and it is often difficult to pin down just what available statistics describe. Based on information available for the US, mode 3 trade (sales by foreign branches of US companies) in financial, insurance and recreational services is considerably larger than mode 1 trade (purchases by foreigners from a US-located source). In business services, trade in the two modes is about equal. Only in telecom services does mode 1 trade – trade across borders – appear to be larger than the corresponding mode 3 trade (Low, Mattoo and Schuknecht, 1999).

[43] Mode 2 appears less important in many areas (except tourism) and commitments there often mirrors mode 1 commitments. Mode 4 (movement of natural persons) commitments are very limited for all countries.

[44] As to how the summary tables were constructed, the category 'Professional Services' in Tables 25 and 26 includes four sectors. Our tabulation covers 105 developing economies and 26 developed economies, hence in Table 27 in the first line, there were a possible total of (a) 105 developing economies times 4 sectors, or 420 access commitments by developing economies and of (b) 26 developed economies times 4 sectors, or 104 access commitments by developed economies.

TABLE 25
Mode 1 Commitments in Selected Services Sectors

Activity	Commitments: Developing Economies[1] Market Access			National Treatment			Commitments: Developed Economies[2] Market Access			National Treatment		
	Full	Partial	None	Full	Partial	None	Full	Partial	None	Full	Partial	None
	Number of Countries						*Number of Countries*					
Professional Services												
Legal	7	17	81	9	14	82	1	24	1	1	24	1
Accounting	12	13	80	15	10	80	4	21	1	4	21	1
Medical and Dental	10	9	86	14	6	85	3	2	21	4	1	21
Total, Professional Services	29	39	247	38	30	247	8	47	23	9	46	23
Communication Services												
Voice Telephone	3	42	60	10	33	62	3	22	1	5	20	1
Private Leased Circuit	3	36	66	15	22	68	3	22	1	5	20	1
Electronic Mail	11	23	71	22	12	71	4	22	0	4	22	0
Total, Communications Services	17	101	197	47	67	201	10	66	2	14	62	2
Distribution Services												
Wholesale	8	6	91	8	7	90	1	24	1	13	12	1
Retail	5	6	94	5	6	94	2	23	1	1	24	1
Total, Distribution Services	13	12	185	13	13	184	3	47	2	14	36	2
Financial Services												
Non-life Insurance	13	17	75	18	13	74	0	4	22	0	4	22
Depositing	16	11	78	19	9	77	0	4	22	0	4	22
Lending	12	16	71	17	12	70	0	15	85	0	15	85
Trading in Securities	13	17	75	18	13	74	0	4	22	0	4	22
Total, Financial Services	47	63	310	62	47	311	1	37	66	2	36	66

Notes:
[1] Total of 105 Members.
[2] Total of 26 Members.

Source: WTO Secretariat.

TABLE 26
Mode 3 Commitments in Selected Services Sectors

Activity	Commitments: Developing Economies[1]						Commitments: Developed Economies[2]					
	Market Access			National Treatment			Market Access			National Treatment		
	Full	Partial	None	Full	Partial	None	Full	Partial	None	Full	Partial	None
	Number of Countries						*Number of Countries*					
Professional Services												
Legal	2	26	77	7	21	77	0	24	2	0	24	2
Accounting	4	36	65	15	24	66	1	25	0	3	23	0
Medical and Dental	8	21	76	16	12	77	0	16	10	1	16	9
Total, Professional Services	14	83	218	38	57	220	1	65	12	4	63	11
Communication Services												
Voice Telephone	4	46	55	8	39	58	0	25	1	2	23	1
Private Leased Circuit	2	39	64	13	24	68	0	25	1	2	23	1
Electronic Mail	3	32	70	20	14	71	1	25	0	3	23	0
Total, Communications Services	9	117	189	41	77	197	1	75	2	7	69	2
Distribution Services												
Wholesale	6	14	85	6	13	86	0	25	1	0	25	1
Retail	2	15	88	3	15	87	1	24	1	0	25	1
Total, Distribution Services	8	29	173	9	28	173	1	49	2	0	50	2
Financial Services												
Non-life Insurance	5	40	60	9	34	62	0	26	0	0	26	0
Depositing	11	44	50	13	42	50	1	24	1	0	25	1
Lending	11	41	53	11	41	53	1	24	1	0	25	1
Trading in Securities	8	37	60	6	39	60	1	25	0	0	26	0
Total, Financial Services	35	162	223	39	156	225	3	99	2	0	102	2

Notes:
[1] Total of 105 Members.
[2] Total of 26 Members.

Source: WTO Secretariat.

TABLE 27

Percentages of Developing and of Developed Economies That Gave *Full* Market Access or *Full* National Treatment Commitments on Selected Service Sectors

Cross-Border Provision (Mode 1)	Market Access		National Treatment	
	Developing Economies	Developed Economies	Developing Economies	Developed Economies
Professional Services	9	10	12	12
Communication Services	5	13	15	18
Distribution Services	6	6	6	27
Financial Services	11	1	15	2
All Selected Sectors	8	7	13	13

Commercial Presence (Mode 3)	Market Access		National Treatment	
	Developing Economies	Developed Economies	Developing Economies	Developed Economies
Professional services	9	10	12	12
Communication services	5	13	15	18
Distribution services	4	2	4	0
Financial services	8	3	9	0
All selected sectors	5	2	10	4

Source: Tabulated from Table 25.

TABLE 28

Percentages of Developing and of Developed Economies That Made *Some* Market Access of *Some* National Treatment Commitments on Selected Service Sectors

Cross-Border Provision (Mode 1)	Market Access		National Treatment	
	Developing Economies	Developed Economies	Developing Economies	Developed Economies
Professional Services	22	71	22	71
Communication Services	37	97	36	97
Distribution Services	12	96	12	96
Financial Services	26	37	26	37
All Selected Sectors	25	70	25	70

Commercial Presence (Mode 3)	Market Access		National Treatment	
	Developing Economies	Developed Economies	Developing Economies	Developed Economies
Professional Services	22	71	22	71
Communication Services	37	97	36	97
Distribution Services	18	96	18	96
Financial Services	47	98	46	98
All Selected Sectors	36	94	35	95

Source: Tabulated from Table 26.

TABLE 29

Tariff Concessions and Levels on All Merchandise, Industrial Goods, Textiles and Clothing, Agricultural Products – Developed Economies and Developing Economies Combined

	Bindings, Post Uruguay Round % of 1989 Imports	Tariff Reductions		Post Uruguay Round Average Tariff	
		Scope % of Imports	Depth $dT/(1+T)$	Bound	Applied
All Merchandise	97	30	1.2	7	4
Industrial Goods	91	32	1.3	6	4
Textiles and Clothing	80	53	1.6	12	10
All Agricultural Products	100	25	2.6	24	14
Tariffed Agricultural Products[a]	100	14	4.2	32	25
Not-Tariffed Agricultural Products[b]	100	32	1.4	19	8

Notes:
[a] Products protected before the Uruguay Round by NTBs – that were converted to tariffs.
[b] Products protected before the Uruguay Round by tariffs – with no NTBs to convert.

not to others. By these standards, the Uruguay Round outcome is more optimistic. The developed economies accepted some cross-border access in more than two-thirds of the instances, and agreed to allow some form of foreign commercial presence in almost all sectors. Developing economy commitments were more restricted, allowing some form of cross-border market access in about one-quarter of instances, allowing some foreign commercial presence and some dimensions of national treatment for foreign establishments in about one-third of the tabulated instances.

The obvious message is that the agreement provides a substantial start towards opening international markets for services, but nearly all liberalisation commitments are qualified in some way, especially commitments by developing economies.

What challenges do these findings pose? Article XIX of the GATS sets 1 January, 2000 as the deadline to start new negotiations in services. Given the relatively limited liberalisation commitments, negotiations should focus on improving market access

TABLE 30

Post Uruguay Round Tariff Rates Developed Economies and Developing Economies – Per cent ad valorem

	Bound		Applied	
	Developed Economies	Developing Economies	Developed Economies	Developing Economies
All Merchandise	4	25	3	13
Industrial Products	4	20	3	13
Textiles and Clothing	11	24	8	21
Agricultural Products[a]	15	60	14	18

Note:
[a] Includes tariffed and not-tariffed products.

TABLE 31

Summary of Uruguay Round Concessions by Developed Economies and by Developing Economies

	All Merchandise	Industrial Products	Textiles and Clothing	All Agricultural Products
Bindings, Post Uruguay Round				
– % of Imports				
Developed Economies	89	92	80	100
Developing Economies	91	84	85	100
Uruguay Round Tariff Cuts				
Scope – % of Imports				
Developed Economies	30	32	53	26
Developing Economies	29	33	49	17
Depth – $dT/(1+T)$ as %				
Developed Economies	1.0	1.0	1.4	1.5
Developing Economies	2.3	2.7	4.1	4.7
Post Uruguay Round Average				
Tariffs – Per cent, Ad Valorem				
Bound				
Developed Economies	4	4	11	15
Developing Economies	25	20	24	60
Applied				
Developed Economies	3	3	8	13
Developing Economies	13	13	21	18

conditions (Croome, 1998). Liberalisation across all sectors, countries and modes should open up considerable new trading opportunities.

Some further development of GATS rules is already mandated in the Agreement itself, and more may be necessary. Effective disciplines on domestic regulation as embedded in professional qualifications, licensing requirements, and technical standards may also be an important issue to prevent such measures from being unnecessarily trade distortive. Furthermore, regulatory principles aiming at effective competition and independent regulatory oversight as agreed for the basic telecom sector, could be a precedent for other sectors where previous monopolies are gradually exposed to competition.

Finally, it is worthwhile mentioning that the trade potential in services is not only constrained by trade policies in many developing countries. A weak services infrastructure and problems in identifying export opportunities can

TABLE 32

Percentages of Anti-dumping Initiations, July 1996–June 1998 Against Different Groups of Economies

Initiating Economy		Targeted Economy		
	China	Developed	Developing	Transition
Developed Economies	19	31	40	11
Developing Economies	25	35	24	15

also be a severe obstacle to services trade development. Nevertheless, it is likely that trade liberalisation in conjunction with technical progress (e.g. electronic commerce) will much expand services trade and the boundary of what is tradable in the future (Bacchetta, Low, Mattoo, Schuknecht, Wager and Wehrens, 1998).

9. SUMMARY FINDINGS

The Uruguay Round was the biggest market access round ever. Measured across its coverage of access to markets for merchandise, its tariff reductions – when the 1997 agreement on information technology products is included – exceeds the approximately 35 per cent shares of world imports covered by the Kennedy and Tokyo Rounds. In addition, the Uruguay Round agreement eliminated VERs and made significant progress to eliminate developed economies' quantitative restrictions on imports of textiles and clothing and all economies' NTBs on imports of agricultural products.

a. Tariff Cuts

Various reports of the round described the depth of the tariff cut as 'one-third,' or even as 'a 40 per cent cut.' When we take into account imports on which tariffs were not reduced (including those duty-free when the round began) and when we follow a formula for the tariff reduction that measures how much more an exporter will be able to retain from a dollar of expenditure by an importer, we come to more modest figures. Export sales to industrial countries will retain about 1 per cent more than without the Uruguay Round cuts, exports sales to developing countries will retain about 2.3 per cent more. Applied to 1997 world imports (excluding intra- trade area imports) of some 3.6 trillion dollars (3.6×10^{12}) that comes to *$50 billion/year more for exporters*.[45]

Developing economies (except for some of the least developed countries) were full participants in the market access negotiations. Their tariff reductions covered as large a share of their imports as did those of the developed economies, their tariff cuts – when measured by how they will affect exporters' receipts – were deeper than those of the developed economies. The percentage of imports covered by GATT-bound rates is now almost as high for the developed economies as for the least developed.

---

[45] 50×10^9.

b. Quantitative Restrictions

The Uruguay Round safeguard agreement requires the phasing out of all existing safeguard (GATT Article XIX) measures and all VERs and other restraints that would not be legal under the Uruguay Round safeguard rules. Good evidence indicates that these measures are indeed on their way out. The safeguards agreement provides for notification of VERs, notification by exporting (i.e., constrained) countries as well as by importing countries. Except for Nigerian restrictions on grain and kaolin imports, for which no elimination date was specified, all notified restrictions will be eliminated by the end of 1999.

As to remaining NTBs of other forms (e.g., restrictive import licensing procedures, price control measures) a 1997 OECD survey of its members found such measures on a small percentage of tariff lines – 4 per cent or lower for the OECD countries covered in the survey. A similar tabulation of NTB incidence among developing economies based on information from WTO Trade Policy Reviews indicates a wider range of NTB incidence among these countries. For Hong Kong and for Singapore, the tabulation found virtually no NTBs, for Brazil, India and Indonesia a relatively high number. The tabulation also indicates that Latin American countries that have undertaken major tariff reductions in the past 10 or 15 years have also significantly reduced their NTBs – e.g., Argentina and Chile.

Some quantitative restrictions remain. Those related to the protection of human, animal and plant health, to the application of industrial standards, or to trade in arms and munitions are clearly GATT-legal. Agreements on the application at the border of health and industrial standards will facilitate the policing of the temptation to use such measures as disguised forms of protection. A few countries maintain restrictive measures under GATT provisions that allow such to protect the balance of payments, but continuing negotiating pressure has significantly reduced the application of such measures.

c. Textiles and Clothing

A major accomplishment of the Uruguay Round is an agreement to eliminate the Multi Fibre Arrangement and an accompanying *bound commitment* by countries that now apply import quotas sanctioned by the MFA *to eliminate these restrictions*. In addition, the developed economies agreed to tariff cuts on textiles that are deeper than those on other industrial products.

There is a dark side to this accomplishment.

- The agreement is written in such a way that the developed economies will be able to legally put off elimination of MFA restrictions until 2005. While the provision of four 'stages' suggests that 33 per cent of the agreed liberalisation should have been in place by the end of 1997, in fact the US has eliminated only one per cent of its MFA quotas, the EU 7 per cent.

- Developed economies' tariffs on textiles and clothing remain two to three times higher than their tariffs on other industrial goods.

The agreement provides for the application of 'transitional safeguards' (MFA-like restraints) on products not under such restraint when the agreement came into effect, but the use of these has been minimal. Three different importing countries through April 1999 have applied a total of 35 such measures; but as of April 1999, only two of these had not been rescinded.

d. Agriculture

The major accomplishment of the agriculture agreement is the creation of a 'tariffs only' regime – the replacement of all NTBs by tariffs plus the binding of all agricultural tariffs (those that replace NTBs as well as those on products previously protected only by tariffs.) This conversion to tariffs was accompanied by reductions of import protection levels that were narrower in scope, but deeper than tariff reductions on industrial products. A special safeguards provision, applicable only to tariffied products, has been minimally used.

A close look at implementation suggests, however, that the public relations dimensions of the agriculture agreement may have outpaced the substance of liberalisation. While the further use of NTBs is explicitly banned, the conversion formulas for setting tariffs 'equivalent' to the NTBs they replaced were negotiating guidelines, not legal obligations.[46] Likewise, the often cited 36 per cent cut by developed economies and 24 per cent cut by developing economies were guidelines, not legal obligations and could be made meaningless for tariffied products by the possibility of setting inflated tariff equivalents. Instances of such inflated tariff equivalents have appeared in the press, e.g., Japan has set a specific tariff[47] on rice that at present prices amounts to 1,000 per cent, *ad valorem*. The post Uruguay Round tariff rates are lower than the tariff equivalent of pre Uruguay Round protection for only 14 per cent of products that underwent tariffication.

Perhaps the most illiberal element in the WTO agricultural regime is the use of tariff quotas to implement minimum access provisions. Except for rice imports by Japan and Korea, the tariff quota system has had little effect on the amount of trade, and it has preserved the old system of political bargaining over the allocation among exporters of restricted import access – managed trade, not liberalised trade.

---

[46] Developing and developed economies alike were required to eliminate NTBs, but the negotiating guidelines allowed developing economies to apply ceiling bindings rather than tariffs equivalent to their NTBs.

[47] Per kilo, rather than *ad valorem*.

The agriculture agreement provides for further negotiations, to begin in 2000. Unlike the textiles and clothing agreement, the agriculture agreement includes no binding commitment for further removal of restrictions.

e. Anti-dumping

In the mid 1980s to early 1990s anti-dumping became the most popular tool for governments seeking a GATT-legal means to accommodate a domestic industry that was clamouring for protection. With the significant strides toward liberalisation achieved at the Uruguay Round, including the banning of VERs (the favoured instrument the previous decade), there were fears that anti-dumping would be even more intensely used.

To now, fears of such a surge have not been realised. The number of anti-dumping measures introduced by the traditional users (Australia, Canada, EU, US) has been less since 1995 than it had been in the years just before. A number of developing economies have, however, become major users – over 30 WTO members have notified anti-dumping actions since the Uruguay Round Agreements came into effect. Argentina, Mexico, Brazil and India have become major users, with numbers of cases per dollar of imports considerably higher than the ratios for traditional users.

China is the most frequent target for anti-dumping actions, followed by the United States. Per dollar of exports, anti-dumping initiations against an economy are much higher against developing economies. Thus the generalisation that describes tariffs can be extended to anti-dumping: it is disproportionally used *by* developing economies, it is disproportionally used *against* developing economies.

Where anti-dumping duties have been applied, they have provided a degree of protection much higher than what was taken away by Uruguay Round tariff reductions. Anti-dumping duties of 30 to 50 per cent are common, many are higher. By comparison, reductions agreed at the Uruguay Round were in the range of two to four percentage points.

f. Countervailing Duties

WTO Members take countervailing measures more often than safeguard actions under Article XIX, but not nearly so often as they use anti-dumping to protect local producers – in 1992–98, some 2,000 anti-dumping investigations were initiated, but there were only 200 countervailing duty investigations. The number of counter-vailing duty cases dropped sharply in the first three years the Uruguay Round Agreements were in force, but incomplete information indicates that in 1998 the number of cases was back up to pre-1995 levels. The US is by far the largest user, more than 40 per cent of initiations in the 1990s were by the US. Developing countries, particularly Brazil, Chile and Mexico, are other frequent users.

g. Safeguards

The major accomplishment of the safeguard agreement is that it has been successful in curtailing protection outside the multilateral framework. VERs that existed when the agreement came into effect have been phased out, and through March 1999, there have been no complaints that the prohibition of grey area measures has been violated. Some WTO Members hoped that in lifting the compensation requirement on time-bound and degressive safeguard measures, the agreement would make safeguard measures more user friendly and perhaps shift usage away from anti-dumping. This seems not to have occurred – in 1995–98, when there were almost 900 anti-dumping initiations, only 19 safeguard investigations were initiated. In only one of the seven countries initiating safeguard investigations did the cases cover as much as one-half of 1 per cent of total imports.

Fourteen of the 19 safeguard initiations were by developing economies.

h. Services

Since the Uruguay Round, the multilateral trading system includes disciplines and liberalisation commitments covering trade in services. Although experts who have reviewed the outcome of the negotiations have concluded that the first round of services negotiations did not result in far-reaching trade liberalisation, they also point out that the importance of bringing services under the multilateral umbrella of the WTO should not be under-estimated. In most countries, at least half of GDP is generated in the services sector and the share is increasing. At the same time, less than one-quarter of reported world trade is in services.

Overall, the Uruguay Round Agreements were a notable step towards opening world markets. Developing economies stepping forward as equal partners with the developing economies in working toward an open global trading system was an equally notable event. The Uruguay Round Agreements preserved and perhaps extended the provisions for imposing new trade restrictions, but so far resort to these provisions has been minimal. Since the entry into force of the Uruguay Round Agreements, use of traditional trade remedies – e.g., anti-dumping, countervailing duties – has been below rates in the decade before. Spread of use of anti-dumping to developing economies – the intensity of their use of this instrument, especially against imports from other developing economies – is, however, a matter of concern.

REFERENCES

Bacchetta, M, P. Low, A. Mattoo, L. Schuknecht, H. Wager and M. Wehrens (1998), *Electronic Commerce and the Role of the WTO* (Geneva: World Trade Organisation).

Croome, J. (1996), *WTO Obligations and Bank Policy Advice: Keeping up with Post-Uruguay*

Round Rules (Washington DC: The World Bank).

Croome, J. (1998), *The Present Outlook for Trade Negotiations in the World Trade Organization*, World Bank Policy Research Working Paper 1992.

Finger, J. M. (1996), 'Legalized Backsliding: Safeguard Provisions in GATT' in W. Martin and L.A. Winters (eds.) *The Uruguay Round and the Developing Countries* (Cambridge: Cambridge University Press), 316–40.

Finger, J.M. (1998), *GATT Experience with Safeguards: Making Economic and Political Sense of the Possibilities that the GATT Allows to Restrict Imports*, Policy Research Working Paper No. 2000 (Washington DC: The World Bank, October).

Finger, J.M. and A. Harrison (1996), 'The MFA Paradox: More Protection and More Trade?' in A.O. Krueger (ed.) *The Political Economy of American Trade Policy* (Chicago: University of Chicago Press), 197–253.

Finger, J. M., M.D. Ingco and U. Reincke (1996), *The Uruguay Round: Statistics on Tariff Concessions Given and Received* (Washington, DC: The World Bank).

General Agreement on Tariffs Trade (GATT) (1993), *Overview of Developments in International Trade and the Trading System*, Annual Report by the Director General (Geneva).

Hathaway, D.E. and M.D. Ingco (1996), 'Agricultural Liberalization and the Uruguay Round,' in W. Martin and L.A. Winters (eds.) *The Uruguay Round and the Developing Countries* (Cambridge: Cambridge University Press), 30–58.

Hoekman, B. (1996), 'Assessing the General Agreement on Trade in Services,' in W. Martin and L.A. Winters (eds.) *The Uruguay Round and the Developing Countries* (Cambridge: Cambridge University Press), 88–124.

Ingco, M.D. (1995), 'Agricultural Trade Liberalization in the Uruguay Round,' *Policy Research Working Paper No. 1500* (August, Washington DC: The World Bank).

Laird, S. (1999), 'Patterns of Protection and Approaches to Liberalization' (WTO, mimeo).

Leidy, M. (1996), Macroeconomic Conditions and Pressures for Protection Under Antidumping and Countervailing Duty Laws: Empirical Evidence from the United States, *IMF Staff Papers*, Washington DC: International Monetary Fund.

Low, P., A. Mattoo and L. Schuknecht (1999), 'Trade Policies for Electronic Commerce' *WTO Working Paper* (forthcoming).

Messerlin P. (1989) 'The EC Antidumping Regulations: A First Economic Appraisal, 1980–85,' *Weltwirtschaftliches Archiv*, **125**, 563–87.

Michalopoulos, C. (1999), 'The Integration of Developing Countries into the Multilateral Trading System: Commercial Policy and Market Acces,' (World Bank, mimeo).

Miranda, J., R. Torres and M. Ruiz (1998), 'The International Use of Antidumping , 1987–1997,' *Journal of World Trade*, **32**, 5–71.

OECD (1997), *Indicators of Tariff and Non-Tariff Trade Barriers* (Paris: Organization for Economic Cooperation and Development).

Snape, R. (1998), 'Reaching Effective Agreements Covering Services', in A.O. Krueger (ed.) *The WTO as an International Organization* (Chicago: The University of Chicago Press), pp. 287–89.

United Nations Conference for Trade and Development and World Trade Organisation (1998), *Market Access Development Since the Uruguay Round: Implications, Opportunities and Challenges, in Particular for Developing Countries and Least Developed Countries, in the Context of Globalization and Liberalization* (Geneva, mimeo).

United States International Trade Commission (1998), *US Antidumping and Countervailing Duty Handbook* (October; Washington DC).

WTO (1997), *Trade Policy Review, United States 1996* (Geneva: World Trade Organisation, February).

WTO (1998), *Trade Policy Review, Japan 1998* (Geneva: World Trade Organization, June).

WTO Secretariat (1999), *Guide to the Uruguay Round Agreements* (The Hague, London, Boston: Kluwer Law International).

Index

accession to WTO
  China and Taiwan 40–1, 46
  complicated nature 109
accounting 76, 89
Advisory Centre on WTO Law (ACWL)
  attitudes towards 110
  dispute settlement 139, 145
  market access 96
Afghanistan 43
African, Caribbean and Pacific (ACP)
      countries 104
African Economic Community (AEC) 100–1
African Economic Research Consortium
      (AERC) 116–17
African Group, WTO 104
agenda-setting process 2
Aggregate Measure of Support (AMS) 31, 32,
      46
Agreement on Agriculture, Uruguay Round
      (URAA) 1, 25, 28–32, 42
  non-trade concerns 52
agriculture 4, 25, 53–5, 276, 305–6
  discipline, need for 26–8
  fairness and comprehensiveness of
      negotiations 11, 12, 18–19
  genetic engineering 18–19
  intent of negotiators 276–7
  interest of developing countries 8
  market access 277–8
  Milliennium Round 45–52, 59–65, 72
  safeguards 282
  tariffs 279–81
  Uruguay Round 1, 3, 11, 12, 25–6, 28–45
aid
  agriculture 42, 44
  cuts 7–8
aircraft manufacturers 21
Algeria 123
Alliance for Global Business 138
aluminium 9, 18
Angola 102
anti-dumping (AD) 5, 282–92, 306
  Asian crisis 286–8
  competition policy 237, 245, 246

dispute settlement 286
environmental and labour standards 193
fairness and comprehensiveness in
      negotiations 16, 17, 18
foreign direct investment 207
hypocrisy 9
textiles and clothing 276
Trade Policy Review Mechanism 151–2
anti-trust laws 17
Argentina
  Advisory Centre on WTO Law 139
  anti-dumping 16, 282, 283, 285, 287, 291,
      306
  intellectual property rights 241
  quantitative restrictions 262, 267, 304
  safeguards 294, 295
  SPS regulations 122, 123, 129
  tariffs 257
Armenia 120
assistance for trade adjustment 20
Association Agreements 209
Association of South East Asian Nations
      (ASEAN) 104, 105–7
Australia
  agriculture 11, 41, 61
  anti-dumping 282, 284, 285, 287, 288, 290,
      291, 306
  competition policy 244
  local content policies 175
  quantitative restrictions 262, 266, 267
  safeguards 294, 295
  textiles and clothing 271
Austria 294
automobiles 175–6

balance of payments 261–3
  services 296
  Trade Policy Review Mechanism 163–4
banana dispute 36, 54, 134, 140, 296
Bangladesh 43, 261
bankruptcy 235
beef hormones dispute 36, 50, 193, 219, 220
Benin 102
Berne Convention 124

Bhutan 43
bilateral investment treaties (BITs) 201, 208
Botswana 102
Brazil
  Advisory Centre on WTO Law 139
  anti-dumping 16, 282, 283, 285, 287, 288,
    290, 291, 306
  capital market crisis 152
  child labour 197
  dispute settlement 131
  intellectual property rights project 126
  quantitative restrictions 266, 267, 268, 304
  safeguards 294, 295
  SPS regulations 123
  tariffs 257
  textiles and clothing 271, 273, 274–5
Bulgaria 209
Burkina Faso 102
Burundi 102
Business and Industry Advisory Committee
  138
business services 76

Cairns Group 3, 11, 26, 59
Cambodia 43, 64
Cameroon 102
Canada
  anti-dumping 282, 285, 287, 291, 306
  dispute settlement 50
  local content policies 175
  MMT additive 220
  quantitative restrictions 267
  safeguards 294
  tariff reductions 259
  textiles and clothing 270, 271
  Trade Policy Review Mechanism 148
capital, benefits of services liberalisation 76–7
capital cities, key staff in 97, 98–101, 104
cartels 237, 242, 246, 247
Cassis de Dijon case 188
Central African Republic 102
Central European Free Trade Area (CEFTA)
  104
Chad 102
cheeses, non-pasteurised 220
child labour 195–7, 199
Chile
  anti-dumping 291, 306
  entry restrictions 82
  quantitative restrictions 262, 267, 304
  tariffs 257
  telecommunications 91
China
  accession to WTO 40–1, 46

agriculture 38–9, 41
  anti-dumping 16, 283, 284, 285, 306
  child labour 196
  manufacturing tariffs 70
  quantitative restrictions 265
  services 302
  SPS regulations 123
  textiles and clothing 34
CITES 194
clothing see textiles and clothing
coalitions 3
Colombia
  anti-dumping 286, 287
  quantitative restrictions 267, 268
  textiles and clothing 271, 273, 274, 275
Common Agricultural Policy (CAP) 28, 29
communications
  entry and ownership 77
  fairness and comprehensiveness in
    negotiations 21
  see also telecommunications
compensation, dispute settlement 135, 141
competition
  law 237
  policy 176–7, 233–47
  promotion 17–18, 22, 78
comprehensiveness of trade negotiations
  11–23
compulsory licences 241
conformity assessment procedures (CAPs)
  225–9
Congo 102
Congo, Democratic Republic 102
construction services 8, 15
Convention on the Settlement of Investment
  Disputes between States and Nationals
  of Other States (ICSID) 209
cooperation 104–7
  competition policy 247
  development and trade agencies 22
  facilitative mechanisms 5
  regional coordination of SSA trade policy
    99–101
  between SSA delegations 104, 108
copyrights 241
Costa Rica
  delegates 103, 108
  dispute settlement 131
  textiles and clothing 272, 274
Côte d'Ivoire 102, 108
Council of Ministers, EU 190–1
countervailing duties 288–92, 306
  fairness and comprehensiveness in
    negotiations 16–17

hypocrisy 9
Trade Policy Review Mechanism 151
couriers 215
creation of WTO 1
credibility
  of developing country policies 150, 209–10
  of domestic reform 152–3
  and participation in WTO 97
Cuba 84
customs and customs officials 215–16, 229–30
  electronic commerce 86, 92
  enforcing regulations 225, 229
  fairness and comprehensiveness in
    negotiations 19, 22
  importance 217, 218–20
  multilateral responses 220, 224–5
Customs Valuation Agreement 118–20, 126–9
Cyprus 262, 264
Czech Republic
  foreign direct investment 209
  safeguards 294
  textiles and clothing 271

Dassonville judgment 188
development agenda 21–2
Dispute Settlement Agreement 25
dispute settlement procedures (DSP) 5, 131–3,
    144–5, 185
  agriculture 25, 33, 35–6, 49
  anti-dumping 286, 288, 292
  enforcement 133–44
  environmental and labour standards 193, 198
  and European Court of Justice, comparisons
    between 191
  intellectual property rights 125
  participation in the WTO 96
  services 296
  SPS Agreement 33
  tariff reductions 260
  technical regulations and customs procedures
    219–20
distilled spirits 259, 260
Djibouti 102
domestic regulation, services 78, 87–91, 92
domestic supply response 96–7
Dominican Republic 272
drug companies see pharmaceuticals trade
dumping laws 9, 16
  see also anti-dumping

East African Cooperation 108
East Asia crisis
  anti-dumping 286–8, 289
  financial institutions 10

rescue packages 9
East Asia miracle 22, 167, 173–4
education
  benefits of liberalisation 76
  child labour 196
  voucher systems 91
Egypt
  customs procedures 219
  safeguards 294, 295
electronic commerce 79, 86–7, 92
elephants 194
El Salvador 272, 274
employment see labour market
energy services 88, 91
entry
  competition policy 234, 235, 236, 243
  investment 205
  services 77–82
environmental effects, agricultural policies 26
environmental services 88
environmental standards 5, 186, 191–5, 197–9
  EU 189
  fairness and comprehensiveness in
    negotiations 19
'ethical' trade 197
Euro-Med Agreement 235
European Accreditation of Certification
    Bodies 228
European Bank for Reconstruction and
    Development (EBRD) 111
European Commission 110, 190
European Cooperation for Accreditation of
    Laboratories 228
European Court of Justice (ECJ) 188, 190,
    191
  mutual recognition 223
European Parliament 190
European Union (EU)
  Advisory Centre on WTO Law 139
  agriculture 27–8, 29–30, 39, 44–5, 46, 64
  anti-dumping 282, 284, 285, 286, 287, 288,
    290, 291–2, 306
  banana dispute 36, 54, 296
  beef hormone dispute 36, 50, 193, 219,
    220
  competition policy 236, 243
  cooperation 104
  dispute settlement 36, 50, 54
  foreign direct investment 207–8, 209
  genetically modified organisms 222
  import surveillance 151
  'mad cow' disease 220
  non-pasteurised cheeses 220
  quantitative restrictions 263, 266, 267

regulation, liberalisation and subsidiarity
    188–91, 198
safeguards 294
Seattle Ministerial meeting 2, 185
single-market programme 88
tariff reductions 259, 260
technical regulations 217, 218, 220, 221,
    223, 224, 226–7
textiles and clothing 34, 53, 270, 271
Trade Policy Review Mechanism 148
Treaty on 190
exchange rates 181
exclusive distribution arrangements 244
exhaustion policies 243–4
exit 235
express mail couriers 215

facilitation of trade 19
factors of production 15, 76
fairness of negotiations 11–23
Fiji 43, 262
financial institutions
    benefits of liberalisation 76, 77
    crises 10
    customs bonds 119
    domestic regulations 90
    entry and ownership 77–81
    fairness and comprehensiveness in
        negotiations 14–15
Finland 220
food prices 27–8, 39–40, 43–4
Ford Foundation 42
Foreign Affairs, Ministry of 99, 103–4
foreign direct investment (FDI) 201–3, 212–13
    architectural argument 210–12
    benefits of services liberalisation 77
    competition policy 177
    and growth of developing countries, trade
        off between 168
    industrial policy 168, 177–80
    issue linkage and the grand bargain 210
    market access 203–5
    market failures and international spillovers
        205–7
    pattern of liberalisation, choosing 77–82
    regional integration spillovers 207–8
    reputation and policy credibility 209–10
    technology transfers 171, 172
foreign labour content entitlements 85–6, 92
France
    Advisory Centre on WTO Law 110
    anti-dumping 285
    labour market 189
    'mad cow' disease 220

mutual recognition agreements 228
tobacco 220
Uruguay Round 12
frictional costs 205
Fuji-Kodak case 238

Gabon 102
Gambia 102
General Agreement on Investment (GAI) 177,
    178, 182
General Agreement on Trade in Services
    (GATS) 1, 75–7, 82–7, 91–2, 296–302
    domestic regulations, dealing with 87–91
    investment 201, 202, 203, 205, 208,
        210–12
    pattern of liberalisation, choosing the 77–82
    technical regulations 226
Generalised System of Preferences 44
genetically modified organisms (GMOs)
    18–19, 51, 219, 222
Geneva delegations
    ownership of rules 117
    SSA countries 97, 101–8, 113
Germany
    Advisory Centre on WTO Law 110
    anti-dumping 283, 285, 291
    'mad cow' disease 220
    quantitative restrictions 265
    subsidiarity 190
Ghana 102
global externalities 194–5
governance structure of WTO 5
government procurement 79
governments as filters, dispute settlement
    133–4, 141
grain self-sufficiency 41
grandfather provisions 77–81
Great Britain see United Kingdom
growth of developing countries
    benefits of services liberalisation 77
    fairness and comprehensiveness in
        negotiations 14–15, 20–1
    and foreign ownership, trade off between
        168
GTAP consortium 160
Guatemala 274, 286
Guinea 102
Guinea-Bissau 102

Harmonised System Convention 120
health
    benefits of liberalisation 76
    fairness in negotiations 20
    intellectual property rights 245

potential exports from developing countries
    84
health insurance 84
Honduras
    delegates 103, 108
    textiles and clothing 272, 273
Hong Kong
    agriculture 41
    delegates 103
    quantitative restrictions 262, 267, 304
    textiles and clothing 273, 274, 275
human capital 76, 77
Hungary
    foreign direct investment 209
    quantitative restrictions 262
    safeguards 294
    SPS regulations 123, 129

Iceland 267
ICIP Treaty 124
India
    Advisory Centre on WTO Law 139
    agriculture 41, 43
    anti-dumping 16, 285, 286, 288, 290, 291,
        306
    child labour 196
    health services 84
    manufacturing 70
    quantitative restrictions 261–3, 267, 304
    safeguards 294, 295
    software industry 83–4
    tariffs 257
    textiles and clothing 271, 273, 275
Indonesia
    agriculture 38, 41
    anti-dumping 16, 287, 289, 292
    child labour 196
    industrial policy 174, 176, 180
    intellectual property rights project 126
    quantitative restrictions 267, 304
industrial policy 167–8, 181–2
    implications for developing countries
        174–81
    theory 168–74
infant industries
    industrial policy 168–9, 180
    promotion of 21
    services 82
information
    anti-dumping and countervailing duties 17
    dispute settlement 134, 137–8, 144
    domestic regulations 89, 90
    Trade Policy Review Mechanism 155–9
    trade-related policies 34–5

information technology 258–9
infrastructure 21–2
insurance 15
    health 84
integrated circuits 124
Integrated Database (IDB)
    tariff reductions 260
    Trade Policy Review Mechanism 156
    transparency 142, 158
    World Bank 160
Integrated Framework for Trade-Related
        Technical Assistance to Least
        Developed Countries 22
Intellectual Property in Respect of Integrated
        Circuits Treaty 124
intellectual property rights (IPRs) 123–9, 234,
        247
    and competition policy, interface between
        239–45
    drug companies 20
    fairness in trade negotiations 20, 21
    multilateral agreement 245–7
    Uruguay Round 1
    see also Trade-Related Intellectual Property
        Rights
International Chamber of Commerce (ICC)
    credibility enhancement 209
    dispute settlement 138
    technical regulations 224
    transparency 143
International Civil Aviation Organisation
        (ICAO) 111
International Conformity Certification
        Programme (ICCP) 227–8
International Labour Organisation (ILO) 111,
        197
International Monetary Fund (IMF)
    agriculture 42
    country monitoring 149
    dissemination of information 158
    resources 111
    voting system 103
International Telecommunication Union (ITU)
        111
intra-firm trade 216
investor confidence 153–4
Italy
    anti-dumping 285, 291
    phosphates 220
ivory trade 194

Jamaica 262, 272
Japan
    Advisory Centre on WTO Law 110

agriculture 27, 28, 39, 41, 45, 64, 280–1,
    305
anti-dumping 283, 285
competition policy 236, 238, 244
quantitative restrictions 262, 263, 264, 266,
    267
tariff reductions 259
textiles and clothing 271
Trade Policy Review Mechanism 148
Japan External Trade Organisation (JETRO)
    174
joint action, facilitative mechanisms 5
joint ventures 237
jute 32

Kennedy Round 106
Kenya 15, 102
Kiribati 43
Korea *see* North Korea; South Korea
Kyoto Convention 225, 229

labelling 187, 199
labour market
    agriculture 31
    mobility *see* people, movement of
        underdevelopment 10
labour standards 5, 186, 191–4, 197–9
    child labour 195–7, 199
    EU 189
    fairness and comprehensiveness in
        negotiations 19
    Seattle Ministerial meeting 2
Laos 43
Lebanon 120
legal services 76
Lesotho 102
licences 241, 242, 247
Liechtenstein 259
lobbying groups *see* special interest groups
local content policies 175–6, 180, 204
Lome Convention 44

Maastricht Treaty 189
Macau 259, 262
Madagascar 102, 123
'mad cow' disease 50, 220, 227
Malawi 102
Malaysia
    agriculture 38, 41
    anti-dumping 287, 289
    quantitative restrictions 267
    services 297
Maldives 43
Mali 102

Malta 262
manufacturing
    and agriculture, comparative distortions 11
    decline 13–14
    fairness and comprehensiveness of
        negotiations 12
    Millennium Round 59–60, 65–72
market access 251–2, 303–7
    agriculture 276–82
    anti-dumping 282–92
    for foreign investors 177–8
    participation in the WTO 96
    quantitative restrictions 260–8
    safeguards 292–3, 294–5
    services 77, 78, 85–7, 293–303
    tariff negotiations 252–60
    textiles and clothing 268–76
    Trade Policy Review Mechanism 151–2
Mauritania 102
Mauritius 102, 103, 107
mergers 237, 245
Mexico
    anti-dumping 282, 283, 285, 286, 287, 288,
        290, 291, 306
    intellectual property rights project 126, 129
    quantitative restrictions 267, 268
    tariffs 257
Micronesia 43
migration *see* people, movement of
Mongolia 43
monopolies 237–8
    services 90, 91
monopoly pricing 242
Montreal Convention on Ozone Depletion 19,
        192, 194
Morocco
    phosphates 220
    quantitative restrictions 262, 267
most favoured nation (MFN) 54
most favoured pricing status 20
Mozambique 102
Multifibre Arrangement (MFA) 33, 268–9
    China 40
    phase-out 1, 34, 53, 252, 304–5
multifunctionality, agricultural 52
multilateral rules 1
multinational corporations 168, 178, 179
    see also foreign direct investment
mutual recognition agreements (MRAs)
    technical regulations and customs procedures
        223–4, 228, 230
    services 79, 89
Myanmar 43

Namibia 102
national initiatives 5
necessity test, domestic regulations 89
negotiating agenda 2, 4
negotiation process 8
Nepal 43
Netherlands 228
New Caledonia 43, 61
New Zealand
  agriculture 41
  anti-dumping 282, 287, 291, 292
  competition policy 244
  quantitative restrictions 262, 266, 267
Niger 102
Nigeria
  delegates 102
  quantitative restrictions 261, 263, 265, 304
  Tariff Board 99
non-governmental organisations (NGOs)
  dispute settlement 140, 141
  technical regulations and customs procedures
    216
  transparency 133, 142, 143, 145
non-pasteurised cheeses 220
non-tariff barriers (NTBs) 266–8
  fairness and comprehensiveness in
    negotiations 16
  Trade Policy Review Mechanism 151–2
non-trade concerns, agriculture 52
Nordic Group 104, 105–6
North American Free Trade Agreement
    (NAFTA)
  advocates of liberalisation 12
  foreign direct investment 179, 207, 209, 211
  mutual recognition 223
North Korea 43
Norway
  agriculture 46
  customs system 119
  delegates 103
  quantitative restrictions 266, 267
  textiles and clothing 270

Office of the US Trade Representative 148
oil 9
oilseeds 32
ombudsmen see special prosecutors
Organisation for Economic Cooperation and
    Development (OECD)
  Business and Industry Advisory Committee
    138
  Multilateral Agreement on Investment
    (MAI) 179, 212, 220
  resources 111

Organisation of African Unity (OAU) 100–1
ownership of WTO reforms 116–18, 128
ownership restrictions 77–82

Padoa-Schippa Report 190
Pakistan
  agriculture 43
  child labour 196
  quantitative restrictions 261, 262
  textiles and clothing 274
Panama 103, 108
Papua New Guinea 43
parallel imports 243–5, 247
Paris Convention for the Protection of
    Industrial Property 124
patents 123–4
  competition policy 234, 239
  TRIPs 240–1
people, movement of 5
  fairness and comprehensiveness in
    negotiations 15
  foreign direct investment 211
  Indian software industry 83
  services 82, 83, 84–6, 92
Peru
  anti-dumping 16
  quantitative restrictions 262
  tariffs 257
pharmaceuticals trade
  intellectual property rights 245
  price discrimination 20
  tariff reductions 259, 260
Philippines
  agriculture 38, 41, 64
  anti-dumping 287, 289
  quantitative restrictions 262
  textiles and clothing 273, 274
Poland 123, 209
political pressures 8–9
political success 12–22
polluter-pays principle 187
port services, monopolised 238
poverty
  child labour 196, 197
  textiles and clothing 53
precommitment to future liberalisation 82
predatory pricing 9, 17
pressure groups see special interest groups
price-fixing 17
private sector
  dispute settlement 133–4, 135, 137–8, 141
  technical regulations and customs procedures
    216, 220–2
  transparency 133, 145

profits 16
public defender body 5

quality issues, export-oriented policies 22
quantitative restrictions 260–8, 304
quotas
  agriculture 31, 47–8
  services 92
  textiles and clothing 33

railways 221–2
regional coordination on SSA trade policy
    99–101
regional integration agreements (RIAs) 203,
    207–8, 209
regional offices 112
regulatory policies 5
regulatory principles 186–8
reputation 209–10
research and development (R&D) 172
research constraints 2
resource constraints 5
  dispute settlement 136–7, 139–40, 144–5
  international economic organisations 111
  SSA countries 98–104, 107–8
  Technical Cooperation and Training
      Division 109–10
  Trade Policy Review Mechanism 149–50
  Uruguay Round 2
reverse engineering 241
Rockefeller Foundation 42
Rome, Treaty of 188
Rome Convention 124
rubber 32
Russia
  aluminium 18
  anti-dumping 9
  capital market crisis 152
  quantitative restrictions 266
  SPS regulations 123
Rwanda 102

safeguards 263, 292–3, 294–5, 307
  agriculture 282
  services 79
  textiles and clothing 269, 271–5
Samoa 43
Sanitary and Phytosanitary Agreement see
    SPS Agreement
Saudi Arabian Standards Organisation (SASO)
    227–8
Seattle Ministerial meeting 2, 7, 185
  Advisory Centre on WTO Law 110
second-best theory 169–70

sectoral comprehensiveness 12–13
sector-by-sector approach to negotiations
    12–13
Senegal 102
sensitivity to developing countries' needs 20
services 293–303, 307
  fairness and comprehensiveness in
      negotiations 13–15
  industrial policy 179
  multilateral trading system 37
  new Round 75–92
  see also General Agreement on Trade in
      Services
Sierra Leone 102
Singapore
  agriculture 41
  quantitative restrictions 267, 304
Single European Act 190
Single Undertaking rule 1
Slovakia 271, 294
Slovenia 265
small and medium enterprises 216
smuggling 119, 120
Social Chapter 189
software industry 83–4
sole agency laws 244
Solomon Islands 43
South Africa
  anti-dumping 285, 287, 288, 290, 291
  delegates 102
  quantitative restrictions 262, 265, 267
Southern African Development Community
    (SADC) 101, 104
South Korea
  agriculture 27, 38, 41, 64, 280–1, 305
  anti-dumping 16, 283, 284, 285, 286, 287,
      288, 289
  industrial policy 174
  quantitative restrictions 262, 263, 264, 265,
      266, 267, 268
  safeguards 294, 295
  textiles and clothing 271, 275
Spain 220
special and differential (S&D) treatment
  agriculture 54
  industrial policy 175, 180–1, 182
special interest groups
  dispute resolution 138, 140
  fairness and comprehensiveness in
      negotiations 13, 18–19
  insulation from 97
special prosecutors 5, 142, 145
spices 32
SPS Agreement 25, 33, 49–51, 121–3, 126–9

risk 192
technical assistance 118
Sri Lanka 43, 273
stakeholders 117
steel 9, 222
strategic trade policy 172–3
sub-Saharan Africa (SSA) 95, 112–13
  dispute settlement 131
  participation in the WTO 95–8, 107–12
  view from capitals 98–101
  view from Geneva 101–7
subsidiarity
  EU 190, 191
  regulatory principles 187
subsidies 288–90
  agriculture 28, 29, 46, 61
  fairness in trade negotiations 21
  industrial policy 168, 169–70, 172–4, 176
  services 79
Subsidies and Countervailing Measures (SCM)
  174
supply response, domestic 96–7
surveillance 131, 132
  Trade Policy Review Mechanism 151
Swaziland 102
Sweden 228
Swiss formula, tariff reduction 46–7, 62
Switzerland
  agriculture 46
  quantitative restrictions 267
  software industry 83
  tariff reductions 259

Taiwan
  accession to WTO 40–1
  agriculture 38, 41
  anti-dumping 283, 285
  textiles and clothing 34
Tanzania 102, 120
tariff rate quotas (TRQs) 47–8, 61, 62–5, 72
tariffs 4, 252–3, 303
  agriculture 29–32, 39–40, 46–7, 61–2, 72,
    274–81, 305
  bindings, increases of 253–4
  industrial policy 168, 169–70, 173, 175–6,
    181
  manufacturing 65–72
  policing the cuts 260
  reductions 254–7, 258–60
  remaining 257–8
  sub-Saharan Africa 97
  textiles and clothing 34, 270–1
taxes 169, 203
technical assistance

commitments 118
dispute settlement 139
sub-Saharan Africa 109–10, 112
Trade Policy Review Mechanism 158, 160,
    161
Technical Barriers to Trade (TBT) Agreement
  219, 221, 227
  agriculture 50, 51
Technical Cooperation and Training Division
  109
technical regulations (TRs) 215–16, 229–30
  enforcing 225–9
  importance 217–18, 219–20
  multilateral responses 220–4
technology
  benefits of services liberalisation 77
  spillovers 77, 171–2, 206
  subsidies 21
  transfers 22, 171–2, 179
telecommunications
  benefits of liberalisation 76, 77
  competition policy 237–8
  domestic regulations 87–8, 89, 90, 91
  entry restrictions 81–2
  precommitment to future liberalisation 82
terms of trade (TOT)
  manufacturing tariff cuts 69, 70
  uncertainty 151
textiles and clothing 5, 268–9, 304–5
  anti-dumping 276
  EU and USA's commitment to 53
  implementation 269–70
  Millennium Round 46
  safeguards 271–5
  tariffs 270–1
  Uruguay Round 1, 3, 33–4
  volume of trade 69
Thailand
  agriculture 38, 41
  anti-dumping 285, 287, 289
  child labour 196
  quantitative restrictions 264, 266, 267, 268
  textiles and clothing 271, 273, 274
tobacco 32, 220
Togo 102
Tonga 43
total factor productivity (TFP) 71
trade intensity 71
trademarks 241
Trade Policies Review Division (TPRD) 149,
    150, 155, 159
Trade Policy Review Mechanism (TPRM) 35,
    147–50, 160–1
  dispute settlement 131, 132, 137–8

domestic reform, credibility 152–3
investor confidence, boosting 153–4
market access 151–2
Marrakesh Agreements 147, 155, 161–4
policy credibility in developing countries
    150
quantitative restrictions 266–8
recommendations 154–60
transparency 142
Trade-Related Intellectual Property Rights
    (TRIPs) 123–9, 234, 239–41, 246
disadvantages for low-income countries 1
industrial policy 174
multilateral trading system 37
parallel imports 243
technical assistance 118
see also intellectual property rights
Trade-Related Investment Measures (TRIMs)
    202
industrial policy 170, 174, 178–80
market access 203–4, 205
multilateral trading system 37
regional integration agreements 207
trade secrets 241
TRAINS 159
transformation of society 8
transition times for liberalisation measures 20
transnational corporations (TNCs) 168, 178,
    179
see also foreign direct investment
transparency
competition policy 247
of governments 35
Trade Policy Review Mechanism 152,
    157–9, 160–1, 162
of WTO operations 5, 35, 131, 133–4,
    142–5
transport
benefits of liberalisation 76
customs procedures 218–19
domestic regulations 88
fairness and comprehensiveness in
    negotiations 21
Trans-Tasman Mutual Recognition
    Arrangement (TTMRA) 223
TRIMs *see* Trade-Related Investment
    Measures
TRIPs *see* Trade-Related Intellectual Property
    Rights
Tunisia
competition policy 234–5, 236, 238
customs reform project 120
quantitative restrictions 261
Turkey

anti-dumping 283
quantitative restrictions 262, 267
SPS regulations 123
textiles and clothing 271, 272
Tuvalu 43

UEMOA 108
Uganda 102
unemployment, developing countries 8, 10
UNICEF 196
United Kingdom
anti-dumping 285
'mad cow' disease 220
manufacturing, decline 14
quantitative restrictions 265
United Nations (UN)
Committee on International Trade Law
    (UNCITRAL) 209
Conference on Trade and Development
    (UNCTAD) 111, 159, 160
resources 111
United States of America
Advisory Centre on WTO Law 110, 139
advocates of liberalisation 12
agriculture 11, 27–8, 29–30, 44–5, 46, 64
anti-dumping 9, 16–17, 151–2, 282–3,
    285–8, 290–2, 306
Bureau of Labor Statistics 159
child labour 196, 197
competition policy 236, 238, 243, 244
dispute settlement 50, 131
Export Enhancement Program 28
FAIR Act 46
Federal Aviation Authority 222
genetically modified organisms 222
health services 84
International Trade Commission 158
labour mobility 85
local content policies 175
manufacturing, decline 13–14
MMT additive 220
non-pasteurised cheeses 220
Office of the US Trade Representative 148
protectionism 10
quantitative restrictions 263, 266, 267
safeguards 294, 295
Seattle Ministerial meeting 2, 185
software industry 83
tariff reductions 259, 260
textiles and clothing 34, 53, 269, 270, 271,
    272–4
Trade Policy Review Mechanism 148
TRIMs 202
universal service obligations 91

Uruguay 257
Uruguay Round (UR) 1, 251–2, 303
  advocates of liberalisation 12
  agriculture 1, 3, 11, 12, 25–6, 28–45, 61,
      278–9, 305–6
  anti-dumping 282–3, 286, 288, 306
  ASEAN 106
  France 12
  negotiations 3
  Nordic Group 106
  quantitative restrictions 260–3, 268, 304
  resource and research capacity constraints of
      developing countries 2
  safeguards 263, 293, 307
  services 85, 301, 307
  sub-Saharan Africa 97, 98, 100
  tariffs 252–7, 303
  technology subsidies 21
  textiles and clothing 268, 271, 304–5
  transition times 20
  TRIMs 202

Vanuatu 43
Venezuela
  anti-dumping 291
  dispute settlement 131
  quantitative restrictions 262
  tariffs 257
Vietnam

  agriculture 43
  SPS regulations 123
  textiles and clothing 34
volatility of developing countries 8
voluntary export restraints (VERs) 1, 151,
      261, 263–6, 304, 307
  textiles and clothing 33
voting system 103
voucher systems 91

Washington Treaty 124
wood 32
World Bank
  assistance for trade adjustment 20
  child labour 196
  country monitoring 149
  project experience 116, 122–3
  resources 111
  voting system 103
  WITS 159–60
World Customs Organisation (WCO) 225, 229
World Food Programme 111
World Intellectual Property Organisation
      (WIPO) 111

Zambia 102, 262
zero-for-zero approach, tariff reduction 47
Zimbabwe 102, 271